Other Books and Series by Jeff Bowen

Cherokee Intermarried White 1906 Volume I thru X

Applications for Enrollment of Creek Newborn Act of 1905
Volumes I thru XIV

Applications for Enrollment of Choctaw Newborn Act of 1905 Volumes I thru XX

Choctaw By Blood Enrollment Cards 1898-1914 Volumes I thru XX

Oglala Sioux Indians Pine Ridge Reservation 1932 Census Book I
Oglala Sioux Indians Pine Ridge Reservation Birth and Death Rolls 1924-1932
Book II

Census of the Sioux and Cheyenne Indians of Pine Ridge Agency
1896 - 1897   Book I
Census of the Sioux and Cheyenne Indians of Pine Ridge Agency
1898 - 1899 Book II

Northern Cheyenne Tongue River, Montana 1904 - 1932 Census
1904-1916 Volume I

Identified Mississippi Choctaw Enrollment Cards 1902-1909 Volume I

Visit our website at **www.nativestudy.com** to learn more about these
and other books and series by Jeff Bowen

Other Books and Series by Jeff Bowen

Compilation of History of the Cherokee Indians and Early History of the Cherokees by Emmet Starr with Combined Full Name Index

1901-1907 Native American Census Seneca, Eastern Shawnee, Miami, Modoc, Ottawa, Peoria, Quapaw, and Wyandotte Indians (Under Seneca School, Indian Territory)

1932 Census of The Standing Rock Sioux Reservation with Births And Deaths 1924-1932

Census of The Blackfeet, Montana, 1897- 1901 Expanded Edition

Eastern Cherokee by Blood, 1906-1910, Volumes I thru XIII

Choctaw of Mississippi Indian Census 1929-1932 with Births and Deaths 1924-1931 Volume I
Choctaw of Mississippi Indian Census 1933, 1934 & 1937, Supplemental Rolls to 1934 & 1935 with Births and Deaths 1932-1938, and Marriages 1936-1938 Volume II

Eastern Cherokee Census Cherokee, North Carolina 1930-1939 Census 1930-1931 with Births And Deaths 1924-1931 Taken By Agent L. W. Page Volume I
Eastern Cherokee Census Cherokee, North Carolina 1930-1939 Census 1932-1933 with Births And Deaths 1930-1932 Taken By Agent R. L. Spalsbury Volume II
Eastern Cherokee Census Cherokee, North Carolina 1930-1939 Census 1934-1937 with Births and Deaths 1925-1938 and Marriages 1936 & 1938 Taken by Agents R. L. Spalsbury And Harold W. Foght Volume III

Seminole of Florida Indian Census, 1930-1940 with Birth and Death Records, 1930-1938

Texas Cherokees 1820-1839 A Document For Litigation 1921

Starr Roll 1894 (Cherokee Payment Rolls) Districts: Canadian, Cooweescoowee, and Delaware Volume One
Starr Roll 1894 (Cherokee Payment Rolls) Districts: Flint, Going Snake, and Illinois Volume Two
Starr Roll 1894 (Cherokee Payment Rolls) Districts: Saline, Sequoyah, and Tahlequah; Including Orphan Roll Volume Three

Cherokee Intruder Cases Dockets of Hearings 1901-1909 Volumes I & II

Indian Wills, 1911-1921 Records of the Bureau of Indian Affairs Books One thru Seven

Other Books and Series by Jeff Bowen

Native American Wills & Probate Records 1911-1921

Turtle Mountain Reservation Chippewa Indians 1932 Census with Births & Deaths, 1924-1932

Chickasaw By Blood Enrollment Cards 1898-1914 Volume I thru V

Cherokee Descendants East An Index to the Guion Miller Applications Volume I
Cherokee Descendants West An Index to the Guion Miller Applications Volume II (A-M)
Cherokee Descendants West An Index to the Guion Miller Applications Volume III (N-Z)

Applications for Enrollment of Seminole Newborn Freedmen, Act of 1905

Eastern Cherokee Census, Cherokee, North Carolina, 1915-1922, Taken by Agent James E. Henderson   Volume I (1915-1916)
Volume II (1917-1918)
Volume III (1919-1920)
Volume IV (1921-1922)

Complete Delaware Roll of 1898

Eastern Cherokee Census, Cherokee, North Carolina, 1923-1929, Taken by Agent James E. Henderson   Volume I (1923-1924)
Volume II (1925-1926)
Volume III (1927-1929)

Applications for Enrollment of Seminole Newborn Act of 1905 Volumes I & II

North Carolina Eastern Cherokee Indian Census 1898-1899, 1904, 1906, 1909-1912, 1914 Revised and Expanded Edition

1932 Hopi and Navajo Native American Census with Birth & Death Rolls (1925-1931) Volume 1 - Hopi
1932 Hopi and Navajo Native American Census with Birth & Death Rolls (1930-1932) Volume 2 - Navajo

Western Navajo Reservation Navajo, Hopi and Paiute 1933 Census with Birth & Death Rolls 1925-1933

Cherokee Citizenship Commission Dockets 1880-1884 and 1887-1889 Volumes I thru V

Applications for Enrollment of Chickasaw Newborn Act of 1905 Volumes I thru VII

Peter Perkins Pitchlynn, 1806-1881
of Folsom lineage and Choctaw interpreter.

IDENTIFIED MISSISSIPPI CHOCTAW ENROLLMENT CARDS 1902 - 1909
VOLUME II

TRANSCRIBED BY
JEFF BOWEN

Copyright © 2021
by Jeff Bowen

ALL RIGHTS RESERVED
No part of this publication can be reproduced
in any form or manner whatsoever
without previous written permission from the
Copyright holder or Publisher.

Native Study LLC
Gallipolis, OH
www.nativestudy.com

Library of Congress Control Number: 2021924446

ISBN: 978-1-64968-124-9

Bookcover: Ha-Tchoo-Tuck-Nee (The Snapping Turtle) or Colonel Peter Perkins Pytchlynn [Pitchlynn]

All images compliments of Smithsonian Institution.

Made in the United States of America.

This series is dedicated to the
Mississippi Choctaw,
and their ancestors who fought for what was theirs.

Table of Contents

Reply of Chief Cobb to Capt. J. J. McRea	vii
Introduction	ix
Treaty of Dancing Rabbit Creek - Original (copy)	xiii
Treaty of Dancing Rabbit Creek - Transcription	xxxix
Dawes Packet of Jack John	lv
Dawes Final Roll of Mississippi Choctaws	lxxxv
Identified Mississippi Choctaw Enrollment Cards	1
Reference Books	309
Index	311

"Brother: When you were young we were strong; we fought by your side; but our arms are now broken. You have grown large. My people have become small.

"Brother: My voice is weak; you can scarcely hear me; it is not the shout of a warrior but the wail of an infant. I have lost it in mourning over the misfortunes of my people. These are their graves, and in those aged pines you hear the ghosts of the departed.--Their ashes are here, and we have been left to protect them. Our warriors are nearly all gone to the far country west; but here are our dead. Shall we go too, and give their bones to the wolves?

. . . .

"Brother: Our hearts are full. Twelve winters ago our chiefs sold our country. Every warrior that you see here was opposed to the treaty. If the dead could have counted, it could never have been made, but alas! though they stood around, they could not be seen or heard. Their tears came in the raindrops, and their voices in the wailing wind, but the pale faces knew it not, and our land was taken away.

". . . .When you took our country, you promised us land. There is your promise in the book. Twelve times have the trees dropped their leaves, and yet we have received no land. Our houses have been taken from us. The white man's plough turns up the bones of our fathers. We dare not kindle our fires; and yet you said we might remain and you would give us land."

The distrust which they felt toward the proposals of the federal officials is shown by the reply of Chief Cobb to Capt. J. J. McRea, who had addressed them in Council in 1843, urging them to remove.

The above from *The Rise And Fall Of The Choctaw Republic*, page 70, by Angie Debo. 1934.

INTRODUCTION

These *Identified Mississippi Choctaw Enrollment Cards* were found in the National Archive film records M-1186, Roll 57, under the heading of Enrollment Cards of the Five Civilized Tribes, 1898-1914. In the Dawes index they are listed as the Final Roll of Mississippi Choctaws September 25, 1902. "After the signing of the Treaty of Dancing Rabbit Creek in 1830, the U.S. government began the methodical removal of the Choctaw Indians from their native land in present-day Mississippi, uprooting about 20,000 of the estimated 25,000 tribesmen in the process. What became of the thousands of people who remained? A few hundred households stayed behind with government approval and were given individual parcels of land reservations as a treaty stipulation. Some other Choctaw--mixed-bloods who had already abandoned their ancestral ways and had chosen white culture as a life-style--simply merged with the incoming white settlers and stayed in the community as white people. Several thousand Indians, however, faded into the wilderness until they were forced out by an expanding white population."[1] As in this quote, it states that a few hundred households stayed behind with government approval to receive their own reservation of 640 acres but it wasn't to be in many cases. Even if they were supplying these surveys for the reservations they were laying out, the plats weren't being supplied so they could formally organize where the Choctaw families could settle. There wasn't going to be any cooperation. But even though they didn't get what was needed to claim their land the government managed to allow the whites to overrun their homes.

After the signing it wasn't that simple, as expected there was dissension almost immediately between the mixed-bloods and the full bloods. The full bloods not wanting to give up their land and the mixed-bloods seeing dollar signs. Andrew Jackson's Secretary of War John Eaton decided to threaten anyone not wanting to cooperate while deciding only to work with those who were willing to sign the treaty. After petrifying the people with a threat of arrest he managed to coax approximately 15,000 to immigrate to Indian Territory while just about 6,000 stayed to fight for their lands, though mostly full-bloods. What's amazing is that after being ratified by Congress President Andrew Jackson signed the Treaty of Dancing Rabbit Creek in February of 1831. Post treaty the Mississippi Choctaw were assigned an agent by the name of William Ward who would almost single handedly destroyed the chance of receiving any form of fair treatment in making their claims for the land promised. The Choctaw had six months to register their claims after ratification. They came from near and far seeking assistance. "Some full-bloods who spoke little if any English probably did not understand the specific procedures or requirements for registering. Even those who did, however, found themselves without effective power to protect their rights. Nevertheless, they refused to abandon their homeland. The majority of the 4,000 Choctaw living in Mississippi today have direct kinship ties to Indians who resisted removal in the 1830s.

The Choctaw who remained in Mississippi after 1833 were victims of one of the most flagrant cases of fraud, intimidation, and speculation in American history. Although the Senate took six months to ratify the treaty, squatters and speculators began

---

[1] *After Removal The Choctaw in Mississippi*; Introduction Pg. vii Para 1.

moving in immediately after the negotiations. As whites inundated the Choctaw cession, the War Department made some efforts to evict the intruders in accordance with the terms of the treaty. The influx of Americans continued, however, and the actions of Agent Ward not only encouraged white squatters and speculators but also blatantly obstructed the treaty rights of the Choctaw."[2]

Even after the removal of 1831 to 1833 many of the Choctaw people continued to travel back and forth between Mississippi and Oklahoma never really feeling settled in at either place because of such pressure from not only the government but also those scheming to take their lands. The intruders were being assisted while the Choctaw were being defrauded daily. The treaty had been signed in 1830 yet massive deception would be applied for decades. The very cards within these pages show that approximately 70 years later the descendants of the original people forced off of their land were still being made to prove who they were. They not only had to prove their heritage but they had to be demeaned by people who could care less. As an example, in the front of this book, you can actually find the documentation of a full blood Mississippi Choctaw named Bob Thomas along with his wife showing what they had to go through on December 18, 1900, titled as "Examination by the Commission". Seventy years previous his ancestors had been forced off of their land and told we'll stand by our word and Article XIV guarantees we'll give you some of your land back. But in realty Bob was in a position where he had to take what they gave him and where. Sadly, his ancestors were never given the land that was promised and Bob was again sitting in front of a Commission being asked questions about whom he was and where he came from. They were once more working to push another Choctaw family out of their home and into Indian Territory. Bob could only guess what his future would be, hoping to receive land from a government that was only concerned with him leaving the very same ground they made his ancestors abandon unwillingly.

There are examples of two different documents (1. the Dawes Folder for Bob Thomas, approximately 35 pages; 2. The full Dawes Index, FINAL ROLL OF MISSISSIPPI CHOCTAWS Ages calculated to September 25, 1902) that can be seen inside the front matter of this book along with the full transcription of the Identified Mississippi Choctaw Cards. You will find full-bloods as well as mixed-bloods on the roll with an extreme amount of full bloods making you think the trouble they were having to go through was just a form of discouragement in hopes they'd give up asking for their home ground. The cards show the person's name, the names of their relations, their ages, blood quantum, parents' names and application numbers. On the cards the settlement addresses show as mostly being in Indian Territory but in the Dawes Folders which not all are complete it shows for many testimony being given in places such as Hattiesburg, Mississippi and as living in Mississippi their whole lives. These in most cases were full bloods asking for the documentation to be rightfully classified by the government as who they were, full-blood Choctaws from Mississippi. But the decision appears to be put off as you can see in letters from the packet to make sure they were going to go west and leave their homes even seventy years later. After all that time the bureaucrats were still

---

[2] *After Removal The Choctaw in Mississippi*; Pg. 8 Para 2-3.

concerned as to whether their ancestors had claimed their own land under a treaty and Article XIV in the year 1830 otherwise we won't let you claim your own racial status.

It seems that Article XIV of the treaty was of the greatest importance in that fight for those that planned to stay. Even though there was never any intention to help them get what was promised, or at least let them keep a part of what was originally theirs in the first place they would have to battle massive corruption and greed because the whites wanted their land to grow cotton and so did Andrew Jackson who saw the Choctaw as a nuisance to progress. The trouble for them was obvious but who would have thought their descendants who lived their whole lives through in Mississippi would inherit the very same circumstances from the very same but different scoundrels many years later. The term repeated for them over and over was, "The Commission has not, up to the present time, reached any opinion or decision relative to the right of the full blood Choctaws residing in Mississippi to be identified as Mississippi Choctaws, but is now considering their applications, and it is probable decisions will be rendered in the near future."

ARTICLE XIV. Each Choctaw head of family being desirous to remain and become a citizen of the States, shall be permitted to do so, by signifying his intention to the Agent within six months from the ratification of this Treaty, and he or she shall thereupon be entitled to a reservation of one section of six hundred and forty acres of land, to be bounded by sectional lines of survey; in like manner shall be entitled to one half that quantity for each unmarried child which is living with him over ten years of age; and a quarter section to, such child as be under 10 years of age, to adjoin the location of the parent. If they reside upon said lands intending to become citizens of the States for years after the ratification of this Treaty, in that case a grant in fee simple shall issue; said reservation shall include the present improvement of the head of the family, or a portion of it. Persons who claim under this article shall not lose the privilege of a Choctaw citizen, but if they ever remove are not to be entitled to any portion of the Choctaw annuity.

Even though Article XIV seems to be extremely clear when it would come time to make those claims the rules would soon be clear as mud for the true owners of the land. For those who planned on staying the deception they'd face from those in power would now prove out their real intentions. These very people the Choctaw of 1830 are the ancestors of those living in Mississippi today.

After reading Grant Foreman's description of the Choctaw removal between the careless timing and terrible treatment of it was nothing short of brutal and deadly. So this quote needs to be left with you so these people will never be forgotten....

"Here they disembarked before the middle of December to organize for their march westward through Washington to the Kiamichi river. Two weeks later, still in camp on the river, Harkins wrote: "...*We sent our horses and oxen by land, and about 250 head of horses have died on the road. We have had very bad weather. Since we landed at this place about twenty of Nail's party have died, and still they are continuing to die. Two of my party have died. We are about 200 miles from my country on Red river. It will be some time in February before we get to where we want to settle. There are 1,200 of us in company, and we are compelled to travel slow, as there are so many sick people. I am afraid a great many will die before we get home. Nail has 400 with him. He had been very sick but now is on the mend."*[3]

It is the hope that these cards and few records will help many and grant the Mississippi Choctaw people the respect they deserved then and their descendants today.

Jeff Bowen
Gallipolis, Ohio
Nativestudy.com

---

[3] *Indian Removal*; Pg. 59 Para 1.

[Copy]

Treaty of Dancing Rabbit Creek

> 1830
> ~~1831~~
>
> Treaty with the Choctaws Sep. 27. 1830
> And 28th Sepr 1830
> Ratified Feby 24th 1831.

A treaty of perpetual friendship, cession and limits entered into by John H. Eaton and John Coffee for and in behalf of the Government of the United States and the Mingoes Chiefs Captains and Warriors of the Choctaw Nation begun and held at Dancing Rabbit Creek on the 15th of September in the year 1830.

Whereas the General Assembly of the State of Mississippi has extended the laws of said State to persons and property within the chartered limits of the same and the President of the United States has said that he cannot protect the Choctaw people from the operation of these laws; Now therefore that the Choctaw may live under their own laws in peace with the United States and the State of Mississippi they have determined to sell their lands east of the Mississippi & have accordingly agreed to the following articles of treaty—

Article 1st

Perpetual peace and friendship is pledged and agreed upon by and between the United States and the Mingoes, Chiefs, & Warriors of the Choctaw Nation of Red People; and that this may be considered the treaty existing between the parties all other treaties heretofore & inconsistent with the provisions of this extinguished hereby declared null and void.—

Article 2nd

The United States under a grant specially to be made by the President of the U.S. shall cause to be conveyed to the Choctaw Nation a tract of Country west of the Mississippi River, beginning near Fort Smith where the Arkansas boundary crosses the Arkansas River, Running thence to the Source of the Canadian fork; if in the limits of the United States, or to those limits; thence due South to Red River, and down Red River to the West boundary of the Territory of Arkansas; thence North along that line to the beginning

the boundary of the same to be agreable to the treaty, made and concluded at Washington City, in the year 1825. The grant to be executed so soon as the present Treaty shall be ratified. — Article 3rd

In consideration of the provisions contained in the several articles of this Treaty, the Choctaw Nation of Indians consent, and hereby cede to the United States, the entire Country they own and possess, East of the Mississippi River; and they agree to remove beyond the Mississippi River, early as practicable, and will so arrange thier removal, that as many as possible of thier people, not exceeding one half of the whole number, shall depart during the falls of 1831 and 1832; the residue to follow during the succeeding fall of 1833; a better opportunity in this manner will be afforded the Government, to extend to them the facilities and comforts which it is desireable should be extended in conveying them to thier New Homes. — Article 4th

The Government and people of the United States are hereby obliged to secure to the said Choctaw Nation of Red People the Jurisdiction and Government of all the Persons & Property that may be within thier limits West, so that no Territory or State shall ever have a right to pass laws for the Government of the Choctaw Nation of Red People & thier Descendants; and that no part of the land granted them shall ever be embraced in any Territory or State; but the U.S. shall forever secure said Choctaw Nation from, & against, all laws except such as from time to time may be enacted in thier own National Councils, not inconsistent with the Constitution, Treaties, and laws of the United States; & except such as may, & which have been enacted by Congress, to the extent that Congress under the Constitution are required to excercise a legislation over Indian affairs. But the Choctaws, should this treaty be ratified, express a wish that Congress may grant to the Choctaws the right of punishing by their own laws, any white man who shall come into their Nation, & infringe any of their National regulations

Article 5th

The United States are obliged to protect the Choctaws from domestic strife & from foreign enemies on the same principles that the Citizens of the United States are protected, so that whatever would be a legal demand upon the U.S. for defence or for wrongs committed by an Enemy, on a Citizen of the U.S, shall be equally binding in favour of the Choctaws, & in all cases where the Choctaws shall be called upon by a legally authorized Officer of the U.S. to fight an Enemy, such Choctaw shall receive the pay & other emoluments, which Citizens of the U.S. receive in such Cases, provided, no war shall be undertaken or prosecuted by said Choctaw Nation but by declaration made in full Council, & to be approved by the U.S. unless it be in self defence against an open rebellion or against an enemy marching into their Country, in which cases they shall defend, until the U.S. are advised thereof

Article 6th

Should a Choctaw or any party of Choctaws commit acts of violence upon the person or property of a Citizen of the U.S, or join any war party against any neighbouring tribe of Indians, without the authority in the preceding Article, & except to oppose an actual or threatened invasion or rebellion, such person so offending shall be delivered up to an Officer of the U.S. if in the power of the Choctaw Nation, that such Offender may be punished as may be provided in such cases, by the laws of the U.S.; but if such Offender is not within the control of the Choctaw Nation, then said Choctaw Nation shall not be held responsible for the injury done by said Offender.

Article 7th

All acts of violence committed upon persons and property of the people of the Choctaw Nation. either by Citizens of the U.S. or neighbouring tribes of Red people, shall be reffered to some authorized agent by him to be reffered to the President of the U.S, who shall examine into such cases and see that every possible degree of justice is done to said Indian party of the Choctaw Nation —

Article 8th

Offenders against the laws of the U.S. or any individual State shall be apprehended & delivered to any duly authorized person where such Offender may be found in the Choctaw Country, having fled from any part of U.S. but in all such cases application must be made to the Agent or Chiefs & the expense of his apprehension and delivery provided for & paid by the U. States,

Article 9th

Any Citizen of the U.S. who may be Ordered from the Nation by the Agent & Constituted authorities of the Nation and refusing to obey or return into the Nation without the Consent of the aforesaid persons, shall be subject to such pains and penalties as may be provided by the laws of the U.S. in such cases. Citizens of the U.S. travelling peaceably under the authority of the laws of the U.S. shall be under the care & protection of the Nation

Article 10th

No person shall expose goods or other article for sale as a trader, without a written permit from the Constituted authorities of the Nation, or authority of the laws of the Congress of the U.S. under penalty of forfeiting the Articles, & the Constituted authorities of the Nation shall grant no license except to such person as reside in the Nation and are answerable to the laws of the Nation. The U.S. shall be particularly obliged to assist in preventing ardent spirits from being introduced into the Nation

Article 11th

Navigable streams shall be free to the Choctaws who shall pay no higher toll or duty than Citizens of the U.S. It is agreed further that the U.S. shall establish one or more Post Offices in said Nation, & may establish such military post roads, and posts, as they may consider necessary

Article 12th

All intruders shall be removed from the Choctaw Nation and kept without it. Private property to be always respected & on no occasion taken for public purposes without just compensation being made therefor to the rightfull owner. If an Indian unlawfully take or steal any property from a white man a citizen of the U.S. the offender shall be punished. And if a white man unlawfully take or steal any thing from an Indian, the property shall be restored & the offender punished. It is further agreed that when a Choctaw shall be given up to be tried for any offence against the laws of the U.S. if unable to employ Counsel to defend him, the U.S. will do it, that his trial may be fair and impartial

Article 13th

It is consented that a qualified Agent shall be appointed for the Choctaws every four Years, unless sooner removed by the President; and he shall be removed on petition of the Constituted authorities of the Nation the President, being satisfied there is sufficient cause shown. The Agent shall fix his residence convenient to the great body of the people; & in the selection of an Agent immediately after the ratification of this Treaty, the wishes of the Choctaw Nation on the subject shall be entitled to great respect.

Article 14th

Each Choctaw head of a family being desirous to remain & become a Citizen of the States, shall be permitted to do so, by signifying his intention to the Agent within Six Months from the ratification of this Treaty: He shall thereupon be entitled to a reservation of one Section of Six Hundred and forty Acres of Land, to be bounded by sectional lines of survey; in like Manner he shall be entitled to one half that quantity for each unmarried child which is living with him over Ten Years of Age; & a quarter section to such child as may be under 10 years of age, to adjoin the location of the Parent. If they reside upon said lands intending to become Citizens of the States for five Years after the ratification of this Treaty in that case a grant in fee simple shall issue; said reservation shall include the present improvements of the head of the family, or a portion of it. Persons who claim under this Article shall not loose the priviledge of a Choctaw Citizen, but if they ever remove are not to be entitled to any portion of the Choctaw Annuity;

Article 15th

To each of the Chiefs in the Choctaw Nation (to wit) Greenwood Lafilore, Nutackachie, and Mushulatubbe there is granted a reservation of four sections of land, two of which shall include and adjoin their present improvements; & the other two located where they please but on unoccupied unimproved lands, such sections shall be bounded by sectional lines, & with the consent of the President they may sell the same. Also to the three principal Chiefs & their successors in office there shall be paid Two Hundred and fifty Dollars annually, while they shall continue in thier respective offices, except to Mushulatubbe who as he has an annuity of One Hundred fifty Dollars for life under a former treaty, shall receive only the additional sum of One Hundred Dollars, while he shall continue in office as Chief; & if in addition to this the Nation shall think propper to elect an additional principal Chief of the whole to superintend and govern upon republican principles he shall receive annually for his services Five Hundred Dollars, which allowance to the chiefs and thier Successors in Office, shall continue for Twenty Years, At any time when in Military service, & while in service by authority of the U.S. the district Chiefs under and by selection of the President shall be entitled to the pay of Majors; the other Chief under the same circumstances shall have the pay of a Lieutenant-Colonel. The speakers of the three districts, shall receive Twenty five Dollars a Year for four Years, & the three Secretaries One to each of the Chiefs, fifty Dollars for four years. Each Captain of the Nation, the number not to exceed Ninety nine, thirty three from each District shall be furnished upon removing to the West, with each a good suit of clothes & a broad sword as an outfit; & for four years commencing with the first of thier removal, shall each receive Fifty Dollars a Year, for four years the trouble of keeping thier people its order in settling; & whenever they shall be in Military service by authority of the U.S. shall receive the pay of a Captain

Article III

In wagons, & with Steam Boats as may be found necessary the U.S. agree to remove the Indians to thier new Homes at thier expense and under the care of discreet and carefull persons, who will be kind & brotherly to them. They agree to furnish them with ample corn and beef, or pork for themselves & families for Twelve Months after reaching thier new homes.

It is agreed further that the U.S. will take all their cattle, at the valuation of some descreet person to be appointed by the President, & the same shall be paid for in money after their arrival at their new homes; or in other cattle such as may be desired shall be furnished them, notice being given through their Agent of their wishes upon this subject before their removal that time to supply the demand may be afforded.

Article 17th

The several Annuities and sums secured under former Treaties to the Choctaw Nation and People shall continue as tho. this Treaty had never been made. And it is further agreed that the U.S. in addition will pay the sum of Twenty thousand Dollars for Twenty Years, Commencing, after their removal to the west, of which, in the first year after their removal, Ten thousand Dollars shall be divided and arranged to such as may not receive reservations under this Treaty.

Article 18th

The U.S. shall cause the lands hereby ceded to be Surveyed, & Surveyors may enter the Choctaw Country for that purpose, conducting themselves properly & disturbing or interrupting, none of the Choctaw people. But no person is to be permitted to settle within the Nation, or the lands to be sold before the Choctaws shall remove. And for the payment of the several amounts secured in this Treaty, the lands hereby ceded are to remain a fund pledged to that purpose, until the debt shall be provided for and arranged. And further it is agreed, that in the construction of this Treaty wherever well founded doubt shall arise, it shall be construed most favourably towards the Choctaws.

Article 19th

The following reservations of land are hereby admitted.
To Col. David Fulsom Four Sections of which Two shall include his present improvements, & two may be located elsewhere, on unoccupied, unimproved land.
To J. Garland, Col. Robert Cole, Tuppanahomer, John Pytchlyn, Charles Juzan, Joh Ke betubbe, Eayochahobia, Ofehoma two sections each, to include their improvements, and to be bounded by sectional lines, & the same may be disposed of and sold with the consent of the President. And that others not provided for, may be provided for, there shall be reserved as follows.

First, One section to each head of a family not exceeding Forty in number, who during the present year, may have had in actual cultivation, with a dwelling House thereon Fifty Acres or more. Secondly three quarter sections after the Manner aforesaid to each head of a family not exceeding Four Hundred and Sixty, as shall have cultivated Thirty Acres and less than Fifty, to be bounded by quarter section lines of survey, & to be contiguous & adjoining.

Third, One half section as aforesaid to those who shall have cultivated from Twenty to Thirty Acres the number not to exceed Four Hundred. Fourth, a quarter section as aforesaid to such as shall have cultivated from twelve to twenty Acres, the number not to exceed three hundred and fifty, and one half that quantity to such as shall have cultivated from two to twelve acres, the number also not to exceed three hundred and fifty persons. Each of said class of cases shall be subject to the limitations contained in the first class, & shall be so located as to include that part of the improvement which contains the dwelling House. If a greater number shall be found to be entitled to reservations under the several classes of this article, than is stipulated for under the limitation prescribed, then & in that case the Chiefs separately or together shall determine the persons who shall be excluded in the respective districts. Fifth; Any Captain the number not to exceed Ninety persons, who under the provisions of this article shall receive less than a section, he shall be entitled, to an additional quantity of half a section adjoining to his other reservation. The several reservations secured under this Article, may be sold with the consent of the President, of the U.S; but should any prefer it; or omit to take a reservation for the quantity he may be entitled to, the U.S. will on his removing pay fifty cents an acre, after reaching thier new homes, provided that before the first of January next they shall adduce to the Agent, or some other authorized person to be appointed, proof of his claim & the quantity of it. Sixth, likewise Children of the Choctaw Nation residing in the Nation, who have neither Father nor Mother a list of which, with satisfactory proof of Parentage and Orphanage being filed with Agent in Six months to be forwarded to the War Department, shall be entitled to a quarter section of Land, to be located under the direction of the President, & with his consent the same may be sold and the proceeds applied to some beneficial purpose for the benefit of said Orphans —

Article 20th.

The U.S. agree & stipulate as follows, that for the benefit, and advantage of the Choctaw people, & to improve thier condition, thier shall be educated under the direction of the President & at the expense of the U.S. forty Choctaw Youths for Twenty years. This number shall be kept at School, & as they finish thier education, others, to supply thier places shall be received for the period stated. The U.S. agree also to erect a Council House for the Nation at some convenient Central point, after thier people shall be settled, & a House for each Chief, also a church for each of the three Districts, to be used also as School

Houses, until the Nation may conclude to build others; & for these purposes Ten thousand Dollars shall be appropriated; Also Fifty thousand Dollars (Viz) Twenty Five Hundred Dollars Annually shall be given for the support of three Teachers of schools for Twenty Years. Likewise there shall be furnished to the Nation, three Black smiths one for each District for Sixteen Years, & a qualified Mill wright for five years, Also there shall be furnished the following articles, Twenty One Hundred Blankets, To each warrior who emigrates a Twelve Hundred rifles, Moulds, wipers and ammunition. One thousand axes, Ploughs, Hoes, Wheels and Cards each; And four Hundred looms. There shall also be furnished One Ton of Iron & two hundred weight of Steel annually to to each District for Sixteen years.

Article 21st

A few Choctaw Warriors yet survive who marched and fought in the Army with General Wayne the whole number stated not to exceed Twenty. These it is agreed shall hereafter while they live receive Twenty Five dollars a year; a list of them to be early as practicable; & within Six Months made out, and presented to the Agent to be forwarded to the War Department, —

Article 22d

The Chiefs of the Choctaws have suggested that their people are in a state of rapid advancement in education and refinements and have expressed a solicitude that they might have the priviledge of a Delegate on the floor of the House of Representatives extended to them. The Commissioners do not feel, that they can under a treaty stipulation accede to the request, but at thier desire, present it in the Treaty, that Congress may consider of and decide the application.

Done and Signed and executed by the Commissioners of the United States and the Chiefs Captains and Head men of the Choctaw Nation at Dancing Rabbit Creek this 27th day of September Eighteen Hundred and Thirty.

his mark

In Presence of   M H Eaton (seal)

E Breathitt Secty   Jno Coffee (seal)
to the Comms=   Greenwood Leflore (seal)
William Ward   Mushulatubbee (seal) X
for Choctaws   Nittuckachee (seal) X
John Pitchlynn   Eyarhokatubbee (seal) X
US Intr   Iyacho hopia (seal) X
M Mackey   Offahooma (seal) X
US Intr   Archatater (seal) X
Geo S Gaines   Onnee hubbee (seal) X
of Alabama   Holarten hoomah (seal) X
R P Currin   Hopiaunchahubbee (seal) X
Jesse Howard   Irhomingo (seal) X
Sam S. Worcester   Captain thalko (seal) X
Jno N Byrn   James Shields (seal) X
John Bell   Pistinubbee (seal) X
Jno Bond   Tobaquenchahubbee (seal) X
   Holubbee (seal)
   Robert Cole (seal) X
   Moshelatarcharhopia (seal) X
   Lewis Perry (seal)
   Artonomanstubbee (seal) X
   Hopiaytubbee (seal) X
   Hoshahoomah (seal) X
   Chuassahoomah (seal) X
   Joseph Kincaide (seal)
   Artookhubbee tubby (seal) X
   Cote tubbee (seal) X
   Arsarkatubbee (seal) X
   Issatahoomah X

Chohtahmatahah	seal	xx
Tummuppashubbee	seal	xx
Okechanyer	seal	xx
Hoshhopia	seal	xx
Warsharthahopia	seal	xx
Maarshunchahubbee	seal	xx
Mishaiguhbee	seal	xx
Daniel McCurtain	seal	xx
Tushkerharcho	seal	xx
Hoktoontubbee	seal	xx
Nukwavehookmarhee		xx
Mingohoomah	seal	xx
Pisinhocuttahhee	seal	xx
Tullarhachen	seal	xx
Little hader	seal	xx
Maashutter	seal	xx
Cowehoomah	seal	xx
Fillamoer	seal	xx
Immellacha	seal	xx
Antopulachubbee	seal	xx
Shushherunchahuthee	seal	xx
Nitterhoomah	seal	xx
Ohklasguthee	seal	xx
Pukumma	seal	xx
Arpatar	seal	xx
Hosher	seal	xx
Hoparmingo	seal	xx
Ispayhoomah	seal	xx
Lieberhoomah	seal	xx
Tohoholanten	seal	xx
Mahayarchubber	seal	xx
Arlanten	seal	xx
Nittehubbee	seal	xx
Tishonowan	seal	xx
Warsharchahoomah	seal	xx

Isaac James
Hopiaintushken
Argokkunner
Shemotar
Hopiaisketuna
Thomas Leflore
Arnoke o hatutbee
Shokeper lukna
Poshenhoomah
Robert Folsom
Arharyotutbee
Kushonolarten
James Vaughan
James James
Tisho ha kubbee
Narkenalar
Perinasha
Inhar gar ken
Motutbee
Narhargubbee
Ishmargubbee
Ammister   James McKing
Lewis Wilson
Istonarker harcho
Hoshinshamantarker
Kunmeashabee
Oyartunstutbee
Saml Garland
Thomas Wall
Saml Worcester
Jacob Folsom
William Foster
Ontien harcho
Hughes Foster
Pierre Juzan

Name	Mark
Mr. Pitchlynn Jr.	Paid
David Folsom	Paid
Sholohammastube	Paid ×
Isho	Paid ×
Lauwechubee	Paid ×
Hoshehomma	Paid ×
Ofenowa	Paid ×
Ahekache	Paid ×
Kaloshaube	Paid ×
Atoko	Paid ×
Ishtonuleche	Paid ×
Onthtohabe	Paid ×
Silos D. Fisher	Paid
Isaac Folsom	Paid +
Hekatube	Paid +
Haksehe	Paid ×
Jerry Carney	Paid +
John Washington	Paid ×
Phiphlip	Paid
Meshamiya	Paid +
Ishtelela	Paid +
Heshohomma	Paid ×
John McKelberry	Paid +
Benjm. James	Paid
Ishbachahambe	Paid ×
Aholihtube	Paid
Walking Wolf	Paid +
John Waiele	Paid ×
Big Ace	Paid +
Bob	Paid ×
Tushkochaubbe	Paid +
Ittabe	Paid ×
Tishowakaiye	Paid

Holehommra (Seal) x
John Garland (Seal) x
Kvshona (Seal) x
Ishteyohomube (Seal) x
Oklanowa (Seal) x
Neta (Seal) x
James Fletcher (Seal) x
Silus D Pitchlynn (Seal)
Mr William Trahern (Seal)
Ivsh Kahem mit ta (Seal) x
Te tha ta yu (Seal) x
Omoklashahopie (Seal) x
Ishoimita (Seal) x
Thomas H. Foster (Seal)
Zadoc Brashears

Name	Seal	Mark
Levi Perkins	Seal	X
Isaac Perry	Seal	X
Ishtonocka Hoomah	Seal	x
Hiram King	Seal	
Ogla Enlah	Seal	X
Nukelahtubbee	Seal	XX
Tuska Hollattah	Seal	XX
Panshestubbee	Seal	X
P P Pitchlynn	Seal	
Sul Hoil	Seal	
Nofaia Stonakey	Seal	+
Ischoomma	Seal	+
William Wade	Seal	+
Pansh Stickulkbee	Seal	+
Ho lit tant chah uhbee	Seal	+
Ka Want chah ukbee	Seal	
Eyarpalukbee	Seal	+
Okintahukbee	Seal	+
Living War Club	Seal	+
John Jones	Seal	
Charles Jones	Seal	
Isaac Jones	Seal	x
Hooklacha	Seal	+
Muscogee	Seal	+
Edan Nelson	Seal	

In the Senate of the United States
February 21st: 1831.

Resolved, (two thirds of the Senators present concurring,) That the Senate do advise and consent to the ratification of the Treaty, between the United States of America and the Mingoes, Chiefs, Captains and Warriors of the Choctaw Nation, concluded at Dancing Rabbit Creek on the 15th of September 1830, together with the supplement thereto, concluded at the same place the 28th of September 1830; with the exception of the preamble.

Attest,
Walter Lowrie

Andrew Jackson,
President of the United States of America,
To all and singular to whom these presents shall come,
Greeting:

Whereas a Treaty between the United States of America, and the Mingoes, Chiefs, Captains and Warriors of the Choctaw Nation was entered into at Dancing Rabbit Creek, on the twenty-seventh day of September in the Year of our Lord one thousand eight hundred and thirty, and of the Independence of the United States, the fifty-fifth, by John H. Eaton and John Coffee, Commissioners on the part of the United

States, and the Chiefs, Captains and Head-Men of the Choctaw Nation, on the part of said Nation;— which Treaty, together with the Supplemental article thereto, is in the words following, To wit:

A Treaty

Various Choctaw persons have been presented by the chiefs of the Nation with a desire that they might be provided for, Being particularly deserving, an earnestness has been manifested that provision might be made for them, It is therefore by the undersigned Commissioners here assented to with the understanding that they are to have no interest in the reservations which are devoted and provided for under the general Treaty, to which this is a Supplement.

As evidence of the liberal and kind feelings of the President and Governments of the United States the Commissioners agree to the request as follows (to wit) Pierre Suzard, Peter Pitchlynn, G. W. Harkins, Jack Pitchlynn, Israel Fulsom, Louis Laflore, Benjamin James, Joel H. Nail, Hopoyuyakubbee, Onorkubbee, Benjamin Laflore, Michael Laflore, Peter Pitchlynn Jun'r & wife shall be entitled to a reservation of two sections of land each to include their improvement where they at present reside, with the exception of the three first named & Benj'n Laflore persons, who are authorized to locate one of their sections on any other unimproved and unoccupied land, within their respective districts.

Article 2d

And to each of the following persons there is allowed a reservation of a section and a half of land, James L. McDonald, Robert Jones, Noah Wall, James Campbell, G. Nelson, and Vaughn Brasheans, R. Harris, Little Leader, I. Foster, J. Vaughn, L. Durant, Samuel Long, I. Magagha, Thos. Everge, Miles Thompson, Thomas Garland, John Bond, William Laflore, and Turner Brasheans; the two first named persons, may locate one section each, and one section jointly on any unimproved and unoccupied land, those not residing in the Nation. The others are to include their present residence and improvement.

Also one section is allowed to the following persons (to wit) Middleton Mackey, Wesley Train, Choweymo, Moses Foster, D McWall, Charles Scott,

Molly Nail, Susan Colbert, who was formerly Susan James, Saml Garland, Silas Fisher, D. McCartain, Oaklahoma, & Polly Fillocathey, to be located in entire sections to include their present residence and improvement, with the exception of Molly Nail & Susan Colberts, who are authorized to locate thiers, on any unimproved unoccupied land.

John Pitchlynn has long and faithfully served the Nation in character of U. States interpreter, he has acted as such for forty years, in Consideration it is agreed, in addition to what has been done for him there shall be granted to two of his Children, (to wit) Silas Pitchlynn, & Thomas Pitchlynn one Section of land each to adjoin the location of their father. Likewise to James Madison and Peter Sons of Mushulatubbee One section of land each to include the Old House and improvement of where their father formerly lived on the Old Military road, adjoining a large Prerarie.

And to Henry Groves Son of the Chief Natticache there is one Section of land given to adjoin his Fathers land.

And to each of the following persons Half a section of land is granted on any unoccupied and unimproved lands in the District where they respectively live (to wit) Willis Harkins, James D. Hamilton, William Pezan, Tobias Lefter Jo Dwarks, Jacob Folsom, P. Hays, Saml Worcester, Geo Curtis, William Train and Robert Nail and Alexander McKee.

And there is given a quarter section of land each to Delila and her five fatherless Children, she being a Choctaw woman residing out of the Nation, also the same quantity to Peggy Trihan another Indian Woman residing out of the Nation & her two fatherless Children; & to the widows of Pushmitahas, & Puck She nubbee who were formerly distinguished Chiefs of Nation and for their Children four quarter sections of land, each in trust for themselves & their Children

All of said last mentioned reservations are to be located under and by direction of the President of the U States

Article 3

The Choctaw people now that they have ceded their lands are solicitous to get to thier new homes early as possible & accordingly they wish that a party may be permitted to proceed this fall to ascertain whereabouts will be most advantageous for thier people to be located

It is therefore agreed that three or four persons (from each of the three districts) under the guidance of some discreet and well qualified persons may proceed during this fall to the West upon an examination of the Country.

For thier time and expenses the U. States agree to allow the said Twelve persons Two Dollars a day each, not to exceed One Hundred days, which is deemed to be ample time to make an examination.

If necessary Pilots acquainted with the Country will be furnished when they arrive in the West

Article 4th

John Donly of Alabama who has several Choctaw grandchildren, and who for twenty years has carried the mail through the Choctaw Nation, a desire by the Chiefs is expressed that he may have a section of land, it is accordingly granted, to be located in one entire section, on any unimproved & unoccupied land. Allen Glover and George S Gaines licensed Traders in the Choctaw Nation, have accounts amounting to upwards of Nine thousand Dollars against the Indians who are unable to pay their said debts without distressing their families, a desire is expressed by the Chiefs that Two sections of land be set apart to be sold and the proceeds thereof to be applied toward the payment of the aforesaid debts. It is agreed that two sections of any unimproved and unoccupied land be granted to George S Gaines who will sell the same for the best price he can obtain and apply the proceeds thereof to the credit of the Indians on their accounts due to the before mentioned Glover and Gaines; ×share make the application to the present Indian Chief

At the earnest and particular request of the Chief Greenwood Laflore there is granted to David Haley one half section of land to be located in a half section on any unoccupied and unimproved land as a compensation for a journey to Washington City with dispatches to the Government and returning others to the Choctaw Nation

The foregoing is entered into, as supplemental to the treaty concluded yesterday.

Done at Dancing Rabbit Creek the 28th day of September 1830

Jn. H. Eaton

In presence of
E. Breathitt Secty to Com:
W. Ward Agt for Choctaws
M Mackey US Intr

John Pitchlynn
US Intr
M Pierin
J A Hogue
G S Gaines

The following words in this supplement were interlined before being signed to wit "& after date ratify" also "Any Sgting" in words, Train— Choctahoma "person or persons"

In presence of
E. Breathitt duly to Com?

Jn Coffee Red P
Greenwood Leflore
Nittuckachee his × mark
Mushulatubbee his × mark
Ofa homma L his × mark
Eyarhoccuttubbee his × mark
Iyachee Hopia his × mark
Holubbee his × mark
Onarhutbee his × mark
Robert Cole his × mark
Hopia unohahtubbe his ×
David Folsom
John Garland his × mark
Hopia homah his × mark
Captain thathle his × mark
Pierre Juzan
Immas tototo his × mark
Hoshuntunmastubee his × mark

Now, therefore, be it known, that I, Andrew Jackson, President of the United States of America, having seen and considered said Treaty, do, in pursuance of the advice and consent of the Senate, as expressed by their Resolution of the twenty-first day of February, one thousand eight hundred and thirty-one, accept, ratify and confirm the same, and every clause and article thereof, with the exception of the Preamble.

In Testimony whereof, I have caused the seal of the United States to be hereunto affixed, having signed the same with my hand.

Done at the City of Washington, this twenty fourth day of February, in the Year of our Lord one thousand eight hundred and thirty-one, and of the Independence of the United States, the fifty-fifth.

Andrew Jackson

By the President,

M. Van Buren,
Secy of State

Treaty of Dancing Rabbit Creek

[Transcription of Original]

Treaty of Dancing Rabbit Creek

1830

~~1831~~

Treaty

with the

Choctaws

Sep. ~~15~~ 27, 1830

And 28th Sep[r] 1930

Ratified Feb[r] 24th 1831

A treaty of perpetual friendship, cession and limits entered into by John H. Eaton and John Coffee for and in behalf of the Government of the United States and the Mingoes Chiefs Captains and Warriors of the Choctaw Nation begun and held at Dancing Rabbit Creek on the 15th of September in the year 1830.

WHEREAS the General Assembly of the State of Mississippi has extended the laws of said State to persons and property within the chartered limits of the same and the President of the United States has said that he cannot protect the Choctaw people from the operation of these laws; Now therefore that the Choctaw may live under their own laws in peace with the United States and the State of Mississippi they have determined to sell their lands east of the Mississippi & have - accordingly agreed to the following articles of treaty ———

Article 1st

Perpetual peace and friendship is pledged and agreed on by and between United States and the Mingoes, Chiefs, & Warriors of the Choctaw Nation of Red People; and that this may be considered the ~~only~~ treaty existing between the parties all other treaties heretofore existing and inconsistent with the provisions of this are hereby declared null and void. ———

Article 2nd

The United States under a grant specially to be made by the President of the U. S. shall cause to be conveyed to the Choctaw Nation a tract of country west of the Mississippi River in fee simple to them & their descendants, to insure to them while they shall, exist as a nation and live on it beginning near Fort Smith where the

Treaty of Dancing Rabbit Creek

Arkansas boundary crosses the Arkansas River, Running thence ~~with~~ to the scource[sic] of the Canadian fork; if in the limits of the United States, or to those limits; thence due South to Red River, and down Red River to the West boundary of the Territory of Arkansas; thence North along that line to the beginning. The boundary of the same to be agreably[sic] to the treaty made and concluded at Washington City in the year 1825 The grant to be executed so soon as the present Treaty shall be ratified ——

Article 3$^{\underline{d}}$

In consideration of the provisions contained in the several articles of this Treaty, the Choctaw Nation of Indians consent and hereby cede to the United States, the entire country they own and possess, East of the Mississippi River; and they agree to remove beyond the Mississippi River, early as practicable, and will so arrange their removal, that as many as possible of thier[sic] people not exceeding one half of the whole number, shall depart during the falls of 1831 and 1832; the residue to follow during the succeeding fall of 1833; a better opportunity in this manner will be afforded the Government, to extend to them the facilities and comforts which it is desirable should be extended in conveying them to thier new Homes. ——

Article 4$^{\underline{th}}$

The Government and people of the United States are hereby obliged to secure to the said Choctaw Nation of Red People the Jurisdiction and Government of all the Persons and Property that may be within thier limits West, so that no territory or State shall ever have a right to pass laws for the Government of the Choctaw Nation of Red People and thier Descendants; and that no part of the land granted them shall ever be embraced in any territory or State; but the U. S. shall forever secure said Choctaw Nation from, & against, all laws except such as from time to time may be enacted in their own National Councils, not inconsistent with the Constitution, Treaties, and laws of the United States; & except such as may, & which have been enacted by Congress, to the extent that Congress under the Constitution are required to exerscise[sic] a legislation over Indian Affairs. But the Choctaws, should this treaty be ratified, express a wish that Congress may grant to the Choctaws the right of punishing by thier own laws, any white man who shall come into thier Nation, & infringe any of their National regulations.

Article 5$^{\underline{th}}$

The United States are obliged to protect the Choctaws from domestic strife & from foreign enemies on the same principles that the citizens of the United States are protected, so that whatever would be a legal demand upon the U. S. for defence[sic] or for wrongs committed by an Enemy, on a Citizen of the U. S, shall be equally binding in favour[sic] of the Choctaws, & in all cases where the Choctaws shall be called upon by a legally authorized officer of the U. S. to fight an Enemy, such Choctaw shall receive the pay & other emoluments, which citizens of the U. S. receive in such cases, provided, no war shall be undertaken or prosecuted by said Choctaw Nation but by declaration made in full Council, & to be approved by the U. S. unless it be in self defence against an open rebellion or against an enemy marching into thier country, in which cases they shall defend, until the U. S. are advised thereof.

Article 6th

Should a Choctaw or any party of Choctaws commit acts of violence upon the person or property of a citizen of the U. S, or join any war party against any neighbouring[sic] tribe of Indians, without the authority in the preceding article; & except to oppose an actual or threatened invasion or rebellion, such person so offending shall be delivered up to an Officer of the U. S. if in the power of the Choctaw Nation, that such offender may be punished as may be provided in such cases, by the laws of the U. S.; but if such Offender is not within the control of the Choctaw Nation, then said Choctaw Nation shall not be held responsible for the injury done by said offender.

Article 7th

All acts of violence committed upon persons and property of the ~~Cho~~ people of the Choctaw Nation either by Citizens of the U. S. or neighbouring[sic] tribes of Red people, shall be referred to some authorized agent by him to be referred to the ~~U.S.~~ President of the U. S, who shall examine into such cases and see that every possible degree of justice is done to said Indian party of the Choctaw Nation.

Article 8th

Offenders against the laws of the U. S. or any individual State shall be apprehended & delivered to any duly authorized person where such offender may be found in the Choctaw Country, having fled from any part of U. S. but in all such cases application must be made to the Agent or Chiefs & the expense of his apprehension and delivery provided for & paid by the U States.

Article 9th

Any citizen of the U. S. who may be ordered from the Nation by the Agent & constituted authorities of the Nation and refusing to obey or return into the Nation without the consent of the aforesaid persons, shall be subject to such pains and penalties as may provided by the laws of the U. S. in such cases. Citizens of the U. S.

travelling peaceably under the authority of the laws of the U. S. shall be under the care and protection of the Nation.

Article 10th

No person shall expose goods or other article for sale as a trader, without a written permit from the constituted authorities of the Nation, or authority of the laws of the Congress of the U. S. under penalty of forfeiting the articles, & the constituted authorities of the Nation shall grant no license except to such persons as reside in the Nation and are answerable to the laws of the Nation. The U. S. shall be particularly obliged to assist to prevent ardent spirits from being introduced into the Nation.

Article 11th

Navigable streams shall be free to the Choctaws who shall pay no higher toll or duty than Citizens of the U. S. It is agreed further that the U. S. shall establish one or more Post Offices in said Nation, & may establish such military post roads, and posts, as they may consider necessary.

Article 12th

All intruders shall be removed from the Choctaw Nation and kept without it. Private property to be always respected & on no occasion taken for public purposes without just compensation being made therefor to the rightful owner. If an Indian unlawfully take or steal any property from a white man a citizen of the U. S. the offender shall be punished. And if a white man unlawfully take or steal any thing from an Indian, the property shall be restored & the offender punished. It is further agreed that when a Choctaw shall be given up to be tried for any offence against the laws of the U. S. if unable to employ Counsel to defend him, the U. S. will do it, that his trial may be fair and impartial.

Article 13th

It is consented that a qualified Agent shall be appointed for the Choctaws every Four Years, unless sooner removed by the President; and he shall be removed on petition of the constituted authorities of the Nation the President being satisfied there is sufficient cause shown. The Agent shall fix his residence convenient to the great body of the people; & in the selection of an Agent immediately after the ratification of this Treaty, the wishes of the Choctaw Nation on the subject shall be entitled to great respect.

Treaty of Dancing Rabbit Creek

Article 14th

Each Choctaw head of a family being desirous to remain & become a Citizen of the States, shall be permitted to do so, by signifying his intention to the Agent within Six Months from the ratification of this Treaty & he or she shall thereupon be entitled to a reservation of one section of Six Hundred and forty Acres of Land, to be bounded by sectional lines of survey; in like manner shall be entitled to one half that quantity for each unmarried child which is living with him over Ten years of Age; & a quarter section to such child as be under 10 years of age, to adjoin the location of the Parent. If they reside upon said lands intending to become Citizens of the States for five Years after the ratification of this Treaty in that case a grant in fee simple shall issue; said reservation shall include the present improvement of the head of the family, or a portion of it. Persons who claim under this article shall not lose the privilege of a Choctaw Citizen, but if they ever remove are not to be entitled to any portion of the Choctaw Annuity;

Article 15th

To each of the Chiefs in the Choctaw Nation (to wit) Greenwood Laflore Nutackachie, and Mushulatubbe there is granted a reservation of four sections of land, two of which shall include and adjoin thier[sic] present improvement, and the other two located where they please but on unoccupied unimproved lands, such sections shall be bounded by sectional lines, & with the consent of the President they may sell the same. Also to the three principal Chiefs & to their successors in office there shall be paid Two Hundred and fifty Dollars annually while they shall continue in their respective offices, except to Mushulatubbe who as he has an annuity of One Hundred & fifty Dollars for life under a former treaty, shall receive only the additional sum of One Hundred Dollars, while he shall continue in office as Chief; & if in addition to this the Nation shall think propper[sic] to elect an additional principal Chief of the whole to superintend and govern upon republican principles he shall receive annually for his services Five Hundred Dollars, which allowance to the Chiefs and their successors in office, shall continue for Twenty Years. At any time when in Military Service, & while in service by authority of the U. S. the district Chiefs under and by selection of the President shall be entitled to the pay of Majors; the other Chief under the same circumstances shall have the pay of a Lieutenant-Colonel. The speakers of the three districts, shall receive Twenty five Dollars a year for four years ~~each~~ for four years each & the three secretaries one to each of the Chiefs, fifty dollars each for four years. Each Captain of the Nation, the number not to exceed ninety nine, thirty three from each District shall be furnished upon removing to the West, with each a good suit of clothes & a broad sword as an outfit, & for four years commencing with the first of thier removal, shall each receive Fifty Dollars a Year, for the trouble of

Treaty of Dancing Rabbit Creek

keeping thier people at order in settling; & whenever they shall be in military service by authority of the U. S. shall receive the pay of a captain.

Article 16th

In wagons; & with steam boats as may be found necessary the U. S. agree to remove the Indians to thier new Homes at thier expense and under the care of discreet and carefull[sic] persons, who will be kind and brotherly to them. They agree to furnish them with ample corn and beef, or pork for themselves & families for Twelve months after reaching thier new homes.

It is agreed further that the U. S. will take all thier cattle, at the valuation of some discreet person to be appointed by the President, & the same shall be paid for in money after thier arrival at thier new homes; or in other cattle such as may be desired shall be furnished them, notice being given through thier Agent of thier wishes upon this subject before thier removal that time to supply the demand may be afforded.

Article 17th

The several annuities and sums secured under former Treaties to the Choctaw Nation and People shall continue as tho. this Treaty had never been made. And it is further agreed that the U. S. in addition will pay the sum of Twenty thousand Dollars for Twenty Years, commencing after thier removal to the west, of which, in the first year after thier removal, Ten thousand Dollars shall be divided and arranged to such as may not receive reservations under this Treaty.

Article 18th

The U. S. shall cause the lands hereby ceded to be surveyed; & surveyors may enter the Choctaw Country for that purpose, conducting themselves properly & disturbing or interrupting none of the Choctaw people. But no person is to be permitted to settle within the Nation, or the lands to be sold before the Choctaws shall remove. And for the payment of the several amounts secured in this Treaty, the lands hereby ceded are to remain a fund pledged to that purpose, until the debt shall be provided for and arranged. And further it is agreed, that in the construction of this Treaty wherever well founded doubt shall arise, it shall be construed most favorably towards the Choctaws.

Treaty of Dancing Rabbit Creek

Article 19ᵗʰ

The following reservations of land are hereby admitted. To Col David Fulsom Four Sections of which Two shall include his present improvement, & two may be located else where, on unoccupied, unimproved land.

To I. Garland, Col Robert Cole, Tuppanahomer, John Pytchlynn[sic], Charles Juzan, Johokebetubbe, Eaychahobia, Ofehoma two sections, each to be include thier improvements, and to be bounded by sectional lines, & the same may be disposed of and sold with the consent of the President. And that others not provided for, may be provided for, there shall be reserved as follows:

First; One section to each head of a family not exceeding Forty in number, who during the present year, may have had in actual cultivation, with a dwelling House thereon Fifty Acres or more. Secondly three quarter sections after the manner aforesaid to each head of a family not exceeding Four Hundred and Sixty, as shall have cultivated Thirty Acres and less than Fifty, to be bounded by quarter section lines of survey, & to be contiguous and adjoining.

Third; One half section as aforesaid to those who shall have cultivated from Twenty to Thirty acres the number not to exceed Four Hundred. Fourth; a quarter section as aforesaid to such as shall have cultivated from twelve to twenty acres, the number not to exceed three hundred and fifty, and one half that quantity to such as shall have cultivated from two to twelve acres, the number also not to exceed three hundred and fifty persons. Each of said class of cases shall be subject to the limitations contained in the first class, & shall be so located as to include that part of the improvement which contains the dwelling House. If a greater number shall be found to be entitled to reservations under the several classes of this article, than is stipulated for under the limitation prescribed, then & in that case the Chiefs separeately[sic] or together shall determine the persons who shall be excluded in the respective districts.

Fifth; Any Captain the number not exceeding ninety persons, who under the provisions of this article shall receive less than a section, he shall be entitled, to an additional quantity of half a section adjoining to his other reservation. The several reservations secured under this article, may be sold with the consent of the President of the U. S; but should any prefer it, or omit to take a reservation for the quantity he may be entitled to the U. S. will on his removing pay fifty cents an acre, after reaching thier new homes, provided that before the first of January next they shall adduce to the Agent; or some other authorized person to be appointed, proof of his claim & the quantity of it. Sixth; likewise children of the Choctaw Nation residing in the Nation, who have neither Father nor Mother a list of which, with satisfactory proof of Parentage and orphanage being filed with Agent in six months to be forwarded to the War Department, shall be entitled to a quarter section of Land, to be located under the direction of the President, & with his consent the same may be sold and the proceeds applied to some beneficial purpose for the benefit of said orphans

Treaty of Dancing Rabbit Creek

Article 20th

The U. S. agree & stipulate as follows, that for the benefit and advantage of the Choctaw people, & to improve thier condition, thier[sic] shall be educated under the direction of the President & at the expense of the U. S. forty Choctaw Youths for Twenty years. This number shall be kept at school, & as they finish thier education others to supply thier places shall be received for the period stated. The U. S. agree also to erect a Council House for the Nation at some convenient central point, after thier people shall be settled; & a House for each Chief, also a church for each of the three Districts, to be used also as school Houses, until the Nation may conclude to build others; & for these purposes Ten thousand Dollars shall be appropriated; also Fifty thousand Dollars (viz) Twenty Five Hundred Dollars annually shall be given for the support of three Teachers of schools for Twenty Years. Likewise there shall be furnished to the Nation, three Blacksmiths one for each District for sixteen years, & a qualified Mill Wright for five years; Also there shall be furnished the following articles, Twenty One Hundred Blankets, To each warrior who emigrates a rifle, moulds, wipers and ammunition. One thousand axes, Ploughs, Hoes, Wheels and Cards each; and four Hundred looms. There shall also be furnished one Ton of iron & two hundred weight of steel annually to each District for sixteen years.

Article 21st

A few Choctaw Warriors yet survive who marched and fought in the Army with General Wayne the whole number stated not to exceed Twenty.
These it is agreed shall hereafter while they live receive Twenty Five dollars a year; a list of them to be early as practicable, & within six months made out, and presented to the Agent to be forwarded to the War Department.—

Article 22d

The Chiefs of the Choctaws have suggested that thier people are in a state of rapid advancement in education and refinement; and have expressed a solicitude that they might have the privilege of a Delegate on the floor of the House of Representatives extended to them. The Commissioners do not feel, that they can under a treaty stipulation accede to the request, but at thier desire, present it in the Treaty, that Congress may consider of and decide the application.

Done and signed and executed by the Commissioners of the United States and the Chiefs Captains and Head Men of the Choctaw Nation, at Dancing Rabbit Creek this 27th day of September Eighteen Hundred and Thirty.

Treaty of Dancing Rabbit Creek

			His Mark
In presence of	Jnº H. Eaton	(Seal)	
E. Breathitt Secty	Jnº. Coffee	(Seal)	
to the Commss^r =	Greenwood Leflore	(Seal)	
William Ward Agt.	Musholatubbee	(Seal)	X
for Choctaws.	Nittucachee	(Seal)	X
John Pitchlynn	Eyarhocuttubbee	(Seal)	X
US Int^r	Iyacherhopia	(Seal)	X
M Mackey	Offahoomah	(Seal)	X
US Intr.	Archalater	(Seal)	X
Geo. S. Gaines	Onnahubbee	(Seal)	X
of Alabama	Holarterhoomah	(Seal)	X
RP Currin	Hopiaunchahubbee	(Seal)	X
Luke Howard	Zishomingo	(Seal)	X
Sam. L. Worchester	Captain thalke	(Seal)	X
Jnº W Byrn	James Shield	(Seal)	X
John Bell	Pistiyubbee	(Seal)	X
Jnº Bond	Yobalarunehahubbee	(Seal)	X
	Holubbee	(Seal)	X
	Robert Cole	(Seal)	X
	Mokelareharhopin	(Seal)	X
	Lewis Perry	(Seal)	X
	Artonamarstubbe	(Seal)	X
	Hopeatubbee	(Seal)	X
	Hoshahoomah	(Seal)	X
	Chuallahoomah	(Seal)	X
	Joseph Kincaide	(Seal)	X
	Artooklubbetushpar	(Seal)	X
	Metubbee	(Seal)	X
	Arsarkatubbee	(Seal)	X
	Issaterhoomah		X
	Chohtahmatahah	(Seal)	X
	Tunnuppashubbee	(Seal)	X
	Okocharyer	(Seal)	X
	Hoshhopia	(Seal)	X
	Warsharshahopia	(Seal)	X
	Maarshunchahubbee	(Seal)	X
	Misharyubbee	(Seal)	X
	Daniel McCurtain	(Seal)	X
	Tushkerharcho	(Seal)	X
	Hoktoontubbee	(Seal)	X
	Nuknacrahookmarhee	(Seal)	X
	Mingohoomah	(Seal)	X
	Pisinhocuttubbee	(Seal)	X
	Tullarhacher	(Seal)	X
	Little leader	(Seal)	X
	Maanhutter	(Seal)	X
	Cowehoomah	(Seal)	X

Treaty of Dancing Rabbit Creek

Name	Seal	Mark
Tillamoer	(Seal)	X
Imnullacha	(Seal)	X
Artopilachubbee	(Seal)	X
Shupherunchahubbee	(Seal)	X
Nitterhoomah	(Seal)	X
Oaklaryubbee	(Seal)	X
Pukumma	(Seal)	X
Arpalar	(Seal)	X
Holber	(Seal)	X
Hoparmingo	(Seal)	X
Isparhoomah	(Seal)	X
Tieberhoomah	(Seal)	X
Tishoholarter	(Seal)	X
Mahayarchubbee	(Seal)	X
Arlarter	(Seal)	X
Nittahubbee	(Seal)	X
Tishonouan	(Seal)	X
Warsharchaboomah	(Seal)	X
Isaac James	(Seal)	X
Hopiaintushker	(Seal)	X
Aryoshkermer		X
Shemotar		X
Hopiaisketina		X
Thomas Leflore		X
Arnokechatubbee		X
Shokoperlukna		X
Posherhoomah		X
Robert Folsom		X
Arharyotubbee		X
Kushonolarter		X
James Vaughan		X
James Karnes		X
Tishohakubbee		X
Narlanalar		X
Pennasha		X
In har yar ker		X
Motubbee		X
Narharyubbee		X
Ishmaryubbee		X
James M King		
Lewis Wilson		X
Istonarkerharcho		X
Hoshinshamartarher		X
Kinsulachubbee		X
Eyarhinstubbee		X
Saml Garlands		
Thomas Wall		
Sam. S. Worcester		

Treaty of Dancing Rabbit Creek

	Jacob Folsom		
	William Foster		
	Ontioerharcho		X
	Hugh A. Foster		
	Pierre Juzan		
	Jno. Pitchlynn Jr.	(Seal)	
	David Folsom	(Seal)	
	Sholohommastube	(Seal)	X
	Tesho	(Seal)	X
	Lauwechubee	(Seal)	X
	Hoshehammo	(Seal)	X
	Ofenowo	(Seal)	X
	Ahekoche	(Seal)	X
	Kaloshoube	(Seal)	X
	Atoko	(Seal)	X
	Ishtemeleche	(Seal)	X
	Emthtohabe	(Seal)	X
	Silas D. Fisher	(Seal)	
	Isaac Folsom	(Seal)	X
	Hekatube	(Seal)	X
	Hakseche	(Seal)	X
	Jerry Carney	(Seal)	X
	John Washington	(Seal)	X
	Phiplip	(Seal)	X
	Meshameye	(Seal)	X
	Ish te he ka	(Seal)	X
	Heshohomme	(Seal)	X
	John McKelbery	(Seal)	X
	Benj^m. James	(Seal)	
	Tik ba cha ham be	(Seal)	X
	Aholiktube	(Seal)	X
	Walking Wolf	(Seal)	X
	John Waide	(Seal)	X
	Big Axe	(Seal)	X
	Bob	(Seal)	X
	Tush ko cha u bbe	(Seal)	X
	It ta be	(Seal)	X
	Tish o wa ka you	(Seal)	
	Folehommo	(Seal)	X
	John Garland	(Seal)	X
	Koshona	(Seal)	X
	Ish le you ham ube	(Seal)	X
	Ok la no wa	(Seal)	X
	Neto	(Seal)	X
	James Fletcher	(Seal)	X
	Silus D Pitchlynn	(Seal)	
	William Trahorn	(Seal)	
	Tosh ka hem mit to	(Seal)	X

Treaty of Dancing Rabbit Creek

	Te the ta yo	(Seal)	X
	Emokloshahopie	(Seal)	X
	Tishoimita	(Seal)	X
	Thomas W Foster	(Seal)	
	Zadoc Brashears		
	Levi Perkins	(Seal)	X
	Isaac Perry	(Seal)	X
	Isblonocka Hoomah	(Seal)	X
	Hiram King	(Seal)	
	Ogla Enlah	(Seal)	X
	Nu1tlahtubbee	(Seal)	X
	Tuska Hollattuh	(Seal)	X
	Panshastubbee	(Seal)	X
	P. P. Pitchlynn	(Seal)	
	Joel H. Nail	(Seal)	
	Hopia Stonakey	(Seal)	X
	Kocohomma	(Seal)	X
	William Wade	(Seal)	X
	Pansh stick ubbee	(Seal)	X
	Ho lit tank chah ubbee	(Seal)	X
	Ko th° ant chah ubbee	(Seal)	X
	Eyarpulubbee	(Seal)	X
	Oken tah ubbe	(Seal)	X
	Living War Club	(Seal)	X
	John Jones	(Seal)	X
	Charles Jones	(Seal)	
	Isaac Jones	(Seal)	X
	Hocklucha	(Seal)	X
	Muscogee	(Seal)	X
	Eden Nelson	(Seal)	

And 28th Sep^t 1830
Ratified Feby 24th 1831.

In the Senate of the United States
February 21st: 1831.

Resolved, (two thirds of the Senators present concurring) That the Senate do advise and consent to the ratification of the Treaty, between the United States of America and the Mingoes, Chiefs, Captains and Warriors of the Choctaw Nation, concluded at Dancing Rabbit Creek on the 15th of September 1830, together with the Supplement thereto, concluded at the same place the 28th of September 1830: with the exception of the preamble.

Attest,   Walter Lowrie

Treaty of Dancing Rabbit Creek

Andrew Jackson,
President of the United States of America,
To all and singular to whom these presents shall come,

Greeting:

Whereas a Treaty between the United States of America, and the Mingoes, Chiefs, Captains and Warriors of the Choctaw Nation was entered into at Dancing Rabbit Creek, on the twenty-seventh day of September in the Year of our Lord one thousand eight hundred and thirty, and of the Independence of the United States, the fifty-fifth, by John H. Eaton and John Coffee, Commissioners on the part of the United States, and the Chiefs, Captains and Head-Men of the Choctaw Nation on the part of said Nation; - which Treaty, together with the supplemental article thereto, is in the words following,
To wit:

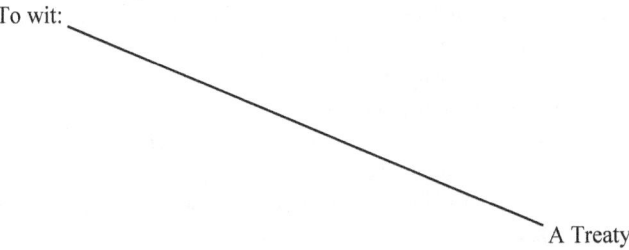

A Treaty

Various Choctaw persons have been presented by the chiefs of the Nation, with a desire that they might be provided for, Being particularly deserving, an earnestness has been manifested that provision might be made for them. It is therefore by the undersigned commissioners here assented to with the understanding that they are to have no interest in the reservations which are directed and provided for under the general Treaty to which this is a supplement.

As evidence of the liberal and kind feelings of the President and Government of the United States the Commissioners agree to the request as follows (to wit) Pierre Juzan, Peter Pitchlynn, G.W. Harkins, Jack Pitchlynn, Israel Fulsom, Louis Laflore, Benjamin James, Joel H. Nail, Hopoynjahubbee, Onorkubbee, Benjamin Laflore, Michael Laflore & Allen Yates & wife shall be entitled to a reservation of two sections of land each to include thier improvement where they at present reside, with the exception of the three first named persons & Benja. Laflore who are authorized to locate one of thier sections on any other unimproved and unoccupied land, within thier respective districts.

Article 2^d

And to each of the following persons there is allowed a reservation of a section and a half of land, (to wit) James L. McDonald, Robert Jones, Noah Wall, James Campbell, G. Nelson, ~~and~~ Vaughn Brashears, R. Harris, Little Leader, S. Foster, J.

Treaty of Dancing Rabbit Creek

Vaughn, L. Durand, Samuel Long, T. Magagha, Thos. Everge, Giles Thompson, Thomas Garland, John Bond, William Laflore, and Turner Brashears; the two first named persons, may locate one section each, and one section jointly on any unimproved and unoccupied land, these not residing in the Nation; The others are to include thier present residence and improvement.

Also one section is allowed to the following persons (to wit) Middleton Mackey, Wesley Train, Choclehomo, Moses Foster, D. W. Wall, Charles Scott, Molly Nail, Susan Colbert, who was formerly Susan James, Samuel Garland, Silas Fisher, D. McCurtain, Oaklahoma, & Polly Fillecuthey, to be located in entire sections to include thier resent residence and improvement, with the exception of Molly Nail and Susan Colbert, who are authorized to locate thiers, on any unimproved unoccupied land.

John Pitchlynn has long and faithfully served the Nation in character of U. States interpreter, he has acted as such for forty years, in consideration it is agreed, in addition to what has been done for him there shall be granted to two of his children, (to wit) Silas Pitchlynn, & Thomas Pitchlynn one section of land each to adjoin the location of thier father likewise to James Madison and Peter sons of Mushulatubbee one section of land each to include the old house and improvement ~~of~~ where thier father formerly lived on the old military road adjoining a large Prerarie[sic].

And to Henry Groves son of the Chief Natticache there is one section of land given to adjoin his father's land.

And to each of the following persons half a section of land is granted on any unoccupied and unimproved lands in the Districts where they respectively live (to wit) Willis Harkins, James D. Hamilton, William Juzan, Tobias Laflore, Jo Doake, Jacob Fulsom, P. Hays, Saml Worcester, Geo. Hunter, William Train ~~and~~ Robert Nail and Alexander McKee.

And there is given a quarter section of land each to Delila and her five fatherless children, she being a Choctaw woman residing out of the Nation; also the same quantity to Peggy Trihan, another Indian woman residing out of the Nation & her two fatherless children; & to the widows of Pushmilaha, & Puck she nubbee, who were formerly distinguished Chiefs of the Nation and for thier children four quarter sections of land, each in trust for themselves & thier children

All of said last mentioned reservations are to be located under and by direction of the President of the U States

Article 3

The Choctaw people now that they have ceded thier[sic] lands are solicitous to act to thier new homes early as possible & accordingly they wish that a party may be permitted to proceed this fall to ascertain where abouts will be most advantageous for thier people to be located.

Treaty of Dancing Rabbit Creek

It is therefore agreed that three or four persons (from each of the three districts) under the guidance of some discreet and well qualified person or persons ~~man~~ may proceed during this fall to the West upon an examination of the country.

For thier time and expenses the U. States agree to allow the said twelve persons Two Dollars a day each, not to exceed one hundred days, which is deemed to be ample time to make an examination.

If necessary Pilots acquainted with the country will be furnished when they arrive in the West.

Article 4th

John Donly of Alabama who has several Choctaw grand children, and who for Twenty years has carried the mail through the Choctaw Nation, a desire by the Chiefs is expressed that he may have a section of land, it is accordingly granted, to be located in one entire section, on any unimproved & unoccupied land.

Allen Glover and George S. Gaines licensed Traders in the Choctaw Nation, have accounts amounting to upwards of Nine thousand Dollars against the Indians who are unable to pay thier said debts without distressing thier families; a desire is expressed by the Chiefs that Two sections of land be set apart to be sold and the proceeds thereof to be applied toward the payment of the aforesaid debts. It is agreed that two sections of any unimproved and unoccupied land be granted to George S. Gaines who will sell the same for the best price he can obtain and apply the proceeds thereof to the credit of the Indians on thier accounts due to the before mentioned Glover and Gaines; & shall make the application to the poorest Indian first.

At the earnest and particular request of the Chief Greenwood Laflore there is granted to David Haley one half section of land to be located in a half section on any unoccupied and unimproved land as a compensation for a journey to Washington City with dispatches to the Government and returning others to the Choctaw Nation.

The foregoing is entered into, as supplemental to the treaty concluded yesterday.

Done at Dancing Rabbit creek the 28th day of September 1830.

In presence of	Jno H Eaton Seal
E. Breathitt Secty to Comr.	Jno. Coffee Seal
W. Ward Agt. for Choctaws	Greenwood Leflore
M Mackey US Intr.	Nittucachee his x mark
John Pitchlynn	Musholatubbee his x mark
US Intr	Ofahoomah his x mark
RP Currin	Eyarhoeuttubbee his x mark
Jno W Byrn	Iyaeherhopia his x mark

Treaty of Dancing Rabbit Creek

Geo. S. Gaines	Holubbee his x mark
The following words in this supplement	Onarhubbee his x mark
were interlined before being signed	Robert Cole his x mark
1st Article "& Allen Yates & wife" also	Hopiaunchahubbee his x mark
& Benjᵃ Laflore	David Folsom
Do. Wesley Train - Choclehomo	John Garland his x mark
	Hopiahoomah his x mark
"person or persons"	Captain Thalko his x mark
	Pierre Juzan
In presence of	Immarstarher his x mark
E. Breathitt Secty to Comʳ.	Hoshimhamarter his x mark

    Now, therefore, be it known, that I, Andrew Jackson, President of the United States of America, having seen and considered said Treaty, do in pursuance of the advice and consent of the Senate, as expressed by their Resolution of the twenty-first day of February, one thousand eight hundred and thirty-one, accept, ratify and confirm the same, and every clause and article thereof, with the exception of the Preamble.

    In Testimony whereof, I have caused the seal of the United States to be hereunto affixed, having signed the same with my hand.

    Done at the City of Washington, this twenty fourth day of February, in the Year of our Lord one thousand eight hundred and thirty-one, and of the Independence of the United States, the fifty-fifth.

                           Andrew Jackson

                           By the President,

                                   M. VanBuren
                                   Secty of State

Dawes Packet
of
Jack John, et al.

In the matter of the application of Jack John, et al.,
for identification as Mississippi Choctaws.

ON IDENTIFICATION AS
A MISSISSIPPI CHOCTAW

Jacb John, et al.,

IDENTIFIED

DECISION RENDERED APR 11 1903

NOTICE OF DECISION MAILED APPLICANT. APR 27 1903

NOTICE OF DECISION MAILED ATTORNEYS
FOR CHOCTAW AND CHICKASAW NATIONS APR 11 1903

DEPARTMENT OF THE INTERIOR,
COMMISSION TO THE FIVE CIVILIZED TRIBES.

In the matter of the application of Jack John, et al., for identification as Mississippi Choctaws, M.C.R.2006.

DEPARTMENT OF THE INTERIOR,
COMMISSION TO THE FIVE CIVILIZED TRIBES.

In the matter of the application of Jack John, et al., for identification as Mississippi Choctaws, M.C.R.2006.

DEPARTMENT OF THE INTERIOR,
COMMISSION TO THE FIVE CIVILIZED TRIBES,
Meridian, Mississippi, May 4, 1901.

In the matter of the application for identification as Mississippi Choctaws of Jack John, his wife and their minor child.
Said Jack John, being first duly sworn through Choctaw Interpreter, Isham Johnston, testified as follows:-

Examination by the Commission.

Q What is your name? A Jack John.
Q How old are you? A 22.
Q Where do you live? A Paulding.
Q What county is that in? A Jasper County.
Q How long have you lived in Mississippi? A A long time.
Q How long? --------
Q Can't you answer that? A I don't know how long.
Q Was you born here? A Yes sir.
Q Never have lived anywhere else? A No sir.
Q What is your father's name? A Billy John.
Q Was your father a full blood Choctaw? A Yes sir.
Q Is he living? A No.
Q Did your father always live here in Mississippi? A Yes sir.
Q Did he have any Choctaw name? A Puchchanunubbee.
Q What is your mother's name? A I don't know.
Q Don't you remember your mother? A No sir.
Q Was she a Choctaw? A Yes sir.
Q Full blood? A Yes.
Q Don't remember her name? A No.
Q Is she living? A No sir.
Q How long has she been dead? A I don't know.
Q Do you know anything about her? A No sir.
Q Don't remember her? A No.
Q Did she die when you were a little fellow? A Yes.
Q Were either your father or mother ever recognized or considered as members of the Choctaw Tribe of Indians? A Yes sir.
Q That is the Choctaw Tribe in the Indian Territory? A Yes.
Q How? A I don't know.
Q They never lived there, did they? A I don't know.
Q Did they ever live in the Indian Territory? (No answer)
Q Did your mother and father ever live out in the Indian Territory?
Q Can't you understand that question? Don't you know whether they lived in Indian Territory or not? A No sir.
Q Always lived here in Mississippi, did they? A Yes sir.
Q Are you married? A Yes sir.
Q What is your wife's name? Sallie John.
Q Is your wife a full blood Choctaw? A Yes.
Q How old is she? A 21.
Q What is her father's name? A Adam Lewis.
Q Is your wife's father living? A No.
Q Was he a full blood Choctaw? A Yes.
Q Did he always live here in Mississippi? A Yes.
Q What is your wife's mother's name? A Eliza Lewis.
Q Is your wife's mother living? A Yes.
Q Is she a full blood Choctaw? A Yes.
Q Did she always live here in Mississippi? A Yes.
Q Were you married to Sallie John? A Yes.
Q How were you married? A About three years ago?
Q How were you married, did you get a license? A No.
Q Married according to Choctaw custom down here? A Yes.
Q Have you any children? A Yes.
Q How many? A One.
Q What is the child's name? A Davis John.

1

Jack John et al -----2

Q How old is he? A About 5 years.
Q That is the only child you have had? A No, had one, he died.
Q This one lives with you, doesn't he? A Yes.
Q Have you or your wife ever been enrolled by the Choctaws in Indian Territory? (No answer)
Q Never lived in the Indian Territory, did you? A No.
Q Have you ever made application for citizenship in the Tribe out there, either you or your wife? Did you ever apply to the Choctaws out there to be enrolled with them? A No.
Q Five years ago, in 1896, did you make an application to the Commission to the Five Civilized Tribes for citizenship in the Choctaw Nation under the Act of Congress of June 10, 1896? A No.
Q Have you, your wife or your child ever been admitted to citizenship in the Choctaw Nation by either the Choctaw Tribal authorities, the Commission to the Five Civilized Tribes, or by the United States Court in Indian Territory? (No answer)
Q You understand that question, don't you? A No.
Q Have you ever been given rights to citizenship in the Choctaw Nation in the Indian Territory? A No sir.
Q This is the first application you have ever made of any kind? A Yes.
Q Has anybody ever made an application for you before? A No sir.
Q You are now making application for the identification of yourself, your wife and your child as Mississippi Choctaws, is that correct? A Yes sir.
Q Claim your rights as beneficiaries under the 14th article of the treaty of 1830? A Yes sir.
Q Did you ever receive any benefits in money or land from the Choctaw Nation? A Yes.
Q When did you ever get and money or land from the Choctaw Nation? A No.
Q Did any of your foreparents, the people that you descended from, ever move from Mississippi out to the Choctaw Nation in Indian Territory when the Choctaws moved out there 65 or 70 years ago? A No.
Q All of them have always lived here in Mississippi? A Yes.
Q Did any of your ancestors ever receive any land from the United States under this 14th article of the treaty of 1830? A No.
Q Have all your ancestors, as far as you remember, always lived here in Mississippi? (No answer)
Q Do you know whether any of your people ever lived anywhere else beside Mississippi? A No.
Q Anything more you want to say? Any statement you want to make? Anything you know about your ancestors or foreparents? (No answer)
Q Is there anything more you want to say, anything you know about your people, your father, your mother, or any of your foreparents? A No sir.
Q Have you any documentary evidence, written testimony of any kind, copies of records, deeds or patents, or any papers, that would show that your ancestors were ever recognized or considered as members of the Choctaw Tribe of Indians or that they ever complied or attempted to comply with the provisions of the 14th article of the treaty of 1830? A No sir.

The appearance of John S. Hagler, the attorney for applicants, noted.

> The applicant in this case is to every appearance a full blood Choctaw Indian and speaks but a little English, the examination having been conducted for a greater part through a sworn Choctaw interpreter. It has been very difficult to elicit any answer from the applicant. It appears from the testimony that the wife and child, for whom application is also made, are both full blood Choctaws and that the applicant, his wife and their ancestors

John Jack et al----3

have always been residents of the State of Mississippi and have not received any benefits as Choctaw Indians. The applicant has no knowledge of the compliance by his ancestors with the provisions of the 14th article of the treaty of 1830.

The decision of the Commission as to your application and the application you make on behalf of your wife and minor child, for identification as Mississippi Choctaws, will be determined at the earliest possible date and report of the same made to the Secretary of the Interior, conformable to the provisions of the 21st section of the Act of Congress of June 28, 1898, and a copy of such decision will be mailed to you at your proper postoffice address as given in your testimony at this time.

Ira S. Niles, being first duly sworn, states that stenographer to the Commission to the Five Civilized Tribes, he reported in full the proceedings had in the above entitled cause, heard at Meridian, Mississippi, May 4, 1901, and that the above and foregoing is a full, true and correct transcription of his stenographic notes in said cause taken the day and date above mentioned.

Subscribed and sworn to before me this the 7th day of May, A.D.1901, at Meridian, Mississippi.

Notary Public.

DEPARTMENT OF THE INTERIOR,
COMMISSION TO THE FIVE CIVILIZED TRIBES,
Meridian, Mississippi, July 5th, 1901.

In the matter of the application of John Jack et al for identification as Mississippi Choctaws, M.C.C.Field No.2006.

Sallie John, being first duly sworn, testified as follows:

Examination by the Commission.

Q What is your name? A Sallie John.
Q How old are you? A Twenty-three.
Q What is your postoffice address? A Paulding, Mississippi.
Q What County? A Jasper County.
Q How long have you lived in the State of Mississippi? A All life
Q Is your father living? A No.
Q What was his name? A Adam Lewis.
Q Did your father always live here in Mississippi? A Yes.
Q How long has he been dead? A Don't know.
Q About how long? A I was three or four years old when he died.
Q About how old a man was he when he died, do you know? A No sir.
Q Do you remember him? A No.
Q Is your mother living? A Don't know if she is living, or not. Heard that my mother was dead not long ago. She has been living in State-Line and I in Kemper. I been raised by my grandmother.
Q You haven't lived with your mother then since the death of your father? A No.
Q Has your mother always lived in the State of Mississippi? A Yes.
Q How much Choctaw blood do you claim to have? A Full blood.
Q Both of your parents were full blood Choctaw Indians? A Yes.
Q You speak and understand the Choctaw language and some English? A Yes.
Q Do you remember the names of any of your grandparents? A Don't know my grandmother's English name; her Choctaw name is Min-ta-ho-nah.
Q Is she living? A Dead.
Q How long has she been dead? A Six years.
Q Is she the one who raised you? A Yes sir.
Q Was she your mother's mother or father's mother? A Father's mother.
Q Do you know the names of any other of your grandparents, do you know your mother's mother's name? A Don't know.
Q Do you know your mother's father's name? A No.
Q Do you know your father's father's name? A Lewis.
Q Didn't he have a Choctaw name? A I don't know, I was too small then; I don't know.
Q He died when you were a child then? A Yes.
Q About how old was your father's mother when she died, your grandmother whom you lived with? A Don't know.
Q Can't you give us an idea of about how old she was? A No.
Q Was she a very old woman when she died, six years ago? A Yes.
Q Had she always lived in the State of Mississippi? A Yes.
Q Do you know the names of any other of your ancestors further back than your grandparents? A No.
Q Do you know whether your father or mother, either of them, were ever recognized in any manner or enrolled as members of the Choctaw Tribe of Indians in Indian Territory by the Choctaw Tribal authorities or by the United States authorities? A Don't know.

John Jack et al-testimony of Sallie John -2

Q Are you married? A Yes.
Q What is your husband's name? A Jack John.
Q Did your husband appear before the Commission here at Meridian on May 4th, last and make application for the identification of himself, you and your child Davis as Mississippi Choctaws? A Yes.

The records of the Commission show that on May 4th, 1901, one Jack John appeared before the Commission at Meridian, Mississippi, and made application for the identification of himself, his wife Sallie and minor child Davis as Mississippi Choctaws, their names appearing on Mississippi Choctaw Card, Field No.R-2006.

Q Does your husband understand the English language? A Not much.
Q He made application for the child named Davis; did you ever have a child by that name? A Yes.
Q Is he living now? A Dead.
Q When did he die? A Three years ago.
Q Do you know the date on which he died? A December.
Q Three years next December? A Yes.
Q Do you remember the day of the month? A Don't know.
Q Have you any children living? A Yes.
Q How many have you living? A One.
Q What is that child's name? A Olevia John.
Q How old is Olevia? A Six months old.
Q What day was she born? A February 6th, 1901.
Q Is Olevia the child you have with you here today before the Commission? A Yes.
Q How did it happen that your husband did not give in the name of this child Olevia? A I don't know. He can't speak English very well.
Q Is that the reason he didn't give in the child's name? A Yes.
Q How do you account for his giving in the name of Davis, whom you say is dead, and not telling us about it? A John Didn't understand much. We thought he give this one in when he gave Davis.
Q You think then that it was because he didn't understand English much that he got mixed up, is that it? A Yes.
Q The application of your husband should have been for him and you and one child, Olevia; is that right? A Yes.
Q Do you know whether your name is on any of the Choctaw Tribal rolls out in Indian Territory? A Don't know.
Q Did you ever make application to the Choctaw Tribal authorities in Indian Territory to be enrolled as a member of that Tribe? A No
Q Did you or your husband, or anyone for either of you, in 1896, make application to the Commission to the Five Civilized Tribes for citizenship in the Choctaw Nation? Did you make such an application five years ago to this Commission? No, this is first time.
Q Do you know whether any of your ancestors or any of your husband's ancestors were living in the old Choctaw Nation here in Mississippi and Alabama in the year 1830 when the treaty of Dancing Rabbit Creek was made? That was nearly 71 years ago, do you know whether any of your ancestors, or forefathers, or any of his forefathers were living here at that time, over 70 years ago? A Don't know.
Q Do you know whether your grandmother Min-ta-ho,nah was living at that time, or not? A Yes.
Q Do you know whether your grandmother Min-ta-ho-nah, or any other of your ancestors, ever received any land from the Government here in Mississippi? A Don't know.

Jack John et al-testimony of Sallie John--3

Q Did your grandmother ever own any land here? A Don't know.
Q Do you understand the 14th article of the treaty of 1830 between the United States and the Choctaw Indians? A Don't know about that

The treaty of Dancing Rabbit Creek was entered into between the United States Government and the Choctaw Tribe of Indians here in Mississippi in the year 1830, September 27, 1830. It was made for the purpose of securing the removal of the Choctaws out to the new country and at that time some of the Choctaws were unwilling to move out there and for their benefit the 14th article was put into the treaty. That article reads as follows:-

"Each Choctaw head of a family being desirous to remain and become a citizen of the States, shall be permitted to do so, by signifying his intention to the Agent within six months from the ratification of this Treaty, and he or she shall thereupon be entitled to a reservation of one section of six hundred and forty acres of land, to be bounded by sectional lines of survey; in like manner shall be entitled to one half that quantity for each unmarried child which is living with him over ten years of age; and a quarter section to such child as may be under ten years of age, to adjoin the location of the parent. If they reside upon said lands intending to become citizens of the States for five years after the ratification of this Treaty, in that case a grant in fee simple shall issue; said reservation shall include the present improvement of the head of the family or a portion of it. Persons who claim under this article shall not lose the privilege of a Choctaw citizen, but if they ever remove are not to be entitled to any portion of the Choctaw annuity."

Q Do you understand that now? A Yes.
Q Have you ever heard whether any of your people, any of your ancestors, ever received any land under this 14th article of the treaty of 1830? A No.
Q If they ever got any land then from the Government under this 14th article of the treaty of 1830, you never heard of it? A No.
Q In 1837 an Act of Congress was passed by which Commissioners were appointed by the Government to come down here in Mississippi and hear the claims of Choctaws who thought they ought to have land under the 14th article of the treaty of 1830. Do you know whether any of your ancestors came before these Commissioners and endeavored to establish their rights to land under that 14th article? Do you know? A Don't know.
Q Another Commission was appointed under the Act of Congress of August 23, 1842, ; do you know whether any of your ancestors appeared before that Commission and attempted to establish their rights ?. A No.
Q Did any of your ancestors remove to the new Choctaw Nation in Indian Territory? A No.
Q So far as you know then, all of your ancestors have always lived here in Mississippi, in what comprised the old Choctaw Nation? A Yes.
Q And you never heard of any of them ever having gotten any land from the Government? A No.
Q Did you ever hear of any of your husband's ancestors ever getting any land from the Government? A No.
Q Is your husband living? A Yes.
Q What is his name? A Billy John.

Jack John et al--testimony of Sallie John--4

Q How old a man is Billy John? A Don't know.
Q Is he an old man? A Yes.
Q Did you ever hear him say whether he ever got any land from the Government or not? A No.
Q You never heard whether he ever got any land or not? A No.
Q Is your husband's mother living? A Yes.
Q Is she an old woman or a young woman? A Old woman.
Q What is her name? A Sohie.
Q Did you ever hear whether she ever got any land from the Government, or not? A No.
Q Do you know the names of any of your husband's grandparents? A No.
Q You don't know then whether any of them ever got any land from the Government? A No.
Q Do you know whether any of your grandparents ever got any scrip from the Government? A Don't know.
Q Do you know whether any of your husband's ancestors ever got any scrip from the Government? A No.
Q Do you know whether any of your husband's ancestors appeared before any of the Commissions appointed by the Act of Congress of March 3, 1837, or August 23, 1842, to which I have above referred, and attempted to establish their rights under the provisions of the 14th article of the treaty of 1830? A Don't know.
Q Are there any further statements you want to make at this time in support of your application? A No.
Q Do you know of any persons that would be apt to know more about your family than you know about them and as to whether any of your people or your husband's people ever got any land from the Government? A No.
Q Have you any documentary evidence, affidavits, written testimony of any description, copies of records, deeds or patents, or any proper papers, showing that any of your ancestors were recognized members of the Choctaw Tribe of Indians in Mississippi in 1830, when the treaty of Dancing Rabbit Creek was made, that they ever complied or attempted to comply with the provisions of the 14th article of that treaty or ever received any benefits thereunder? A No.
Q Did you ever see any deeds or patents from the United States Government giving land to any of your people or any of your husband's people? A No.

    This applicant and her child Olevia are both present before the Commission at this time and both have every appearance and characteristic of full blood Indians. The applicant speaks and understands the Choctaw language and also speaks and understands English fairly well, the examination having been conducted partially in English and partially through a sworn Choctaw interpreter.

------- -----

 Ira S. Niles, being first duly sworn, states that as stenographer to the Commission to the Five Civilized Tribes he reported in full the proceedings had in the above entitled cause, heard at Meridian, Mississippi, July 5th, 1901, and that the above and foregoing is a full, true and correct transcript of his stenographic notes taken in said proceedings on said date.
Subscribed and sworn to before me this the 26th day of July, 1901, at Meridian, Mississippi.

                 Notary Public.

(COPY)

Department of the Interior
Commission to the Five Civilized Tribes
Chickasaw Land Office
Tishomingo, I.T.
Sep. 26, 1903.

In the matter of the declaration and proof of settlement within the Choctaw Chickasaw Country of Jack John and his minor child Olevia John.

Mississippi Choctaw card 430.   Mississippi Choctaw roll numbers 1249 and 1251.

Jack John being first duly sworn testified as follows:

Examination by the Commission.

Q   What is your name?   A Jack John.
Q   What is your age?   A About twenty five.
Q. What is your post office address?   A Kemp.
Q. What is your father's name?   A Billy John.
Q. What is your mother's name?   A Sookey.
Q. Are you married?   A Yes.
Q. What is your wife's name?   A Maggie. Davis.
Q   Were you married before you married her?   A Yes.
Q   What was your other wife's name?   A Sallie.
Q. What is the name of Sallie's father?   A Adam.
Q. Who was her mother?   A I dont know.
Q   Is Sallie dead?   A Yes.
Q   When did Sallie die?   A March 16th 1902.
Q. Have you any children?   A Yes.
Q   How many?   A One.
Q   What is its name?   A Olevia John.
Q   Who is Olevia's mother?   A Sallie.
Q. Is Olevia living now?   A Yes.
Q. How old was Olevia when Sallie died?   A One year old.
Q   How old is Olevia now?   A The 9th of February she was two years old.
Q   What age did you give for Olevia when you made application to the Commission to be enrolled?   A Four months.
Q   Have you had any other children besides this one?   A No.
A   Just that one.
Q   It appears from the records of the Commission that you gave the age of Olevia at the time you made application for enrollment as six years of age; is this a mistake?   A Yes
Q. What was your post office address in Mississippi?   A Paulding.
Q   When did you leave Mississippi to go to the Choctaw Chickasaw Country?   A February.
Q. Did you come directly to Indian Territory?   A Yes.
Q   Did you bring Olevia with you?---A--Yes
Q   Where did you locate in Indian Territory?   A Cale.
Q   Did you bring Olevia with you?   A Yes sir.

Q   Did you bring Sallie with you?   A   She was dead.
Q   Is Olevia living with you now?   A   Yes sir
Q   Did you bring your household goods with you from Mississippi?   A   Yes.
Q.   Have you any home in Mississippi at the present time?   A   No.
Q   Do you intend to reside permanently in Indian Territory?

A   Yes sir.
Q   What will be your permanent post office address?   A   Kemp.
Q   Are you the identical Jack John who with his wife Sallie and his child Olevia were identified by the Commission as Mississippi Choctaws on April 11, 1903:   A   Yes.
Q   Have you made any agreement with a view to leasing the land which you are about to select?   A   No.

Clara Mitchell Wood being first duly sworn upon her oath states that she reported the above proceedings on the 26th day of September 1903 and that this is a correct transcript of her stenographic notes.

                (Signed) Clara Mitchell Wood.

Subscribed and sworn to before me this 2nd day of October 1903.

                (Signed) J. E. Williams
                       Notary Public.

DEPARTMENT OF THE INTERIOR,

COMMISSIONER TO THE FIVE CIVILIZED TRIBES,

----oOo----

Muskogee, Indian Territory, February 5, 1907.

----oOo----

IN THE MATTER of the application for the identification of Maggie John, nee Maggie Nickey, Lizzie, Billy, Sam, Bettie, Russel and Mollie Mass Nickey as Mississippi Choctaws.

....

Rehearing had at the office of the Commissioner to the Five Civilized Tribes at Muskogee, Indian Territory, on the above date in conformity with Departmental instructions of January 12, 1907 (I T D 12338-1904, 82-1907), due notice of which hearing has heretofore been furnished the principal applicant, L. D. Horton, her attorney, and the attorneys for the Choctaw and Chickasaw Nations.

....

APPEARANCES: Maggie John, applicant.
L. D. Horton, attorney of record.
No appearance on behalf of the Choctaw and Chickasaw Nations.

----------oOo----------

MAGGIE JOHN, being first duly sworn, testified as follows:

By the Commissioner:

Q What is your name ? A Maggie John.
Q How old are you ? A I don't know.
Q Don't you have some idea about how old you are ? A. No.
Q What is your post office address ? A Paucaunla.
Q Is that in the Chickasaw Nation, Indian Territory ? A Yes sir.
Q What is the name of your father ? A Nickey.
Q Did he have any other name besides Nickey ? A Yes sir.
Q What did they call him ? A Nickey Davis.
Q Is he living or dead ? A Dead.
Q How long ago did he die ? A I don't know.
Q Can you remember when he died ? A No sir.
Q You know where he died ? A Yes sir.
Q Where ? A Mississippi.
Q He never came to the Indian Territory, did he ? A No.
Q What is the name of your mother ? A Nickey.
Q What is her first name - - what other name did she have besides Nickey ? A Nancy Davis.

- Q Is she living ? A Yes sir.
- Q Where does she live ? A State of Mississippi.
- Q Near what town does she live; where does she get her mail? A Missionary.
- Q How much Choctaw blood did your father have, Nickey Davis? A (No response).
- Q He was an Indian, wasn't he ? A Yes sir.
- Q Was he a full blood ? A Yes sir.
- Q Are you sure that he was a full blood Mississippi Choctaw? A Yes sir.
- Q How do you know that ? A (No response).
- Q Did you ever see your father ? A Yes sir.
- Q Do you know the name of your father's father ? A Yes sir.
- Q What was his name, your grandfather's name ? A (No response).
- Q Have you any brothers ? A Yes sir.
- Q What are their names ? A Billy, Sam.
- Q Are these all the brothers you have ?A Yes sir.
- Q Have you some sisters ? A Yes sir.
- Q What are their names ? A Bettie, Mollie and Lizzie.
- Q Are all your brothers and sisters living ? A No.
- Q Which ones are dead ? A Lizzie.
- Q Is that all ? A Yes sir, all the rest are dead.
- Q Do you know when Lizzie died, how long ago ? A 6 years.
- Q Did any of your brothers or sisters ever come to the Indian Territory from Mississippi ? A They stayed in Mississippi.
- Q Never removed to the Indian Territory - never came out here from Mississippi ? A No sir.
- Q These children that you have named are your full brothers and sisters, are they ? A Yes sir.
- Q You had the same father and the same mother ? A Yes sir.
- Q Are your brothers and sisters younger than you are or older ? A Younger.
- Q Wasn't Lizzie older than you are ? A Yes sir.
- Q And Billy was to, wasn't he ? A Yes sir.
- Q Then you were the next child after Billy ? A Yes sir.
- Q Are you married ? A Yes sir.
- Q What is the name of your husband ? A Jack John.
- Q How long have you been married to Jack John ? A 4 years.
- Q Did you marry him in Mississippi ? A Yes sir.
- Q And you came out here together to the Indian Territory, you and your husband ? A Yes sir.

    By the Commissioner to Mr. Horton:
- Q. Mr. Horton this applicant does not make any claim under the 14th article ?
- A. None whatever.
- Q. Her claim is as a full blood ?
- A. Yes sir.

- Q Did Jack John have a wife named Sallie ? A Yes sir.
- Q Sallie died and then you married Jack John ? A Yes sir.
- Q Did he have a child by Sallie named Olevia John ? A Yes sir.

    The name of Jack John appears upon a schedule of identified Mississippi Choctaws opposite No. 1249 approved by the Secretary of the Interior June 1, 1903, and upon a final roll of Mississippi Choctaws opposite No. 702 approved by the Secretary of the Interior January 13, 1905.

By Mr. Horton:

Q How big was you, Maggie, when your father died; about how high was you when your father died ? A 10 years old.
Q Do you remember him well, remember how he looked; you remember what kind of a looking man he was ? A Yes sir.
Q Well how did he look - - I mean by that did he look just like those other Indians out there ? A Yes sir.
Q Well now Maggie do you remember when the Dawes Commission were in Mississippi five or six years ago ? A Yes sir.
Q Did your mother leave home to go before that Commission or not ? A Yes sir.
Q Do you know the name of the place that she said she went to; you know a town by the name of Meridian ? A Yes sir.
Q How long have you been living in the Indian Territory, Maggie ? A Three years.
Q Did you come with your husband, Jack John, when he came ? A Yes sir.

By the Commissioner:

> The applicant, Maggie John, has all the appearance and physical characteristics of a full blood Mississippi Choctaw.

--------------- oOo---------------

Wm. L. Martin, stenographer to the Commissioner to the Five Civilized Tribes, on oath states that he recorded the testimony and proceedings had in this cause, and that the above and foregoing is a full, true and correct transcript of his stenographic notes thereof.

Wm L Martin

Subscribed and sworn to before me this the 11th day of February, 1907.

My Commission Expires June 17 1908

Oliver C Hinkle
Notary Public.

DEPARTMENT OF THE INTERIOR,
COMMISSIONER TO THE FIVE CIVILIZED TRIBES.

In the matter of the removal to and settlement within the Choctaw-Chickasaw country, Indian Territory, of Maggie Nickey (now Maggie John), schedule of identified Mississippi Choctaws, No. . . . .

The evidence herein shows that Maggie Nickey (now Maggie John) was identified as a full-blood Mississippi Choctaw by the Commissioner to the Five Civilized Tribes March 4, 1907; that she removed to and established her residence in the Choctaw-Chickasaw country, Indian Territory in the month of February 1903; that satisfactory proof of such removal and settlement was submitted to the Commissioner to the Five Civilized Tribes February 5, 1907, and that she is, therefore, entitled to enrollment as a Mississippi Choctaw under the provisions of Section 41 of the Act of Congress approved July 1, 1902 (32 Stats., 641).

Commissioner.

Muskogee, Indian Territory,
MAR - 1 1907

DEPARTMENT OF THE INTERIOR,
COMMISSION TO THE FIVE CIVILIZED TRIBES.

In the matter of the application of Jack John, et al., for identification as Mississippi Choctaws, M.C.R.2006.

......D E C I S I O N......

It appears from the record herein that application for identification as Mississippi Choctaws was made to this Commission on May 4, 1901, by Jack John for himself, his wife, Sallie John, and his minor child, Davis John, under the following provision of the act of Congress approved June 28, 1898, (30 Stats., 495):

> "Said Commission shall have authority to determine the identity of Choctaw Indians claiming rights in the Choctaw lands under article fourteen of the treaty between the United States and the Choctaw Nation, concluded September twenty-seventh, eighteen hundred and thirty, and to that end may administer oaths, examine witnesses and perform all other acts necessary thereto and make report to the Secretary of the Interior."

It further appears that on July 5, 1901, Sallie John, wife of the principal applicant herein, appeared before this Commission and testified that at the time her said husband made application for the identification of himself, wife and child, the child Davis John had been dead three years, and that their child then living,

8

and who should have been applied for, was named Olevia John, who was born on February 6, 1901.

From the evidence submitted in support of said application it appears that all the applicants are full-blood Mississippi Choctaw Indians.

Section forty-one of the act of Congress entitled "An Act To ratify and confirm an agreement with the Choctaw and Chickasaw tribes of Indians, and for other purposes," approved July 1, 1902, (32 Stats., 641), and ratified by the Choctaw and Chickasaw Nations September 25, 1902, provides as follows:

> "The application of no person for identification as a Mississippi Choctaw shall be received by said Commission after six months subsequent to the date of the final ratification of this agreement and in the disposition of such applications all full-blood Mississippi Choctaw Indians and the descendants of any Mississippi Choctaw Indians whether of full or mixed blood who received a patent to land under the said fourteenth article of the said treaty of eighteen hundred and thirty who had not moved to and made bona fide settlement in the Choctaw-Chickasaw country prior to June twenty-eighth, eighteen hundred and ninety-eight, shall be deemed to be Mississippi Choctaws, entitled to benefits under article fourteen of the said treaty of September twenty-seventh, eighteen hundred and thirty, and to identification as such by said Commission, but this direction or provision shall be deemed to be only a rule of evidence and shall not be invoked by or operate to the advantage of any applicant who is not a Mississippi Choctaw of the full blood, or who is not the descendant of a Mississippi Choctaw who received a patent to land under said treaty, or who is otherwise barred from the right of citizenship in the Choctaw Nation, all of said Mississippi Choctaws so enrolled by said Commission shall be upon a separate roll."

It is, therefore, the opinion of this Commission that Jack John, Sallie John and Olevia John should be identified as

-3-

Mississippi Choctaws, and it is so ordered.

COMMISSION TO THE FIVE CIVILIZED TRIBES,

_____
Acting Chairman.

_____
Commissioner.

_____
Commissioner.

Muskogee, Indian Territory,

APR 11 1903

_____
Commissioner.

COMMISSIONERS:
HENRY L. DAWES,
TAMS BIXBY,
THOMAS B. NEEDLES,
C. R. BRECKINRIDGE.

ALLISON L. AYLESWORTH,
SECRETARY.

DEPARTMENT OF THE INTERIOR,
COMMISSION TO THE FIVE CIVILIZED TRIBES.

ADDRESS ONLY THE
COMMISSION TO THE FIVE CIVILIZED TRIBES.

Carthage, Mississippi, December 18th, 1901.

Commission to the Five Civilized Tribes,
    Muskogee, Indian Territory,
Gentlemen:-

    Referring to M.C.C.Field No.517, I have to advise that from information received by me in Jasper County, I have reason to believe that these are the same persons whose names appear upon M.C.C.Field No.R-2006. Their names appear upon page 106 of the schedule, being numbers 1862 and 1863 thereon.

                Yours truly,

                      Guy L. V. Emerson

COMMISSION
No.
17658
1901   DEC 23 1901

Emerson, Guy V.,
Carthage, Miss.
Dec 16, 1901

CHOCTAW

States that names on M.C.R.
Field No. 517 are same as those
that appear on M.C.R. Field
No. R-2006.

DEPARTMENT OF THE INTERIOR,
COMMISSION TO THE FIVE CIVILIZED TRIBES.
FILED
DEC 27 1901

ACTING CHAIRMAN.

MCR 2006

M.C.R. 8006.

COPY

Muskogee, Indian Territory, April 11, 1903.

Mansfield, McMurray & Cornish,
    Attorneys for the Choctaw and Chickasaw Nation,
        South McAlester, Indian Territory.

Gentlemen:

    Enclosed herewith you will find a copy of the decision of the Commission rendered April 11, 1903, identifying Jack John, his wife, Sallie John, and minor child, Clevia John, as Mississippi Choctaw Indians under the provisions of the act of Congress approved July 1, 1902, (32 Stats., 641).

    You are hereby advised that you will be allowed fifteen days from the date hereof, in which to file with this Commission such protest as you desire to make against the action of the Commission in identifying the said Jack John, his wife and child as Mississippi Choctaws, and make satisfactory proof of service of said protest upon the applicants herein.

    If you fail to file such protest within the time allowed, the names of the applicants herein will be placed upon the schedule of duly identified Mississippi Choctaws now being prepared by this Commission.

                      Respectfully,
                      (SIGNED) *Tams Bixby.*
                              Chairman.

Registered.
Enc.8006.

COPY. M.C.R. 2006

Muskogee, Indian Territory, April 27, 1903.

Jack John,
  Paulding, Mississippi.

Dear Sir:

    Enclosed herewith you will find a copy of the decision of the Commission to the Five Civilized Tribes, rendered April 11, 1903, identifying yourself, your wife, Sallie John, and minor child, Olevia John, as Mississippi Choctaw Indians under the provisions of article 41 of the Act of Congress approved July 1, 1902, (32 Stats., 641).

    If you remove to the Choctaw-Chickasaw country, Indian Territory, before October 11, 1903, you will have six months from that date, or until April 11, 1904, within which to make proof of such removal and settlement at the office of the Commission at Atoka, Choctaw Nation, or Tishomingo, Chickasaw Nation.

                              Respectfully,

                              (SIGNED):

                              Tams Bixby,
                                Chairman.

Registered.
Enc. 2006.

M C R 2006

Muskogee, Indian Territory, February 26, 1904.

Sedley S. Lowe,
    Attorney at Law,
        Sterrett, Indian Territory.

Dear Sir:

    Receipt is hereby acknowledged of your letter of the 22nd instant, stating that Jack John, a Mississippi Choctaw, requests you to inquire if his wife, known as Maggie John, Maggie Davis, or Maggie Russell Davis, is "on the roll."

    In reply you are advised that on April 11, 1903, the Commission rendered a decision identifying Jack John, his wife, Sallie John, and minor child, Olevia John, as full blood Mississippi Choctaws, of which action Jack John was duly notified on April 27, 1903.

    Our records do not show that any person by the name of Maggie John, Maggie Davis, or Maggie Russell Davis, wife of Jack John, is an applicant to this Commission for identification as a Mississippi Choctaw.

                   Respectfully,

                                  Commissioner in Charge.

M.C.R.2006

Muskogee, Indian Territory, April 8, 1904.

Jack John,
    In care of S. T. Johns,
        Box 46,
           Kemp, Indian Territory.

Dear Sir:

    Receipt is hereby acknowledged of your letter of April 1, 1904, in which you ask if you can be permitted to make selection of allotment for your deceased wife, Sally John, and if your present wife, Maggy John, is entitled to a share in the lands of the Choctaw and Chickasaw Nations.

    In reply to your letter you are advised that it appears from our records that on April 11, 1903, the Commission rendered a decision identifying you, your wife, Sallie John, and minor child, Olevia John, as full-blood Mississippi Choctaws, of which action you were duly notified on April 27, 1903.

    It further appears from our records that on September 26, 1903, you appeared at the Chickasaw Land Office, at Tishomingo, Indian Territory, and testified relative to the removal to and settlement within the Choctaw-Chickasaw country of yourself and minor child, Olevia John. At that time you stated that your

J. J., 2.

wife, Sallie, died March 16, 1902.

    As your wife, Sallie John, died prior to the date of the rendition of the decision by the Commission, identifying her as a Mississippi Choctaw, it cannot be presumed that she acquired any right to share in the distribution of the tribal property of the Choctaw and Chickasaw Nations. Therefore you cannot be permitted to make selection of allotment in her name.

    Our records do not show that any person by the name of Maggie John is an applicant before the Commission for identification as a Mississippi Choctaw, and under the following provision of the act of Congress approved July 1, 1902, which was ratified by the citizens of the Choctaw and Chickasaw Nations September 25, 1902:-

> "The application of no person for identification as a Mississippi Choctaw shall be received by said Commission after six months subsequent to the date of the final ratification of this agreement......"

this Commission is now without authority to receive or consider the application of any person for identification as a Mississippi Choctaw.

    Respectfully,

    Commissioner in Charge.

No. 2006

For Identification as a Mississippi Choctaw.

Date MAY -4 1901

Name Jack John.

Age 22. Blood full.

Post Office Paulding, Miss.

Father: Billy John - dead.

Mother: (don't know). - dead

Claims through both parents -

WIFE: Sallie John (full) 21

FATHER: Adam Lewis - dead.

MOTHER: Eliza Lewis - ✓

Children:
Davis John   5.

Claims for himself, his wife and one child.

Stenographer
G. S. Niles.

FINAL ROLL

OF

MISSISSIPPI CHOCTAWS

Ages calculated to September 25, 1902.

[Dawes]

FINAL ROLL OF MISSISSIPPI CHOCTAWS.

Ages calculated to September 25, 1902.

Roll No.	Name	Age	Sex	Blood
1	Hussey, William Hancock	5	M	1-16
2	Hussey, Alvin McDowell	3	M	1-16
3	Roe, J. Folsom	44	M	1-4
4	Roe, Jeannette C.	17	F	1-8
5	Hancock, Jubal A.	26	M	1-8
6	Gibson, Alex	24	M	Full
7	Johnson, Frank	12	M	Full
8	Johnson, Allen	9	M	Full
9	Johnson, Lela	7	F	Full
10	Baptiste, Joseph, Jr.	30	M	Full
11	Taylor, Baptiste	30	M	Full
12	Taylor, Elizabeth	28	F	Full
13	Taylor, Lem	10	M	Full
14	Taylor, Stanley	5	M	Full
15	Taylor, Louisa	3	F	Full
16	Tom, Lina	30	F	Full
17	Tom, Amos	11	M	Full
18	Tom, Leona	5	F	Full
19	Dansby, Jacob	26	M	Full
20	Billey, Cornelius	15	M	Full
21	Billey, Eliza	33	F	Full
22	Bob, Jim	10	M	Full
23	Billey, Wicks	6	M	Full
24	Cuttie, Annie	12	F	Full
25	Wallace, Tom	21	M	Full
26	Isom, John	47	M	Full
27	Isom, Mary	41	F	Full
28	Isom, Rosie	6	F	Full
29	Isom, John, Jr.	6	M	Full
30	Philip, Nancy	14	F	Full
31	Davis, Tom	47	M	Full
32	Davis, Rena	47	F	Full
33	Davis, Walton	19	M	Full
34	Davis, Alice	17	F	Full
35	Davis, Emma	18	F	Full
36	Davis, Oscar	10	M	Full
37	Davis, John	6	M	Full
38	Ellis, Habett	19	M	Full
39	Gibson, Walter	20	F	Full
40	In-pun-nuhbee, Mingo	60	M	Full
41	Chubbee, Cully	35	M	Full
42	Kelly, Joe	24	M	Full
43	Kelly, Lizzie	23	F	Full
44	Willis, Mary	32	F	Full
45	Willis, Silly	13	F	Full
46	Willis, Mandy	9	F	Full
47	Willis, Anna	6	F	Full
48	Willis, Abel	4	M	Full
49	Thomas, Bob	37	M	Full
50	Thomas, Daley	32	F	Full
51	Thomas, Ransom	15	M	Full
52	Thomas, Berry	13	F	Full
53	Thomas, Emeline	10	F	Full
54	Thomas, Sam	6	M	Full
55	Thomas, Samawail	8	M	Full
56	Cooper, Jacob	41	M	Full
57	Cooper, Julia	36	F	Full
58	Cooper, Foster	19	M	Full
59	Cooper, Janie	3	F	Full
60	Cooper, Susie	5	F	Full
61	Cooper, Georgie	7	F	Full
62	Davis, Alex	22	M	Full
63	Joshua, Levisa	18	F	Full
64	Toby, William	27	M	Full
65	Jackson, Melvins	46	F	Full
66	Jackson, Marcelene	19	F	Full
67	Solomon, Winnie	68	F	Full
68	Jackson, Henry	23	M	Full
69	Jackson, Sealy	21	F	Full
70	Tom, Ahlean	30	F	Full
71	Tom, John	14	M	Full
72	Tom, Sallie	3	F	Full
73	Sampson, Johnson	42	M	Full
74	Sampson, Sallie	41	F	Full
75	Sampson, Senie	16	F	Full
76	Sampson, Jim	14	M	Full
77	Sampson, George	12	M	Full
78	Sampson, Sealy Ann	10	F	Full
79	Sampson, Pauline	5	F	Full
80	Sampson, Gus	6	M	Full
81	Sampson, Bennie	4	M	Full
82	Sampson, Mary Ann	2	F	Full
83	Golden, Abe	26	M	Full
84	Golden, Louisa	27	F	Full
85	Golden, Mollie	8	F	Full
86	Byrnes, Cricket	23	F	Full
87	Sweeney, Robert	26	M	Full
88	Sweeney, Ara Ann	23	F	Full
89	Sweeney, Joseph	5	M	Full
90	Sweeney, Frank	1	M	Full
91	Smith, Seborn	38	M	Full
92	Smith, Emma	40	F	Full
93	Amos, Dan	12	M	Full
94	Sam, Huddleston	21	M	Full
95	Willis, John (Tom-tah-tubbee)	53	M	Full
96	Willis, Susie Ann (or Susie Ann)	42	F	Full
97	Willis, Lee	14	M	Full
98	Willis, Adolphus	8	M	Full
99	Willis, Will	6	M	Full
100	Willis, Walter	5	M	Full
101	Willis, Mary	1	F	Full
102	Hawkins, Billy	48	M	Full
103	Hawkins, Jerden	12	M	Full
104	York, Dixon	42	M	Full
105	York, Josephine	28	F	Full
106	York, Sydney	19	M	Full
107	York, Bettie	14	F	Full
108	York, Sallie	11	F	Full
109	York, Lee	9	M	Full
110	York, Alice	4	F	Full
111	York, Lola	1	F	Full
112	Wallace, Jim	27	M	Full
113	Wallace, Mary	22	F	Full
114	Toby, Lewis	50	M	Full
115	Toby, Ellen	50	F	Full
116	Wallace, Jim	38	M	Full
117	Wallace, Lizzie	22	F	Full
118	Wallace, Walter	11	M	Full
119	Wallace, David	5	M	Full
120	Wallace, Mary	1	F	Full
121	Isaac, John	42	M	Full
122	Isaac, Lucy	35	F	Full
123	Isaac, Clinton	18	M	Full
124	Isaac, Tennis	15	M	Full
125	Isaac, Hatmond	12	M	Full
126	Isaac, Hollis	8	M	Full
127	Isaac, Nabors	4	M	Full
128	Isaac, Tommie	6	M	Full
129	Isaac, Mandy	2	F	Full
130	Foley, Davis	21	M	Full
131	Jim, Lucy (Lo-nah)	21	F	Full
132	Phillip, Wesley	20	M	Full
133	Phillip, Maggie	4	F	Full
134	Wilkerson, Sam (or John)	38	M	Full
135	Wilkerson, Annie	27	F	Full
136	Wilkerson, Mollie	9	F	Full
137	Wilkerson, Lemie	8	F	Full
138	Wilkerson, Isetralen	5	F	Full
139	Wilkerson, Mary	3	F	Full
140	Wilkerson, Cora	1	F	Full
141	Postoak, Jack	57	M	Full
142	Postoak, Fee Kelly	6	M	Full
143	Postoak, Sam	3	M	Full
144	Willis, Mack	31	M	Full
145	Dixon, John	38	M	Full
146	Dixon, Feely	25	F	Full
147	Guss, Nancy	30	F	Full
148	Guss, Sina	18	F	Full
149	Guss, Rafe	15	M	Full
150	Guss, Alice	9	F	Full
151	Shoemaker, Jackson (La-we-tubbee)	48	M	Full
152	Shoemaker, Jennie	29	F	Full
153	Shoemaker, Watson	7	M	Full

INDEX AND FINAL ROLLS OF CITIZENS AND FREEDMEN

Roll No.	Name	Age	Sex	Blood
154	Shoemake, Ernest	3	M	Full
155	Shoemake, Mansi	5	F	Full
156	Shoemake, Ada	1	F	Full
157	Shoemake, Rhoda	1	F	Full
158	Phillip, Sock	32	M	Full
159	Phillip, Plea Tinsley	20	M	Full
160	Phillip, Bettie	18	F	Full
161	Phillip, Lewis	10	M	Full
162	Phillip, Celia Ann	7	F	Full
163	Sockey, Will	22	M	Full
164	Willis, John	38	M	Full
165	Willis, Hickman	19	M	Full
166	Willis, Margaret	17	F	Full
167	Willis, Lillie	8	F	Full
168	Willis, Fannie	5	F	Full
169	Willis, Elpa	3	F	Full
170	Willis, Sam Houston	1	M	Full
171	Wilson, Billy	38	M	Full
172	Wilson, Maggie	35	F	Full
173	Wilson, Sampson	11	M	Full
174	Wilson, Sammie	9	M	Full
175	Wilson, Jimmie	7	M	Full
176	Wilson, Freeman	4	M	Full
177	Wilson, Dick Russell	1	M	Full
178	Toby, John	22	M	Full
179	Sampson, John	37	M	Full
180	Sampson, Louisiana	35	F	Full
181	Sampson, Emeline	16	F	Full
182	Sampson, Steve	14	M	Full
183	Sampson, Oscar	11	M	Full
184	Sampson, Arlone	9	F	Full
185	Sampson, Spence	7	M	Full
186	Sampson, Artis	5	M	Full
187	Sampson, Cenie	3	F	Full
188	Billey, Ben	40	M	Full
189	Bull, John (On-ta-tubbee)	80	M	Full
190	Willie, Billy	29	M	Full
191	Simmons, Leona	18	F	Full
192	Simmons, Robert	3	M	Full
193	Simmons, Maggie	8	F	Full
194	Simmons, King	6	M	Full
195	Simmons, Pigfoot	3	M	Full
196	Simmons, Mamie	1	F	Full
197	Johnson, Louis	30	M	Full
198	Johnson, Mettie	15	F	Full
199	Wallace, John	52	M	Full
200	Wallace, Leona	20	F	Full
201	Wallace, William	15	M	Full
202	Baptiste, Joseph	45	M	Full
203	Baptiste, Felice	40	F	Full
204	Baptiste, Louise	14	F	Full
205	Baptiste, Madline	12	F	Full
206	Baptiste, Sammy	10	M	Full
207	Baptiste, Johnnie	5	M	Full
208	Lewis, Smith	26	M	Full
209	Lewis, Chuly	18	F	Full
210	Lewis, Jacob	6	M	Full
211	Charley, Emil	15	M	Full
212	Postoak, Sarah	35	F	Full
213	Chubbee, Leanna	60	F	Full
214	Wallace, Comby	17	M	Full
215	John, Sidney	28	M	Full
216	John, Bettie	28	F	Full
217	John, Eva	5	F	Full
218	John, Elia	2	F	Full
219	Jackoway, Cora	12	F	Full
220	Johnson, Henry	28	M	Full
221	Johnson, Reezy	25	F	Full
222	Johnson, Amos	3	M	Full
223	Johnson, Thomas	1	M	Full
224	Johnson, Will	24	M	Full
225	Johnson, Frank	60	M	Full
226	Johnson, John	73	M	Full
227	Johnson, Margaret	40	F	Full
228	Johnson, Fayette	28	M	Full
229	Johnson, Isly	27	F	Full
230	Johnson, Oscar	5	F	Full
231	Johnson, Jimmie	3	M	Full
232	Johnson, Lona	2	F	Full
233	A-me-ah-tubbee, Lewis	52	M	Full
234	A-me-ah-tubbee, Henry	20	M	Full
235	A-me-ah-tubbee, Sidney	12	M	Full
236	Pistonah, Nancy	75	F	Full
237	Gibson, Ona	40	F	Full
238	York, Scott	40	M	Full
239	York, John	19	M	Full

Roll No.	Name	Age	Sex	Blood
240	York, Taylor	17	M	Full
241	York, Evan	15	M	Full
242	Bob, Winnie	60	F	Full
243	Lewis, Young	10	M	Full
244	Jim, Ellen	46	F	Full
245	Austin, Stewart	21	M	Full
246	Austin, Alice	12	F	Full
247	Phillips, Meeka	28	M	Full
248	Wickson, Sim	24	M	Full
249	Wickson, David	3	M	Full
250	Bob, Morris	45	M	Full
251	Johnson, Andy	24	M	Full
252	Allen, John (or Dixey John) (A-chok-mat-ek-tubbee)	45	M	Full
253	Polk, Jim	54	M	Full
254	Polk, Melissie	33	F	Full
255	Morris, Clemmans	16	M	Full
256	Morris, Frank	14	M	Full
257	Morris, Tracy	12	M	Full
258	Davis, Jeff	32	M	Full
259	Primus, Ben	22	M	Full
260	Elix, Davis	22	M	Full
261	Ned, Annie (Mehiotimah)	33	F	Full
262	Ned, John	16	M	Full
263	Ned, Francis	12	M	Full
264	Ned, Frank	8	M	Full
265	Ned, Ernest	5	M	Full
266	Ned, Reuben	1	M	Full
267	Simpson, Jefferson	47	M	Full
268	Simpson, Sallie	30	F	Full
269	Simpson, Marcelline	8	F	Full
270	Simpson, Backus	7	M	Full
271	Simpson, Barnett	5	M	Full
272	Simpson, Mary Corria	1	F	Full
273	Billey, William	38	M	Full
274	Billey, Fannie	30	F	Full
275	Billey, Oma	12	F	Full
276	Billey, Wilson	6	M	Full
277	Billey, Katie	3	F	Full
278	Billey, Enoch	1	M	Full
279	Boston, Lizzie	30	F	Full
280	Boston, Bennie	10	M	Full
281	Boston, Dora	8	F	Full
282	Betsey, Wilson	27	M	Full
283	Betsey, Nannie	24	F	Full
284	Betsey, Preston	6	M	Full
285	Betsey, Eva	4	F	Full
286	Betsey, Crecellus	2	M	Full
287	Tonny, Frankson	30	M	Full
288	Tonny, Fannie	28	F	Full
289	Tonny, Sibena	6	F	Full
290	Tonny, Limmer	1	M	Full
291	Morris, Watkins	38	M	Full
292	Jackson, Becky	60	F	Full
293	Thomas, Smith	22	M	Full
294	Barcus, Bob	28	M	Full
295	Old Hannah	75	F	Full
296	Tookolo, Sealy	60	F	Full
297	Tookolo, Leo Jim	2	M	Full
298	Williamson, Ben (Ni-noc-e-tubbee)	41	M	Full
299	Williamson, Amie	41	F	Full
300	Williamson, Joe	16	M	Full
301	Williamson, Pres	11	M	Full
302	Williamson, Rosie	6	F	Full
303	Neal, Jeff D.	28	M	Full
304	Neal, Dora	20	F	Full
305	Neal, Cora	2	F	Full
306	Neal, Earnest	1	M	Full
307	Lewis, David	35	M	Full
308	Lewis, Emely	22	F	Full
309	Simpson, Beeley	6	F	Full
310	Simpson, Leslie	3	F	Full
311	Billey, Alice	28	F	Full
312	Billey, Nannie	8	F	Full
313	Billey, Clay	4	M	Full
314	Meely, Leanna	45	F	Full
315	Meely, Kelley	16	M	Full
316	Meely, Botman	14	M	Full
317	Meely, Eunice	8	F	Full
318	Meely, Salie	6	F	Full
319	Willis, Riley	30	M	Full
320	Willis, Lena	28	F	Full
321	Arkansas, Susan	47	F	Full
322	Reese, Salina	21	F	Full

OF THE CHOCTAW AND CHICKASAW TRIBES.

Roll No.	Name	Age	Sex	Blood	Roll No.	Name	Age	Sex	Blood
321	Reese, Manusi		M	Full	407	Neal, Nancy		F	Full
322	Johnson, John	60	M	Full	408	Tennoa, Sallie	60	F	Full
323	Johnson, Nancy	50	F	Full	409	John, Lewis	28	M	Full
324	Johnson, Hickman	10	M	Full	410	John, Simpson	8	M	Full
325	Johnson, Albert	4	M	Full	411	Wilson, Sam		M	Full
326	Smith, Mollie	30	F	Full	412	Stephen, Jim Polk	22	M	Full
327	Smith, Aeno	11	M	Full	413	Stephen, Agnes	10	F	Full
328	Smith, Sibbie	5	F	Full	414	Rasha, Mary	37	F	Full
329	Smith, Martin	3	M	Full	415	Rasha, Jim	13	M	Full
330	Postoak, William	30	M	Full	416	Rasha, John	12	M	Full
331	Davis, Frank	30	M	Full	417	Williams, Jack	25	M	Full
332	Neal, John (Me-ah-ta-kubbee)	53	M	Full	418	Williams, Emaline	22	F	Full
					419	Williams, Mamie	7	F	Full
333	Lewis, Sina	16	F	Full	420	Williams, Smith	4	M	Full
334	Bob, Sallie	5	F	Full	421	Stricken from roll.			
335	Billey, Frank	24	M	Full	422	Johnnie, Lucy	30	F	Full
336	Billey, Lilly	23	F	Full	423	Johnnie, Hickman	14	M	Full
337	Bertis, Bill	51	M	Full	424	Johnnie, Sutt	11	M	Full
338	Bertis, Nab	30	F	Full	425	Johnnie, Criset		F	Full
339	Bertis, Sam	12	M	Full	426	Johnnie, George O.	5	M	Full
340	Bertis, Dixie	3	F	Full	427	Johnnie, Presney	1	F	Full
341	Brokeshoulder, Morris	26	M	Full	428	Johnson, Willie	24	M	Full
342	Brokeshoulder, Martha	27	F	Full	429	Jackson, Elder	70	M	Full
343	Brokeshoulder, Obediah W.	4	M	Full	430	Willis, Jim	12	M	Full
344	Brokeshoulder, Severs M.	2	F	Full	431	Jeff, Eliza	30	F	Full
345	Jim, Stephen	88	M	Full	432	Primus, Seaby	21	F	Full
346	Jim, Betsy	60	F	Full	433	Willis, Wallace	37	M	Full
347	Billey, Rena	30	F	Full	434	Willis, Nancy	27	F	Full
348	Billey, Charles E.	12	M	Full	435	Willis, Fannie	14	F	Full
349	Billey, Dawson	7	M	Full	436	Willis, Charlie	8	M	Full
350	Billey, Ormond	2	M	Full	437	Willis, Eddie	6	M	Full
351	James, Mollie	24	F	Full	438	Willis, Moses	4	M	Full
352	James, Jeff	1	M	Full	439	Frazer, Jacoway	30	M	Full
353	Johnson, Wallace	27	M	Full	440	Frazer, Frank	7	M	Full
354	Johnson, Mary	26	F	Full	441	Frazer, John		M	Full
355	Johnson, Effie	6	F	Full	442	Frazer, Sudie	4	F	Full
356	Tuffarnah, Ishaman	65	M	Full	443	Frazer, Henry	2	M	Full
357	Tuffarnah, Suella	51	F	Full	444	Baptiste, Emily (Chumpahonah)	78	F	Full
358	Tuffarnah, Moses	3	M	Full					
359	Tuffarnah, Emma	1	F	Full	445	Umber, Ida	23	F	Full
360	Jackson, Jim	20	M	Full	446	Umber, Joe	7	M	Full
361	Reese, Fannie	19	F	Full	447	Umber, Minnie	5	F	Full
362	Willis, Robison	30	M	Full	448	Horton, Bob	11	M	Full
363	Willis, Lizzie	24	F	Full	449	York, Pauline	20	F	Full
364	Willis, Davie	7	M	Full	450	York, William	2	M	Full
365	Willis, Ballison	5	M	Full	451	Pis-tubbee, Horace	40	M	Full
366	Thompson, Isaac	30	M	Full	452	Pis-tubbee, Lena	22	F	Full
367	Thompson, Betsy	31	F	Full	453	Pis-tubbee, Mattie		F	Full
368	Thompson, Juznie	16	F	Full	454	Pis-tubbee, Seleah		F	Full
369	Thompson, Sarah	14	F	Full	455	Pis-tubbee, Maggie		F	Full
370	Thompson, Arthur	11	M	Full	456	Philip, Nancy		F	Full
371	Thompson, Leona	8	F	Full	457	Williamson, Fimmo		M	Full
372	Johnson, Jim	24	M	Full	458	Williams, Smith		M	Full
373	Johnson, Amie	6	F	Full	459	Jim, Austin		M	Full
374	Johnson, Lotie	2	F	Full	460	Jim, Ott		M	Full
375	Smith, Jeff	22	M	Full	461	Jim, Martha	10	F	Full
376	Smith, Mary Jane	20	F	Full	462	Jim, Bessie	8	F	Full
377	Smith, Williamson	4	M	Full	463	Shoemaker, Willie	30	M	Full
378	Smith, Emma	1	F	Full	464	Shoemaker, Lucy	25	F	Full
379	Smith, Isabel		F	Full	465	Shoemaker, Joe	13	M	Full
380	Smith, Richardson	27	M	Full	466	Shoemaker, Amie	9	F	Full
381	Smith, Bettie	22	F	Full	467	Shoemaker, Dock	6	M	Full
382	Smith, Doyle	3	M	Full	468	Shoemaker, Fannie	4	F	Full
383	Smith, Louisa	1	F	Full	469	Shoemaker, Dan	2	M	Full
384	Williamson, Joe	45	M	Full	470	Philip, Thomas	14	M	Full
385	Williamson, Deanna	42	F	Full	471	Philip, Louisa		F	Full
386	Williamson, Steve Smith	16	M	Full	472	Philip, John Lumpkin		M	Full
387	Williamson, Malissa		F	Full	473	Tom, Thomas		M	Full
388	Hickman, Jim	30	M	Full	474	Johnson, Isaac	60	M	Full
389	Hickman, Dennis	15	M	Full	475	Johnson, Susie (Ah-bi-ho-ka)	45	F	Full
390	Hickman, Ben	8	M	Full	476	Johnson, Sallie	10	F	Full
391	Williams, Rainy	22	F	Full	477	Johnson, Pixiey		F	Full
392	Williams, Bessie		F	Full	478	Johnson, Mattie		F	Full
393	Williams, Maggie		F	Full	479	Peter, Emely	30	F	Full
394	Williams, Lethlena		F	Full	480	Peter, Nathan	3	M	Full
395	Williams, Micheal	1	M	Full	481	Thompson, Simmons	30	M	Full
396	Janison, Hattie	20	F	Full	482	Thompson, Callie	25	F	Full
397	Alex, Polly	65	F	Full	483	Billy, George		M	Full
398	Lewis, Jim	50	M	Full	484	Billy, Minerva	25	F	Full
399	Lewis, Moseley	15	M	Full	485	Billy, Lee		M	Full
400	Lewis, Mary	7	F	Full	486	Tubbee, Columbus	45	M	Full
401	Lewis, Sarah	14	F	Full	487	Tubbee, Willis	40	M	Full
402	Shoemaker, Billy	77	M	Full	488	Tubbee, Martha	45	F	Full
403	Shoemaker, Eliza	55	F	Full	489	Tubbee, Lucy	12	F	Full
404	Scott, Emil	13	M	Full	490	Tubbee, Ada		F	Full

INDEX AND FINAL ROLLS OF CITIZENS AND FREEDMEN

Roll No.	Name	Age	Sex	Blood
491	Cunnatomby, Thompson	64	M	Full
492	Cunnatomby, Sealy	33	F	Full
493	Robinson, Dilsee	40	F	Full
494	Robinson, Annie	9	F	Full
495	Simpson, Jennie	21	F	Full
496	Simpson, Lewis	3	M	Full
497	Simpson, Adaline	30	F	Full
498	Simpson, George	20	M	Full
499	Simpson, Sinms	12	M	Full
500	Simpson, Johnnie	10	M	Full
501	Simpson, Celia	7	F	Full
502	Simpson, Leta	5	F	Full
503	Simpson, Cinda	1	F	Full
504	Bull, Robert E.	22	M	Full
505	York, Pickens	23	M	Full
506	York, Nannie	10	F	Full
507	Tookolo, William O.	33	M	Full
508	Tookolo, Lillie	16	F	Full
509	Bob, Willis	57	M	Full
510	Bob, Betsie	42	F	Full
511	Sam, Tilwa	24	M	Full
512	Bob, Johnnie	7	M	Full
513	Ah-no-sa-chubbee	52	M	Full
514	Lewis, John	61	M	Full
515	Taylor, Lawrence	21	M	Full
516	Post-Oak, Malissa	41	F	Full
517	Wickson, Mike	26	M	Full
518	Wickson, Amie	22	F	Full
519	Wickson, Cleo	7	F	Full
520	Wickson, Leotie	5	F	Full
521	Wickson, Nancy	3	F	Full
522	Wickson, Holleton	1	M	Full
523	Stemona, Eliza	48	F	Full
524	Foley, Betsie	48	F	Full
525	Foley, Oscar	18	M	Full
526	Foley, Stella	4	F	Full
527	Chubbee, Susie	40	F	Full
528	Chubbee, Rosanna	24	F	Full
529	Chubbee, Julia	22	F	Full
530	Chubbee, Lucy	19	F	Full
531	Chubbee, Agnes	17	F	Full
532	Chubbee, Anna	9	F	Full
533	Chubbee, Janie	7	F	Full
534	Chubbee, Willie	6	M	Full
535	Chubbee, Pink	2	F	Full
536	Washington, Billy	41	M	Full
537	Washington, Liza	19	F	Full
538	Washington, Hannah	17	F	Full
539	Washington, Martha	14	F	Full
540	York, Solomon (Tuck-a-lum-bee)	90	M	Full
541	Waiter, Martha	20	F	Full
542	Waiter, Robert	1	M	Full
543	Sampson, Lillie	23	F	Full
544	Sampson, Salonie	3	F	Full
545	Simpson, Gill	28	M	Full
546	Simpson, Mertine	17	F	Full
547	York, Rufus	52	M	Full
548	York, Malissa	46	F	Full
549	York, Ida	16	F	Full
550	York, Izmison	12	M	Full
551	York, Jesse	7	M	Full
552	York, Annie	4	F	Full
553	John, Sam	26	M	Full
554	John, Nancy	42	F	Full
555	West, John	28	M	Full
556	Carter, Nettie Frances	21	F	1/8
557	Lewis, Jim	40	M	Full
558	Thompson, Ben	50	M	Full
559	Thompson, Martha	36	F	Full
560	Thompson, Leona	18	F	Full
561	Thompson, Thomas	11	M	Full
562	Thompson, Maggie	9	F	Full
563	Morris, P.	22	M	Full
564	Morris, Bessie	18	F	Full
565	Billey, Young	66	M	Full
566	Billey, Sallie	40	F	Full
567	Billey, Fable	17	M	Full
568	Billey, Alan	15	M	Full
569	Billey, Betty	6	F	Full
570	Billey, Ina	4	F	Full
571	Billey, Charley	2	M	Full
572	Willis, John (Bi-le-an-Tuhbee)	50	M	Full
573	Williams, Tom	48	M	Full
574	Williams, Mary		F	Full
575	Williams, Chlorie	17	F	Full
576	Williams, Sam	16	M	Full
577	Williams, Harvey	6	M	Full
578	Williams, Susan	4	F	Full
579	Wickson, John (Con-ne-ma-tubbee)	60	M	Full
580	Bull, Pink	23	M	Full
581	Bull, Emma	17	F	Full
582	Willis, Charley	34	M	Full
583	Billey, Sam	34	M	Full
584	Alderman, Christian	25	M	Full
585	Johnson, Taylor	66	M	Full
586	Johnson, Jennie	70	F	Full
587	Cooper, James	32	M	Full
588	Cooper, Annie	30	F	Full
589	Cooper, Lonnie	8	M	Full
590	Cooper, Nancy	2	F	Full
591	Cooper, Mary	1	F	Full
592	Simon, Albert	26	M	Full
593	Simon, Mary Jane	25	F	Full
594	Simon, Amos	3	M	Full
595	Mose, John	49	M	Full
596	Mose, Lula	32	F	Full
597	Mose, Steen	20	M	Full
598	Mose, Frank	12	M	Full
599	Mose, William Davis	3	M	Full
600	Mose, Lark Davis	1	M	Full
601	John, Big (Ondocha-tubbee)	74	M	Full
602	John, Sally	68	F	Full
603	John, Charley	21	M	Full
604	John, Lena	9	F	Full
605	John, Julie	7	F	Full
606	Jack, Jim	24	M	Full
607	Dansby, Lewis	32	M	Full
608	Jack, Billy	53	M	Full
609	Jack, Leanna	68	F	Full
610	Jack, Minnie	17	F	Full
611	Jack, Nettie	15	F	Full
612	Jack, Camille	7	F	Full
613	Sturdevant, Charley J.	30	M	Full
614	Johnson, John F.	20	M	Full
615	Dixon, Julia	22	F	Full
616	Dixon, Columbus	49	M	Full
617	Dixon, Sallie	65	F	Full
618	Martin, Bettie	13	F	Full
619	Phillip, Mack	26	M	Full
620	Phillip, Sallie	22	F	Full
621	Phillip, Arlena	5	F	Full
622	Phillip, Mary	1	F	Full
623	Phillip, Winston	24	M	Full
624	Philip, Tom	21	M	Full
625	Dansby, Isom	63	M	Full
626	Dixon, John	30	M	Full
627	Dixon, Mary	29	F	Full
628	Dixon, Leanna	3	F	Full
629	Dixon, Sarah Jane	6	F	Full
630	Dixon, Lens	1	F	Full
631	Dixon, Beauty	1	F	Full
632	Billey, Richmond	30	M	Full
633	Billey, Martha	25	F	Full
634	Billey, Lizzie	9	F	Full
635	Billey, Harrison	4	M	Full
636	Billey, Sallie	40	F	Full
637	Sam, Deanis	18	M	Full
638	Sam, Acy	15	F	Full
639	Bull, Houston	20	M	Full
640	Sam, Thomas	58	M	Full
641	Sam, Minnie	32	F	Full
642	Sam, Amos	18	M	Full
643	Sam, Joe	15	M	Full
644	Sam, George	13	M	Full
645	Sam, Delia	11	F	Full
646	Sam, Nancy	8	F	Full
647	Sam, Sis	4	F	Full
648	Parker, Logan	18	M	Full
649	Parker, Sidney	8	M	Full
650	Parker, Jim	6	M	Full
651	James, Wash	26	M	Full
652	James, Easter	27	F	Full
653	James, Harbar	2	M	Full
654	Ellis, Jim	30	M	Full
655	Ellis, Nancy	32	F	Full
656	Ellis, Mary	3	F	Full
657	Ellis, Leroy	2	M	Full
658	Dixon, Doctor	66	M	Full

OF THE CHOCTAW AND CHICKASAW TRIBES.

Roll No.	Name	Age	Sex	Blood	Roll No.	Name	Age	Sex	Blood
659	Dixon, Nancy	68	F	Full	744	Lewis, John	7	M	Full
660	Jackson, Cornelia	9	F	Full	745	Johnson, Cook	38	M	Full
661	Lise, Lissie	3	F	Full	746	Johnson, Eliza	20	F	Full
662	Billy, Moss	22	M	Full	747	Meely, Jim	24	M	Full
663	Billy, Ada	18	F	Full	748	Meely, Lola	26	F	Full
664	Billy, Bullson	1	M	Full	749	Meely, Amos	3	M	Full
665	Bob, Johnnie	26	M	Full	750	Meely, Fannie	2	F	Full
666	Bob, Martha	20	F	Full	751	Martin, Sallie	63	F	Full
667	Adam, Toney	32	M	Full	752	Martin, Jacob	19	M	Full
668	Thomas, Elijah	62	M	Full	753	Isaac, King	21	M	Full
669	Stephen, Frank	32	M	Full	754	Isaac, Eliza	30	F	Full
670	Stephen, Lissie	27	F	Full	755	Isaac, Sias	9	F	Full
671	Stephen, Allie	3	F	Full	756	Cotton, Willie	5	M	Full
672	Stephen, Eliza	2	F	Full	757	Jack, Tom	27	M	Full
673	Sockey, Solomon	60	M	Full	758	Jack, Eliza	76	F	Full
674	Sockey, Phoebe	58	F	Full	759	Jack, Ethel	3	F	Full
675	Sockey, Mary	13	F	Full	760	Jack, Silman	7	M	Full
676	John, Simon	30	M	Full	761	Jack, Evaline	4	F	Full
677	John, Georgia	22	F	Full	762	Gibson, Ben	47	M	Full
678	John, Johnnie	4	M	Full	763	Gibson, Sallie	45	F	Full
679	John, Minnie	2	F	Full	764	Gibson, Mullen	19	M	Full
680	John, Alex	1	M	Full	765	Gibson, Lena	17	F	Full
681	Jack, Allen	27	M	Full	766	Gibson, Lulu	14	F	Full
682	Simpson, Sookie	30	F	Full	767	Gibson, Sammon	11	M	Full
683	Okchi-tubbee, Josephine	40	F	Full	768	Isaac, George	22	M	Full
684	Jim, Filleah	15	F	Full	769	Isaac, Mary	67	F	Full
685	Jim, Rosie	12	F	Full	770	Martin, Sam B.	29	M	Full
686	Jim, Thomas	10	M	Full	771	Martin, Winnie	22	F	Full
687	Jim, Salena	8	F	Full	772	Meely, Clark	21	M	Full
688	Biley, Jim	48	M	Full	773	Meely, Mary	20	F	Full
689	Biley, Bud	11	M	Full	774	Jackson, Annie	13	F	Full
690	Lewis, Leanna	28	F	Full	775	Isaac, Wilson	34	M	Full
691	Lewis, William	12	M	Full	776	Isaac, Siney	30	F	Full
692	Lewis, Thomas	10	M	Full	777	Isaac, Gift	12	M	Full
693	Lewis, Nelson	8	M	Full	778	Isaac, Ellen	7	F	Full
694	Lewis, Mary	6	F	Full	779	Isaac, Jim	5	M	Full
695	Lewis, Annie	4	F	Full	780	Isaac, Lela	2	F	Full
696	Lewis, Easter	2	F	Full	781	Simpson, Sam	86	M	Full
697	Ha-cubbee, Mollie	60	F	Full	782	Amos, Wes	60	M	Full
698	Thomas, John E.	28	M	Full	783	Amos, Lizas	58	F	Full
699	Thomas, Emma	26	F	Full	784	Amos, Jasper	20	M	Full
700	Thomas, Ada	3	F	Full	785	Amos, Dora	19	F	Full
701	Thomas, Henry	1	M	Full	786	Amos, Cleveland	17	M	Full
702	John, Jack	22	M	Full	787	Amos, Bennett	14	M	Full
703	John, Olevia	6	F	Full	788	Amos, Willie	8	M	Full
704	Bob, Mollie	52	F	Full	789	Lewis, Noble	10	M	Full
705	Orah-fal-e-ma-tubbee	52	F	Full	790	Lewis, Webb	20	M	Full
706	Jacob, Charley	24	M	Full	791	Anderson, Lucy	40	F	Full
707	Jacob, Louisa	21	F	Full	792	Anderson, Artie	9	M	Full
708	Jacob, Ebbie	2	F	Full	793	Anderson, John Harrison	6	M	Full
709	James, Ora	1	F	Full	794	Anderson, John Amos	3	M	Full
710	Jim, Simpson	50	M	Full	795	Anderson, Lola	1	F	Full
711	Jim, Eliza	40	F	Full	796	Toonubbee, Allen	53	M	Full
712	Jim, Robert	18	M	Full	797	Toonubbee, Sias	16	F	Full
713	Jim, Egburt	13	M	Full	798	Toonubbee, Rissie	3	F	Full
714	Jim, Tessie	10	F	Full	799	Gilmore, Nettie Bessie	21	F	Full
715	Jim, Clemmon	7	M	Full	800	Gilmore, Ramond	4	M	Full
716	Jim, Evan	3	M	Full	801	Gilmore, Emma	2	F	Full
717	Moses, Ike	35	M	Full	802	Gilmore, Mabell	1	F	Full
718	Moses, Ann	27	F	Full	803	Gibson, Leona	18	F	Full
719	Moses, Nicey	14	F	Full	804	Gibson, Billie	35	M	Full
720	Moses, Lattie	13	F	Full	805	Gibson, Christiana	30	F	Full
721	Moses, Edna	5	F	Full	806	Gibson, Ethan S.	4	M	Full
722	Moses, Elsie	1	F	Full	807	Gibson, Mattie	3	F	Full
723	Porter, Jesse	45	M	Full	808	Gibson, Ennie	40	F	Full
724	Porter, Betsey	40	F	Full	809	Gibson, Sallie	3	F	Full
725	Porter, Jenkins	16	M	Full	810	Gibson, Willie	26	M	Full
726	Porter, Thornton	9	M	Full	811	Gibson, Mollie	24	F	Full
727	Lewis, Mollie	24	F	Full	812	Gibson, Mike	4	M	Full
728	Lewis, Martha	1	F	Full	813	Shoemaker, Ben	41	M	Full
729	Robison, Mary Jane	40	F	Full	814	Shoemaker, Mary (Stonah)			
730	Robison, Alice	7	F	Full			39	F	Full
731	Robison, Eula	5	F	Full	815	Shoemaker, Sister	17	F	Full
732	Lewis, Caroline	45	F	Full	816	Shoemaker, Coleman	14	M	Full
733	Lewis, Ollie	10	F	Full	817	Shoemaker, Henry	10	M	Full
734	Lewis, Martha	7	F	Full	818	Shoemaker, Selest	8	F	Full
735	Lewis, Charles (Kon-ni-sh-tubbee)	53	M	Full	819	Shoemaker, Will	4	M	Full
736	Lewis, Lila	80	F	Full	820	Shoemaker, Sally	1	F	Full
737	Davis, Edna	27	F	Full	821	Phillips, Caroline	30	F	Full
738	Davis, Linnie	6	F	Full	822	Phillips, Lena	15	F	Full
739	Davis, Louella	4	F	Full	823	Phillips, Sealis	12	F	Full
740	Lewis, Sim	20	M	Full	824	Phillips, Germain	9	M	Full
741	Lewis, Minnie	19	F	Full	825	Phillips, Custer	7	M	Full
742	Lewis, Lonie	1	F	Full	826	Philip, Sallie	4	F	Full
743	Lewis, Jesse	28	M	Full	827	Arkansas, Jim	36	M	Full

INDEX AND FINAL ROLLS OF CITIZENS AND FREEDMEN

Roll No.	Name	Age	Sex	Blood
828	Arkansas, Catherine (Tish-ah-yah-honah)	27	F	Full
829	Arkansas, Marzalina	8	F	Full
830	Arkansas, Fannie	5	F	Full
831	Arkansas, Missie	3	F	Full
832	Arkansas, Linnie	1	F	Full
833	Jacoway, Charlie	62	M	Full
834	Jacoway, Mandy	34	F	Full
835	Jacoway, Martin	6	M	Full
836	Jacoway, Oma	4	F	Full
837	Jacoway, Elsie	3	F	Full
838	Jacoway, Opus	1	M	Full
839	Johnson, Big Wiley	56	M	Full
840	Johnson, Patsie	42	F	Full
841	Gilmore, Allen	9	M	Full
842	Farmer, Solomon	41	M	Full
843	Farmer, Louisa	38	F	Full
844	Pittlebeam, Nancy	60	F	Full
845	Gibson, Ben	50	M	Full
846	Gibson, Sealy	50	F	Full
847	Jackson, Billie	36	M	Full
848	Jackson, Jennie	28	F	Full
849	Jackson, Leroy	7	M	Full
850	Jackson, Mary	3	F	Full
851	Stollby, Folsom	18	M	Full
852	Thompson, Allison	40	M	Full
853	Thompson, Martha	55	F	Full
854	Austin, Hortense Thompson	18	F	Full
855	Thompson, Lena	14	F	Full
856	Gibson, Jeff	28	M	Full
857	Gibson, Lucy	29	F	Full
858	Gibson, William	6	M	Full
859	Gibson, Ellis	4	M	Full
860	Gibson, Snowdon	3	M	Full
861	Gibson, Amy	1	F	Full
862	Davis, Julia	44	F	Full
863	Davis, Mary	16	F	Full
864	Stallaby, Anderson	45	M	Full
865	Scott, Chubby	28	M	Full
866	Bob, Nancy Jane	42	F	Full
867	Houston, Willie	20	M	Full
868	Bob, Woodward	8	M	Full
869	Bob, Lena	7	F	Full
870	Thomas, Charlie	38	M	Full
871	Thomas, Mary	28	F	Full
872	Thomas, Peter Foster	14	M	Full
873	Thomas, Esau	13	M	Full
874	Thomas, Risher	5	M	Full
875	Thomas, Enoch	3	M	Full
876	Thomas, Nicholas	1	M	Full
877	Ned, Willie	28	M	Full
878	Ned, Lona	24	F	Full
879	Ned, Marvin	9	M	Full
880	Ned, Russell	2	M	Full
881	Wilson, Willie	30	M	Full
882	Wilson, Janie	26	F	Full
883	Wilson, John	2	M	Full
884	Wilson, Donald	1	M	Full
885	Shook, Bettie	18	F	Full
886	Bob, Boyd	44	M	Full
887	Bob, Lishy	28	F	Full
888	Bob, Preston	13	M	Full
889	Bob, Stainey	8	F	Full
890	Bob, Lexis	2	M	Full
891	Billey, Nolie	50	F	Full
892	Billey, Charley Columbus	10	M	Full
893	Billey, Paulina	4	F	Full
894	Billey, Frank Bishop	18	M	Full
895	Billy, Perwood	28	M	Full
896	Billy, Fannie	21	F	Full
897	Billy, John	2	M	Full
898	Wilkinson, Harrison	47	M	Full
899	Gilmore, Tom	28	M	Full
900	Gilmore, Martha	26	F	Full
901	Gilmore, Jahmie	9	M	Full
902	Gilmore, Mamie	3	F	Full
903	Gilmore, Ludie	1	F	Full
904	Gilmore, Benjamin	27	M	Full
905	Gilmore, Jane	24	F	Full
906	Ha-cubbee, Annie (Il-le-mah-ho-ki)		F	Full
907	Pistubbee, Tinsley	75	F	Full
908	Pistubbee, Archie	17	M	Full
909	Henry, John	38	M	Full
910	Henry, Sarah	8	F	Full
911	Henry, Dennis	1	M	Full
912	Lewis, Mary	18	F	Full
913	Lewis, Jim	30	M	Full
914	Lewis, Jeffe	9	M	Full
915	Himonubbe, Shook	50	M	Full
916	Himonubbe, Bobbie	19	F	Full
917	Himonubbe, Laben	12	M	Full
918	Tom, Nicholas	38	M	Full
919	Tom, Watson	15	M	Full
920	Tom, Moses	12	M	Full
921	Tom, Sicily	8	F	Full
922	Johnston, Isham	43	M	Full
923	Johnston, Lemma	11	F	Full
924	Johnston, Jesse	16	M	Full
925	Johnston, Lena	10	F	Full
926	Johnston, Mallsie	1	F	Full
927	Tom, Willis	38	M	Full
928	Taylor, Willie	26	M	Full
929	Taylor, Jennie	38	F	Full
930	Taylor, Elizabeth	3	F	Full
931	Taylor, Johnson	2	M	Full
932	Jeff, Alice	11	F	Full
933	Brokeshoulder, Adam (Ox-lah-ush-nubbee)	70	M	Full
934	Jackson, Charlie	49	M	Full
935	Jackson, Frances	43	F	Full
936	Jackson, Ben	9	M	Full
937	Jackson, Stephen	6	M	Full
938	Jacoway, Davis	50	M	Full
939	Jacoway, Sealy	38	F	Full
940	Jacoway, Rose	1	F	Full
941	James, Lula	12	F	Full
942	Lick, John (Hintubbee)	72	M	Full
943	Morris, Elizabeth	36	F	Full
944	Philip, George	23	M	Full
945	Philip, Bettie	18	F	Full
946	Philip, Sissy	1	F	Full
947	Hochemah, Mary	57	F	Full
948	Jack, Martha	75	F	Full
949	Him-o-nubbe, Davis	52	M	Full
950	Him-o-nubbe, Emmon	20	M	Full
951	Him-o-nubbe, Ela	19	F	Full
952	Him-o-nubbe, Carson	15	F	Full
953	Him-o-nubbe, Larbin	14	M	Full
954	Jack, Lena	16	F	Full
955	Jack, Sarah Jane	1	F	Full
956	Jack, Willie	28	M	Full
957	Jack, Nancy	21	F	Full
958	Jack, Ellen	12	F	Full
959	Jack, Lillie	8	F	Full
960	Jack, Robert	3	M	Full
961	Jackson, Tecumseh	47	M	Full
962	Jackson, Sophie	34	F	Full
963	Jackson, Walter	11	M	Full
964	Jackson, McElroy	8	M	Full
965	Jackson, Salina	4	F	Full
966	Jackson, Winnie	1	F	Full
967	Lewis, Sam	30	M	Full
968	Lewis, Pollie	27	F	Full
969	Lewis, Jim	11	M	Full
970	Lewis, Dorano	7	M	Full
971	Lewis, Ump	5	M	Full
972	Lewis, Claire	1	F	Full
973	Lewis, Charlie	45	M	Full
974	Lewis, Sallie	36	F	Full
975	Lewis, Larnie	10	M	Full
976	Lewis, Minnie	8	F	Full
977	Lewis, Bud	6	M	Full
978	Lewis, Rody	2	F	Full
979	Shoemaker, Wilson	30	M	Full
980	Shoemaker, Margaret (Tah-te-mah)	30	F	Full
981	Shoemaker, Emerson	1	M	Full
982	Lewis, Betty	2	F	Full
983	Johnson, Jesse Porter	1	M	Full
984	Reese, Lelia	3	F	Full
985	Williams, Telas	1	F	Full
986	Simpson, William	33	M	Full
987	Simpson, Caroline	28	F	Full
988	Simpson, Ben	7	M	Full
989	Simpson, Fannie	5	F	Full
990	Simpson, Ira	3	M	Full
991	Simpson, Mabel	1	F	Full
992	Smith, Mack	10	M	Full
993	York, Anne	28	F	Full
994	York, Bettie Lee	5	F	Full

OF THE CHOCTAW AND CHICKASAW TRIBES.

Roll No.	Name	Age	Sex	Blood	Roll No.	Name	Age	Sex	Blood
956	Bob, Sallie	22	F	Full	1051	Phillip, Lucie	42	F	Full
956	Bob, Emma	1	F	Full	1052	Phillip, Lena	10	F	Full
957	Johnson, Wiley	21	M	Full	1053	Blue-eye, Amos	44	M	Full
958	Johnson, Stella	18	F	Full	1054	Blue-eye, Adolphe	6	M	Full
959	Jackson, Willis	50	M	Full	1055	Blue-eye, Ida	3	F	Full
960	Jackson, Jameson	25	M	Full	1056	Womack, Maggie	38	F	Full
961	Jackson, Ida	13	F	Full	1057	Henry, John	67	M	Full
962	Jackson, Albert			Full	1058	Kelly, Fannie	45	F	Full
963	Jackson, Nixie	4	F	Full	1059	Sam, Jim	45	M	Full
964	Phillip, Williamson	65	M	Full	1060	Taylor, Madeline	45	F	Full
965	Phillip, Jinnie	55	F	Full	1061	Taylor, Nettie	12	F	Full
966	Phillip, Loanna	30	F	Full	1062	Taylor, Mary	10	F	Full
967	Phillip, Sina	14	F	Full	1063	Peter, Thompson	52	M	Full
968	Phillip, Albert	10	M	Full	1064	Peter, Richardson	8	M	Full
969	Phillip, Dibin	7	M	Full	1065	Jimmerson, Lucy	50	F	Full
970	Phillip, Rob	5	M	Full	1066	Arkansas, Louisa	36	F	Full
971	Williamson, Tom	28	M	Full	1067	Arkansas, Freeman	14	M	Full
972	Williamson, Mary	19	F	Full	1068	Arkansas, Lawyer	12	M	Full
973	Williamson, Davie	1	M	Full	1069	Arkansas, Lawson	10	M	Full
974	Tom, Willie	38	M	Full	1070	Arkansas, Irene	8	F	Full
975	Emi-yah-tubbe, Wallace	65	M	Full	1071	Henry, George	4	M	Full
976	Emi-yah-tubbe, Nancy	54	F	Full	1072	Lewis, John	60	M	Full
977	Emi-yah-tubbe, Martha	13	F	Full	1073	Lewis, Lucy			Full
978	Emi-yah-tubbe, Minnie	10	F	Full	1074	Lewis, Dan		M	Full
979	Emi-yah-tubbe, Flemmon	14	M	Full	1075	Lewis, Jim	5	M	Full
980	Emi-yah-tubbe, Johnnie	11	M	Full	1076	Thomas, Anison		M	Full
981	Billey, Lem	21	M	Full	1077	Williamson, Edmund	2	M	Full
982	Sam, Wallace	81	M	Full	1078	Sockey, Rafe	24	M	Full
983	Thompson, Lem	21	M	Full	1079	Billey, Oscar	39	M	Full
984	Thompson, Susla	18	F	Full	1080	Billey, Beauty	27	F	Full
985	Thompson, Lonie	16	F	Full	1081	Stricken from roll.			
986	Thompson, Sydney	14	M	Full	1082	Stricken from roll.			
987	Thompson, Leona	12	F	Full	1083	Stricken from roll.			
988	Thompson, Marsaline	10	F	Full	1084	Billey, Louisa	5	F	Full
989	Wallace, Wesley	27	M	Full	1085	Billey, Sallie Dora	3	F	Full
990	Wallace, Letitia	22	F	Full	1086	Billey, Emerson	1	M	Full
991	Jackson, Tom	21	M	Full	1087	Postoak, Johnson	39	M	Full
992	Wallace, Lemmie	1	F	Full	1088	Postoak, Susie	40	F	Full
993	Wallace, Kariey	1	M	Full	1089	Postoak, Eli	10	M	Full
994	Jackson, Nancy	60	F	Full	1090	Postoak, Sweeney	6	M	Full
995	Jackson, Bessie	8	F	Full	1091	Thomas, Silman	10	F	Full
996	Jackson, Palsey	6	F	Full	1092	Thomas, Beckey	8	F	Full
997	Reed, Kit	37	M	Full	1093	Burton, Susan S.	72	F	1-8
998	Reed, Victoria	26	F	Full	1094	Burton, Henry D.	29	M	1-8
999	Hawkins, Sillie	4	F	Full	1095	Burton, Austin G.	11	M	1-32
1000	Tom, Sealy Ann	18	F	Full	1096	Burton, Susan G.		F	1-16
1001	Solomon, Fannie	30	F	Full	1097	Burton, Florence A.	9	F	1-16
1002	Dincy, Jim	7	M	Full	1098	Burton, Jewel A.	5	F	1-16
1003	Wallace, John B.	22	M	Full	1099	Marshall, Susan Cornelia	37	F	1-16
1004	Wallace, Lillie	20	F	Full	1100	Marshall, Valentine			1-16
1005	Wallace, Ayns	1	F	Full	1101	Marshall, John H.	3	M	1-16
1006	Wallace, Ora		F	Full	1102	Lafontain, Victoria	32	F	Full
1007	Gibson, Sarah	27	F	Full	1103	Taylor, Henry	37	M	Full
1008	Gibson, Robison	9	M	Full	1104	Faure, Mayie	37	F	Full
1009	Gibson, Mary Jane	3	F	Full	1105	Stribling, Frank	32	M	Full
1010	Frenchman, Lotie	12	F	Full	1106	Tonubbe, Jackson	45	M	Full
1011	Frenchman, Mollie	8	F	Full	1107	Hawkins, Rollin	7	M	Full
1012	Billey, Jesse	40	M	Full	1108	Dixon, John	30	M	Full
1013	Billey, John Atmon	18	M	Full	1109	Dixon, Manie	20	F	Full
1014	Billey, Lewis	12	M	Full	1110	Gibson, Ennis		F	Full
1015	Parker, John	45	M	Full	1111	Marshall, Charles Harold	1	M	1-16
1016	Parker, Mary	38	F	Full	1112	Benton, Jim T.		M	Full
1017	Parker, Joseph	17	M	Full	1113	Willis, Solomon	50	M	Full
1018	Parker, Frances	11	F	Full	1114	Brokeshoulder, Minore	10	F	Full
1019	Parker, Ninnie	7	F	Full	1115	McCormick, Sarah Jane	30	F	Full
1020	Parker, Susieline	4	F	Full	1116	Lewis, Lewis	40	M	Full
1021	Jeff, George	21	M	Full	1117	Jefferson, Thomas		M	Full
1022	Jeff, Lula	18	F	Full	1118	Lewis, Dan		M	Full
1023	Willis, Tishomingo	56	M	Full	1119	McDonald, Susanna		F	Full
1024	Renicawa, Ben	20	M	Full	1120	McDonald, Lucy		F	Full
1025	Henry, Pearly	20	F	Full	1121	Stout, Sis		F	Full
1026	Jimmerson, Joe	40	M	Full	1122	Stout, Terase Annie		F	Full
1027	Jimmerson, Martha	30	F	Full	1123	John, Emil		M	Full
1028	Jack, Marsaline	12	F	Full	1124	Mingo, Samuel Alexander	64	M	Full
1029	Jack, Joe	9	M	Full	1125	Jamison, Lula	21	F	Full
1030	Jack, Tom	3	M	Full	1126	Jamison, Finis	13	M	Full
1031	Jack, Jane	1	F	Full	1127	Jamison, Mike	11	M	Full
1032	Henry, Wallace	29	M	Full	1128	Jamison, Reuben	3	M	Full
1033	Henry, Lillie		F	Full	1129	Boaks, Jack	30	M	Full
1034	Henry, Josie	2	M	Full	1130	Morris, Pergy		F	Full
1035	Taylor, Frank	21	M	Full	1131	Faye, Amelia		F	Full
1036	Taylor, Lulie	1	F	Full	1132	Jackson, Joe		M	Full
1037	Johnson, Sealy	20	F	Full	1133	Cooper, Spencer		M	Full
1038	Johnson, Maggie	17	F	Full	1134	Postoak, Jim		M	Full
1039	Johnson, Sam	13	M	Full	1135	Postoak, Mary		F	Full
1040	Johnson, Tatum	7	M	Full	1136	Postoak, Jim Brown	8	M	Full

Roll No.	Name	Age	Sex	Blood	Roll No.	Name	Age	Sex	Blood
1167	Clover, Matilda	70	F	1-2	1252	Seals, Annie	2	F	1-4
1168	Clover, Josiah M.	44	M	1-4	1253	Folsom, Andy	30	M	Full
1169	Clover, Nettie Lee	11	F	1-8	1254	Plummer, Frank E.	43	M	1-8
1170	Clover, Robert Arthur	9	M	1-4	1255	Plummer, Frank S.	5	M	1-16
1171	Clover, Leander Louis	2	M	1-8	1256	Plummer, Raymond S.	3	M	1-16
1172	McClosky, Charlie	2	M	1-16	1257	Plummer, Joseph R.	1	M	1-16
1173	Tucker, George	34	M	1-8	1258	Marris, Jim	28	M	3-4
1174	Wilson, Katie	28	F	1-4	1259	Marris, Arch	3	M	15-16
1175	Wilson, William C.	2	M	1-16	1260	Marris, Annie	2	F	15-16
1176	Karr, Nancy F.	50	F	1-4	1261	Marris, Dibbin	60	M	1-2
1177	Karr, Lon	18	M	1-8	1262	Marris, Wench	19	M	3-4
1178	Franklin, Lou	26	F	1-8	1263	Marris, Steve	17	M	3-4
1179	Franklin, Alfus R.	6	M	1-16	1264	Marris, Nancy	17	F	3-4
1180	Franklin, Homer Lee	3	M	1-16	1265	Marris, Missy	13	F	3-4
1181	Franklin, Quinon Hubert	1	M	1-16	1266	Marris, Mat	10	M	3-4
1182	Draper, Rosie	25	F	1-8	1267	Marris, Lisa	6	M	3-4
1183	Draper, Maggie	2	F	1-16	1268	McDonald, Indian	62	M	1-2
1184	Pebworth, William	42	M	14174	1269	McDonald, Lee	37	M	3-4
1185	Pebworth, William H.	19	M	1-8	1270	McDonald, Lee Poe	2	M	7-8
1186	Pebworth, Lillie May	15	F	1-8	1271	McDonald, William	26	M	3-4
1187	Pebworth, Pearl	13	F	1-8	1272	McDonald, Mack	7	M	7-8
1188	Pebworth, Zelma	7	M	1-8	1273	McDonald, Viney	5	F	7-8
1189	Pebworth, Maggie	6	F	1-8	1274	McDonald, Hugh	21	M	3-4
1190	Pebworth, Josie	3	F	1-8	1275	McDonald, Sealy	20	F	3-4
1191	Pebworth, David	36	M	1-4	1276	McDonald, John Patty	4	M	3-4
1192	Pebworth, Artie	14	M	1-8	1277	McDonald, Mollie	17	F	3-4
1193	Pebworth, Charley	11	M	1-8	1278	McDonald, Jane	23	F	3-4
1194	Pebworth, Lee	8	M	1-8	1279	Jack, Bicey	14	F	7-8
1195	Pebworth, Clarence	2	M	1-8	1280	Davis, Bissie	7	F	7-8
1196	Pebworth, Joe	39	M	1-4 A	1281	Davis, Fronie	4	F	7-8
1197	Pebworth, Josie Viola	6	F	1-8	1282	Tonubbee, Sissie	45	F	3-4
1198	Clover, Earnest O.	17	M	1-16	1283	Tonubbee, Lewis	17	M	7-8
1199	Clover, Thomas L.	14	M	1-16	1284	Tonubbee, Robert	14	M	7-8
1200	Clover, Eugia B.	6	F	1-16	1285	Tonubbee, Murphy	10	M	7-8
1201	Hunter, Joewillie	23	F	1-8	1286	Tonubbee, Lottie	4	F	7-8
1202	Hunter, Mary	2	F	1-16	1287	Marris, Tom H.	37	M	3-4
1203	Hunter, Pearl	1	F	1-16	1288	Marris, Christian	4	M	7-8
1204	Clover, Mary	70	F	1-2	1289	Marris, Winner	1	F	7-8
1205	Clover, William Marshall	54	M	1-4	1290	Marris, Coleman	40	M	3-4
1206	Barr, Mary Ann	35	F	1-4	1291	Marris, Nannie	10	F	7-8
1207	Guice, Benjamin J.	33	M	1-8	1292	Marris, Jane	9	F	7-8
1208	Lehow, Willie Ann	22	F	1-4	1293	Marris, Lillie	7	F	7-8
1209	Lehow, Floyd	3	M	1-16	1294	Marris, Tennis	4	M	7-8
1210	Lehow, Ophelia	1	F	1-16	1295	Kelley, Sealy	36	F	3-4
1211	Ricketts, Freddie C.	17	M	1-8	1296	Kelley, Presley	12	F	7-8
1212	Ricketts, Dossie	16	F	1-4	1297	Kelley, Lloyd	10	M	5-8
1213	Jordon, William G.	42	M	1-4	1298	Kelley, Eula	8	F	5-8
1214	Patterson, Dorah A.	31	F	1-8	1299	Marris, Robb	28	M	3-4
1215	Patterson, Shelby A.	6	M	1-8	1300	Marris, Otis	3	M	3-4
1216	Patterson, Howell M.	4	M	1-8	1301	Marris, Sanderson	30	M	3-4
1217	Pebworth, Vassie V.	13	F	1-8	1302	Morris, Lula	1	F	7-8
1218	Pebworth, Void Preston	7	M	1-4	1303	Buel, Susan	36	F	3-4
1219	Pebworth, Roscoe W.	14	M	1-4	1304	Marris, Marris	30	M	5-8
1220	Pebworth, Jepthar A.	12	M	1-4	1305	Sockey, Bettie	26	F	5-8
1221	Pebworth, Marshal H.	10	M	1-8	1306	Sookey, Maggie	4	F	13-16
1222	Roe, Harry F.	22	M		1307	Sockey, Rafe	3	M	13-16
1223	Roe, Tannie T.	11	M		1308	Sockey, Ned	4	M	13-16
1224	Meely, John G.	1	M	Full	1309	Marris, Sam	11	M	3-4
1225	Sorkey, John	28	M	Full	1310	Marris, George	26	M	3-4
1226	Frenchman, Sally	22	F	Full	1311	Bell, Jane	56	F	1-4
1227	Thompson, Chatman	46	M	Full	1312	Bell, Rufus	18	M	1-8
1228	Bull, Ase Elmon	38	M	Full	1313	Bell, Callie	13	F	7-8
1229	Lewis, Little Tom	60	M	Full	1314	Thompson, Austin	31	M	Full
1230	Lewis, Lonie	50	F	Full	1315	Barcus, Sanders	33	M	Full
1231	Lewis, William	4	M	Full	1316	Moore, Ellen	46	F	1-2
1232	Lewis, Rufus	2	M	Full	1317	Moore, John N.	26	M	1-4
1233	Thomas, Sincum	30	M	Full	1318	Moore, Lizzie B.	24	F	1-4
1234	Thomas, Martha	2	F	Full	1319	Moore, Callie H.	22	F	1-4
1235	Johnson, Jimmie	25	M	Full	1320	Moore, Elisha N.	20	M	1-4
1236	Johnson, Amy	23	F	Full	1321	Moore, Mattie J.	16	F	1-4
1237	Johnson, Freezum	19	M	Full	1322	Moore, Maggie M.	14	F	1-4
1238	Shoemaker, Susie	2	F	Full	1323	Moore, Rufus E.	10	M	1-4
1239	Scott, Liza	21	F	Full	1324	Moore, Willie N.	8	M	1-4
1240	Scott, Aline	6	F	Full	1325	Moore, Lee A.	5	M	1-4
1241	Marris, Minerva	26	F	Full	1326	Farmer, Wilson	30	M	Full
1242	Yearby, Thomas	17	M	Full	1327	Gift, Jim	78	M	1-2
1243	Yearby, Christie	14	M	Full	1328	Gift, Movella	12	F	1-4
1244	Byars, Loisa	22	F	Full	1329	Gift, Sarah	15	F	1-4
1245	Tucker, Henry	29	M	1-4	1330	Gift, Johnson	20	M	1-4
1246	Clover, Henry H.	11	M	1-16	1331	Gift, Effie	7	F	1-4
1247	Clover, Josie	7	F	3-16	1332	Gift, Donnie	11	F	1-4
1248	Philip, Elijah	30	M	Full	1333	Mosely, Maggie	34	F	1-4
1249	Philip, Edmond (or Father)	4	M	Full	1334	Seals, Emma	16	F	1-4
					1335	Seals, James	10	M	1-4
1250	McMillan, Lonie	4	F	Full	1336	Seals, Ora	14	F	1-4
1251	Willis, Hugh	13	M	Full	1337	Seals, Kernell	11	M	1-4

OF THE CHOCTAW AND CHICKASAW TRIBES. 409

Roll No.	Name	Age	Sex	Blood	Roll No.	Name	Age	Sex	Blood
1373	Seals, Ada	6	F	1-4	1393	McPhail, Myra	23	F	1-32
1339	Seals, Talmadge	4	M	1-8	1393	McPhail, Fannie	21	F	1-32
1340	Jones, Annie C.	35	F	1-16	1394	McPhail, Grace	19	F	1-32
1341	Jones, Maud	10	F	1-32	1395	McPhail, Gates	17	M	1-32
1342	Jones, May	18	F	1-32	1396	McPhail, Preston	15	M	1-32
1343	Jones, Leonard H.	2	M	1-32	1397	McPhail, Virgil	10	M	1-32
1344	Wampler, Amanda L.	42	F	1-8	1398	McPhail, Homer	4	M	1-32
1345	Lenochan, Campbell	18	M	1-16	1399	Dees, Mary E.	47	F	1-16
1346	Wampler, George W.	12	M	1-16	1400	Dees, Henry H.	27	M	1-32
1347	Wampler, John	9	M	1-16	1401	Wood, Mary E.	25	F	1-32
1348	Wampler, Daniel Edgar	6	M	1-16	1402	Dees, George A.	22	M	1-32
1349	Smith, Victoria	22	F	1-16	1403	Dees, Edgar R.	18	M	1-32
1350	Stafford, Tinnie	5	F	1-32	1404	Dees, Oscar E.	12	M	1-32
1351	Snider, Sarah Pearl	17	F	1-16	1405	Dees, Fannie E.	9	F	1-32
1352	Snider, Esther D.	15	F	1-16	1406	Dees, Katiebelle	6	F	1-32
1353	Snider, Beulah Lee	13	F	1-16	1407	Fountain, Lillie M.	29	F	1-16
1354	Jackson, Bob	29	M	3-4	1408	Wiltshire, Fannie E.	51	F	1-16
1355	Jackson, Birdie	5	F	7-8	1409	Marx, Sallie V.	21	F	1-32
1356	Jackson, Mazeline	1	F	7-8	1410	Marx, Moses	7	M	1-32
1357	Guss, Leanna	42	F	Full	1411	Marx, Miriam	5	M	1-32
1358	Lewis, Jennie	77	F	Full	1412	Marx, Philic Aaron	6	M	1-32
1359	Shoemaker, Jim	6	M	Full	1413	Willis, William	30	M	Full
1360	Lewis, Frank	12	M	Full	1414	Moncrief, Joseph	40	M	1-8
1361	Reese, John	25	M	Full	1415	Amos, Jeff	34	M	Full
1362	Jamison, Arden	32	M	Full	1416	Amos, Lucinda	2	F	Full
1363	Chubbee, John	54	M	Full	1417	Amos, Roselle	1	F	Full
1364	Golden, Margaret Ann	1	F	Full	1418	Wallace, Bill	11	M	Full
1365	Tookolo, John Henry	1	M	Full	1419	Jefferson, Mary Jane	35	F	Full
1366	Reed, Linnie	1	F	Full	1420	Jefferson, Ike	38	M	Full
1367	Bob, Alex	37	M	Full	1421	Jefferson, Velma	10	F	Full
1368	Bob, Edna	47	F	Full	1422	Jefferson, Susie	8	F	Full
1369	Chubbee, Sallie	13	F	Full	1423	Jefferson, Abbey	6	M	Full
1370	Phillip, Sis	16	F	Full	1424	Pratoak, Bessie	20	F	Full
1371	Hawkins, William	33	M	Full	1425	Yearby, Nancy	75	F	Full
1372	Hawkins, Jane	21	F	Full	1426	Isaac, Rogers	18	M	Full
1373	Wallace, Aben	23	M	Full	1427	Washington, Sallie	60	F	Full
1374	Wallace, Sota	18	F	Full	1428	Lewis, Mary	4	F	Full
1375	Yearby, Jesse J.	20	M	Full	1429	Peter, Sooky	32	F	Full
1376	Huff, Zeno	45	M	Full	1430	Arkansas, Reuben	17	M	Full
1377	Johnson, Mamie	18	F	Full	1431	Lewis, Lonie	13	M	Full
1378	Johnson, Nochee	21	F	Full	1432	Stout, Usan	60	M	Full
1379	Murria, Sealy	26	F	Full	1433	Tubbee, Robert	30	M	Full
1380	Thompson, Arba Luvenia	1	F	Full	1434	Yearby, Joseph	13	M	Full
1381	Beck, Frances	42	F	Full	1435	Jackson, Lizzie	22	F	Full
1382	Brokeshoulder, James	23	M	7-8	1436	Bell, Sallie	25	F	Full
1383	Brokeshoulder, John	26	M	3-4	1437	Willis, Nannie	4	F	Full
1384	Brokeshoulder, Adam, Jr.	12	M	3-4	1438	Sampson, Selfa	3	F	Full
1385	Brokeshoulder, Cammack	6	M	3-4	1439	Bonaham, Ed	31	M	3-4
1386	Morrison, George W.	37	M	1-16	1440	Taylor, Mollie	33	F	Full
1387	Morrison, Emma Z.	10	F	1-32	1441	Brokeshoulder, Lee	18	M	3-4
1388	Morrison, Annax May	8	F	1-32	1442	Patterson, Emma	2	F	1-4
1389	Morrison, Henry B.	5	M	1-32	1443	Brewer, Frank	28	M	Full
1390	McPhail, Laura K.	48	F	1-16	1444	Wilmond, Raymond	14	F	Full
1391	McPhail, Frank	25	M	1-32	1445	Dees, Walter T.	18	M	1-32

MISSISSIPPI CHOCTAW ROLL, CITIZENS BY BLOOD

(Enrolled under provisions of the Act of Congress Approved
August 1, 1914. Public No. 160)

No.	Name	Age	Sex	Blood	Census Card No.	No.	Name	Age	Sex	Blood	Census Card No.
1446	Farve, Geneheene	57	F	Full	915	1457	McDaniel, Houston	36	M	Full	919
1447	Farve, Elizabeth	31	F	Full	915	1458	McDaniel, Joe	16	M	Full	919
1448	Adams, Mitchell C.	56	M	Full	914	1459	Taylor, Joseph	6	M	Full	920
1449	Adams, Lillie M.	23	F	1-2	916	1460	Charles, Sallie	63	F	3-4	921
1450	Adams, Nora M.	21	F	1-2	916	1461	Charles, Minnie	30	F	7-8	921
1451	Nickey, Maggie now Jolly	27	F	Full	917	1462	Charles, Bettie	22	F	7-8	921
1452	Nickey, Billy	29	M	Full	917	1463	Charles, Louisa	16	F	7-8	921
1453	Nickey, Sam	26	M	Full	917	1464	Charles, James	12	M	7-8	921
1454	Nickey, Bettie Russell (Nickey, Bettie)	24	F	Full	917	1465	John, Lillie Jackson	24	F	Full	922
1455	Nickey, Mollie Mae	22	F	Full	917	1466	Adams, William C. (born May 28, 1902)	12	M	1-2	916
1456	Davis, Mond Amos	26	M	Full	918		(Age as shown hereon is computed to May 28, 1914. Approved November 15, 1914.)				

Memo:
Ages appearing on this schedule are shown as of August 1, 1914, except those of persons who died prior to said date in which cases the ages are shown as of date of death. See notations hereon.

FINAL ROLL OF NEW BORN MISSISSIPPI CHOCTAWS.

Enrolled under Act of March 3, 1905 (33 Stat. L., 1048).

Ages calculated to March 4, 1905.

No.	Name	Age	Sex	Blood	Census Card No	No.	Name	Age	Sex	Blood	Census Card No
1	Meely, Lillian	1	F	Full	7	7	Wilson, Arvin Velma	1	M	1-16	71
2	Jacob, Caroline	1	F	Full	5	8	Thomas, Bennie	2	M	Full	70
3	Meely, Green	1	M	Full	33	9	Ned, Colbert	1	M	Full	85
4	John, Johnson	2	M	Full	47	10	Henry, Lony	2	M	Full	117
5	Isaac, Lennie	2	F	Full	49	11	Petworth, David Clifford	2	M	1-8	63
6	Smith, Susie Ann	2	F	Full	66						

FINAL ROLL OF MINOR MISSISSIPPI CHOCTAWS.

Enrolled under Act of April 26, 1906 (34 Stat. L., 137).

Ages calculated to March 4, 1906.

No.	Name	Age	Sex	Blood	Census Card No	No.	Name	Age	Sex	Blood	Census Card No
1	Johnson, Effie	3	F	Full	3	7	Johnson, Lula	3	F	Full	26
2	Phillip, Joe	3	M	Full	10	8	Brokeshoulder, Arthur Mellen	3	M	Full	32
3	Phillip, Nannie	1	F	Full	11	9	Bob, Gertrude	4	F	Full	42
4	Shoemaker, Arlie	3	M	Full	20	10	Bob, Bicey	4	F	Full	42
5	Billey, Charley	1	M	Full	24	11	Bob, Leana	2	F	Full	44
6	Sam, Abel	2	M	Full	25						

OF THE CHOCTAW AND CHICKASAW TRIBES.

No.	Name	Age	Sex	Blood	Census Card No
12	Philip, Asie	3	F	Full	46
13	Wilson, Lelia	3	F	Full	51
14	Scott, Luciel	3	F	7-8	58
15	Lafontain, Cecilia May	1	F	7-8	66
16	Lafontain, Sidney	12	M	7-8	67
17	Lafontain, Oscar	8	M	7-8	69
18	Lafontain, Victoria J.	4	F	7-8	70
19	Morris, Sam	1	M	15-16	86
20	Byars, Amiel	7	M	3-4	93
21	Thompson, Ida Jewell	1	F	1-8	105
22	Kelley, Annie	3	F	5-8	112
23	Philip, Sid	3	M	Full	116
24	Wickson, Winnie	4	F	Full	118
25	Wickson, James	2	M	Full	119
26	Wallace, Ida	1	F	Full	120
27	Billey, Leona	3	F	Full	124
28	Tonubbee, Lizzie	4	F	7-8	126
29	Jack, Billy	3	M	Full	128
30	Billy, Fannie	3	F	Full	129
31	Neal, Willie	1	M	Full	131
32	Jackson, Clark	3	M	Full	136
33	Jackson, LeFlore	1	M	Full	137
34	Henry, Bonnie	1	F	Full	139
35	Jackson, Emmett	1	M	Full	140
36	Johnson, Lester	4	M	Full	141
37	Johnson, Charley	2	M	Full	142
38	Isaac, Emily	1	F	Full	143
39	Lehuw, Mary M.	1	F	1-16	144
40	Taylor, Mamie Annie	1	F	Full	145
41	Lewis, Annie	1	F	Full	146
42	Morris, Nela	2	F	Full	149
43	Risher, None	1	F	1-2	150
44	Isaac, Sadie	1	F	Full	151
45	Marshall, Paul	1	M	1-16	153
46	Philip, Eli	1	M	Full	154
47	Williams, James	2	M	Full	156
48	Post-oak, May Jane	1	F	Full	158
49	Draper, Effie Ethel May	1	F	1-16	159
50	Austin, Jimerson	3	M	Full	160
51	Thompson, Will	6	M	Full	161
52	Willis, Willis	2	M	Full	1
53	Lewis, Hattie	1	F	Full	3
54	Sweeney, Minna	1	F	Full	6
55	Golden, Allie Mamie	1	F	Full	13
56	Willis, Mary	3	F	Full	15
57	Simpson, Easton	1	M	Full	16
58	Lewis, Corher	2	M	Full	17
59	Betsey, Alice	1	F	Full	21
60	Jacoway, Sammie	3	F	Full	22
61	Betsey, Jessie	4	M	Full	23
62	Neal, Isa A.	3	F	Full	27
63	Jack, Ida	1	F	Full	28
64	Gibson, Jimmie	3	M	Full	29
65	Arkansas, Emer	3	F	Full	30
66	Dixon, Mian	4	M	Full	32
67	Smith, Martha Jane	1	F	Full	34
68	Smith, William B.	3	M	Full	35
69	Billy, Dewet	3	M	Full	37
70	York, Annice	2	F	Full	41
71	Lewis, Venie	2	F	Full	50
72	Wilkerson, Lonnie	1	M	Full	52
73	Wallace, Neeley	2	F	Full	53
74	Wallace, Annie	1	F	Full	54
75	Marshall, William H.	3	M	1-16	56
76	Gillard, John Lollie	1	M	1-2	59
77	Hunter, Bruce	3	M	1-16	60
78	Billey, Hampton	2	M	Full	61
79	Franklin, Authie Lois	3	F	1-16	62
80	Lafontain, Salena	10	F	7-8	68
81	Wilson, Marvin Alma	1	M	1-16	75
82	Post-oak, Lena	2	F	Full	18
83	Davis, Emmett	1	M	Full	26
84	Lewis, Bob	2	M	Full	40
85	Simpson, Barnard	1	M	Full	46
86	John, George	1	M	Full	48
87	Seals, Willie	3	M	1-8	92
88	McDonald, Phintahhonah	1	F	7-8	172
89	Isaac, Mitchell	3	M	Full	290
90	Stephen, Wade	2	M	Full	272
91	Hughes, Ovillar	2	F	1-4	101
92	Morris, Ida	4	F	1-8	109
93	Clover, Joe Cole	2	M	1-8	110
94	Seals, Anna	1	F	1-8	122
95	Draper, Evie Minnie May	1	F	1-16	152
96	Thompson, Sallie	1	F	Full	163
97	Phillip, Minnie	1	F	Full	164
98	Sam, Rhody	1	F	Full	165
99	Philip, Adam	1	M	Full	170
100	Johnson, Tony	1	F	Full	171
101	McDonald, Cola	1	F	7-8	173
102	Karr, Nina Virgul Lee	1	F	1-8	174
103	Hughes, Carrie	1	F	1-8	175
104	Lewis, Mack D.	1	M	Full	176
105	Morris, Mart	1	M	7-8	177
106	Billey, Lonie	1	F	Full	180
107	Williamson, Tom Frank	1	M	Full	182
108	Henry, Norman	1	M	Full	183
109	Arkansas, Nora	1	F	Full	187
110	Jorden, Linnie M.	1	F	1-2	189
111	Morris, Annie	1	F	Full	191
112	Shoemake, Labon	1	M	Full	225
113	Frenchman, Clarence	4	M	7-8	198
114	Frenchman, Atlas	3	M	7-8	199
115	Frenchman, Agnes	2	F	7-8	200
116	Billey, Sidney	1	M	Full	202
117	Bull, Foreman	2	M	Full	227
118	James, Johnie	1	M	Full	208
119	Thompson, Jim	1	M	Full	209
120	Morris, Gilbert	1	M	7-8	210
121	Jamus, Jodie	1	M	1-2	225
122	Franklin, General D.	1	M	1-16	226
123	Parker, Sam	4	M	Full	4
124	Parker, Elizabeth	1	F	Full	5
125	Tookolo, Ida Rena	2	F	Full	11
126	Lacoway, Rhoda	3	F	Full	19
127	Post-oak, Sam	1	M	Full	31
128	Cooper, Mandy	2	F	Full	39
129	McDonald, Bettie	3	F	7-8	57
130	Tucker, Docia May	1	F	1-16	73
131	Gift, E. F.	4	M	1-8	99
132	Gift, Johnson, Jr.	2	M	1-8	100
133	Phillips, Joseph	4	M	Full	122
134	Moss, Margaret	10	F	Full	178
135	Lewis, Mettie	1	F	Full	186
136	York, Wm. Baston	2	M	Full	195
137	Johnson, Ed	2	M	Full	204
138	John, Ida	2	F	Full	322
139	Gibson, Mita Mulen	2	F	Full	5
140	John, Becca	2	F	Full	14
141	Sockey, Robert	1	M	1-2	44
142	McCormick, Hettie	3	F	1-4	76
143	McCormick, Lizzie	11	F	1-4	77
144	Taylor, Emily F.	5	F	7-8	78
145	Taylor, Ritchard	4	M	7-8	79
146	Taylor, Dewey W.	2	M	7-8	80
147	James, Cora	4	F	Full	81
148	Hickman, Gaston	1	M	7-8	82
149	McDonald, Ollie	1	F	3-4	87
150	McDonald, Lavada	3	F	3-4	88
151	Plommer, Charles W., Jr.	1	M	1-16	90
152	Morris, Hale	3	M	7-8	91
153	Pis-tubbee, Stinnes	3	M	Full	106
154	Mingo, Douglas	18	M	1-2	107
155	Wallace, Newt	3	M	Full	113
156	Wallace, Lee	1	M	Full	121
157	Bob, Mary	1	F	Full	133
158	Gibson, Ross	4	F	Full	162
159	Stribling, Jimmie Jefferson	6	M	5-8	196
160	Willis, Nellie	1	F	Full	212
161	Tubbee, Lena	1	F	Full	221
162	Post-oak, Lena	6	F	Full	253
163	Post-oak, Oscar	9	M	Full	254
164	Willis, Willie	11	M	5-8	315
165	Willis, Sarah Jane	9	F	5-8	316
166	Willis, Henney Lee	7	M	5-8	317
167	Davis, Maliss Wadlington	3	F	Full	355
168	Morrison, Frank L.	3	M	1-32	361
169	Morrison, Fannie H.	1	F	1-32	361
170	Dees, Willie W.	1	M	1-32	932
171	Dees, Tommie W.	5	M	1-32	932
172	Dees, Herbert	3	M	1-32	932
173	Wood, Sammie D.	3	M	1-32	942
174	Marx, Susan Burton	4	F	1-32	365
175	Marx, Ruby	1	F	1-32	369

INDEX AND FINAL ROLLS OF CITIZENS AND FREEDMEN

No.	Name	Age	Sex	Blood	Census Card No.
176	Wallace, Jennie	1	F	Full	190
177	Farve, Forest	14	M	3/4	71
178	Farve, Elvener	9	F	3/4	72
179	Sampson, Jennie	3	F	Full	385
180	Taylor, Celestine	1	F	Full	870
181	Patterson, Joseph Allen	8	M	1/4	890
182	Tubbee, Effie	17	F	5/8	371
183	Tubbee, Rachel	15	F	5/8	271
184	Tubbee, Annie	14	F	5/8	271
185	Tubbee, Maisie (or Bessie)	11	F	5/8	271
186	Tubbee, Betsey	8	F	5/8	271
187	Patterson, Ruby Elnora	1	F	1/4	896

FINAL ROLL OF CHICKASAWS BY BLOOD.

Ages calculated to September 25, 1902.

No.	Name	Age	Sex	Blood	Census Card No.
1	Walker, Tandy C.	62	M	1-8	1
2	Walker, J. T.	38	M	1-16	1
3	Walker, J. C.	30	M	1-16	1
4	Byrd, Ida	20	F	1-16	1
5	Walker G. C.	17	M	1-16	1
6	Walker, Minnie	16	F	1-16	1
7	Byrd, Eugean				
8	Byrd, Chester Temple	1	M	1-32	1
9	Walker, Mary Cornelia		F	1-32	2
10	Walker, Robert T.	27	M	1-16	3
11	Mayer, Cornelia	3	F	1-16	3
12	Mayer, Myrtle J.		F	1-32	3
13	Colbert, Humphrey	64	M	3-4	4
14	Colbert, Salina	48	F		4
15	Colbert, Jackson R.	30	M	Full	7
16	Colbert, Mary Wolfe	22	F	Full	7
17	Cuberry, Davis	23	M	Full	7
18	Colbert, Lucy	7	F	Full	7
19	Colbert, Amanda	1	F	Full	7
20	Loving, Isabelle	54	F	3-4	8
21	Ayakatubby, Thompson	48	M	Full	9
22	Ayakatubby, Mina	44	F	Full	9
23	Ayakatubby, Agnes	22	F	Full	9
24	Ayakatubby, Mary	19	F	Full	9
25	Ayakatubby, Dixson	8	M	Full	9
26	Ayakatubby, Dorene		F	Full	9
27	Ayakatubby, Minnie	18	F	Full	9
28	Davis, Martha	31	F	1-4	10
29	Davis, Maggie P.	10	F	1-4	10
30	Benton, Peter	58	M	Full	11
31	Benton, Ellen	22	F	Full	11
32	Yancey, Minnie	26	F	1-16	12
33	Yancey, Lillian	2	F	1-32	12
34	Yancey, Clara		F	1-32	12
35	Stricken from roll.				
36	Yancey, Jean Archer	1	M	1-32	12
37	Apala, Kizzie	20	F	Full	14
38	Apala, Henrietta	10	F	Full	14
39	Apala, Ophelia	7	F	Full	14
40	Apala, Lemuel	4	M	Full	14
41	Apala, Mulbery	1	M	Full	14
42	Underwood, George	49	M	Full	16
43	Stricken from roll.				
44	Folsom, Charlie	19	M	Full	16
45	Harris, Walton	11	M	1-4	16
46	Brown, Levi	24	M	Full	16
47	Brown, Elizabeth	26	F	Full	16
48	Boaza, Rosa	9	F	Full	16
49	Brown, Scott	5	M	Full	16
50	Brown, Andy	3	M	Full	16
51	Holloway, Kittie	21	F	1-4	17
52	Alberson, Cornelia	24	F		17
53	Chapman, Harriet E. G.	42	F	1-16	18
54	Chapman, Charles J.	21	M	1-16	18
55	Chapman, James W.	17	M	1-16	18
56	Chapman, Virginia C.	16	F	1-16	18
57	Chapman, Clara C.			1-16	18
58	Chapman, Richard F.	9	M	1-16	18
59	Lewis, Galloway	73	M	Full	19
60	Lewis, Turner		M	Full	19
61	Lewis, Wilson		M	Full	19
62	Lewis, Nancy	36	F	Full	19
63	Trentham, Henderson	31	M	1-16	20
64	Trentham, Lena	6	F	1-32	20
65	Trentham, Mary	1	F	1-32	20
66	Colbert, Wahoo	29	M	3-4	21
67	Colbert, Louisa	54	F	Full	21
68	Colbert, Amanda	15	F	7-8	21
69	Colbert, Minnie	13	F	7-8	21
70	Colbert, Frank	12	M	7-8	21
71	Colbert, Serena	10	F	7-8	21
72	Colbert, Nora	5	F	7-8	21
73	Colbert, Mack	5	M	7-8	21
74	Stricken from roll.				
75	Perry, Albert	34	M	1-2	23
76	Perry, Charles Guy	11	M	3-4	23
77	Perry, Ella	9	M	3-4	23
78	Perry, Billie	60	M	3-4	23
79	Perry, Eliza	50	F	1-2	23
80	Perry, James	18	M	5-8	23
81	Perry, Lee	15	M	6-8	23
82	Perry, Tena	12	F	5-8	23
83	Perry, Wilson	8	M	5-8	23
84	Sealy, Eli	34	M	Full	24
85	Sealy, Annie	19	F	Full	24
86	Sealy, Josephine	9	F	Full	24
87	Stricken from roll.				
88	Sealy, Sampson	3	M	Full	24
89	Hawkins, Morris H.	32	M	Full	25
90	Hawkins, Charlie	1	M	1-2	25
91	Phillips, Sallie Walker	41	F	1-8	26
92	Phillips, Ada	17	F	1-16	26
93	Phillips, Louisa	15	F	1-16	26
94	Phillips, Lucy	14	F	2-16	26
95	Phillips, Hill, Jr.	11	M	1-16	26
96	Phillips, Elmer	8	M	1-16	26
97	Phillips, Robert E.	6	M	1-16	26
98	Phillips, Winona	2	F	1-16	26
99	Walker, David	23	M	1-16	27
100	Brown, Margaret	9	F	Full	29
101	Collins, Odus Lynn	26	M	Full	30
102	Collins, Wm. B.	13	M	1-8	30
103	Collins, S. C.	11	M	1-8	30
104	Collins, George R., Jr.	9	M	1-8	30
105	Stricken from roll.				
106	Nelson, Ward	36	M	1-2	
107	Alberson, Nicholas	49	M	Full	
108	Alberson, Pannie	34	F	Full	
109	Johnson, Napoleon B.	44	M	1-2	
110	Johnson, Leewellyn	9	M	1-4	
111	Johnson, Geftrude	4	F	1-4	
112	Truax, Mary	38	F	1-4	
113	Truax, Pearl E.	11	F	1-4	
114	Truax, Ruby G.	7	F	1-4	
115	Truax, William B.	5	M	1-4	
116	Truax, Jewel	2	F	1-4	
117	Underwood, Gabriel	47	M	Full	
118	Underwood, Nancy	46	F	Full	
119	Underwood, Wesley	21	M	Full	
120	Underwood, Alice	18	F	Full	
121	Underwood, Bina	16	F	Full	
122	Underwood, Hazen	14	M	Full	
123	Underwood, Louis	12	M	Full	
124	Gully, Jim	14	M	1-2	
125	Sealy, Sallie	30	F	Full	
126	Dyer, Dawes	4	M	Full	
127	Underwood, Phoebe	3	F	Full	
128	Crosbey, Annie	22	F	1-2	
129	King, Walt	49	M	Full	
130	King, Celian		M	Full	
131	King, Patsey		F	Full	
132	Grayson, Gibson T.	58	M	Full	
133	Grayson, Emi	27	F	Full	
134	Grayson, Felix	26	M	Full	
135	Grayson, James J.	23	M	Full	
136	Grayson, Annie	19	F	Full	
137	Stricken from roll.				

IDENTIFIED MISSISSIPPI CHOCTAWS 1902 - 1909
Volume II

IDENTIFIED MISSISSIPPI CHOCTAWS   CARD NO. 308

IDENTIFICATION ADDRESS Tucker, Miss.   SETTLEMENT ADDRESS Atoka, I.T.
DATE OF IDENTIFICATION Feb. 14, 1903.   DATE OF PROOF OF SETTLEMENT Aug. 17, 03

APPROVED ROLL No.	DAWES ROLL NO.	NAME	RELATIONSHIP TO PERSON FIRST NAMED	AGE	SEX	BLOOD
		1 Simpson, Lewis		51	M	Full
		2 " Adaline	Wife	30	F	Full
		3 " George	Son	20	M	Full
		4 " Simms	Son	12	M	Full
		5 " Johnnie	Son	10	M	Full
		6 " Celia	Dau	7	F	Full
		7 " Leta	Dau	3	F	Full
		8 " Cinda	Dau	7mo	F	Full

CITIZENSHIP CERTIFICATE
ISSUED FOR NO 1-2-3-4-5-6-
AUG 17 1903   7-8   APPROVED BY SECRETARY OF INTERIOR.

NAME OF FATHER	LIVING OR DEAD	NAME OF MOTHER	LIVING OR DEAD	APPLICATION NO.	REMARKS
1 John Simpson		Mollie Simpson	Dead	4893	
2 William	Dead	Lucy	"	"	
3 No.1		Meely Simpson	"	"	
4 No.1		No.2		"	
5 No.1		No.2			
6 No.1		No.2		"	
7 No.1		No.2		"	
8 No.1		No.2		"	
9					
10 ENROLLMENT OF NOS. 1 2 3 4 5 6 7 & 8 HEREON APPROVED BY THE SECRETARY					
11 OF INTERIOR JAN 13 1905					

Nos 1,2,4,5 and 7: Testimony relative to continuous residence for a period of three years submitted October 11, 1906.
No.6: died November 13, 1905; No8: died September 11, 1905;
Testimony relative to their continuous residence up to the time of their death submitted October 11, 1906.

"No 3 Testimony as to continuous residence for a period of three years submitted October 6, 1906."

IDENTIFIED MISSISSIPPI CHOCTAWS 1902 - 1909
Volume II

IDENTIFIED MISSISSIPPI CHOCTAWS CARD NO. 309

IDENTIFICATION ADDRESS Franks, Miss. SETTLEMENT ADDRESS
DATE OF IDENTIFICATION Feb. 14, 1903. DATE OF PROOF OF SETTLEMENT

APPROVED ROLL No.	DAWES ROLL NO.	NAME	RELATIONSHIP TO PERSON FIRST NAMED	AGE	SEX	BLOOD
		1 Jimmy, Will		25	M	Full
		2 " Viola	Wife	23	F	Full
		3 " Mabel	Dau	2	F	Full
		4				
		5				
		6 APPROVED BY SECRETARY OF INTERIOR.				
		7				
		8 DID NOT SUBMIT PROOF OF				
		9 REMOVAL AND BONA-FIDE SET- TLEMENT WITHIN ONE YEAR				
		10 FROM DATE OF IDENTIFICATION.				
		11				

NAME OF FATHER	LIVING OR DEAD	NAME OF MOTHER	LIVING OR DEAD	APPLICATION NO.	REMARKS
1 Tobe Jimmy	Dead	Louisa Philip		4855	
2 Madison Ben		Eliza Ben	Dead	"	
3 No.1		No.2		"	
4					
5					
6					
7					
8					
9					
10					
11					

IDENTIFIED MISSISSIPPI CHOCTAWS 1902 - 1909
Volume II

IDENTIFIED MISSISSIPPI CHOCTAWS   CARD NO. 310

IDENTIFICATION ADDRESS Coffadeliah, Miss.   SETTLEMENT ADDRESS
DATE OF IDENTIFICATION Feb. 14, 1903.   DATE OF PROOF OF SETTLEMENT

APPROVED ROLL No.	DAWES ROLL NO.	NAME	RELATIONSHIP TO PERSON FIRST NAMED	AGE	SEX	BLOOD
		1 Jackson, Alex		40	M	Full
		2 " Solomon	Son	18	M	Full
		3 " Fannie	Dau	14	F	Full
		4 " Franklin	Son	12	M	Full
		5 " Sonie	Dau	5	F	Full
		6 " Caway	Son	4	M	Full
		7				
		8 APPROVED BY SECRETARY OF INTERIOR.				
		9 DID NOT SUBMIT PROOF OF				
		10 REMOVAL AND BONA-FIDE SETTLEMENT WITHIN ONE YEAR				
		11 FROM DATE OF IDENTIFICATION				

	NAME OF FATHER	LIVING OR DEAD	NAME OF MOTHER	LIVING OR DEAD	APPLICATION NO.	REMARKS
1		Dead		Dead	5097	
2	No.1		Mary Jackson	"	"	
3	No.1		" "	"	"	
4	No.1		" "	"	"	
5	No.1		Callie Jackson	"	"	
6	No.1		" "	"	"	
7						
8						
9						
10						
11						

IDENTIFIED MISSISSIPPI CHOCTAWS 1902 - 1909
Volume II

IDENTIFIED MISSISSIPPI CHOCTAWS CARD NO. 311

IDENTIFICATION ADDRESS Roscoe, Miss.   SETTLEMENT ADDRESS Ardmore, Ind. Ter.
DATE OF IDENTIFICATION Feb. 14, 1903.   DATE OF PROOF OF SETTLEMENT March 16, 1904

APPROVED ROLL No.	DAWES ROLL NO.		NAME	RELATIONSHIP TO PERSON FIRST NAMED	AGE	SEX	BLOOD
		1	Wallace, Aben		22	M	Full
		2	" Sota	Wife	16	F	Full
		3					
		4					
		5	APPROVED BY SECRETARY OF INTERIOR.				
		6					
		7					
		8					

CITIZENSHIP CERTIFICATE
ISSUED FOR NO 1 & 2
OCT 27 1903

ENROLLMENT
OF NOS. 1 & 2 HEREON
APPROVED BY THE SECRETARY
OF INTERIOR Feb. 27 1907

NAME OF FATHER	LIVING OR DEAD	NAME OF MOTHER	LIVING OR DEAD	APPLICATION NO.	REMARKS
1 John Wallace		Sarah Wallace	Dead	2272	
2 Jim Jackson	Dead	Latisha Wallace		"	
3					
4					
5					
6		Enrolled under Act of Congress approved			
7		June 21, 1906 (34 Stats. 325).			
8					
9		Nos 1 and 2 - Testimony relative to continuous residence			
10		for a period of three years submitted September 25, 1908.			
11					

See Commission Letter - File #87[illegible]

IDENTIFIED MISSISSIPPI CHOCTAWS 1902 - 1909
Volume II

IDENTIFIED MISSISSIPPI CHOCTAWS CARD NO. 312

IDENTIFICATION ADDRESS Rio, Miss.   SETTLEMENT ADDRESS Story I.T.
DATE OF IDENTIFICATION Feb. 14, 1903.   DATE OF PROOF OF SETTLEMENT Sept. 30, 1903.

APPROVED ROLL No.	DAWES ROLL NO.	NAME	RELATIONSHIP TO PERSON FIRST NAMED	AGE	SEX	BLOOD
		1 Bull, Robert E.		22	M	Full
		2				
		3				
		4				
		5 APPROVED BY SECRETARY OF INTERIOR.				
		6 ENROLLMENT OF NOS. ~~1~~ HEREON				
		7 APPROVED BY THE SECRETARY OF INTERIOR JAN 13 1905.				
		8				
CITIZENSHIP CERTIFICATE		9				
ISSUED FOR NO 1						
SEP 30		10				
		11				

NAME OF FATHER	LIVING OR DEAD	NAME OF MOTHER	LIVING OR DEAD	APPLICATION NO.	REMARKS
1 John Bull			Dead	2524	
2					
3					
4					
5					
6 Testimony relative to continuous residence for a					
7 period of three years submitted September 30, 1908.					
8					
9					
10					
11					

IDENTIFIED MISSISSIPPI CHOCTAWS 1902 - 1909
Volume II

IDENTIFIED MISSISSIPPI CHOCTAWS CARD NO. 313

IDENTIFICATION ADDRESS Philadelphia, Miss.   SETTLEMENT ADDRESS
DATE OF IDENTIFICATION Feb. 14, 1903.   DATE OF PROOF OF SETTLEMENT

APPROVED ROLL No.	DAWES ROLL NO.	NAME	RELATIONSHIP TO PERSON FIRST NAMED	AGE	SEX	BLOOD
		1 Billey, Welsh		28	M	Full
		2				
		3				
		4				
		5 APPROVED BY SECRETARY OF INTERIOR.				
		6				
		7 DID NOT SUBMIT PROOF OF				
		8 REMOVAL AND BONA-FIDE SET-				
		9 TLEMENT WITHIN ONE YEAR				
		10 FROM DATE OF IDENTIFICATION.				
		11				

NAME OF FATHER	LIVING OR DEAD	NAME OF MOTHER	LIVING OR DEAD	APPLICATION NO.	REMARKS
1 Jesse Billey		Amy Billey	Dead	2098	
2					
3					
4					
5					
6					
7					
8					
9					
10					
11					

IDENTIFIED MISSISSIPPI CHOCTAWS 1902 - 1909
Volume II

IDENTIFIED MISSISSIPPI CHOCTAWS   CARD NO. 314

IDENTIFICATION ADDRESS Thomastown, Miss.   SETTLEMENT ADDRESS Marlow I.T.
DATE OF IDENTIFICATION Feb. 14, 1903.   DATE OF PROOF OF SETTLEMENT Oct. 23, 1903.

APPROVED ROLL No.	DAWES ROLL NO.	NAME	RELATIONSHIP TO PERSON FIRST NAMED	AGE	SEX	BLOOD
		1. York, Pickens		29	M	Full
		2. " Nannie	Dau	10	F	Full
		3.				
		4.				
		5. APPROVED BY SECRETARY OF INTERIOR.				
		6. ENROLLMENT				
		7. OF NOS. 1&2 HEREON APPROVED BY THE SECRETARY				
		8. OF INTERIOR				
CITIZENSHIP CERTIFICATE ISSUED FOR NO 1-2 OCT 23 1903		9.				
		10.				
		11.				

	NAME OF FATHER	LIVING OR DEAD	NAME OF MOTHER	LIVING OR DEAD	APPLICATION NO.	REMARKS
1	Charley York		Nicey York	Dead	4407	
2	No.1		Annie York	"	"	
3						
4						
5						
6						
7						
8						
9						
10	"Nos 1 and 2: Proof of continuous residence for a					
11	period of three years submitted July 1-1907."					

IDENTIFIED MISSISSIPPI CHOCTAWS 1902 - 1909
Volume II

IDENTIFIED MISSISSIPPI CHOCTAWS CARD NO. 315

IDENTIFICATION ADDRESS Hays, Miss. SETTLEMENT ADDRESS
DATE OF IDENTIFICATION Feb. 14, 1903. DATE OF PROOF OF SETTLEMENT

APPROVED ROLL No.	DAWES ROLL NO.	NAME	RELATIONSHIP TO PERSON FIRST NAMED	AGE	SEX	BLOOD
		1 Tom, Martha		80	F	Full
		2				
		3				
		4				
		5 APPROVED BY SECRETARY OF INTERIOR.				
		6 DID NOT SUBMIT PROOF OF REMOVAL AND BONA-FIDE SETTLEMENT WITHIN ONE YEAR FROM DATE OF IDENTIFICATION.				
		7				
		8				
		9				
		10				
		11				

NAME OF FATHER	LIVING OR DEAD	NAME OF MOTHER	LIVING OR DEAD	APPLICATION NO.	REMARKS
1 Billy Nubbee	Dead	Jennie Nubbee	Dead	4268	
2					
3					
4					
5					
6					
7					
8					
9					
10					
11					

IDENTIFIED MISSISSIPPI CHOCTAWS 1902 - 1909
Volume II

IDENTIFIED MISSISSIPPI CHOCTAWS CARD NO. 316

IDENTIFICATION ADDRESS Toles, Miss.   SETTLEMENT ADDRESS Kiowa, Ind. Ter.
DATE OF IDENTIFICATION Feb. 14, 1903.   DATE OF PROOF OF SETTLEMENT May 20, 1903.

APPROVED ROLL No.	DAWES ROLL NO.	NAME	RELATIONSHIP TO PERSON FIRST NAMED	AGE	SEX	BLOOD
		1. Tookolo, William O.		23	M	Full
		2. " Lillie	Wife	16	F	Full
		3.				
		4.				
		5. APPROVED BY SECRETARY OF INTERIOR.				
		6. ENROLLMENT OF NOS. 1&2 HEREON				
		7. APPROVED BY THE SECRETARY OF INTERIOR JAN 13 1905				
		8.				
CITIZENSHIP CERTIFICATE ISSUED FOR NO 1-2 MAY 20 1903		9.				
		11.				

NAME OF FATHER	LIVING OR DEAD	NAME OF MOTHER	LIVING OR DEAD	APPLICATION NO.	REMARKS
1. Elan Tookolo		Lissie Tookolo	Dead	2668	
2. Sam Philip	Dead	Sallie Philip		"	
3.					
4.					
5.					
6.					
7. No2: Testimony as to continuous residence up to her death submitted April 18, 1905.					
9. "No.1 - Testimony as to continuous residence of No.1 for a period of 3 years submitted January 10, 1906."					
11.					

IDENTIFIED MISSISSIPPI CHOCTAWS 1902 - 1909
Volume II

IDENTIFIED MISSISSIPPI CHOCTAWS   CARD NO. 317

IDENTIFICATION ADDRESS Engine, Miss.   SETTLEMENT ADDRESS Atoka Ind. Ter.
DATE OF IDENTIFICATION Feb. 14, 1903.   DATE OF PROOF OF SETTLEMENT Aug. 17, 03.

APPROVED ROLL No.	DAWES ROLL NO.	NAME	RELATIONSHIP TO PERSON FIRST NAMED	AGE	SEX	BLOOD
		1 Bob, Willis		57	M	Full
		2 " Betsie	Wife	42	F	Full
		3 Sam, Tilwa	S.Son	14	M	Full
		4 Bob, Johnnis	G.Son	7	M	Full
		5				
		6				
		7 APPROVED BY SECRETARY OF INTERIOR				
		8				

CITIZENSHIP CERTIFICATE ISSUED FOR NO 1-2-3-4 AUG 17 1903

ENROLLMENT OF NOS. 1 2 3 & 4 HEREON APPROVED BY THE SECRETARY OF INTERIOR JAN 13 1905

NAME OF FATHER	LIVING OR DEAD	NAME OF MOTHER	LIVING OR DEAD	APPLICATION NO.	REMARKS
1 Pis-an-tubbee	Dead	Amy Bob (Ama)	Dead	2206	
2 Sam (Ima-cah-tubbee)	"	Ache-ho-nah	"	"	
3		No.2		"	
4 John Bob	Dead	Amy Bob	Dead	"	
5					
6					
7					
8					
9					
10					
11					

Nos 1, 2, 3 & 4 Testimony as to continuous residence for a period of three years submitted Aug. 15, 1906.

IDENTIFIED MISSISSIPPI CHOCTAWS 1902 - 1909
Volume II

IDENTIFIED MISSISSIPPI CHOCTAWS   CARD NO. 318

IDENTIFICATION ADDRESS Decatur, Miss.   SETTLEMENT ADDRESS Ardmore I.T.
DATE OF IDENTIFICATION Feb. 14, 1903.   DATE OF PROOF OF SETTLEMENT Nov. 11, 03.

APPROVED ROLL No.	DAWES ROLL NO.	NAME	RELATIONSHIP TO PERSON FIRST NAMED	AGE	SEX	BLOOD
		1 Ah-no-sa-chubbee		82	M	Full
		2				
		3				
		4				
		5 APPROVED BY SECRETARY OF INTERIOR.				
		6 ENROLLMENT OF NOS. ~~1~~ HEREON				
		7 APPROVED BY THE SECRETARY OF INTERIOR JAN. 13 1905.				
		8				
CITIZENSHIP CERTIFICATE 9 ISSUED FOR NO ~~1~~ MAR 29 1904						
		11				

NAME OF FATHER	LIVING OR DEAD	NAME OF MOTHER	LIVING OR DEAD	APPLICATION NO.	REMARKS
1 On-cha-ley	Dead			3919	
2					
3					
4					
5					
6		Testimony relative to continuous residence from			
7		date of settlement until date of death submitted			
8		September 25, 1908.			
9					
10					
11					

IDENTIFIED MISSISSIPPI CHOCTAWS 1902 - 1909
Volume II

IDENTIFIED MISSISSIPPI CHOCTAWS

CARD NO. 319

IDENTIFICATION ADDRESS Avera, Miss. SETTLEMENT ADDRESS
DATE OF IDENTIFICATION Feb. 14, 1903. DATE OF PROOF OF SETTLEMENT

APPROVED ROLL No.	DAWES ROLL NO.	NAME	RELATIONSHIP TO PERSON FIRST NAMED	AGE	SEX	BLOOD
		1 Londine, Julie		52	F	Full
		2 " James	Husband	67	M	Full
		3				
		4				
		5				
		6 APPROVED BY SECRETARY OF INTERIOR.				
		7				
		8 DID NOT SUBMIT PROOF OF				
		9 REMOVAL AND BONA-FIDE SET- TLEMENT WITHIN ONE YEAR				
		10 FROM DATE OF IDENTIFICATION.				
		11				

NAME OF FATHER	LIVING OR DEAD	NAME OF MOTHER	LIVING OR DEAD	APPLICATION NO.	REMARKS
1	Dead	Polly	Dead	2556	
2	"	Sallie	"	"	
3					
4					
5					
6					
7					
8					
9					
10					
11					

IDENTIFIED MISSISSIPPI CHOCTAWS 1902 - 1909
Volume II

IDENTIFIED MISSISSIPPI CHOCTAWS

CARD NO. 320

IDENTIFICATION ADDRESS Avera, Miss.   SETTLEMENT ADDRESS No1 Durwood I.T.
DATE OF IDENTIFICATION Feb. 14, 1903.   DATE OF PROOF OF SETTLEMENT No1 Sept 15/03.

APPROVED ROLL No.	DAWES ROLL NO.	NAME	RELATIONSHIP TO PERSON FIRST NAMED	AGE	SEX	BLOOD
		1 Lewis, John		51	M	Full
		2 " Alice	Dau	14	F	Full
		3 " Mamie	Dau	10	F	Full
		4				
		5 APPROVED BY SECRETARY OF INTERIOR.				
		6 ENROLLMENT				
		7 OF NOS. ~~1~~ HEREON APPROVED BY THE SECRETARY				
		8 OF INTERIOR JAN 13 1905 .				
CITIZENSHIP CERTIFICATE ISSUED FOR NO 1 SEP 15 1903		9 No 2&3 DID NOT SUBMIT PROOF OF REMOVAL AND BONA-FIDE SET-TLEMENT WITHIN ONE YEAR FROM DATE OF IDENTIFICATION				
		10				
		11				

	NAME OF FATHER	LIVING OR DEAD	NAME OF MOTHER	LIVING OR DEAD	APPLICATION NO.	REMARKS
1	Lewis	Dead	Betsy Lewis	Dead	1959	
2	No.1		Jennie Lewis	"	"	
3	No.1		" "	"		
4						
5						
6						
7						
8						
9						
10						
11						

Declaration & proof of settlement of Sept 15-03 apply to No1 only -

"No1: Proof of continuous residence for a period of three years submitted May 29 - 09" -

IDENTIFIED MISSISSIPPI CHOCTAWS 1902 - 1909
Volume II

IDENTIFIED MISSISSIPPI CHOCTAWS   CARD NO. 321

IDENTIFICATION ADDRESS Bay St. Lewis, Miss.   SETTLEMENT ADDRESS Durwood I.T.
DATE OF IDENTIFICATION Feb. 14, 1903.   DATE OF PROOF OF SETTLEMENT Nov. 19/03.

APPROVED ROLL No.	DAWES ROLL NO.	NAME	RELATIONSHIP TO PERSON FIRST NAMED	AGE	SEX	BLOOD
		1 Taylor, Lawrence		21	M	Full
		2				
		3				
		4				
		5 APPROVED BY SECRETARY OF INTERIOR.				
		6				
		7				
		8				
CITIZENSHIP CERTIFICATE ISSUED FOR NO 1 NOV 19 1903		9				
		10				
		11				

ENROLLMENT OF NOS ~~1~~ HEREON APPROVED BY THE SECRETARY OF INTERIOR JAN 13 1905.

NAME OF FATHER	LIVING OR DEAD	NAME OF MOTHER	LIVING OR DEAD	APPLICATION NO.	REMARKS
1 Sam Taylor	Dead	Madeline Taylor		2394	
2					
3					
4					
5					
6					
7		Testimony as to continuous residence for a period of three years submitted August 11, 1908.			
8					
9					
10					
11					

IDENTIFIED MISSISSIPPI CHOCTAWS 1902 - 1909
Volume II

IDENTIFIED MISSISSIPPI CHOCTAWS CARD NO. 322

IDENTIFICATION ADDRESS Philadelphia, Miss. SETTLEMENT ADDRESS
DATE OF IDENTIFICATION Feb. 14, 1903. DATE OF PROOF OF SETTLEMENT

APPROVED ROLL No.	DAWES ROLL NO.	NAME	RELATIONSHIP TO PERSON FIRST NAMED	AGE	SEX	BLOOD
		1. Mingo, Gibson		24	M	Full
		2.				
		3.				
		4.				
		5.				
		6. APPROVED BY SECRETARY OF INTERIOR.				
		7. DID NOT SUBMIT PROOF OF				
		8. REMOVAL AND BONA-FIDE SET-				
		9. TLEMENT WITHIN ONE YEAR				
		10. FROM DATE OF IDENTIFICATION.				
		11.				

NAME OF FATHER	LIVING OR DEAD	NAME OF MOTHER	LIVING OR DEAD	APPLICATION NO.	REMARKS
1. Mingo Monk		Susie Monk	Dead	4891	
2.					
3.					
4.					
5.					
6.					
7.					
8.					
9.					
10.					
11.					

IDENTIFIED MISSISSIPPI CHOCTAWS 1902 - 1909
Volume II

IDENTIFIED MISSISSIPPI CHOCTAWS   CARD NO. 323

IDENTIFICATION ADDRESS Hickory, Miss.   SETTLEMENT ADDRESS Ardmore I.T.
DATE OF IDENTIFICATION Feb. 14, 1903.   DATE OF PROOF OF SETTLEMENT May 21/03

APPROVED ROLL No.	DAWES ROLL NO.	NAME	RELATIONSHIP TO PERSON FIRST NAMED	AGE	SEX	BLOOD
		1 Post-Oak, Malissa		41	F	Full
		2				
		3				
		4				
		5				
		6 APPROVED BY SECRETARY OF INTERIOR.				
		7				
		8				
CITIZENSHIP CERTIFICATE ISSUED FOR NO 1 MAY 23 1903		9				
		10				
		11				

NAME OF FATHER (Momintubbee)	LIVING OR DEAD	NAME OF MOTHER (Siel-la-honah)	LIVING OR DEAD	APPLICATION NO.	REMARKS
1 Tom Mehah	Dead	Sally Mehah	Dead	3069	
2					
3					
4					
5					
6					
7					
8					
9					
10 No. 1: Proof of continuous residence for a period					
11 of three years submitted February 18-1907.					

IDENTIFIED MISSISSIPPI CHOCTAWS 1902 - 1909
Volume II

IDENTIFIED MISSISSIPPI CHOCTAWS   CARD NO. 324

IDENTIFICATION ADDRESS Conehatta, Miss.　　SETTLEMENT ADDRESS Atoka I.T.
DATE OF IDENTIFICATION Feb. 14, 1903.　　DATE OF PROOF OF SETTLEMENT Aug. 19/03.

APPROVED ROLL No.	DAWES ROLL NO.	NAME		RELATIONSHIP TO PERSON FIRST NAMED	AGE	SEX	BLOOD
		1	Wickson, Mike		26	M	Full
		2	" Amie	Wife	28	F	Full
		3	" Cleo	Dau	7	F	Full
		4	" Leotie	Dau	5	F	Full
		5	" Nancy	Dau	3	F	Full
		6	" Holiston	Son	1	M	Full
		7	APPROVED BY SECRETARY OF INTERIOR.				
		8	ENROLLMENT				
CITIZENSHIP CERTIFICATE ISSUED FOR NO 1-2-3-4-5-6 AUG 19 1903		9	OF NOS. 1 2 3 4 5 6 HEREON APPROVED BY THE SECRETARY OF INTERIOR JAN 13 1905.				
		11					

NAME OF FATHER	LIVING OR DEAD	NAME OF MOTHER	LIVING OR DEAD	APPLICATION NO.	REMARKS
1 John Wickson		Malinda Wickson	Dead	3067	
2 Jim Billey	Dead	Mary Billey		"	
3 No.1		No.2		"	
4 No.1		No.2		"	
5 No.1		No.2		"	
6 No.1		No.2		"	
7					
8					
9 "Nos 1,2,3,4,5 and 6: Testimony as to continuous					
10 residence for a period of three years submitted					
11 August 22, 1906."					

IDENTIFIED MISSISSIPPI CHOCTAWS 1902 - 1909
Volume II

IDENTIFIED MISSISSIPPI CHOCTAWS   CARD NO. 325

IDENTIFICATION ADDRESS Tucker, Miss.   SETTLEMENT ADDRESS Hubbard, Ind. Ter.
DATE OF IDENTIFICATION Feb. 14, 1903.   DATE OF PROOF OF SETTLEMENT May 16, 1903.

APPROVED ROLL No.	DAWES ROLL NO.	NAME	RELATIONSHIP TO PERSON FIRST NAMED	AGE	SEX	BLOOD
		1 Stemona, Eliza		48	F	Full
		2				
		3				
		4				
		5 APPROVED BY SECRETARY OF INTERIOR.				
		6				
		7				
		8				
		9				
		10				
		11				

NAME OF FATHER	LIVING OR DEAD	NAME OF MOTHER	LIVING OR DEAD	APPLICATION NO.	REMARKS
1 Jim Stemona	Dead	Sallie Stemona		1986	
2					
3					
4					
5					
6					
7					
8 "No.1: testimony relative to continuous					
9 residence for a period of three years submitted					
10 September 11, 1906."					
11					

IDENTIFIED MISSISSIPPI CHOCTAWS 1902 - 1909
Volume II

IDENTIFIED MISSISSIPPI CHOCTAWS CARD NO. 326

IDENTIFICATION ADDRESS Saint Anns[sic], Miss.   SETTLEMENT ADDRESS

DATE OF IDENTIFICATION Feb. 14, 1903.   DATE OF PROOF OF SETTLEMENT

APPROVED ROLL No.	DAWES ROLL NO.	NAME	RELATIONSHIP TO PERSON FIRST NAMED	AGE	SEX	BLOOD
		1 Barney, George		32	M	Full
		2 " Martha	Wife	18	F	Full
		3 " Eve	Dau	1½	F	Full
		4 " Jinnie	Dau	3wks	F	Full
		5				
		6				
		7 APPROVED BY SECRETARY OF INTERIOR.				
		8 DID NOT SUBMIT PROOF OF				
		9 REMOVAL AND BONA-FIDE SET-				
		10 TLEMENT WITHIN ONE YEAR				
		11 FROM DATE OF IDENTIFICATION.				

NAME OF FATHER	LIVING OR DEAD	NAME OF MOTHER	LIVING OR DEAD	APPLICATION NO.	REMARKS
1 Alex Barney	Dead	Eliza Boley		2133	
2 Wes Amos		Stemala Amos		"	
3 No.1		No.2			
4 No.1		No.2			
5					
6					
7					
8					
9					
10					
11					

IDENTIFIED MISSISSIPPI CHOCTAWS 1902 - 1909
Volume II

IDENTIFIED MISSISSIPPI CHOCTAWS CARD NO. 327

IDENTIFICATION ADDRESS Coffadeliah, Miss.   SETTLEMENT ADDRESS
DATE OF IDENTIFICATION Feb. 14, 1903.   DATE OF PROOF OF SETTLEMENT

APPROVED ROLL No.	DAWES ROLL NO.		NAME	RELATIONSHIP TO PERSON FIRST NAMED	AGE	SEX	BLOOD
		1	Frazer, Echols		25	M	Full
		2	" Mollie	Wife	23	F	Full
		3	" Winston	Son	3	M	Full
		4	" Will Marshall	Son	1	M	Full
		5					
		6					
		7					
		8	APPROVED BY SECRETARY OF INTERIOR.				
		9	DID NOT SUBMIT PROOF OF REMOVAL AND BONA-FIDE SET-				
		10	TLEMENT WITHIN ONE YEAR FROM DATE OF IDENTIFICATION				
		11					

	NAME OF FATHER	LIVING OR DEAD	NAME OF MOTHER	LIVING OR DEAD	APPLICATION NO.	REMARKS
1	Forbes Frazer	Dead	Mary Frazer		1891	
2		"	Martha		"	
3	No.1		No.2		"	
4	No.1		No.2		"	
5						
6						
7						
8						
9						
10						
11						

IDENTIFIED MISSISSIPPI CHOCTAWS 1902 - 1909
Volume II

IDENTIFIED MISSISSIPPI CHOCTAWS CARD NO. 328

IDENTIFICATION ADDRESS Mardis, Miss. SETTLEMENT ADDRESS
DATE OF IDENTIFICATION Feb. 14, 1903. DATE OF PROOF OF SETTLEMENT

APPROVED ROLL No.	DAWES ROLL NO.	NAME	RELATIONSHIP TO PERSON FIRST NAMED	AGE	SEX	BLOOD
		1 Frazer, John		70	M	Full
		2				
		3				
		4				
		5 APPROVED BY SECRETARY OF INTERIOR.				
		6 DID NOT SUBMIT PROOF OF				
		7 REMOVAL AND BONA-FIDE SET-				
		8 TLEMENT WITHIN ONE YEAR FROM DATE OF IDENTIFICATION.				
		9				
		10				
		11				

NAME OF FATHER	LIVING OR DEAD	NAME OF MOTHER	LIVING OR DEAD	APPLICATION NO.	REMARKS
1 Frazer	Dead		Dead	1792	
2					
3					
4					
5					
6					
7					
8					
9					
10					
11					

IDENTIFIED MISSISSIPPI CHOCTAWS 1902 - 1909
Volume II

IDENTIFIED MISSISSIPPI CHOCTAWS   CARD NO. 329

IDENTIFICATION ADDRESS Tucker, Miss.   SETTLEMENT ADDRESS
DATE OF IDENTIFICATION Feb. 14, 1903.   DATE OF PROOF OF SETTLEMENT

APPROVED ROLL No.	DAWES ROLL NO.	NAME	RELATIONSHIP TO PERSON FIRST NAMED	AGE	SEX	BLOOD
		1 Polk, Winston		31	M	Full
		2				
		3				
		4				
		5 APPROVED BY SECRETARY OF INTERIOR.				
		6 DID NOT SUBMIT PROOF OF				
		7 REMOVAL AND BONA-FIDE SET-				
		8 TLEMENT WITHIN ONE YEAR				
		9 FROM DATE OF IDENTIFICATION.				
		10				
		11				

NAME OF FATHER	LIVING OR DEAD	NAME OF MOTHER	LIVING OR DEAD	APPLICATION NO.	REMARKS
1 Jim Polk	Dead	Mary Polk	Dead	1994	
2					
3					
4					
5					
6					
7					
8					
9					
10					
11					

IDENTIFIED MISSISSIPPI CHOCTAWS 1902 - 1909
Volume II

IDENTIFIED MISSISSIPPI CHOCTAWS CARD NO. 330

IDENTIFICATION ADDRESS Hope, Miss. SETTLEMENT ADDRESS
DATE OF IDENTIFICATION Feb. 14, 1903. DATE OF PROOF OF SETTLEMENT

APPROVED ROLL No.	DAWES ROLL NO.	NAME	RELATIONSHIP TO PERSON FIRST NAMED	AGE	SEX	BLOOD
		1 Wait, Nancy		28	F	Full
		2 " Sawil	Son	15	M	Full
		3 " Liza	Dau	13	F	Full
		4				
		5				
		6 ~~APPROVED BY SECRETARY OF INTERIOR.~~				
		7 ~~DID NOT SUBMIT PROOF OF~~				
		8 ~~REMOVAL AND BONA-FIDE SET-~~				
		9 ~~TLEMENT WITHIN ONE YEAR~~				
		10 ~~FROM DATE OF IDENTIFICATION.~~				
		11				

	NAME OF FATHER	LIVING OR DEAD	NAME OF MOTHER	LIVING OR DEAD	APPLICATION NO.	REMARKS
1	Jim Isaac (Tin-cha)		Mary Isaac		4495	
2	Wait	Dead	No.1		"	
3	"	"	No.1		"	
4						
5						
6						
7						
8						
9						
10						
11						

IDENTIFIED MISSISSIPPI CHOCTAWS 1902 - 1909
Volume II

IDENTIFIED MISSISSIPPI CHOCTAWS   CARD NO. 331

IDENTIFICATION ADDRESS Rose Hill, Miss.   SETTLEMENT ADDRESS Atoka Ind. Ter.
DATE OF IDENTIFICATION Feb. 14, 1903.   DATE OF PROOF OF SETTLEMENT Aug. 17/03.

APPROVED ROLL No.	DAWES ROLL NO.	NAME	RELATIONSHIP TO PERSON FIRST NAMED	AGE	SEX	BLOOD
		1 Foley, Betsie		48	F	Full
		2 " Oscar	Son	18	M	Full
		3 " Stella	Dau	6	F	Full
		4				
		5				
		6 APPROVED BY SECRETARY OF INTERIOR.				
		7				
		8 ENROLLMENT OF NOS. 1, 2 & 3 HEREON				
CITIZENSHIP CERTIFICATE ISSUED FOR NO 1-2-3 AUG 17 1903		9 APPROVED BY THE SECRETARY OF INTERIOR JAN 13 1905				
		11				

NAME OF FATHER (Che-fa-no-ah)	LIVING OR DEAD	NAME OF MOTHER	LIVING OR DEAD	APPLICATION NO.	REMARKS
1 Tom Parker	Dead	Sally Parker	Dead	1936	
2 John Foley	"	No.1	"		
3 " "	"	No.1	"		
4					
5					
6					
7					
8					
9					
10 "No.2 Died September 5, 1904: Testimony as to continuous					
11 residence up to his death submitted August 22, 1906."					

"Nos 1 and 3: Testimony as to continuous residence for a period of three years submitted August 22, 1906."

IDENTIFIED MISSISSIPPI CHOCTAWS 1902 - 1909
Volume II

IDENTIFIED MISSISSIPPI CHOCTAWS

See other side of card for notations.

CARD NO. 332

IDENTIFICATION ADDRESS Ravia, Ind. Ter. SETTLEMENT ADDRESS Ravia, Ind. Ter.
DATE OF IDENTIFICATION Feb. 14, 1903. DATE OF PROOF OF SETTLEMENT July 11, 1903.

APPROVED ROLL No.	DAWES ROLL NO.		NAME	RELATIONSHIP TO PERSON FIRST NAMED	AGE	SEX	BLOOD
1363		1	Chubbee, John		54	M	Full
CITIZENSHIP CERTIFICATE ISSUED FOR NO ~~10~~		2	" Susie	Wife	49	F	Full
JUN 13 1904		3	" Rosanna	Dau	24	F	Full
CITIZENSHIP CERTIFICATE ISSUED FOR NO ~9~		4	" Julia	Dau	22	F	Full
MAY 3 1904		5	" Lucy	Dau	19	F	Full
CITIZENSHIP CERTIFICATE ISSUED FOR NO ~~7~~		6	" Agnes	Dau	17	F	Full
FEB 4 1904		7	" Anna	Dau	8	F	Full
CITIZENSHIP CERTIFICATE ISSUED FOR NO ~1~		8	" Janie	Dau	7	F	Full
SEP 5- 1906		9	" Willie	Son	6	M	Full
CITIZENSHIP CERTIFICATE ISSUED FOR NO 3 - 5		10	" Pink	Dau	2	F	Full

APPROVED BY SECRETARY OF INTERIOR.

	NAME OF FATHER	LIVING OR DEAD	NAME OF MOTHER	LIVING OR DEAD	APPLICATION NO.	REMARKS
1	Sam Chubbee	Dead	Sallie Chubbee	Dead	1617	
2	Dr. Jim	"	Sophie Jim	"	"	
3	No.1		No.2		"	
4	No.1		No.2		"	ENROLLMENT OF NOS. 2,3,4,5,6,7,8,9&10 HEREON APPROVED BY THE SECRETARY OF INTERIOR JAN 13 1905
5	No.1	Sept 18, 06	No.2		"	
6	No.1		No.2		"	
7	No.1		No.2		"	
8	No.1		No.2		"	
9	No.1		No.2		"	
10	No.1		No.2		"	
11						

CITIZENSHIP CERTIFICATE ISSUED FOR NO 4
SEP 19
CITIZENSHIP CERTIFICATE ISSUED FOR NO 2
JUL 11 1903
CITIZENSHIP CERTIFICATE ISSUED FOR NO ~~6~~
JAN 29 1904
CITIZENSHIP CERTIFICATE ISSUED FOR NO ~~8~~
FEB 15 1904

No6 wife No1 card 295
No3: Proof of continuous residence for a period of three years submitted April-13-1907.
No4: Proof of continuous residence for a period of three years submitted February 4-1907.
No7: Proof of continuous residence for a period of three years submitted March 26-1907.
"No1 Proof of death filed showing No1 died July 5-1903."
No1 Proof of settlement taken June 19, 1906 under authority of Act of Congress approved April 26-1906.
Settlement add No.6 Ravia I.T.
Date proof settlement No6 Jan. 29-04

IDENTIFIED MISSISSIPPI CHOCTAWS 1902 - 1909
Volume II

Notations continued form front of previous card #332:

Declaration and proof of settlement of July 11, 1903 applies to Nos. 2,5,7,8,9 and 10 only.
No3   Settlement address Ravia I.T.
No3   Declaration and proof of settlement Sept 18/03.
No4   Settlement address [Illegible] I.T.
No4   declaration and proof of settlement Sept 19/03.

No6   Testimony as to continuous residence for a period of three years submitted 4/5,06.

Notations from back of previous card #332:

No.5:   Testimony relative to continuous residence for a period of three years submitted February 17, 1908.

No.1.   Proof of settlement taken June 19, 1906, under authority of Act of Congress approved April 26, 1906, and to be considered as proof of continuous residence.

No.2:   Testimony relative to continuous residence from date of settlement until date of death submitted September 24 & 25, 1908.

Nos. 8-9-10:   Testimony relative to continuous residence for a period of three years submitted September 24 & 25, 1908.

IDENTIFIED MISSISSIPPI CHOCTAWS 1902 - 1909
Volume II

IDENTIFIED MISSISSIPPI CHOCTAWS CARD NO. 333

IDENTIFICATION ADDRESS Rose Hill, Miss.
SETTLEMENT ADDRESS Nos 1,2,3,4 Durwood I.T. No2. Oct. 21/03
DATE OF IDENTIFICATION Feb. 14, 1903.
DATE OF PROOF OF SETTLEMENT Nos1&4 Sept 18/03

APPROVED ROLL No.	DAWES ROLL NO.	NAME		RELATIONSHIP TO PERSON FIRST NAMED No3 Nov 24/03	AGE	SEX	BLOOD
		1	Washington, Billy		41	M	Full
		2	" Liza	Dau	19	F	Full
		3	" Hannah	Dau	17	F	Full
		4	" Martha	Dau	14	F	Full

CITIZENSHIP CERTIFICATE
ISSUED FOR NO 1-4
SEP 18 1903

APPROVED BY SECRETARY OF INTERIOR.

~~CITIZENSHIP CERTIFICATE~~
~~ISSUED FOR NO 2~~
~~OCT 22 1903~~

ENROLLMENT OF NOS. 1,2,3 HEREON APPROVED BY THE SECRETARY OF INTERIOR JAN. 13, 1905.

~~CITIZENSHIP CERTIFICATE~~
~~ISSUED FOR NO 3~~
~~NOV 25 1903~~

	NAME OF FATHER	LIVING OR DEAD	NAME OF MOTHER	LIVING OR DEAD	APPLICATION NO.	REMARKS
1	George Washington	Dead	Susan Washington	Dead	1602	
2	No.1		Lucy Washington	"	"	
3	No.1		" "	"	"	
4	No.1		" "	"	"	
5						
6						
7						
8	~~"No3: Proof of continuous residence for a period of three years submitted December 20, 1906."~~					
9	"No4: Proof of continuous residence for a period of three years submitted December 21, 1906."					
10	~~"No2: Proof of continuous residence for a period of three years submitted December 21, 1906."~~					

Declaration and proof of settlement of Sept 18/03 apply to Nos. 1 & 4 only.

Declaration and proof of settlement of Oct. 21, 03 apply to No2 only.

Declaration & proof of settlement of Nov. 24, 03 apply to No.3 only.

"No.1: Proof of continuous residence for a period of three years submitted August 18, 1906."

IDENTIFIED MISSISSIPPI CHOCTAWS 1902 - 1909
Volume II

IDENTIFIED MISSISSIPPI CHOCTAWS   CARD NO. 334

IDENTIFICATION ADDRESS Sandersville, Miss.   SETTLEMENT ADDRESS
DATE OF IDENTIFICATION Feb. 14, 1903.   DATE OF PROOF OF SETTLEMENT

APPROVED ROLL No.	DAWES ROLL NO.		NAME		RELATIONSHIP TO PERSON FIRST NAMED	AGE	SEX	BLOOD
		1	Thomas, George			47	M	Full
		2	" Susie		Wife	49	F	Full
		3	" Lewis		Son	20	M	Full
		4						
		5						
		6	APPROVED BY SECRETARY OF INTERIOR.					
		7	DID NOT SUBMIT PROOF OF					
		8	REMOVAL AND BONA-FIDE SET-					
		9	TLEMENT WITHIN ONE YEAR					
		10	FROM DATE OF IDENTIFICATION.					
		11						

	NAME OF FATHER	LIVING OR DEAD	NAME OF MOTHER	LIVING OR DEAD	APPLICATION NO.	REMARKS
1	Thomas	Dead	Sally Thomas	Dead	1604	
2	Istubbee	"	Janie	"	"	
3	No.1		No.2		"	
4						
5						
6						
7						
8						
9						
10						
11						

IDENTIFIED MISSISSIPPI CHOCTAWS 1902 - 1909
Volume II

IDENTIFIED MISSISSIPPI CHOCTAWS   CARD NO. 335

IDENTIFICATION ADDRESS Conway, Miss.   SETTLEMENT ADDRESS
DATE OF IDENTIFICATION Feb. 14, 1903.   DATE OF PROOF OF SETTLEMENT

APPROVED ROLL No.	DAWES ROLL NO.		NAME	RELATIONSHIP TO PERSON FIRST NAMED	AGE	SEX	BLOOD
		1	Sockey, John		42	M	Full
		2	" Ethel	Dau	8	F	Full
		3	" Riley	Son	7	M	Full
		4	" Sarah	Dau	4	F	Full
		5					
		6					
		7	APPROVED BY SECRETARY OF INTERIOR.				
		8	DID NOT SUBMIT PROOF OF				
		9	REMOVAL AND BONA-FIDE SET-				
		10	TLEMENT WITHIN ONE YEAR				
		11	FROM DATE OF IDENTIFICATION.				

	NAME OF FATHER	LIVING OR DEAD	NAME OF MOTHER	LIVING OR DEAD	APPLICATION NO.	REMARKS
1	Louis Sockey	Dead	Sally (or Martha) Sockey	Dead	1591	
2	No.1		Elsie Sockey	"	"	
3	No.1		" "	"	"	
4	No.1		" "	"	"	
5						
6						
7						
8						
9						
10						
11						

IDENTIFIED MISSISSIPPI CHOCTAWS 1902 - 1909
Volume II

IDENTIFIED MISSISSIPPI CHOCTAWS   CARD NO. 336

IDENTIFICATION ADDRESS Standing Pine, Miss.   SETTLEMENT ADDRESS Marietta I.T.
DATE OF IDENTIFICATION Feb. 14, 1903.   DATE OF PROOF OF SETTLEMENT Oct. 13, 1903.

APPROVED ROLL No.	DAWES ROLL NO.	NAME	RELATIONSHIP TO PERSON FIRST NAMED	AGE	SEX	BLOOD
		1 York, Solomon (Tuck-a-lum-bee)		90	M	Full
		2				
		3				
		4 APPROVED BY SECRETARY OF INTERIOR.				
		5				
		6				
		7	ENROLLMENT OF NOS. ~~1~~ HEREON APPROVED BY THE SECRETARY OF INTERIOR JAN 13 1905			
		8				
CITIZENSHIP CERTIFICATE ISSUED FOR NO 1 OCT 13 1903		9				
		10				
		11				

NAME OF FATHER	LIVING OR DEAD	NAME OF MOTHER	LIVING OR DEAD	APPLICATION NO.	REMARKS
1 Ya-con-ya York	Dead	Ah-che-bah	Dead	3013	
2					
3					
4					
5					
6					
7					
8					
9					
10 No1: Proof of death filed showing No1 died February 11, 1904.					

No1: Proof of continuous residence from date of settlement
until date of death submitted January 11-1907.

IDENTIFIED MISSISSIPPI CHOCTAWS 1902 - 1909
Volume II

IDENTIFIED MISSISSIPPI CHOCTAWS   CARD NO. 337

IDENTIFICATION ADDRESS High Hill, Miss.   SETTLEMENT ADDRESS Roff, I.T.
DATE OF IDENTIFICATION Feb. 14, 1903.   DATE OF PROOF OF SETTLEMENT Oct. 16/03.

APPROVED ROLL No.	DAWES ROLL NO.	NAME	RELATIONSHIP TO PERSON FIRST NAMED	AGE	SEX	BLOOD
		1 Waiter, Martha		26	F	Full
		2 " Robert	Son	5	M	Full
		3				
		4				
		5 APPROVED BY SECRETARY OF INTERIOR.				
		6				
		7				
		8				
CITIZENSHIP CERTIFICATE ISSUED FOR OR NO 1-2- OCT 16 1903		9				
		11				

NAME OF FATHER	LIVING OR DEAD	NAME OF MOTHER	LIVING OR DEAD	APPLICATION NO.	REMARKS
1 Captain Billey	Dead	Sallie Billey		3059	
2 Caleb Waiter	"	No.1		"	
3					
4					
5					
6					
7					
8					
9					
10		"Nos 1 and 2: Proof of continuous residence for a period of three years submitted April 12-1907."			
11					

IDENTIFIED MISSISSIPPI CHOCTAWS 1902 - 1909
Volume II

IDENTIFIED MISSISSIPPI CHOCTAWS   CARD NO. 338

IDENTIFICATION ADDRESS Vernon, Miss.   SETTLEMENT ADDRESS Mill Creek, I.T.
DATE OF IDENTIFICATION Feb. 14, 1903.   DATE OF PROOF OF SETTLEMENT Aug. 26/03.

APPROVED ROLL No.	DAWES ROLL NO.		NAME	RELATIONSHIP TO PERSON FIRST NAMED	AGE	SEX	BLOOD
		1	Sampson, Lillie		21	F	Full
		2	" Salonie	Son	5	M	Full
		3					
		4					
		5	APPROVED BY SECRETARY OF INTERIOR.				
		6					
		7					
		8					

CITIZENSHIP CERTIFICATE
ISSUED FOR NO 1-2
AUG 26 1903

	NAME OF FATHER	LIVING OR DEAD	NAME OF MOTHER	LIVING OR DEAD	APPLICATION NO.	REMARKS
1	Johnson Sampson		Sallie Sampson		2459	
2	Wash Jim		No.1		"	
3						
4						
5						
6						
7						
8						
9						
10			"Nos 1&2: Proof of continuous residence for a period of three years submitted June 20-1906."			
11						

IDENTIFIED MISSISSIPPI CHOCTAWS 1902 - 1909
Volume II

IDENTIFIED MISSISSIPPI CHOCTAWS

CARD NO. 339

IDENTIFICATION ADDRESS Dossville, Miss. SETTLEMENT ADDRESS Atoka I.T.
DATE OF IDENTIFICATION Feb. 14, 1903. DATE OF PROOF OF SETTLEMENT Aug 17, 03.

APPROVED ROLL No.	DAWES ROLL NO.	NAME	RELATIONSHIP TO PERSON FIRST NAMED	AGE	SEX	BLOOD
		1. Simpson, Gill		28	M	Full
		2. " Sissie	Wife	18	F	Full
		3. " Mertine	Dau	8	F	Full
		4. " Rosie	Dau	10mo	F	Full
		5.				
		6.				
		7. APPROVED BY SECRETARY OF INTERIOR				
		8.				
1-3 AUG 17 1903		9. 1 & 3.				
		10.				
		11.				

NAME OF FATHER	LIVING OR DEAD	NAME OF MOTHER	LIVING OR DEAD	APPLICATION NO.	REMARKS
1. John Simpson		Minnie Simpson	Dead	2158	
2. Billy Oscar	Dead	Milljean Sisman		"	
3. No.1		Leanna Simpson	Dead	"	
4. No.1		No.2		"	
5.					
6.					
7.					
8.					
9. "Nos 1 and 3. Testimony relative to continuous residence					
10. residence[sic] for a period of three years submitted July 13-1907."					
11. Declaration and proof of settlement apply to Nos. 1 & 3 only.					

IDENTIFIED MISSISSIPPI CHOCTAWS 1902 - 1909
Volume II

IDENTIFIED MISSISSIPPI CHOCTAWS CARD NO. 340

IDENTIFICATION ADDRESS Trapp, Miss.　　　SETTLEMENT ADDRESS
DATE OF IDENTIFICATION Feb. 14, 1903.　　DATE OF PROOF OF SETTLEMENT

APPROVED ROLL No.	DAWES ROLL NO.		NAME	RELATIONSHIP TO PERSON FIRST NAMED	AGE	SEX	BLOOD
		1	Willis, Louisa		25	F	Full
		2	" Ely	Son	5	M	Full
		3	" Camblin	Son	3	M	Full
		4					
		5					
		6					
		7	APPROVED BY SECRETARY OF INTERIOR.				
		8	DID NOT SUBMIT PROOF OF				
		9	REMOVAL AND BONA-FIDE SET-				
		10	TLEMENT WITHIN ONE YEAR				
		11	FROM DATE OF IDENTIFICATION.				

	NAME OF FATHER	LIVING OR DEAD	NAME OF MOTHER	LIVING OR DEAD	APPLICATION NO.	REMARKS
1	Dixon Isaac		Margaret Isaac	Dead	4904	
2	Gus Willis		No.1		"	
3	" "		No.1		"	
4						
5						
6						
7						
8						
9						
10						
11						

IDENTIFIED MISSISSIPPI CHOCTAWS 1902 - 1909
Volume II

IDENTIFIED MISSISSIPPI CHOCTAWS CARD NO. 341

IDENTIFICATION ADDRESS Philadelphia, Miss. SETTLEMENT ADDRESS
DATE OF IDENTIFICATION Feb. 14, 1903. DATE OF PROOF OF SETTLEMENT

APPROVED ROLL No.	DAWES ROLL NO.	NAME	RELATIONSHIP TO PERSON FIRST NAMED	AGE	SEX	BLOOD
		1 Waiter, Tom		34	M	Full
		2 " Jane	Wife	35	F	Full
		3 " Minnie	Dau	15	F	Full
		4				
		5				
		6 APPROVED BY SECRETARY OF INTERIOR.				
		7				
		8				
		9				
		10				
		11				

DID NOT SUBMIT PROOF OF REMOVAL AND BONA-FIDE SETTLEMENT WITHIN ONE YEAR FROM DATE OF IDENTIFICATION

NAME OF FATHER (A-mish-tubbee)	LIVING OR DEAD	NAME OF MOTHER	LIVING OR DEAD	APPLICATION NO.	REMARKS
1 John Waiter	Dead		Dead	4892	
2 Alex Ah-bin-ah-tubbee	"		"	"	
3 No.1		No.2		"	
4					
5					
6					
7					
8					
9					
10					
11					

IDENTIFIED MISSISSIPPI CHOCTAWS 1902 - 1909
Volume II

IDENTIFIED MISSISSIPPI CHOCTAWS CARD NO. 342

IDENTIFICATION ADDRESS Trapp, Miss. SETTLEMENT ADDRESS
DATE OF IDENTIFICATION Feb. 14, 1903. DATE OF PROOF OF SETTLEMENT

APPROVED ROLL No.	DAWES ROLL NO.	NAME	RELATIONSHIP TO PERSON FIRST NAMED	AGE	SEX	BLOOD
		1 Rush, Eliza		50	F	Full
		2 Isaac, Malissa	Ward	19	F	Full
		3 Lewis, Ed.	Ward	18	M	Full
		4				
		5				
		6 APPROVED BY SECRETARY OF INTERIOR.				
		7				
		8				
		9				
		10				
		11				

NAME OF FATHER	LIVING OR DEAD	NAME OF MOTHER	LIVING OR DEAD	APPLICATION NO.	REMARKS
1 Isaac Lewis		Becky Lewis	Dead	4905	
2 Dixon Isaac		Maggie Isaac	"	"	
3 Sam Lewis	Dead	Emma Lewis	"	"	
4					
5					
6					
7					
8					
9					
10					
11					

DID NOT SUBMIT PROOF OF SETTLEMENT WITHIN ONE YEAR FROM DATE OF IDENTIFICATION

IDENTIFIED MISSISSIPPI CHOCTAWS 1902 - 1909
Volume II

IDENTIFIED MISSISSIPPI CHOCTAWS CARD NO. 343

IDENTIFICATION ADDRESS Thomastown, Miss. SETTLEMENT ADDRESS Marlow I T.
DATE OF IDENTIFICATION Feb. 14, 1903. DATE OF PROOF OF SETTLEMENT Mar 7/03.

APPROVED ROLL No.	DAWES ROLL NO.	NAME	RELATIONSHIP TO PERSON FIRST NAMED	AGE	SEX	BLOOD
		1 York, Rufus		53	M	Full
		2 " Malissa	Wife	46	F	Full
		3 " Ida	Dau	16	F	Full
		4 " Jamison	Son	12	M	Full
		5 " Jesse	Son	7	M	Full
		6 " Annie	Dau	6	F	Full

APPROVED BY SECRETARY OF INTERIOR.

CITIZENSHIP CERTIFICATE ISSUED FOR NO 1-2-3-4-5-6 SEP 2 1903

NAME OF FATHER	LIVING OR DEAD	NAME OF MOTHER	LIVING OR DEAD	APPLICATION NO.	REMARKS
1 Tom York	Dead	Mimie York		2168	
2 Charles Bob		Sophie Bob	Dead	"	
3 No.1		No.2		"	
4 No.1		No.2		"	
5 No.1		No.2		"	
6 No.1		No.2		"	

"No4: Proof of death filed showing No4 died February 17-1907."
"No4: Proof of continuous residence for a period of three years submitted August 1-1907."
No3 now wife of No1 on card 48 - See test 8-1-07

Supplimental[sic] proof of settlement taken at the Chickasaw Land Office Sept 2/03.
"No3: Proof of continuous residence for a period of three years submitted August 1-1907."

IDENTIFIED MISSISSIPPI CHOCTAWS 1902 - 1909
Volume II

IDENTIFIED MISSISSIPPI CHOCTAWS CARD NO. 344

IDENTIFICATION ADDRESS Vernon, Miss. SETTLEMENT ADDRESS Ravia I.T.
DATE OF IDENTIFICATION Feb. 14, 1903. DATE OF PROOF OF SETTLEMENT Sept 1/03.

APPROVED ROLL No.	DAWES ROLL NO.		NAME	RELATIONSHIP TO PERSON FIRST NAMED	AGE	SEX	BLOOD
		1	John, Sam		68	M	Full
		2	" Nancy	Wife	62	F	Full
		3					
		4					
		5					
		6					
		7					
		8					
CITIZENSHIP CERTIFICATE ISSUED FOR NO 1-2 SEP 2 1903		9					
		10					
		11					

APPROVED BY SECRETARY OF INTERIOR ENROLLMENT OF NOS. 1&2 HEREON APPROVED BY ANNE SECRETARY OF INTERIOR

	NAME OF FATHER	LIVING OR DEAD	NAME OF MOTHER	LIVING OR DEAD	APPLICATION NO.	REMARKS
1	John (Ille-nowah)	Dead	Polly John	Dead	2181	
2	John	"	Phyllis	"	"	
3						
4						
5						
6						
7						
8						
9						
10	No2: Proof of continuous residence for a period of three years					
11	submitted January 25, 1907.					

No1: Proof of death filed showing that No1 died November 21, 1906.

No1: Proof of continuous residence from date of settlement until date of death submitted January 25, 1907.

IDENTIFIED MISSISSIPPI CHOCTAWS 1902 - 1909
Volume II

IDENTIFIED MISSISSIPPI CHOCTAWS   CARD NO. 345

IDENTIFICATION ADDRESS Cooksey, Miss.   SETTLEMENT ADDRESS Atoka, Ind. Ter.
DATE OF IDENTIFICATION Feb. 14, 1903.   DATE OF PROOF OF SETTLEMENT April 30, 1903.

APPROVED ROLL No.	DAWES ROLL NO.	NAME	RELATIONSHIP TO PERSON FIRST NAMED	AGE	SEX	BLOOD
		1 West, John		25	M	Full
		2 " Ollie	Wife	21	F	Full
		3				
		4				
		5 APPROVED BY SECRETARY OF INTERIOR				
		6 ENROLLMENT				
		7				
		8 OF INTERIOR JAN. 13, 1905				
CITIZENSHIP CERTIFICATE ISSUED ROLL NO.		9				
		10				
		11				

NAME OF FATHER	LIVING OR DEAD	NAME OF MOTHER	LIVING OR DEAD	APPLICATION NO.	REMARKS
1 West	Dead	West	Dead	2285	
2 Sam Lewis	"	Martha Lewis		"	
3					
4					
5					
6					
7					
8	No1 testimony relative to continuous residence for a period of three				
9	years submitted July 15-1907.				
10	Declaration and proof of settlement applies to No1 only.				
11					

No2 DID NOT SUBMIT PROOF OF REMOVAL AND BONA-FIDE SETTLEMENT WITHIN ONE YEAR FROM DATE OF IDENTIFICATION

IDENTIFIED MISSISSIPPI CHOCTAWS 1902 - 1909
Volume II

IDENTIFIED MISSISSIPPI CHOCTAWS   CARD NO. 346

IDENTIFICATION ADDRESS Saint Anns[sic], Miss.   SETTLEMENT ADDRESS
DATE OF IDENTIFICATION Feb. 14, 1903.   DATE OF PROOF OF SETTLEMENT

APPROVED ROLL No.	DAWES ROLL NO.		NAME	RELATIONSHIP TO PERSON FIRST NAMED	AGE	SEX	BLOOD
		1	Weshock, Sampson		30	M	Full
		2	" Jane	Wife	40	F	Full
		3	" Sallie	Dau	12	F	Full
		4	" Massy	Son	9	M	Full
		5	" Nona	Dau	7	F	Full
		6					
		7					
		8	APPROVED BY SECRETARY OF INTERIOR.				
		9	DID NOT SUBMIT PROOF OF REMOVAL AND BONA FIDE SET-				
		10	TLEMENT WITHIN ONE YEAR				
		11	FROM DATE OF IDENTIFICATION.				

	NAME OF FATHER	LIVING OR DEAD	NAME OF MOTHER	LIVING OR DEAD	APPLICATION NO.	REMARKS
1	John Weshock	Dead		Dead	2159	
2	Willis Barney	"		"	"	
3	No.1		No.2		"	
4	No.1		No.2		"	
5	No.1		No.2		"	
6						
7						
8						
9						
10						
11						

IDENTIFIED MISSISSIPPI CHOCTAWS 1902 - 1909
Volume II

IDENTIFIED MISSISSIPPI CHOCTAWS — CARD NO. 347

IDENTIFICATION ADDRESS: Mobile, Alabama
SETTLEMENT ADDRESS: Byars I.T.
DATE OF IDENTIFICATION: Dec. 4, 1902, 153 Marine St.
DATE OF PROOF OF SETTLEMENT: Sept. 22, 03.

APPROVED ROLL No.	DAWES ROLL NO.		NAME	RELATIONSHIP TO PERSON FIRST NAMED	AGE	SEX	BLOOD
		1	Carter, Nettie Frances		21	F	1/8
		2					
		3					
		4	APPROVED BY SECRETARY OF INTERIOR.				
		5					
		6					
		7					
		8					

CITIZENSHIP CERTIFICATE ISSUED FOR NO 1 SEP 22 1903

	NAME OF FATHER	LIVING OR DEAD	NAME OF MOTHER	LIVING OR DEAD	APPLICATION NO.	REMARKS
1	Jubal Braxton Carter	Dead	Laura Belle Goldthorpe	Dead	1929	
2						
3						
4						
5						
6						
7						
8		Testimony as to continuous residence for a period of 3 years submitted Mch 13, [?].				
9						
10						
11						

IDENTIFIED MISSISSIPPI CHOCTAWS 1902 - 1909
Volume II

IDENTIFIED MISSISSIPPI CHOCTAWS   CARD NO. 348

IDENTIFICATION ADDRESS Rio, Miss.   SETTLEMENT ADDRESS
DATE OF IDENTIFICATION Feb. 14, 1903.   DATE OF PROOF OF SETTLEMENT

APPROVED ROLL No.	DAWES ROLL NO.	NAME	RELATIONSHIP TO PERSON FIRST NAMED	AGE	SEX	BLOOD
		1 Bull, Leah		28	F	Full
		2				
		3				
		4				
		5 APPROVED BY SECRETARY OF INTERIOR.				
		6 DID NOT SUBMIT PROOF OF REMOVAL AND BONA-FIDE SETTLEMENT WITHIN ONE YEAR FROM DATE OF IDENTIFICATION.				
		7				
		8				
		9				
		10				
		11				

NAME OF FATHER	LIVING OR DEAD	NAME OF MOTHER	LIVING OR DEAD	APPLICATION NO.	REMARKS
1 John Bull			Dead	2527	
2					
3					
4					
5					
6					
7					
8					
9					
10					
11					

IDENTIFIED MISSISSIPPI CHOCTAWS 1902 - 1909
Volume II

IDENTIFIED MISSISSIPPI CHOCTAWS CARD NO. 349

IDENTIFICATION ADDRESS Violin, La.   SETTLEMENT ADDRESS Ardmore, Ind. Ter.
DATE OF IDENTIFICATION Feb. 14, 1903.   DATE OF PROOF OF SETTLEMENT Dec. 10th, 1903.

APPROVED ROLL No.	DAWES ROLL NO.	NAME	RELATIONSHIP TO PERSON FIRST NAMED	AGE	SEX	BLOOD
		1 Lewis, Jim		40	M	Full
		2				
		3				
		4				
		5 APPROVED BY SECRETARY OF INTERIOR.				
		6				
		7				
		8				

CITIZENSHIP CERTIFICATE
ISSUED FOR NO 1
DEC 10 1903

NAME OF FATHER	LIVING OR DEAD	NAME OF MOTHER	LIVING OR DEAD	APPLICATION NO.	REMARKS
1 Jim	Dead		Dead	2270	
2					
3					
4					
5					
6					
7 Testimony taken December 10, 1908, as to continuous residence within the Choctaw-Chickasaw country.					
8 Additional testimony as to continuous residence taken					
9 January 12, 1909.					
10					
11					

IDENTIFIED MISSISSIPPI CHOCTAWS 1902 - 1909
Volume II

IDENTIFIED MISSISSIPPI CHOCTAWS   CARD NO. 350

IDENTIFICATION ADDRESS Ennis, Miss.   SETTLEMENT ADDRESS Kiowa, I.T.
DATE OF IDENTIFICATION Feb. 14, 1903.   DATE OF PROOF OF SETTLEMENT Nov. 16/03.

APPROVED ROLL No.	DAWES ROLL NO.		NAME	RELATIONSHIP TO PERSON FIRST NAMED	AGE	SEX	BLOOD
		1	Thompson, Ben		36	M	Full
		2	" Martha	Wife	36	F	Full
		3	" Leona	Dau	15	F	Full
		4	" Thomas	Son	11	M	Full
		5	" Maggie	Dau	5	F	Full
		6					
		7					
		8	APPROVED BY SECRETARY OF INTERIOR.				

CITIZENSHIP CERTIFICATE
ISSUED FOR NO 1-2-3-4-5
NOV 16 1903

ENROLLMENT
OF NOS. 1 2 3 4 & 5
APPROVED BY THE SECRETARY
OF INTERIOR JAN 13 1905

	NAME OF FATHER (Fee-lah-kah-tubbe)	LIVING OR DEAD	NAME OF MOTHER	LIVING OR DEAD	APPLICATION NO.	REMARKS
1	Bill Thompson	Dead	Sookie Thompson	Dead	2536	
2	Jacob	"	Betsey	"	"	
3	No.1		No.2		"	
4	No.1		No.2		"	
5	No.1		No.2		"	

Nos 1 to 5 testimony as to continuous residence of Nos. 1 to 5, inclusive, for a period of 3 years submitted February 10, 1906.

IDENTIFIED MISSISSIPPI CHOCTAWS 1902 - 1909
Volume II

IDENTIFIED MISSISSIPPI CHOCTAWS   CARD NO. 351

IDENTIFICATION ADDRESS Roscoe, Miss.   SETTLEMENT ADDRESS Ardmore, Ind. Ter.
DATE OF IDENTIFICATION Feb. 14, 1903.   DATE OF PROOF OF SETTLEMENT July 1, 1903.

APPROVED ROLL No.	DAWES ROLL NO.	NAME	RELATIONSHIP TO PERSON FIRST NAMED	AGE	SEX	BLOOD
		1. Morris, J. P.		22	M	Full
		2. " Bessie	Wife	18	F	Full
		3.				
		4.				
		5. APPROVED BY SECRETARY OF INTERIOR.				
		6.				
		7.	1 & 2			
		8.				
		9.				
	1 & 2	10.				
		11.				

NAME OF FATHER	LIVING OR DEAD	NAME OF MOTHER	LIVING OR DEAD	APPLICATION NO.	REMARKS
1. Morris			Dead	2271	
2. John Wallace		Sarah Wallace	"	"	
3.					
4.					
5.					
6.					
7.					
8.					
9. Declaration and proof of settlement applies to Nos. 1&2.					
10. "Nos. 1 and 2: Proof of continuous residence for a period of three years submitted October 25, 1906."					
11.					

IDENTIFIED MISSISSIPPI CHOCTAWS 1902 - 1909
Volume II

IDENTIFIED MISSISSIPPI CHOCTAWS CARD NO. 352

IDENTIFICATION ADDRESS Tucker, Miss.   SETTLEMENT ADDRESS Atoka, Ind. Ter.
DATE OF IDENTIFICATION Feb. 14, 1903.   DATE OF PROOF OF SETTLEMENT Aug. 18/1903.

APPROVED ROLL No.	DAWES ROLL NO.		NAME	RELATIONSHIP TO PERSON FIRST NAMED	AGE	SEX	BLOOD
		1	Billey, Young		66	M	Full
		2	" Sallie	Wife	40	F	Full
		3	" Fabie	Son	17	M	Full
		4	" Alam	Son	13	M	Full
		5	" Betty	Dau	6	F	Full
		6	" Ina	Dau	4	F	Full
		7	" Charley	Son	2	M	Full
		8					

CITIZENSHIP CERTIFICATE ISSUED FOR NO 1-2-3-4-5-6-7 AUG 18 1903

APPROVED BY SECRETARY OF INTERIOR
ENROLLMENT OF NOS. 1 2 3 4 5 6 & 7 HEREON APPROVED BY THE SECRETARY OF INTERIOR JAN 13 1905.

	NAME OF FATHER (Thlopotubbee)	LIVING OR DEAD	NAME OF MOTHER	LIVING OR DEAD	APPLICATION NO.	REMARKS
1	Yahfin Billey	Dead	Ahbehoke	Dead	2014	
2	Tom	"		"	"	
3	No.1		No.2		"	
4	No.1		No.2		"	
5	No.1		No.2		"	
6	No.1		No.2		"	
7	No.1		No.2		"	

No3 is female, see test. 8/18/03.
No3 is wife of No1 on card 404.
No1 died August 28, 1904: Testimony relative to continuous
residence up to his death submitted September 10, 1906.
"Nos 2 to 7 inclusive: Testimony relative to continuous
residence for a period of three years submitted September 10, 1906."

IDENTIFIED MISSISSIPPI CHOCTAWS 1902 - 1909
Volume II

IDENTIFIED MISSISSIPPI CHOCTAWS CARD NO. 353

IDENTIFICATION ADDRESS Saint Anns[sic], Miss.   SETTLEMENT ADDRESS
DATE OF IDENTIFICATION Feb. 14, 1903.   DATE OF PROOF OF SETTLEMENT

APPROVED ROLL No.	DAWES ROLL NO.	NAME	RELATIONSHIP TO PERSON FIRST NAMED	AGE	SEX	BLOOD
		1 Allen, Newton		26	M	Full
		2 " Rosie	Wife	19	F	Full
		3 " Martha	Dau	2wks	F	Full
		4				
		5				
		6 APPROVED BY SECRETARY OF INTERIOR.				
		7				
		8 DID NOT SUBMIT PROOF OF				
		9 REMOVAL AND BONA-FIDE SET-				
		10 TLEMENT WITHIN ONE YEAR FROM DATE OF IDENTIFICATION.				
		11				

NAME OF FATHER	LIVING OR DEAD	NAME OF MOTHER	LIVING OR DEAD	APPLICATION NO.	REMARKS
1 Kit Allen	Dead	Missouri Stoliby		4440	
2 Simon Joshua		Lucy Joshua		"	
3 No.1		No.2		"	
4					
5					
6					
7					
8					
9					
10					
11					

IDENTIFIED MISSISSIPPI CHOCTAWS 1902 - 1909
Volume II

IDENTIFIED MISSISSIPPI CHOCTAWS   CARD NO. 354

IDENTIFICATION ADDRESS Remus, Miss.   SETTLEMENT ADDRESS
DATE OF IDENTIFICATION Feb. 14, 1903.   DATE OF PROOF OF SETTLEMENT

APPROVED ROLL No.	DAWES ROLL NO.	NAME	RELATIONSHIP TO PERSON FIRST NAMED	AGE	SEX	BLOOD
		1 Sam, Oscar		38	M	Full
		2 " Mattie	Wife	28	F	Full
		3 " Jimsie	Dau	1½	F	Full
		4 " Raymond	Son	17	M	Full
		5 " Houston	Son	14	M	Full
		6				
		7				
		8 APPROVED BY SECRETARY OF INTERIOR.				
		9 DID NOT SUBMIT PROOF OF				
		10 REMOVAL AND BONA-FIDE SETTLEMENT WITHIN ONE YEAR				
		11 FROM DATE OF IDENTIFICATION.				

	NAME OF FATHER	LIVING OR DEAD	NAME OF MOTHER	LIVING OR DEAD	APPLICATION NO.	REMARKS
1	Sam	Dead	Sophie Sam		2174	
2	Sampson Tubbee		Caroline Tubbee		"	
3	No.1		No.2		"	
4	No.1		Eliza Sam	Dead	"	
5	No.1		" "	"	"	
6						
7						
8						
9						
10						
11						

IDENTIFIED MISSISSIPPI CHOCTAWS 1902 - 1909
Volume II

IDENTIFIED MISSISSIPPI CHOCTAWS CARD NO. 355

IDENTIFICATION ADDRESS Franks, Miss.   SETTLEMENT ADDRESS
DATE OF IDENTIFICATION Feb. 14, 1903.   DATE OF PROOF OF SETTLEMENT

APPROVED ROLL No.	DAWES ROLL NO.		NAME	RELATIONSHIP TO PERSON FIRST NAMED	AGE	SEX	BLOOD
		1	Tuf-fa-mah, Willis		60	M	Full
		2	" Lucy	Wife	40	F	Full
		3	" Exa	StepDau	11	F	Full
		4					
		5					
		6	APPROVED BY SECRETARY OF INTERIOR.				
		7					
		8	DID NOT SUBMIT PROOF OF				
		9	REMOVAL AND BONA-FIDE SET-				
		10	TLEMENT WITHIN ONE YEAR				
		11	FROM DATE OF IDENTIFICATION.				

	NAME OF FATHER	LIVING OR DEAD	NAME OF MOTHER	LIVING OR DEAD	APPLICATION NO.	REMARKS
	(On-ta-mah-chubbee)		(Po-ki)			
1	John	Dead	Nancy	Dead	4844	
2	Sam (Tish-o-cubbee)	"	Casey	"	"	
3	Amos Tuf-fa-mah	"	No.2		"	
4						
5						
6						
7						
8						
9						
10						
11						

IDENTIFIED MISSISSIPPI CHOCTAWS 1902 - 1909
Volume II

IDENTIFIED MISSISSIPPI CHOCTAWS   CARD NO. 356

IDENTIFICATION ADDRESS Toles, Miss.   SETTLEMENT ADDRESS Kiowa I.T.
DATE OF IDENTIFICATION Feb. 14, 1903.   DATE OF PROOF OF SETTLEMENT Aug 21, 03

APPROVED ROLL No.	DAWES ROLL NO.		NAME	RELATIONSHIP TO PERSON FIRST NAMED	AGE	SEX	BLOOD
		1	Willis, John (Il-le-ah-tubbee)		59	M	Full
		2					
		3					
		4					
		5	APPROVED BY SECRETARY OF INTERIOR.				
		6	ENROLLMENT				
		7	OF NOS. ~~1~~ HEREON APPROVED BY THE SECRETARY				
		8	OF INTERIOR JAN 13 1905				
CITIZENSHIP CERTIFICATE ISSUED FOR NO 1 DEC 16 1903		9					
		10					
		11					

NAME OF FATHER	LIVING OR DEAD	NAME OF MOTHER	LIVING OR DEAD	APPLICATION NO.	REMARKS
1 Ma-shone-tah-tubbee	Dead	Cun-ne-o-te-mah	Dead	5198	
2					
3					
4					
5					
6					
7 No.1-Testimony as to continuous residence of No.1,					
8 up to his death submitted May 4, 1905.					
9					
10					
11					

IDENTIFIED MISSISSIPPI CHOCTAWS 1902 - 1909
Volume II

IDENTIFIED MISSISSIPPI CHOCTAWS

CARD NO. 357

IDENTIFICATION ADDRESS Kullituklo, Ind. Ter.   SETTLEMENT ADDRESS Kullituklo I.T.
DATE OF IDENTIFICATION Feb. 14, 1903.   DATE OF PROOF OF SETTLEMENT Aug 12/03

APPROVED ROLL No.	DAWES ROLL NO.	NAME		RELATIONSHIP TO PERSON FIRST NAMED	AGE	SEX	BLOOD
		1	Williams, Tom		69	M	Full
		2	" Mary	Wife		F	Full
		3	" Chlorie	Dau	17	F	Full
		4	" Sam	Son	16	M	Full
		5	" Harvey	Son	8	M	Full
		6	" Susan	Dau	4	F	Full

CITIZENSHIP CERTIFICATE ISSUED FOR NO 1-3-4-5-6 JAN 6 190

APPROVED BY SECRETARY OF INTERIOR.
1 2 3 4 5 & 6

NAME OF FATHER	LIVING OR DEAD	NAME OF MOTHER	LIVING OR DEAD	APPLICATION NO.	REMARKS
1 Williams	Dead		Dead	5798	
2 Thompson	"		"	"	
3 No.1		No.2		"	
4 No.1		No.2		"	
5 No.1		No.2		"	
6 No.1		No.2		"	
7					
8	No.1: Testimony relative to continuous residence				
9	from date of settlement until date of death				
10	submitted September 22, 1908.				

Nos. 2-3-4-5 and 6: Testimony relative to continuous residence for a period of three years submitted September 22, 1908.

IDENTIFIED MISSISSIPPI CHOCTAWS 1902 - 1909
Volume II

IDENTIFIED MISSISSIPPI CHOCTAWS   CARD NO. 358

IDENTIFICATION ADDRESS   North Bend, Miss.   SETTLEMENT ADDRESS
DATE OF IDENTIFICATION   Feb. 14, 1903.   DATE OF PROOF OF SETTLEMENT

APPROVED ROLL No.	DAWES ROLL NO.	NAME	RELATIONSHIP TO PERSON FIRST NAMED	AGE	SEX	BLOOD
		1 Lahbin, Elizabeth		60	F	Full
		2 " Ben	Son	20	M	Full
		3				
		4				
		5				
		6 APPROVED BY SECRETARY OF INTERIOR.				
		7 ~~DID NOT SUBMIT PROOF OF~~				
		8 ~~REMOVAL AND BONA-FIDE SET-~~				
		9 ~~TLEMENT WITHIN ONE YEAR~~				
		10 ~~FROM DATE OF IDENTIFICATION.~~				
		11				

NAME OF FATHER	LIVING OR DEAD	NAME OF MOTHER	LIVING OR DEAD	APPLICATION NO.	REMARKS
1	Dead		Dead	5107	
2 Lahbin	"	No.1		"	
3					
4					
5					
6					
7					
8					
9					
10					
11					

IDENTIFIED MISSISSIPPI CHOCTAWS 1902 - 1909
Volume II

IDENTIFIED MISSISSIPPI CHOCTAWS   CARD NO. 359

IDENTIFICATION ADDRESS Conehatta, Miss.   SETTLEMENT ADDRESS Atoka, I.T.
DATE OF IDENTIFICATION Feb. 14, 1903.   DATE OF PROOF OF SETTLEMENT Aug. 18/03.

APPROVED ROLL No.	DAWES ROLL NO.	NAME	RELATIONSHIP TO PERSON FIRST NAMED	AGE	SEX	BLOOD
		1. Wickson, John (Con-ne-ma-tubbee)		60	M	Full
		2.				
		3.				
		4.				
		5. APPROVED BY SECRETARY OF INTERIOR.				
		6. ENROLLMENT				
		7. OF NOS. ~~1~~ HEREON APPROVED BY THE SECRETARY OF INTERIOR JAN				
		8.				
CITIZENSHIP CERTIFICATE		9.				
ISSUED FOR NO 1		10.				
AUG 19		11.				

NAME OF FATHER (Ah-be-tu-tah)	LIVING OR DEAD	NAME OF MOTHER	LIVING OR DEAD	APPLICATION NO.	REMARKS
1. John Davis	Dead	Conne-ma-honah	Dead	4009	
2.					
3.					
4.					
5.					
6.					
7.					
8.					
9. "No1: Testimony as to continuous residence					
10. for a period of three years submitted					
11. August 25, 1906."					

IDENTIFIED MISSISSIPPI CHOCTAWS 1902 - 1909
Volume II

IDENTIFIED MISSISSIPPI CHOCTAWS   CARD NO. 360

IDENTIFICATION ADDRESS Rio, Miss.   SETTLEMENT ADDRESS Story I.T.
DATE OF IDENTIFICATION Feb. 14, 1903.   DATE OF PROOF OF SETTLEMENT Sept 30/03.

APPROVED ROLL No.	DAWES ROLL NO.	NAME	RELATIONSHIP TO PERSON FIRST NAMED	AGE	SEX	BLOOD
		1 Bull, Pink		23	M	Full
		2 " Emma	Wife	17	F	Full
		3				
		4				
		5 APPROVED BY SECRETARY OF INTERIOR.				
		6 ENROLLMENT OF NOS. 1&2 HEREON APPROVED BY THE SECRETARY OF INTERIOR J 1905				
		7				
		8				
CITIZENSHIP CERTIFICATE ISSUED FOR NO 1-2 SEP 30 1903		9 10 11				

NAME OF FATHER	LIVING OR DEAD	NAME OF MOTHER	LIVING OR DEAD	APPLICATION NO.	REMARKS
1 John Bull			Dead	2525	
2 Giffin Amos	Dead		"	"	
3					
4					
5					
6					
7					
8 Nos. 1 and 2: Testimony relative to continuous residence for a period of three years submitted September 30, 1908.					
9					
10					
11					

IDENTIFIED MISSISSIPPI CHOCTAWS 1902 - 1909
Volume II

IDENTIFIED MISSISSIPPI CHOCTAWS   CARD NO. 361

IDENTIFICATION ADDRESS Ennis, Miss.   SETTLEMENT ADDRESS Ardmore I.T.
DATE OF IDENTIFICATION Feb. 14, 1903.   DATE OF PROOF OF SETTLEMENT Aug 28/03.

APPROVED ROLL No.	DAWES ROLL NO.	NAME	RELATIONSHIP TO PERSON FIRST NAMED	AGE	SEX	BLOOD
		1. Willis, Charley		34	M	Full
		2.				
		3.				
		4.				
		5. APPROVED BY SECRETARY OF INTERIOR.				
		6. ENROLLMENT				
		7. OF NOS. ~~~	~~~ HEREON APPROVED BY THE SECRETARY				
		8. OF INTERIOR JAN 13 1905				
CITIZENSHIP CERTIFICATE		9.				
ISSUED FOR NO 1						
AUG 28 1903						
		11.				

NAME OF FATHER	LIVING OR DEAD	NAME OF MOTHER	LIVING OR DEAD	APPLICATION NO.	REMARKS
1. John Willis		Sookey Willis	Dead	2865	
2.					
3.					
4.					
5.					
6.					
7.					
8.					
9.					
10. "No 1: proof of continuous residence for a period of three years submitted January 5, 1907."					
11.					

IDENTIFIED MISSISSIPPI CHOCTAWS 1902 - 1909
Volume II

IDENTIFIED MISSISSIPPI CHOCTAWS CARD NO. 362

IDENTIFICATION ADDRESS Doolittle, Miss. SETTLEMENT ADDRESS Paucaunla, Ind. Ter.
DATE OF IDENTIFICATION Feb. 14, 1903. DATE OF PROOF OF SETTLEMENT July 25, 1903.

APPROVED ROLL No.	DAWES ROLL NO.	NAME	RELATIONSHIP TO PERSON FIRST NAMED	AGE	SEX	BLOOD
		1 Billey, Sam		34	M	Full
		2				
		3				
		4				
		5 APPROVED BY SECRETARY OF INTERIOR.				
		6				
		7				
		8				
CITIZENSHIP CERTIFICATE ISSUED FOR NO 1 AUG 27 1903		9				
		10				
		11				

NAME OF FATHER	LIVING OR DEAD	NAME OF MOTHER	LIVING OR DEAD	APPLICATION NO.	REMARKS
1 Thompson Billey	Dead	Lilie Billey		3478	
2					
3					
4					
5					
6					
7					
8					
9 Testimony as to continuous residence for period of 3 years submitted Mch 29, 06.					
10					
11					

IDENTIFIED MISSISSIPPI CHOCTAWS 1902 - 1909
Volume II

IDENTIFIED MISSISSIPPI CHOCTAWS   CARD NO. 363

IDENTIFICATION ADDRESS Cushtusa, Miss.   SETTLEMENT ADDRESS Wilson I.T.
DATE OF IDENTIFICATION Feb. 14, 1903.   DATE OF PROOF OF SETTLEMENT May 18/03

APPROVED ROLL No.	DAWES ROLL NO.	NAME	RELATIONSHIP TO PERSON FIRST NAMED	AGE	SEX	BLOOD
		1. Alderman, Christian		25	M	Full
		2.				
		3.				
		4.				
		5. APPROVED BY SECRETARY OF INTERIOR.				
		6.				
		7.				
		8.				
CITIZENSHIP CERTIFICATE 9.						
ISSUED FOR NO 1 MAY 19 1903						
		11.				

NAME OF FATHER	LIVING OR DEAD	NAME OF MOTHER	LIVING OR DEAD	APPLICATION NO.	REMARKS
1. John Alderman	Dead	Sealy Alderman	Dead	2897	
2.					
3.					
4.					
5.					
6.					
7.					
8.					
9. No.1: Proof of continuous residence for a period of three years submitted January 29-1907.					
10.					
11.					

IDENTIFIED MISSISSIPPI CHOCTAWS 1902 - 1909
Volume II

IDENTIFIED MISSISSIPPI CHOCTAWS — CARD NO. 364

IDENTIFICATION ADDRESS Byram, Miss.　　SETTLEMENT ADDRESS Colbert, I.T.
DATE OF IDENTIFICATION Feb. 14, 1903.　　DATE OF PROOF OF SETTLEMENT Aug. 4/03.

APPROVED ROLL No.	DAWES ROLL NO.	NAME	RELATIONSHIP TO PERSON FIRST NAMED	AGE	SEX	BLOOD
		1. Johnson, Taylor		66	M	Full
		2. " Jennie	Wife	70	F	Full
		3. " Freeman	Son	19	M	Full
		4.				
		5. **APPROVED BY SECRETARY OF INTERIOR.**				

CITIZENSHIP CERTIFICATE
ISSUED FOR NO ~~1~~
AUG 4 1903

1&2

JAN 13 1905

CITIZENSHIP CERTIFICATE　　12/12-1904 No.3　DID NOT SUBMIT PROOF OF
ISSUED FOR NO ~~2~~　　　　　　　　　　　　REMOVAL AND BONA-FIDE SET-
MAR 18 1904　　　　　　　　　　　　　　　　TLEMENT WITHIN ONE YEAR
　　　　　　　　　　　　　　　　　　　　　　FROM DATE OF IDENTIFICATION.

NAME OF FATHER	LIVING OR DEAD	NAME OF MOTHER	LIVING OR DEAD	APPLICATION NO.	REMARKS
1. Jim	Dead		Dead	2686	
2. Willis	"		"	"	
3. No.1		No.2		"	
4.					
5.					
6.		No.1 - Testimony relative to continuous residence from date of settlement until date of death submitted September 18, 1908."			

CITIZENSHIP CERTIFICATE
ISSUED FOR NO ~~1~~
JUN 8- 1906

8. See Commission Letter - File #5713

9. ~~3~~
10. June 19-1906　　of Aug 4,03
11. Decl. & Proof of settlement applies to Nos 1&2 only.
　　　"　　"　　"　　"　　"　　"　　" 3 also.

No.3= Testimony relative to continuous residence for a period of
three years submitted September 18, 1908.
Sept 25, 1905 Commissioner held that proof of settlement had
been submitted for No. 3 on Aug 4, 1903.
"No.2 died December 13, 1904: testimony as to continuous residence
up to her death submitted July 23, 1906."

IDENTIFIED MISSISSIPPI CHOCTAWS 1902 - 1909
Volume II

IDENTIFIED MISSISSIPPI CHOCTAWS   CARD NO. 365

IDENTIFICATION ADDRESS Shady point, Ind. Ter.   SETTLEMENT ADDRESS Connerville I.T.
DATE OF IDENTIFICATION Feb. 14, 1903.   DATE OF PROOF OF SETTLEMENT Oct 8/03.

APPROVED ROLL No.	DAWES ROLL NO.	NAME		RELATIONSHIP TO PERSON FIRST NAMED	AGE	SEX	BLOOD
		1	Cooper, James		32	M	Full
		2	" Annie	Wife	20	F	Full
		3	" Lonnie	Son	8	M	Full
		4	" Nancy	Dau	2	F	Full
		5	" Mary	Dau	1	F	Full
		6					

CITIZENSHIP CERTIFICATE ISSUED FOR NO 1-3-4 OCT 8 1903

APPROVED BY SECRETARY OF INTERIOR.
ENROLLMENT OF NOS. 1 2 3 4 & 5 HEREON
APPROVED BY THE SECRETARY OF INTERIOR JAN 13 1905

CITIZENSHIP CERTIFICATE ISSUED FOR NO 2-5 OCT 27 1909

	NAME OF FATHER	LIVING OR DEAD	NAME OF MOTHER	LIVING OR DEAD	APPLICATION NO.	REMARKS
1	Peter Cooper	Dead	Betsey Cooper	Dead	1138	
2	Lewis Hawkins	"	Nancy Hawkins	"	"	
3	No.1		No.2		"	
4	No.1		No.2		"	
5	No.1		No.2		"	
6						
7						
8						
9	Nos. 1,2,3,4 and 5: Proof of continuous residence for a					
10	period of three years submitted March 4, 1907.					
11						

IDENTIFIED MISSISSIPPI CHOCTAWS 1902 - 1909
Volume II

IDENTIFIED MISSISSIPPI CHOCTAWS   CARD NO. 366

IDENTIFICATION ADDRESS Hickory, Miss.   SETTLEMENT ADDRESS Kemp, Ind. Ter.
DATE OF IDENTIFICATION Feb. 14, 1903.   DATE OF PROOF OF SETTLEMENT July 11, 1903

APPROVED ROLL No.	DAWES ROLL NO.		NAME	RELATIONSHIP TO PERSON FIRST NAMED	AGE	SEX	BLOOD
		1	Simon, Albert		26	M	Full
		2	" Mary Jane	Wife	25	F	Full
		3	" Amos	Son	6	M	Full
		4	" Fannie	Dau	8mo	F	Full
		5	APPROVED BY SECRETARY OF INTERIOR.				
		6	ENROLLMENT				
		7	OF NOS. 1 2 & 3 HEREON APPROVED BY THE SECRETARY				
		8	OF INTERIOR.				

CITIZENSHIP CERTIFICATE   No.4   DID NOT SUBMIT PROOF OF
ISSUED FOR NO 1-2-3   REMOVAL AND BONA-FIDE SET-
     JUL 11 1903   TLEMENT WITHIN ONE YEAR
                        FROM DATE OF IDENTIFICATION.

	NAME OF FATHER	LIVING OR DEAD	NAME OF MOTHER	LIVING OR DEAD	APPLICATION NO.	REMARKS
1	Simon Charley		Jane Simon		1571	
2		Dead		Dead	"	
3	No.1		No.2		"	
4	No.1		No.2		"	
5						
6			N°s 1&3 Testimony relative to continuous residence			
7			for a period of three years submitted February 19-1908.			
8						
9			Declaration and proof of settlement applies to Nos 1,2 and 3 only.			
10						
11						

"No2 died November 18, 1903: testimony as to continuous residence up to her death submitted June 21, 1906."

IDENTIFIED MISSISSIPPI CHOCTAWS 1902 - 1909
Volume II

IDENTIFIED MISSISSIPPI CHOCTAWS CARD NO. 367

Nos 1-2-3-4-5-6
IDENTIFICATION ADDRESS Rose Hill, Miss.   SETTLEMENT ADDRESS McMillan I.T.
DATE OF IDENTIFICATION Feb. 14, 1903.   DATE OF PROOF OF SETTLEMENT Aug. 28/03 1-2-4-5-6

APPROVED ROLL No.	DAWES ROLL NO.		NAME	RELATIONSHIP TO PERSON FIRST NAMED	AGE	SEX	BLOOD
		1	Mose, John	No3 Nov 14 03	49	M	Full
		2	" Lula	Wife	32	F	Full
		3	" Steen	Son	20	M	Full
		4	" Frank	Son	8	M	Full
		5	" William Davis	Son	3	M	Full
		6	" Lark	Son	1	M	Full

CITIZENSHIP CERTIFICATE
ISSUED FOR NO 1-2-4-5-6
~~AUG 28 1903~~   **APPROVED BY SECRETARY OF INTERIOR.**

CITIZENSHIP CERTIFICATE   ENROLLMENT
~~ISSUED FOR NO 3~~   OF NOS. 1 2 3 4 5 & 6 HEREON
NOV 14 1903   APPROVED BY THE SECRETARY
                           OF INTERIOR JAN 13 1905

	NAME OF FATHER	LIVING OR DEAD	NAME OF MOTHER	LIVING OR DEAD	APPLICATION NO.	REMARKS
1	Mose	Dead		Dead	1145	
2	Jackson			"	"	
3	No.1		No.2		"	
4	No.1		No.2		"	
5	No.1		No.2		"	
6	No.1		No.2		"	
7						
8			Nos 1, 5 and 6: Proof of continuous residence for a			
9			period of three years submitted February 5, 1907.			
10	Declaration and proof of settlement applies to Nos 1-2-4-5-6 only.					
11	" " " "		of Nov 14/03 applies to No.3 only.			

Nos. 2 and 4: Testimony relative to continuous residence from date of settlement until date of death submitted September 24, 1908.

No.3: Testimony relative to continuous residence for a period of three years submitted September 24, 1908.

IDENTIFIED MISSISSIPPI CHOCTAWS 1902 - 1909
Volume II

IDENTIFIED MISSISSIPPI CHOCTAWS   CARD NO. 368

IDENTIFICATION ADDRESS Dill, Miss.   SETTLEMENT ADDRESS Ardmore, I.T.
DATE OF IDENTIFICATION Feb. 14, 1903.   DATE OF PROOF OF SETTLEMENT June 3, 1903

APPROVED ROLL No.	DAWES ROLL NO.	NAME	RELATIONSHIP TO PERSON FIRST NAMED	AGE	SEX	BLOOD
		1 Yearby, Jesse		20	M	Full
		2				
		3				
		4 APPROVED BY SECRETARY OF INTERIOR.				
		5				
	Jan. 13, 1905 No.1 6					
		7				
		8				
	~1~ 9 DEC 27 1908	~1~	Feb. 27-1907			
		11				

NAME OF FATHER	LIVING OR DEAD	NAME OF MOTHER	LIVING OR DEAD	APPLICATION NO.	REMARKS
1 Ellis Yearby	Dead	Margaret Yearby	Dead	1141	
2					
3					
4					
5		Testimony relative to continuous residence			
6		from date of settlement until date of death			
7		submitted September 25, 1908.			
8					
9					
10					
11					

As to proof of settlement see department letter of Jan. 30, 1906.

IDENTIFIED MISSISSIPPI CHOCTAWS 1902 - 1909
Volume II

IDENTIFIED MISSISSIPPI CHOCTAWS   CARD NO. 369

IDENTIFICATION ADDRESS Mansfield, Miss.   SETTLEMENT ADDRESS Ardmore, Ind. Ter.
DATE OF IDENTIFICATION Feb. 14, 1903.   DATE OF PROOF OF SETTLEMENT July 13, 1903.

APPROVED ROLL No.	DAWES ROLL NO.	NAME	RELATIONSHIP TO PERSON FIRST NAMED	AGE	SEX	BLOOD
		1 John, Big (Ondochatubbee)		74	M	Full
		2 " Sally	Full	63	F	Full
		3 " Charley	Son	21	M	Full
		4 " Lena	Dau	9	F	Full
		5 " Julia	Dau	7	F	Full
		6 APPROVED BY SECRETARY OF INTERIOR.				
		7 ENROLLMENT				
CITIZENSHIP CERTIFICATE ISSUED FOR NO 1-2-4-5-3- JUL 1903		8 OF NOS. 1,2,3,4&5 HEREON APPROVED BY THE SECRETARY OF INTERIOR JAN 13 1905				
		11				

NAME OF FATHER	LIVING OR DEAD	NAME OF MOTHER	LIVING OR DEAD	APPLICATION NO.	REMARKS
1 Kaniatubbee	Dead	Lucy (Amelia)	Dead	1135	
2 Anchaunubbee	"	Pelionah	"	"	
3 No.1		No.2		"	
4 No.1		No.2		"	
5 No.1		No.2		"	
6					
7					
8	"No3 testimony as to continuous residence for a period of three years submitted February 25, 07."				
9	Declaration and proof of settlement applies to Nos. 1 to 5 inc. Also see testimony of Lucy John, Miss. Choc. card no. 412 as to Nos. 4&5				
10	"No1: Proof of death filed showing No1 died November 1, 1903."				

"No1: Proof of continuous residence from date of settlement until date of death submitted August 3, 1906."

"Nos 2,4 and 5: Proof of continuous residence for a period of three years submitted August 3, 1906."

No3: Proof of continuous residence for a period of three years submitted February 25-1907.

IDENTIFIED MISSISSIPPI CHOCTAWS 1902 - 1909
Volume II

IDENTIFIED MISSISSIPPI CHOCTAWS

CARD NO. 370

IDENTIFICATION ADDRESS Tucker, Miss.   SETTLEMENT ADDRESS Durwood, Ind. Ter.
DATE OF IDENTIFICATION Feb. 14, 1903.   DATE OF PROOF OF SETTLEMENT July 16, 1903.

APPROVED ROLL No.	DAWES ROLL NO.	NAME	RELATIONSHIP TO PERSON FIRST NAMED	AGE	SEX	BLOOD
		1 Jack, Jim		24	M	Full
		2 " Liza	Wife	26	F	Full
		3				
		4				
		5 APPROVED BY SECRETARY OF INTERIOR.				
		6 ENROLLMENT				
		7 OF NOS. ~~1~~ HEREON APPROVED BY THE SECRETARY				
		8 OF INTERIOR JAN 13 1905				

CITIZENSHIP CERTIFICATE   No. 2
ISSUED FOR NO 1
JUL 18 1903

NAME OF FATHER	LIVING OR DEAD	NAME OF MOTHER	LIVING OR DEAD	APPLICATION NO.	REMARKS
1 Billy Jack		Leanna Jack		1995	
2 Pistubbee	Dead	Amy Pistubbee		"	
3					
4					
5					
6					
7					
8					
9		Declaration and proof of settlement applies to No. 1 only.			
10					
11		"No. 1: Proof of continuous residence for a period of three years submitted May 7, 1906."			

IDENTIFIED MISSISSIPPI CHOCTAWS 1902 - 1909
Volume II

IDENTIFIED MISSISSIPPI CHOCTAWS CARD NO. 371

IDENTIFICATION ADDRESS Toles, Miss. SETTLEMENT ADDRESS Kiowa, I.T.
DATE OF IDENTIFICATION Feb. 14, 1903. DATE OF PROOF OF SETTLEMENT Nov. 11/03.

APPROVED ROLL No.	DAWES ROLL NO.	NAME	RELATIONSHIP TO PERSON FIRST NAMED	AGE	SEX	BLOOD
		1 Dansby, Lewis		32	M	Full
		2				
		3				
		4				
		5 APPROVED BY SECRETARY OF INTERIOR.				
		6				
		7				
		8				
		9				
		10				
		11				

NAME OF FATHER	LIVING OR DEAD	NAME OF MOTHER	LIVING OR DEAD	APPLICATION NO.	REMARKS
1 Isom Dansby		Betsie Dansby	Dead	1757	
2					
3					
4					
5					
6		Testimony relative to continuous residence of No.1			
7		from date of settlement until date of death			
8		submitted September 16, 1908.			
9					
10					
11					

IDENTIFIED MISSISSIPPI CHOCTAWS 1902 - 1909
Volume II

IDENTIFIED MISSISSIPPI CHOCTAWS   CARD NO. 372

IDENTIFICATION ADDRESS Franks, Miss.   SETTLEMENT ADDRESS
DATE OF IDENTIFICATION Feb. 14, 1903.   DATE OF PROOF OF SETTLEMENT

APPROVED ROLL No.	DAWES ROLL NO.	NAME	RELATIONSHIP TO PERSON FIRST NAMED	AGE	SEX	BLOOD
		1 Jimmy, Ike		28	M	Full
		2				
		3				
		4				
		5 APPROVED BY SECRETARY OF INTERIOR.				
		6				
		7 DID NOT SUBMIT PROOF OF REMOVAL AND BONA-FIDE SETTLEMENT WITHIN ONE YEAR FROM DATE OF IDENTIFICATION				
		8				
		9				
		10				
		11				

NAME OF FATHER	LIVING OR DEAD	NAME OF MOTHER	LIVING OR DEAD	APPLICATION NO.	REMARKS
1 Tobe Jimmy (Shun-i-o-tubbee)	Dead	Louisa Philip		4497	
2					
3					
4					
5					
6					
7					
8					
9					
10					
11					

IDENTIFIED MISSISSIPPI CHOCTAWS 1902 - 1909
Volume II

IDENTIFIED MISSISSIPPI CHOCTAWS CARD NO. 373

IDENTIFICATION ADDRESS SETTLEMENT ADDRESS Ardmore, Ind. Ter.
DATE OF IDENTIFICATION Feb. 14, 1903. DATE OF PROOF OF SETTLEMENT No.3 July 21, 1903. "

APPROVED ROLL No.	DAWES ROLL NO.		NAME	RELATIONSHIP TO PERSON FIRST NAMED	AGE	SEX	BLOOD
		1	Jack, Billy		53	M	Full
		2	" Leanna	Wife	53	F	Full
		3	" Minnie	Dau	17	F	Full
		4	" Nettie	Dau	15	F	Full
		5	" Camille	Dau	7	F	Full
		6					

No.3 Nov 7/03

CITIZENSHIP CERTIFICATE ISSUED FOR NO 1-2-4-5
JUL 21 1903

APPROVED BY SECRETARY OF INTERIOR.

ENROLLMENT OF NOS. 1 2 3 4 & 5 HEREON APPROVED BY THE SECRETARY OF INTERIOR JAN 13 1905.

CITIZENSHIP CERTIFICATE ISSUED FOR NO 3
NOV 7 1903

	NAME OF FATHER	LIVING OR DEAD	NAME OF MOTHER	LIVING OR DEAD	APPLICATION NO.	REMARKS
1	Big Jack	Dead		Dead	1996	
2		"	Mealy	"	"	
3	No.1		No.2		"	
4	No.1		No.2		"	
5	No.1		No.2		"	
6						
7						
8	"No4: Proof of continuous residence for a					
9	period of three years submitted August 14, 1906."					
10						
11			Declaration and proof of settlement applies to Nos 1,2,4&5 only			

" " " " " of Nov 7/03 applies to No3 only.

No3: Testimony as to continuous residence of No3 for period of 3 years submitted Mch 24, 06.

No's 1 2 & 5: Testimony as to continuous residence for a period of three years submitted Mch 24, 06.

IDENTIFIED MISSISSIPPI CHOCTAWS 1902 - 1909
Volume II

IDENTIFIED MISSISSIPPI CHOCTAWS   CARD NO. 374

IDENTIFICATION ADDRESS Point, Miss.   SETTLEMENT ADDRESS Kiowa I.T.
DATE OF IDENTIFICATION Feb. 14, 1903.   DATE OF PROOF OF SETTLEMENT Nov. 16/03

APPROVED ROLL No.	DAWES ROLL NO.		NAME	RELATIONSHIP TO PERSON FIRST NAMED	AGE	SEX	BLOOD
		1	Sturdevant, Charley		60	M	Full
		2					
		3					
		4	APPROVED BY SECRETARY OF INTERIOR.				
		5					
		6					
		7					
		8					
CITIZENSHIP CERTIFICATE		9					
ISSUED FOR NO 1 NOV 16 1903		10					
		11					

	NAME OF FATHER	LIVING OR DEAD	NAME OF MOTHER	LIVING OR DEAD	APPLICATION NO.	REMARKS
1		Dead	Sukey	Dead	1778	
2						
3						
4						
5	No.1: Testimony relative to continuous residence within					
6	the Choctaw-Chickasaw country for a period of three					
7	years submitted July 1, 1905.					
8						
9						
10						
11						

IDENTIFIED MISSISSIPPI CHOCTAWS 1902 - 1909
Volume II

IDENTIFIED MISSISSIPPI CHOCTAWS

CARD NO. 375

IDENTIFICATION ADDRESS Hero, Miss.　　SETTLEMENT ADDRESS Ardmore, I.T.
DATE OF IDENTIFICATION Feb. 14, 1903.　　DATE OF PROOF OF SETTLEMENT April 29, 1904.

APPROVED ROLL No.	DAWES ROLL NO.	NAME	RELATIONSHIP TO PERSON FIRST NAMED	AGE	SEX	BLOOD
		1. Huff, Zeno		45	M	Full
		2.				
		3.				
		4. APPROVED BY SECRETARY OF INTERIOR.				
		5. DID NOT SUBMIT PROOF OF				
		6. REMOVAL AND BONA-FIDE SET-				
		7. TLEMENT WITHIN ONE YEAR FROM DATE OF IDENTIFICATION.				
		8.				
CITIZENSHIP CERTIFICATE ISSUED FOR NO. ~~1~~ Nov. 12, 1906		9. ENROLLMENT ... APPROVED BY SECRETARY Feb. 27, 1907				
		10.				
		11.				

NAME OF FATHER	LIVING OR DEAD	NAME OF MOTHER	LIVING OR DEAD	APPLICATION NO.	REMARKS
1.	Dead	Phyllis Huff	Dead	1930	
2.					
3.					
4.					
5.		Testimony relative to continuous residence for a period of three years submitted September 25, 1908.			
6.					
7.					
8.					
9.					
10.					
11. June 11, 1906 - I.T.D. 1539	1905	10236 1906			

Department directs Commission to make allotment to Zeno Huff.

Testimony as to removal and settlement taken Apr 29/04.

IDENTIFIED MISSISSIPPI CHOCTAWS 1902 - 1909
Volume II

IDENTIFIED MISSISSIPPI CHOCTAWS CARD NO. 376

IDENTIFICATION ADDRESS Stateline, Miss. SETTLEMENT ADDRESS Ardmore, Ind. Ter.
DATE OF IDENTIFICATION Feb. 14, 1903. DATE OF PROOF OF SETTLEMENT July 22, 1903.

APPROVED ROLL No.	DAWES ROLL NO.	NAME	RELATIONSHIP TO PERSON FIRST NAMED	AGE	SEX	BLOOD
		1 Johnson, John P.		20	M	Full
		2				
		3				
		4				
		5 **APPROVED BY SECRETARY OF INTERIOR**.				
		6 ENROLLMENT				
		7 OF Nos. 1 PERSON APPROVED BY THE SECRETARY				
		8 OF INTERIOR				
		9 CITIZENSHIP CERTIFICATE				
		ISSUED FOR NO 1				
		JUL 22 1903 10				
		11				

NAME OF FATHER	LIVING OR DEAD	NAME OF MOTHER	LIVING OR DEAD	APPLICATION NO.	REMARKS
1 Frank Johnson			Dead	1951	
2					
3					
4					
5					
6					
7					
8					
9					
10					
11					

"No1: Proof of continuous residence for a period of three years submitted December 15, 1906."

IDENTIFIED MISSISSIPPI CHOCTAWS 1902 - 1909
Volume II

IDENTIFIED MISSISSIPPI CHOCTAWS CARD NO. 377

IDENTIFICATION ADDRESS Stamper, Miss. SETTLEMENT ADDRESS
DATE OF IDENTIFICATION Feb. 14, 1903. DATE OF PROOF OF SETTLEMENT

APPROVED ROLL No.	DAWES ROLL NO.	NAME	RELATIONSHIP TO PERSON FIRST NAMED	AGE	SEX	BLOOD
		1 Davis, Culberson		35	M	Full
		2 " Leanna	Wife	28	F	Full
		3 " Anna	Dau	8	F	Full
		4 " Beny[sic]	Dau	6	F	Full
		5 " Thomas	Son	2	M	Full
		6				
		7				
		8 APPROVED BY SECRETARY OF INTERIOR.				
		9				
		10				
		11				

NAME OF FATHER	LIVING OR DEAD	NAME OF MOTHER	LIVING OR DEAD	APPLICATION NO.	REMARKS
(Ah-le-mo-tubbee)		(Ish-ma-te-mah)			
1 John Davis	Dead	Nancy Davis	Dead	3020	
2 John Meely	"	Ma-te-ho-nah	"	"	
3 No.1		No.2	"	"	
4 No.1		No.2	"	"	
5 No.1		No.2	"	"	
6					
7					
8					
9					
10					
11					

IDENTIFIED MISSISSIPPI CHOCTAWS 1902 - 1909
Volume II

IDENTIFIED MISSISSIPPI CHOCTAWS   CARD NO. 378

IDENTIFICATION ADDRESS Conehatta, Miss.   SETTLEMENT ADDRESS
DATE OF IDENTIFICATION Feb. 14, 1903.   DATE OF PROOF OF SETTLEMENT

APPROVED ROLL No.	DAWES ROLL NO.	NAME	RELATIONSHIP TO PERSON FIRST NAMED	AGE	SEX	BLOOD
		1 Cooper, Billy		32	M	Full
		2				
		3				
		4 APPROVED BY SECRETARY OF INTERIOR.				
		5				
		6				
		7				
		8				
		9				
		10				
		11				

NAME OF FATHER	LIVING OR DEAD	NAME OF MOTHER (Imathlehonah)	LIVING OR DEAD	APPLICATION NO.	REMARKS
1 George Cooper		Jennie Cooper		3988	
2					
3					
4					
5					
6					
7					
8					
9					
10					
11					

IDENTIFIED MISSISSIPPI CHOCTAWS 1902 - 1909
Volume II

IDENTIFIED MISSISSIPPI CHOCTAWS CARD NO. 379

IDENTIFICATION ADDRESS Hays, Miss.   SETTLEMENT ADDRESS
DATE OF IDENTIFICATION Feb. 14, 1903.   DATE OF PROOF OF SETTLEMENT

APPROVED ROLL No.	DAWES ROLL NO.		NAME	RELATIONSHIP TO PERSON FIRST NAMED	AGE	SEX	BLOOD
		1	Charlie, Dave		31	M	Full
		2	" Donie	Wife	21	F	Full
		3	" Lillie	Dau	6	F	Full
		4	" Nettie	Dau	2	F	Full
		5					
		6					
		7	APPROVED BY SECRETARY OF INTERIOR.				
		8	DID NOT SUBMIT PROOF OF				
		9	REMOVAL AND BONA-FIDE SET-				
		10	TLEMENT WITHIN ONE YEAR				
		11	FROM DATE OF IDENTIFICATION.				

	NAME OF FATHER	LIVING OR DEAD	NAME OF MOTHER	LIVING OR DEAD	APPLICATION NO.	REMARKS
1	Charley Johnson	Dead	Eliza Johnson	Dead	4270	
2	John Wesley		Louisa Wesley		"	
3	No.1		No.2		"	
4	No.1		No.2		"	
5						
6						
7						
8						
9						
10						
11						

IDENTIFIED MISSISSIPPI CHOCTAWS 1902 - 1909
Volume II

IDENTIFIED MISSISSIPPI CHOCTAWS CARD NO. 380

IDENTIFICATION ADDRESS Eady, Miss. SETTLEMENT ADDRESS No1 Atoka I.T.
DATE OF IDENTIFICATION Feb. 14, 1903. DATE OF PROOF OF SETTLEMENT No1 Aug 19/03

APPROVED ROLL No.	DAWES ROLL NO.	NAME	RELATIONSHIP TO PERSON FIRST NAMED	AGE	SEX	BLOOD
		1 Dixon, Julia		22	F	Full
		2 " Simpson		3	M	Full
		3				
		4				
		5 APPROVED BY SECRETARY OF INTERIOR.				
		6				
		7				
		8				
CITIZENSHIP CERTIFICATE ISSUED FOR NO		9 No.2				
		10				
		11				

NAME OF FATHER	LIVING OR DEAD	NAME OF MOTHER	LIVING OR DEAD	APPLICATION NO.	REMARKS
1 Jeff Jackson (Illayoeubbee)		Eliza Jackson	Dead	4011	
2 Benjamin Dixon		No.1		"	
3					
4					
5					
6					
7					
8					
9					
10 Declaration and proof of settlement applies to No. 1 only					
11 No1 is now wife of No.5 on card 519.					

No.2 died in August 1902.
See testimony of Folsom Stoliby of Aug 19/03 on file in
jacket Miss. Choc. 1102.
No1: Testimony as to continuous residence for a period of three
years submitted Aug. 15, 1906

IDENTIFIED MISSISSIPPI CHOCTAWS 1902 - 1909
Volume II

IDENTIFIED MISSISSIPPI CHOCTAWS   CARD NO. 381

IDENTIFICATION ADDRESS   SETTLEMENT ADDRESS
DATE OF IDENTIFICATION Feb. 14, 1903. DATE OF PROOF OF SETTLEMENT

APPROVED ROLL No.	DAWES ROLL NO.	NAME	RELATIONSHIP TO PERSON FIRST NAMED	AGE	SEX	BLOOD
		1. Charlie, Johnson		28	M	Full
		2. " Leona		18	F	Full
		3. " Jane		3	F	Full
		4. " Herman E.		2mo	M	Full
		5.				
		6.				
		7. APPROVED BY SECRETARY OF INTERIOR.				
		8.				
		9.				
		10.				
		11.				

NAME OF FATHER	LIVING OR DEAD	NAME OF MOTHER	LIVING OR DEAD	APPLICATION NO.	REMARKS
1. Charlie Johnson	Dead	Eliza Johnson	Dead	4271	
2. John Wesley		Louisa Wesley		"	
3. No.1		No.2		"	
4. No.1		No.2		"	
5.					
6.					
7.					
8.					
9.					
10.					
11.					

IDENTIFIED MISSISSIPPI CHOCTAWS 1902 - 1909
Volume II

IDENTIFIED MISSISSIPPI CHOCTAWS   CARD NO. 382

IDENTIFICATION ADDRESS Carthage, Miss.   SETTLEMENT ADDRESS Calloway, Ind. Ter.
DATE OF IDENTIFICATION Feb. 14, 1903.   DATE OF PROOF OF SETTLEMENT May 12, 1903.

APPROVED ROLL No.	DAWES ROLL NO.		NAME	RELATIONSHIP TO PERSON FIRST NAMED	AGE	SEX	BLOOD
		1	Dixon, Columbus		49	M	Full
		2	" Sallie	Wife	58	F	Full
		3	Martin, Bettie	G. Child	13	F	Full
		4					
CITIZENSHIP CERTIFICATE ISSUED FOR NO 1 MAY 12 1903		5					
		6	APPROVED BY SECRETARY OF INTERIOR.				
	2	7	ENROLLMENT OF NOS. 12 & 3 HEREON APPROVED BY THE SECRETARY OF INTERIOR				
		8					
CITIZENSHIP CERTIFICATE ISSUED FOR NO 3 JAN 4 1904		9					
		10					
		11					

	NAME OF FATHER	LIVING OR DEAD	NAME OF MOTHER	LIVING OR DEAD	APPLICATION NO.	REMARKS
1	Dixon (Ho-pah-ka)	Dead	Sealy Dixon	Dead	4408	
2	Solomon York		Martha York	"	"	
3	Ed. Martin	Dead	Louisa Martin	"	"	
4						
5						
6			"No.1 - - Testimony as to continuous residence of			
7			No 1 for a period of 3 years submitted February 10, 1905."			
8			"Declaration and proof of settlement of May 12, 1903, applies to No.1 only."			
9			No 2&3: Testimony as to continuous residence of Nos 2 for a period			
10			of three year[sic] submitted 2/3 06.			
11			Settlement address of Nos 2 and 3 Atoka, Ind. Ter.			

Date of proof of settlement #2&3 July 2, 1903.

IDENTIFIED MISSISSIPPI CHOCTAWS 1902 - 1909
Volume II

IDENTIFIED MISSISSIPPI CHOCTAWS   CARD NO. 383

IDENTIFICATION ADDRESS Hope, Miss.   SETTLEMENT ADDRESS
DATE OF IDENTIFICATION Feb. 14, 1903.   DATE OF PROOF OF SETTLEMENT

APPROVED ROLL No.	DAWES ROLL NO.	NAME	RELATIONSHIP TO PERSON FIRST NAMED	AGE	SEX	BLOOD
		1 Jim, Sallie		23	F	Full
		2 " Mary	Dau	9mo	F	Full
		3				
		4				
		5 APPROVED BY SECRETARY OF INTERIOR.				
		6				
		7				
		8				
		9				
		10				
		11				

DID NOT SUBMIT PROOF OF REMOVAL AND BONA-FIDE SETTLEMENT WITHIN ONE YEAR FROM DATE OF IDENTIFICATION.

NAME OF FATHER	LIVING OR DEAD	NAME OF MOTHER	LIVING OR DEAD	APPLICATION NO.	REMARKS
1 Steve Jim		Lillie Jim		4500	
2 Goodman Jim		No.1			
3					
4					
5					
6					
7					
8					
9					
10					
11					

IDENTIFIED MISSISSIPPI CHOCTAWS 1902 - 1909
Volume II

IDENTIFIED MISSISSIPPI CHOCTAWS   CARD NO. 384

IDENTIFICATION ADDRESS Laurel Hill, Miss.   SETTLEMENT ADDRESS
DATE OF IDENTIFICATION Feb. 14, 1903.   DATE OF PROOF OF SETTLEMENT

APPROVED ROLL No.	DAWES ROLL NO.	NAME	RELATIONSHIP TO PERSON FIRST NAMED	AGE	SEX	BLOOD
		1 Willis, Katie		10	F	Full
		2				
		3				
		4				
		5 APPROVED BY SECRETARY OF INTERIOR.				
		6				
		7 DID NOT SUBMIT PROOF OF REMOVAL AND BONA-FIDE SETTLEMENT WITHIN ONE YEAR FROM DATE OF IDENTIFICATION.				
		8				
		9				
		10				
		11				

NAME OF FATHER	LIVING OR DEAD	NAME OF MOTHER	LIVING OR DEAD	APPLICATION NO.	REMARKS
1 Sampson Jacoway	Dead	Mahala Willis	Dead	4359	
2					
3					
4					
5					
6					
7					
8					
9					
10					
11					

IDENTIFIED MISSISSIPPI CHOCTAWS 1902 - 1909
Volume II

IDENTIFIED MISSISSIPPI CHOCTAWS   CARD NO. 385

IDENTIFICATION ADDRESS Ennis, Miss.   SETTLEMENT ADDRESS Ardmore, Ind. Ter.
DATE OF IDENTIFICATION Feb. 14, 1903.   DATE OF PROOF OF SETTLEMENT July 21, 1903

APPROVED ROLL No.	DAWES ROLL NO.	NAME		RELATIONSHIP TO PERSON FIRST NAMED	AGE	SEX	BLOOD
		1	Phillip, Mack		25	M	Full
		2	" Sallie	Wife	23	F	Full
		3	" Arlena	Dau	2	F	Full
		4	" Mary	Dau	8mo	F	Full
		5					
		6					
		7	APPROVED BY SECRETARY OF INTERIOR				
		8	ENROLLMENT				

CITIZENSHIP CERTIFICATE   OF NOS. 1 2 3&4 HEREON
ISSUED FOR NO 1-2-3-4   APPROVED BY THE SECRETARY
JUL 21 1903   OF INTERIOR JAN 13 1905

	NAME OF FATHER	LIVING OR DEAD	NAME OF MOTHER	LIVING OR DEAD	APPLICATION NO.	REMARKS
1	Williamson Phillip		Jinnie Phillip		2045	
2	Jesse Porter		Betsie Porter		"	
3	No.1		No.2		"	
4	No.1		No.2		"	
5						
6						
7						
8						
9	Nos 1 2 3&4: Testimony as to continuous residence					
10	of Nos 1 2 3&4 for a period of 3 years submitted [Illegible]					
11						

IDENTIFIED MISSISSIPPI CHOCTAWS 1902 - 1909
Volume II

IDENTIFIED MISSISSIPPI CHOCTAWS CARD NO. 386

IDENTIFICATION ADDRESS Moscow, Miss.   SETTLEMENT ADDRESS Story I.T.
DATE OF IDENTIFICATION Feb. 14, 1903.   DATE OF PROOF OF SETTLEMENT Oct 1/03.

APPROVED ROLL No.	DAWES ROLL NO.	NAME	RELATIONSHIP TO PERSON FIRST NAMED	AGE	SEX	BLOOD
		1 Philip, Winston		25	M	Full
		2				
		3				
		4				
		5 APPROVED BY SECRETARY OF INTERIOR.				
		6				
		7				
		8				
CITIZENSHIP CERTIFICATE ISSUED FOR NO 1 OCT 1 19		9				
		10				
		11				

NAME OF FATHER	LIVING OR DEAD	NAME OF MOTHER	LIVING OR DEAD	APPLICATION NO.	REMARKS
1 Sam Philip	Dead	Sallie Philip		2793	
2					
3					
4					
5					
6					
7					
8					
9					
10					
11					

"No.1. Proof of death filed showing No1 died September 10, 1905."
"No1 Proof of continuous residence from date of settlement until date of death submitted July 25, 1906."

IDENTIFIED MISSISSIPPI CHOCTAWS 1902 - 1909
Volume II

IDENTIFIED MISSISSIPPI CHOCTAWS CARD NO. 387

IDENTIFICATION ADDRESS Ennis, Miss. SETTLEMENT ADDRESS Kiowa I.T.
DATE OF IDENTIFICATION Feb. 14, 1903. DATE OF PROOF OF SETTLEMENT Feb. 10-04

APPROVED ROLL No.	DAWES ROLL NO.	NAME	RELATIONSHIP TO PERSON FIRST NAMED	AGE	SEX	BLOOD
		1 Philip, Tom		21	M	Full
		2				
		3				
		4				
		5 APPROVED BY SECRETARY OF INTERIOR.				
		6				
		7				
		8				

CITIZENSHIP CERTIFICATE
ISSUED FOR NO 1
FEB 12 1904

NAME OF FATHER	LIVING OR DEAD	NAME OF MOTHER	LIVING OR DEAD	APPLICATION NO.	REMARKS
1 Sam Philip	Dead	Sallie Philip		2727	
2					
3					
4					
5					
6					
7					
8					
9					
10					
11					

"No.1 Proof of continuous residence for a period of three years submitted January 9, 1907."

IDENTIFIED MISSISSIPPI CHOCTAWS 1902 - 1909
Volume II

IDENTIFIED MISSISSIPPI CHOCTAWS CARD NO. 388

IDENTIFICATION ADDRESS Toles, Miss. SETTLEMENT ADDRESS Kiowa I.T.
DATE OF IDENTIFICATION Feb. 14, 1903. DATE OF PROOF OF SETTLEMENT [Illegible]/03.

APPROVED ROLL No.	DAWES ROLL NO.		NAME	RELATIONSHIP TO PERSON FIRST NAMED	AGE	SEX	BLOOD
		1	Dansby, Isom		53	M	Full
		2					
		3					
		4					
		5	APPROVED BY SECRETARY OF INTERIOR.				
		6	~~ 1 ~~				
		7					
		8					
	1	9					
		10					
		11					

	NAME OF FATHER (Teh-e-cubbee)	LIVING OR DEAD	NAME OF MOTHER (Low-ah-hoka)	LIVING OR DEAD	APPLICATION NO.	REMARKS
1	Squire Solomon	Dead	Sallie Solomon	Dead	1755	
2						
3						
4						
5						
6	No.1 - Testimony as to continuous residence of No.1					
7	for a period of	[sic]	submitted February 20-1906			
8						
9						
10						
11						

IDENTIFIED MISSISSIPPI CHOCTAWS 1902 - 1909
Volume II

IDENTIFIED MISSISSIPPI CHOCTAWS   CARD NO. 389

IDENTIFICATION ADDRESS Prospect, Miss.   SETTLEMENT ADDRESS Byars, Ind. Ter.
DATE OF IDENTIFICATION Feb. 14, 1903.   DATE OF PROOF OF SETTLEMENT July 13, 1903.

APPROVED ROLL No.	DAWES ROLL NO.	NAME	RELATIONSHIP TO PERSON FIRST NAMED	AGE	SEX	BLOOD
		1. Dixon, John		30	M	Full
		2. " Mary	Wife	29	F	Full
		3. " Leanna	Dau	8	F	Full
		4. " Sarah Jane	Dau	5	F	Full
		5. " Lena	Dau	4	F	Full
		6. " Beauty	Dau	1	F	Full

APPROVED BY SECRETARY OF INTERIOR.

CITIZENSHIP CERTIFICATE ISSUED FOR NO 1-2-3-4-5-6 JUL 13 1903

ENROLLMENT OF NOS. 1 2 3 4 5 & 6 HEREON APPROVED BY THE SECRETARY OF INTERIOR JAN 13 1905.

	NAME OF FATHER	LIVING OR DEAD	NAME OF MOTHER	LIVING OR DEAD	APPLICATION NO.	REMARKS
1	Doctor Dixon			Dead	4056	
2	John Farmer	Dead	Polly Farmer		"	
3	No.1		No.2		"	
4	No.1		No.2		"	
5	No.1		No.2		"	
6	No.1		No.2		"	

Nos 1&2: Proof of continuous residence for a period of three years submitted March 16, 1906.
Nos 3,4,5 and 6: Proof of continuous residence for a period of three years submitted February 6, 1907.

IDENTIFIED MISSISSIPPI CHOCTAWS 1902 - 1909
Volume II

IDENTIFIED MISSISSIPPI CHOCTAWS

CARD NO. 390

IDENTIFICATION ADDRESS Hays, Miss.   SETTLEMENT ADDRESS
DATE OF IDENTIFICATION Feb. 14, 1903.   DATE OF PROOF OF SETTLEMENT

APPROVED ROLL No.	DAWES ROLL NO.	NAME	RELATIONSHIP TO PERSON FIRST NAMED	AGE	SEX	BLOOD
		1 Charlie, William		38	M	Full
		2 " Fannie	Wife	32	F	Full
		3 " Seaborn	Son	13	M	Full
		4 " Lula	Dau	0	F	Full
		5 " John H	Son	8	M	Full
		6 " Salena	Dau	7	F	Full
		7				
		8 APPROVED BY SECRETARY OF INTERIOR.				
		9 DID NOT SUBMIT PROOF OF				
		10 REMOVAL AND BONA-FIDE SET- TLEMENT WITHIN ONE YEAR				
		11 FROM DATE OF IDENTIFICATION				

NAME OF FATHER	LIVING OR DEAD	NAME OF MOTHER	LIVING OR DEAD	APPLICATION NO.	REMARKS
1 Charley Johnson	Dead	Eliza Johnson	Dead	4272	
2 John Wesley		Louisa Wesley		"	
3 No.1		No.2		"	
4 No.1		No.2		"	
5 No.1		No.2		"	
6 No.1		No.2		"	
7					
8					
9					
10					
11					

IDENTIFIED MISSISSIPPI CHOCTAWS 1902 - 1909
Volume II

IDENTIFIED MISSISSIPPI CHOCTAWS CARD NO. 391

IDENTIFICATION ADDRESS Freetrade[sic], Miss.　　SETTLEMENT ADDRESS Roff, I.T.
DATE OF IDENTIFICATION Feb. 14, 1903.　　DATE OF PROOF OF SETTLEMENT Sept 4-1903

APPROVED ROLL No.	DAWES ROLL NO.	NAME	RELATIONSHIP TO PERSON FIRST NAMED	AGE	SEX	BLOOD
		1. Billey, Richmond		28	M	Full
		2. " Martha	Wife	25	F	Full
		3. " Lizzie	Dau	9	F	Full
		4. " Harrison	Son	6	M	Full
		5. " Esther	Dau	1	F	Full

APPROVED BY SECRETARY OF INTERIOR.
ENROLLMENT OF NOS. 1 2 3 & 4 HEREON APPROVED BY THE SECRETARY OF INTERIOR JAN 13 1905.

CITIZENSHIP CERTIFICATE ISSUED FOR NO 1-2-3-4 SEP 4 1903

NAME OF FATHER	LIVING OR DEAD	NAME OF MOTHER	LIVING OR DEAD	APPLICATION NO.	REMARKS
1. Captain Billey	Dead	Sallie Billey		3060	
2. Ellis			Dead	"	
3. No.1		No.2		"	
4. No.1		No.2		"	
5. No.1		No.2		"	
8. No.5					

DID NOT SUBMIT PROOF OF REMOVAL AND BONA-FIDE SETTLEMENT WITHIN ONE YEAR FROM DATE OF IDENTIFICATION

Proof of settlement applies to 1-2-3 & 4 only.
Nos 1 2 3 and 4: Proof of continuous residence for a period of three years submitted April 12-1907.

IDENTIFIED MISSISSIPPI CHOCTAWS 1902 - 1909
Volume II

IDENTIFIED MISSISSIPPI CHOCTAWS   CARD NO. 392

IDENTIFICATION ADDRESS High Hill, Miss.   SETTLEMENT ADDRESS No1 Roff I.T.
DATE OF IDENTIFICATION Feb. 14, 1903.   DATE OF PROOF OF SETTLEMENT No1 Oct 16/03

APPROVED ROLL No.	DAWES ROLL NO.	NAME	RELATIONSHIP TO PERSON FIRST NAMED	AGE	SEX	BLOOD
		1 Billey, Sallie		80	F	Full
		2 Sam, Dennis	Grand Child	18	M	Full
		3 " Acy	Grand Child	16	F	Full
		4				
		5				
		6 APPROVED BY SECRETARY OF INTERIOR.				
		7 ~~CITIZENSHIP CERTIFICATE~~ ENROLLMENT				
		ISSUED FOR NO 8 OF NOS. 1 2 & 3 HEREON ~~APPROVED BY THE SECRETARY~~				
		OCT 16 1903 OF INTERIOR JAN				
		9 CITIZENSHIP CERTIFICATE				
		~~ISSUED FOR NO~~ 2 & 3				
		DEC 21 1903				

NAME OF FATHER	LIVING OR DEAD	NAME OF MOTHER	LIVING OR DEAD	APPLICATION NO.	REMARKS
1	Dead	Betsey (Ah-che-bah)	Dead	3058	
2 Wash Sam	"	Rena Sam	"	"	
3 " "	"	" "	"	"	
4					
5					
6					
7					
8		"No.1: Proof of continuous residence for a period of three years submitted April 12-1907."			
9		"No.2: Proof of continuous residence for a period of three years submitted April 12-1907."			
10		Declaration and proof of settlement of Oct 16/03 apply to No.1 only.			
11					

"No3: Proof of continuous residence for a period of three years submitted April 12-1907"

Settlement address Nos 2&3 Roff, I.T.
Date of proof of settlement Nos 2&3 Dec. 26, 1903.

Declaration and proof of settlement of Dec. 21/03 apply to Nos 2&3 only.

IDENTIFIED MISSISSIPPI CHOCTAWS 1902 - 1909
Volume II

IDENTIFIED MISSISSIPPI CHOCTAWS   CARD NO. 393

IDENTIFICATION ADDRESS Kosciusco[sic], Miss.   SETTLEMENT ADDRESS
DATE OF IDENTIFICATION Feb. 14, 1903.   DATE OF PROOF OF SETTLEMENT

APPROVED ROLL No.	DAWES ROLL NO.	NAME	RELATIONSHIP TO PERSON FIRST NAMED	AGE	SEX	BLOOD
		1 Bell, Bud		19	M	Full
		2				
		3				
		4				
		5 APPROVED BY SECRETARY OF INTERIOR.				
		6				
		7 DID NOT SUBMIT PROOF OF				
		8 REMOVAL AND BONA-FIDE SET-				
		9 TLEMENT WITHIN ONE YEAR				
		10 FROM DATE OF IDENTIFICATION.				
		11				

NAME OF FATHER	LIVING OR DEAD	NAME OF MOTHER	LIVING OR DEAD	APPLICATION NO.	REMARKS
1 Kelly Bell	Dead	Sally Bell	Dead	1583	
2					
3					
4					
5					
6					
7					
8					
9					
10					
11					

IDENTIFIED MISSISSIPPI CHOCTAWS 1902 - 1909
Volume II

IDENTIFIED MISSISSIPPI CHOCTAWS   CARD NO. 394

IDENTIFICATION ADDRESS Toles, Miss.   SETTLEMENT ADDRESS Ardmore, Ind. Ter.
DATE OF IDENTIFICATION Feb. 14, 1903.   DATE OF PROOF OF SETTLEMENT May 21, 1903

APPROVED ROLL No.	DAWES ROLL NO.	NAME	RELATIONSHIP TO PERSON FIRST NAMED	AGE	SEX	BLOOD
		1 Bull, Houston		20	M	Full
		2				
		3				
		4				
		5 APPROVED BY SECRETARY OF INTERIOR.				
		6 ENROLLMENT				
		7 OF NOS. ~~1~~ HEREON APPROVED BY THE SECRETARY				
		8 OF INTERIOR JAN 13 1905 .				

CITIZENSHIP CERTIFICATE
ISSUED FOR NO 1
MAY 21 1903

NAME OF FATHER	LIVING OR DEAD	NAME OF MOTHER	LIVING OR DEAD	APPLICATION NO.	REMARKS
1 John Bull	Dead	Susan Bull	Dead	1646	
2					
3					
4					
5			Testimony relative to continuous residence for a period of three years submitted July 28, 1908.		
6					
7					
8					
9					
10					
11					

IDENTIFIED MISSISSIPPI CHOCTAWS 1902 - 1909
Volume II

IDENTIFIED MISSISSIPPI CHOCTAWS CARD NO. 395

IDENTIFICATION ADDRESS Rose Hill, Miss.   SETTLEMENT ADDRESS Hennepin, I.T.
DATE OF IDENTIFICATION Feb. 14, 1903.   DATE OF PROOF OF SETTLEMENT Aug. 11/03.

APPROVED ROLL No.	DAWES ROLL NO.	NAME	RELATIONSHIP TO PERSON FIRST NAMED	AGE	SEX	BLOOD
		1. Sam, Thomas		58	M	Full
		2. " Minnie	Wife	38	F	Full
		3. " Amos	Son	18	M	Full
		4. " Joe	Son	15	M	Full
		5. " George	Son	13	M	Full
		6. " Delia	Dau	11	F	Full
		7. " Nancy	Dau	8	F	Full
		8. " Sis	Dau	4	F	Full

CITIZENSHIP CERTIFICATE ISSUED FOR NO 1,2,3,4,5,6,7&8
AUG 11 1903   APPROVED BY SECRETARY OF INTERIOR.

	NAME OF FATHER	LIVING OR DEAD	NAME OF MOTHER	LIVING OR DEAD	APPLICATION NO.	REMARKS
1	Sam	Dead	Ann	Dead	1640	
2		Dead	Liza		"	
3	No.1		No.2		"	
4	No.1		No.2		"	
5	No.1		No.2		"	
6	No.1		No.2		"	
7	No.1		No.2		"	
8	No.1		No.2		"	

9. ENROLLMENT
10. OF NOS. 1,2,3,4,5,6,7&8 HEREON APPROVED BY THE SECRETARY
11. OF INTERIOR JAN 13 1905.

"Nos. 1,2,4,5,6,7&8: Proof of continuous residence for a period of three years submitted May 16, 1906."
No.3: Proof of continuous residence for a period of three years submitted March 27-1907.

IDENTIFIED MISSISSIPPI CHOCTAWS 1902 - 1909
Volume II

IDENTIFIED MISSISSIPPI CHOCTAWS No. of Durwood, I.T. 396

IDENTIFICATION ADDRESS Stringer, Miss.
DATE OF IDENTIFICATION Feb. 14, 1903.
SETTLEMENT ADDRESS Nos 2&3 Durwood, I.T. No1 Sept 30/03
DATE OF PROOF OF SETTLEMENT Nos 2&3 Dec 17, 1903

APPROVED ROLL No.	DAWES ROLL NO.	NAME		RELATIONSHIP TO PERSON FIRST NAMED	AGE	SEX	BLOOD
		1	Parker, Logan		18	M	Full
		2	" Sidney	Bro	9	M	Full
		3	" Jim	Bro	6	M	Full
		4	" Susan	Grand Mother	65	F	Full
		5					

CITIZENSHIP CERTIFICATE
ISSUED FOR NO 1
SEP 30 1903

CITIZENSHIP CERTIFICATE
ISSUED FOR NO 2-3
DEC 17 1903

APPROVED BY SECRETARY OF INTERIOR.

ENROLLMENT OF NOS. 1 2&3 HEREON APPROVED BY THE SECRETARY OF INTERIOR JAN ...

	NAME OF FATHER	LIVING OR DEAD	NAME OF MOTHER	LIVING OR DEAD	APPLICATION NO.	REMARKS
1	John Parker		Lizzie Parker	Dead	1668	
2	" "		" "	"	"	
3	" "		" "	"	"	
4		Dead		Dead	"	
5						
6						
7						
8						
9						
10						
11						

Declaration and proof of settlement of Sept 30/03 apply to No1 only

Settlement address of Nos. 2&3, Durwood I.T.
Date of proof of settlement of Nos 2&3 Dec 17, 1903

Nos 2 and 3: Proof of continuous residence for a period of three years submitted October 12th 1907

No1 Proof of continuous residence for a period of three years submitted Mch 29-1906.

IDENTIFIED MISSISSIPPI CHOCTAWS 1902 - 1909
Volume II

IDENTIFIED MISSISSIPPI CHOCTAWS   CARD NO. 397

IDENTIFICATION ADDRESS Sandersville, Miss.   SETTLEMENT ADDRESS Ravia, Ind. Ter.
DATE OF IDENTIFICATION Feb. 14, 1903.   DATE OF PROOF OF SETTLEMENT July 11, 1903.

APPROVED ROLL No.	DAWES ROLL NO.		NAME	RELATIONSHIP TO PERSON FIRST NAMED	AGE	SEX	BLOOD
		1	James, Wash		26	M	Full
		2	" Easter	Wife	27	F	Full
		3	" Harbar	Son	2	M	Full
		4	Billey, Mack	S.Son	4	M	Full
		5	APPROVED BY SECRETARY OF INTERIOR.				
		6	ENROLLMENT				
CITIZENSHIP CERTIFICATE ISSUED FOR NO 1 JUL 11 1903		7	OF NOS. 1 2 & 3 HEREON APPROVED BY THE SECRETARY OF INTERIOR JAN 13 1905				
		8					
CITIZENSHIP CERTIFICATE ISSUED FOR NO 2-3 SEP 12 1903		9	No. 4 DID NOT SUBMIT PROOF OF REMOVAL AND BONA-FIDE SETTLEMENT WITHIN ONE YEAR FROM DATE OF IDENTIFICATION.				
		10					
		11					

	NAME OF FATHER	LIVING OR DEAD	NAME OF MOTHER	LIVING OR DEAD	APPLICATION NO.	REMARKS
1	Doctor James	Dead	Sophie James	Dead	1645	
2	David		Sukey John		"	
3	No.1		No.2		"	
4	Billey Jackson		No.2		"	
5						
6						
7						
8						
9						
10						
11						

Declaration and proof of settlement applies to Nos 1, 2 and 3 only.
<u>Nos. 1, 2 and 3</u>: Proof of continuous residence for a period of three years submitted June 19, 1906.

IDENTIFIED MISSISSIPPI CHOCTAWS 1902 - 1909
Volume II

IDENTIFIED MISSISSIPPI CHOCTAWS CARD NO. 398

IDENTIFICATION ADDRESS Bond, Miss. SETTLEMENT ADDRESS
DATE OF IDENTIFICATION Feb. 14, 1903. DATE OF PROOF OF SETTLEMENT

APPROVED ROLL No.	DAWES ROLL NO.		NAME	RELATIONSHIP TO PERSON FIRST NAMED	AGE	SEX	BLOOD
		1	Forbes, William		55	M	Full
		2	" Lala	Dau	18	F	Full
		3	" Alice	Dau	16	F	Full
		4					
		5					
		6	APPROVED BY SECRETARY OF INTERIOR.				
		7					
		8	DID NOT SUBMIT PROOF OF REMOVAL AND BONA-FIDE SETTLEMENT WITHIN ONE YEAR FROM DATE OF IDENTIFICATION				
		9					
		10					
		11					

	NAME OF FATHER	LIVING OR DEAD	NAME OF MOTHER	LIVING OR DEAD	APPLICATION NO.	REMARKS
1	Forbes	Dead	Mary Forbes	Dead	1641	
2	No.1		Josephine Forbes	"	"	
3	No.1		" "	"	"	
4						
5						
6						
7						
8						
9						
10						
11						

IDENTIFIED MISSISSIPPI CHOCTAWS 1902 - 1909
Volume II

IDENTIFIED MISSISSIPPI CHOCTAWS CARD NO. 399

IDENTIFICATION ADDRESS Heidelberg, Miss. SETTLEMENT ADDRESS Ravia I.T.
DATE OF IDENTIFICATION Feb. 14, 1903. DATE OF PROOF OF SETTLEMENT Sept 1st 1903

APPROVED ROLL No.	DAWES ROLL NO.	NAME	RELATIONSHIP TO PERSON FIRST NAMED	AGE	SEX	BLOOD
		1 Ellis, Jim		39	M	Full
		2 " Nancy	Wife	33	F	Full
		3 " Mary	Dau	7	F	Full
		4 " Leroy	Son	2	M	Full
		5				
		6				
		7 APPROVED BY SECRETARY OF INTERIOR.				
		8 ENROLLMENT OF NOS. 1 2 3 & 4 HEREON				
CITIZENSHIP CERTIFICATE ISSUED FOR NO 1-2-3-4 SEP 1 1903		9 APPROVED BY THE SECRETARY OF INTERIOR JAN 13 1905				
		10				
		11				

NAME OF FATHER	LIVING OR DEAD	NAME OF MOTHER	LIVING OR DEAD	APPLICATION NO.	REMARKS
1 Porter Sam		Nancy Sam		1647	
2 John Chubbee		Susan Chubbee		"	
3 No.1		No.2		"	
4 No.1		No.2		"	
5					
6					
7					
8					
9					
10 "Nos. 1,2,3 and 4: Proof of continuous residence for a					
11 period of three years submitted December 18, 1906."					

IDENTIFIED MISSISSIPPI CHOCTAWS 1902 - 1909
Volume II

IDENTIFIED MISSISSIPPI CHOCTAWS   CARD NO. 400

IDENTIFICATION ADDRESS DeKalb, Miss.   SETTLEMENT ADDRESS
DATE OF IDENTIFICATION Feb. 14, 1903.   DATE OF PROOF OF SETTLEMENT

APPROVED ROLL No.	DAWES ROLL NO.	NAME	RELATIONSHIP TO PERSON FIRST NAMED	AGE	SEX	BLOOD
		(Oon-te-ah-tubbe)				
		1 Jones, Joe		90	M	Full
		2				
		3				
		4				
		5 APPROVED BY SECRETARY OF INTERIOR.				
		6				
		7				
		8				
		9				
		10				
		11				

DID NOT SUBMIT PROOF OF REMOVAL AND BONA-FIDE SETTLEMENT WITHIN ONE YEAR FROM DATE OF IDENTIFICATION

NAME OF FATHER	LIVING OR DEAD	NAME OF MOTHER	LIVING OR DEAD	APPLICATION NO.	REMARKS
1 Nun-ta-o-tubbee	Dead	O-mollie-hoke	Dead	1739	
2					
3					
4					
5					
6					
7					
8					
9					
10					
11					

IDENTIFIED MISSISSIPPI CHOCTAWS 1902 - 1909
Volume II

IDENTIFIED MISSISSIPPI CHOCTAWS   CARD NO. 401

IDENTIFICATION ADDRESS Lucern, Miss. SETTLEMENT ADDRESS Byars, Ind. Ter.
DATE OF IDENTIFICATION Feb. 14, 1903. DATE OF PROOF OF SETTLEMENT July 10, 1903.

APPROVED ROLL No.	DAWES ROLL NO.	NAME	RELATIONSHIP TO PERSON FIRST NAMED	AGE	SEX	BLOOD
		1 Dixon, Doctor		56	M	Full
		2 " Nancy	Wife	68	F	Full
		3 Jackson, Cornelia	G.Dau	9	F	Full
		4 Lise, Lissie	G.Dau	8	F	Full
		5				
		6				

CITIZENSHIP CERTIFICATE ISSUED FOR NO 1 and 2 JUL 10 1903

APPROVED BY SECRETARY OF INTERIOR
ENROLLMENT OF NOS. 1 2 3 & 4 HEREON APPROVED BY THE SECRETARY OF INTERIOR JAN 13 1905

CITIZENSHIP CERTIFICATE ISSUED FOR NO 3-4 NOV 1 1903

NAME OF FATHER	LIVING OR DEAD	NAME OF MOTHER	LIVING OR DEAD	APPLICATION NO.	REMARKS
1 Hotinlubbee	Dead	Sallie	Dead	2989	
2	"	Ithlahoke	"	"	
3 Henry Jackson		Lulie Jackson		"	
4 John Lise		Mary J. Lise	Dead	"	
5					
6					
7					
8					
9	Nos 1 2 3 & 4 Testimony as to continuous residence				
10	for Nos 1 2 3 & 4 for a period of 3 years submitted				
11	[Illegible].				

IDENTIFIED MISSISSIPPI CHOCTAWS 1902 - 1909
Volume II

IDENTIFIED MISSISSIPPI CHOCTAWS   CARD NO. 402

IDENTIFICATION ADDRESS Tucker, Miss.   SETTLEMENT ADDRESS Atoka, I.T.
DATE OF IDENTIFICATION Feb. 14, 1903.   DATE OF PROOF OF SETTLEMENT Aug 18/03.

APPROVED ROLL No.	DAWES ROLL NO.	NAME	RELATIONSHIP TO PERSON FIRST NAMED	AGE	SEX	BLOOD
		1 Billy, Moss		23	M	Full
		2 " Ada	Wife	18	F	Full
		3 " Hullison	Son	1	M	Full
		4				
		5 APPROVED BY SECRETARY OF INTERIOR.				
		6				
		7 JAN				
		8				
CITIZENSHIP CERTIFICATE ISSUED FOR NO 1-2-3 AUG 18 1903		9				
		10				
		11				

NAME OF FATHER	LIVING OR DEAD	NAME OF MOTHER	LIVING OR DEAD	APPLICATION NO.	REMARKS
1 Young Billy		Isbey Billy	Dead	2022	
2 John Alman	Dead	Mollie Bob		"	
3 No.1		No.2		"	
4					
5					
6					
7					
8					
9					
10	"Nos 1, 2 and 3: Testimony relative to continuous residence for a period of three years submitted September 10, 1906."				
11					

IDENTIFIED MISSISSIPPI CHOCTAWS 1902 - 1909
Volume II

IDENTIFIED MISSISSIPPI CHOCTAWS CARD NO. 403

IDENTIFICATION ADDRESS Tucker, Miss. SETTLEMENT ADDRESS Atoka I.T.
DATE OF IDENTIFICATION Feb. 14, 1903. DATE OF PROOF OF SETTLEMENT Aug. 15/03.

APPROVED ROLL No.	DAWES ROLL NO.	NAME	RELATIONSHIP TO PERSON FIRST NAMED	AGE	SEX	BLOOD
		1. Bob, Johnnie		26	M	Full
		2. " Martha	Wife	20	F	Full
		3.				
		4.				
		5. APPROVED BY SECRETARY OF INTERIOR.				
		6. ENROLLMENT OF NOS. 1 & 2 HEREON				
		7. APPROVED BY THE SECRETARY OF INTERIOR JAN 13 1905				
		8.				
CITIZENSHIP CERTIFICATE ISSUED FOR NO 1-2 AUG 15 1903		9.				
		10.				
		11.				

NAME OF FATHER	LIVING OR DEAD	NAME OF MOTHER	LIVING OR DEAD	APPLICATION NO.	REMARKS
1. William Bob	Dead	Amy Bob	Dead	2020	
2. John Maley		Noley Maley	"	"	
3.					
4.					
5.					
6.					
7.					
8.					
9.		Nos 1 and 2: Testimony relative to continuous residence for a period of three years submitted September 11, 1906.			
10.					
11.					

IDENTIFIED MISSISSIPPI CHOCTAWS 1902 - 1909
Volume II

IDENTIFIED MISSISSIPPI CHOCTAWS   CARD NO. 404

IDENTIFICATION ADDRESS Tucker, Miss.   SETTLEMENT ADDRESS Atoka, I.T.
DATE OF IDENTIFICATION Feb. 14, 1903.   DATE OF PROOF OF SETTLEMENT Aug 18/03

APPROVED ROLL No.	DAWES ROLL NO.	NAME	RELATIONSHIP TO PERSON FIRST NAMED	AGE	SEX	BLOOD
		1 Adam, Toney		33	M	Full
		2				
		3				
		4				
		5 APPROVED BY SECRETARY OF INTERIOR.				
		6 ENROLLMENT OF NOS. ~ 1 ~ HEREON APPROVED BY THE SECRETARY OF INTERIOR JAN 13 1905				
CITIZENSHIP CERTIFICATE ISSUED FOR NO 1 AUG 18 1903						

NAME OF FATHER	LIVING OR DEAD	NAME OF MOTHER	LIVING OR DEAD	APPLICATION NO.	REMARKS
1 Adam	Dead	Betsie	Dead	2330	
2					
3					
4					
5					
6					
7					
8					
9					
10					
11					

No.1 is husband of No3 on Miss Choc card 352.

No.1 - Testimony as to continuous residence of No.1 up to his death, submitted May 24, 1906.
No1 died February 1, 1904

IDENTIFIED MISSISSIPPI CHOCTAWS 1902 - 1909
Volume II

IDENTIFIED MISSISSIPPI CHOCTAWS   CARD NO. 405

IDENTIFICATION ADDRESS Conehatta, Miss.   SETTLEMENT ADDRESS
DATE OF IDENTIFICATION Feb. 14, 1903.   DATE OF PROOF OF SETTLEMENT

APPROVED ROLL No.	DAWES ROLL NO.	NAME	RELATIONSHIP TO PERSON FIRST NAMED	AGE	SEX	BLOOD
		1 Jackson, Jeff		40	M	Full
		2 " Martha	Wife	32	F	Full
		3 " Sam	Son	18	M	Full
		4 " Tom	Son	12	M	Full
		5 " Lottie	Dau	8	F	Full
		6				
		7				
		8 APPROVED BY SECRETARY OF INTERIOR.				
		9 DID NOT SUBMIT PROOF OF				
		10 REMOVAL AND BONA-FIDE SET- TLEMENT WITHIN ONE YEAR				
		11 FROM DATE OF IDENTIFICATION.				

NAME OF FATHER (Ha-na-ka-ubbee)	LIVING OR DEAD	NAME OF MOTHER (Elah-pe-ah)	LIVING OR DEAD	APPLICATION NO.	REMARKS
1 Sam Jackson	Dead	Lucy Williamson		1866	
2 Un-teh-yah-bee	"	He-le-ho-nah	Dead	"	
3 No.1		No.2		"	
4 No.1		No.2		"	
5 No.1		No.2		"	
6					
7					
8					
9					
10					
11					

IDENTIFIED MISSISSIPPI CHOCTAWS 1902 - 1909
Volume II

IDENTIFIED MISSISSIPPI CHOCTAWS CARD NO. 406

IDENTIFICATION ADDRESS Hugo, I.T.   SETTLEMENT ADDRESS Spencerville, I.T.
DATE OF IDENTIFICATION Feb. 14, 1903.   DATE OF PROOF OF SETTLEMENT Jany 19, 04

APPROVED ROLL No.	DAWES ROLL NO.	NAME	RELATIONSHIP TO PERSON FIRST NAMED	AGE	SEX	BLOOD
		1. Thomas, Elijah		52	M	Full
		2.				
		3.				
		4.				
		5. APPROVED BY SECRETARY OF INTERIOR.				
		6.				
		7. OF NOS. ~~1~~ HEREON APPROVED BY THE SECRETARY OF INTERIOR JAN 13 1905				
		8.				
CITIZENSHIP CERTIFICATE 9.						
ISSUED FOR NO 1 JAN 19 1903 10.						
		11.				

NAME OF FATHER	LIVING OR DEAD	NAME OF MOTHER	LIVING OR DEAD	APPLICATION NO.	REMARKS
1. Jake Thomas	Dead	Martha Thomas	Dead	2008	
2.					
3.					
4.					
5.					
6.					
7.					
8.		Testimony relative to continuous residence for a period			
9.		of three years submitted September 21, 1908.			
10.					
11.					

IDENTIFIED MISSISSIPPI CHOCTAWS 1902 - 1909
Volume II

IDENTIFIED MISSISSIPPI CHOCTAWS CARD NO. 407

IDENTIFICATION ADDRESS Engine, Miss. SETTLEMENT ADDRESS Atoka I.T.
DATE OF IDENTIFICATION Feb. 14, 1903. DATE OF PROOF OF SETTLEMENT Aug 18/03.

APPROVED ROLL No.	DAWES ROLL NO.		NAME	RELATIONSHIP TO PERSON FIRST NAMED	AGE	SEX	BLOOD
		1	Stephen, Frank		32	M	Full
		2	" Lissie	Wife	27	F	Full
		3	" Allie	Dau	5	F	Full
		4	" Eliza	Dau	2	F	Full
		5					
		6					
		7	APPROVED BY SECRETARY OF INTERIOR.				
		8	ENROLLMENT				
CITIZENSHIP CERTIFICATE ISSUED FOR NO 1-2-3-4 AUG 18 1903		9	OF NOS. 1-2-3&4 HEREON APPROVED BY THE SECRETARY OF INTERIOR JAN 13 1905				
		11					

	NAME OF FATHER	LIVING OR DEAD	NAME OF MOTHER	LIVING OR DEAD	APPLICATION NO.	REMARKS
1	Jim Stephen		Betsie Stephen		2291	
2	Allen		Lucy	Dead	"	
3	No.1		No.2		"	
4	No.1		No.2		"	
5						
6						
7						
8						
9						
10	Nos 1,2,3 and 4: testimony relative to continuous					
11	residence for a period of three years submitted November 9, 1906."					

IDENTIFIED MISSISSIPPI CHOCTAWS 1902 - 1909
Volume II

IDENTIFIED MISSISSIPPI CHOCTAWS CARD NO. 408

IDENTIFICATION ADDRESS Coffadeliah, Miss.   SETTLEMENT ADDRESS
DATE OF IDENTIFICATION Feb. 14, 1903.   DATE OF PROOF OF SETTLEMENT

APPROVED ROLL No.	DAWES ROLL NO.	NAME	RELATIONSHIP TO PERSON FIRST NAMED	AGE	SEX	BLOOD
		1 Willis, Mose W.		23	M	Full
		2 " Rachael	Wife	24	F	Full
		3 " Almond	Son	6mo	M	Full
		4				
		5				
		6				
		7 APPROVED BY SECRETARY OF INTERIOR.				
		8 DID NOT SUBMIT PROOF OF				
		9 REMOVAL AND BONA-FIDE SET-				
		10 TLEMENT WITHIN ONE YEAR				
		11 FROM DATE OF IDENTIFICATION				

NAME OF FATHER	LIVING OR DEAD	NAME OF MOTHER	LIVING OR DEAD	APPLICATION NO.	REMARKS
1 Willis Tubbee	Dead		Dead	1895	
2 Richard				"	
3 No.1		No.2		"	
4					
5					
6					
7					
8					
9					
10					
11					

IDENTIFIED MISSISSIPPI CHOCTAWS 1902 - 1909
Volume II

IDENTIFIED MISSISSIPPI CHOCTAWS   CARD NO. 409

IDENTIFICATION ADDRESS Goodman, Miss.   SETTLEMENT ADDRESS Marietta, Ind. Ter.
DATE OF IDENTIFICATION Feb. 14, 1903.   DATE OF PROOF OF SETTLEMENT Dec. 16, 1903

Aug. 20/03

APPROVED ROLL No.	DAWES ROLL NO.	NAME	RELATIONSHIP TO PERSON FIRST NAMED	AGE	SEX	BLOOD
		1 Sockey, Solomon		60	M	Full
		2 " Phoebe	Wife	58	F	Full
		3 " Mary	Dau	13	F	Full
		4				
		5				
		6				
		7				
		8				

APPROVED BY SECRETARY OF INTERIOR.

CITIZENSHIP CERTIFICATE ISSUED FOR NO 1-2-3 DEC 16 1903

ENROLLMENT OF NOS. 1, 2 & 3 HEREON APPROVED BY THE SECRETARY OF INTERIOR JAN 13 1905

NAME OF FATHER	LIVING OR DEAD	NAME OF MOTHER	LIVING OR DEAD	APPLICATION NO.	REMARKS
1 Wallace Sockey	Dead	Liza Sockey	Dead	3393	
2 Lewis Pisamby	Dead	Polly Isaac (Illahotimah)	Dead	"	
3 No.1		No.2		"	
4					
5					
6					
7					
8					
9					
10					
11					

Test of Aug 20/03 taken at Choc. Land Office
Subsequet[sic] testimony as to proof of settlement
taken at Tishomingo Land Office Dec 16, 1903
"Nos 1,2 and 3: Testimony relative to continuous residence
for a period of three years submitted July 1-1907."

IDENTIFIED MISSISSIPPI CHOCTAWS 1902 - 1909
Volume II

IDENTIFIED MISSISSIPPI CHOCTAWS

CARD NO. 410

IDENTIFICATION ADDRESS Rose Hill, Miss.　　SETTLEMENT ADDRESS

DATE OF IDENTIFICATION Feb. 14, 1903.　　DATE OF PROOF OF SETTLEMENT

APPROVED ROLL No.	DAWES ROLL NO.	NAME	RELATIONSHIP TO PERSON FIRST NAMED	AGE	SEX	BLOOD
		1 Weeks, Masleke			F	Full
		2 " John	Son	10mo	M	"
		3				
		4				
		5				
		6 APPROVED BY SECRETARY OF INTERIOR.				
		7				
		8 DID NOT SUBMIT PROOF OF				
		9 REMOVAL AND BONA FIDE SET-				
		10 TLEMENT WITHIN ONE YEAR				
		11 FROM DATE OF IDENTIFICATION.				

NAME OF FATHER	LIVING OR DEAD	NAME OF MOTHER	LIVING OR DEAD	APPLICATION NO.	REMARKS
1 Lewis Chatham	Dead	Eliza Chatham		1905	
2 John Weeks	"	No.1		"	
3					
4					
5					
6					
7					
8					
9					
10					
11					

IDENTIFIED MISSISSIPPI CHOCTAWS 1902 - 1909
Volume II

IDENTIFIED MISSISSIPPI CHOCTAWS   CARD NO. 411

IDENTIFICATION ADDRESS Avera, Miss.   SETTLEMENT ADDRESS Hugo, Indian Territory
DATE OF IDENTIFICATION Feb. 14, 1903.   DATE OF PROOF OF SETTLEMENT Nov. 3-1906

APPROVED ROLL No.	DAWES ROLL NO.	NAME	RELATIONSHIP TO PERSON FIRST NAMED	AGE	SEX	BLOOD
		1. Johnson, Mamie		16	F	Full
		2.				
		3.				
		4.				
		5.				
		6. APPROVED BY SECRETARY OF INTERIOR.				
		7.				
		8. ENROLLMENT OF NOS. ~~~1~~~ HEREON				
CITIZENSHIP CERTIFICATE ISSUED FOR NO 1 JUN 27 1907		9. APPROVED BY THE SECRETARY OF INTERIOR JAN 13 1905				
		10.				
		11.				

NAME OF FATHER	LIVING OR DEAD	NAME OF MOTHER	LIVING OR DEAD	APPLICATION NO.	REMARKS
1. Frank Johnson		Josephine Johnson	Dead	1882	
2.					
3.					
4.					
5. Testimony relative to removal and settlement submitted					
6. November 3rd & 17th 1906, to be considered as proof of					
7. three years continuous residence in the Choctaw-Chickasaw country.					
8.					
9.					
10.					
11. Proof of removal to and settlement submitted under Act of Congress of June 21-1906.					

IDENTIFIED MISSISSIPPI CHOCTAWS 1902 - 1909
Volume II

IDENTIFIED MISSISSIPPI CHOCTAWS   CARD NO. 412

IDENTIFICATION ADDRESS Masengale, Miss.   SETTLEMENT ADDRESS Ardmore, Ind. Ter.
DATE OF IDENTIFICATION Feb. 14, 1903.   DATE OF PROOF OF SETTLEMENT July 14, 1903

APPROVED ROLL No.	DAWES ROLL NO.	NAME	RELATIONSHIP TO PERSON FIRST NAMED	AGE	SEX	BLOOD
		1 John, Simon		30	M	Full
		2 " Georgia	Wife	22	F	Full
		3 " Johnnie	Son	4	M	Full
		4 " Minnie	Dau	2	F	Full
		5 " Alex	Son	2mo	M	Full
		6				
		7				
		8				

CITIZENSHIP CERTIFICATE ISSUED FOR NO 1-2-3-4-5 JUL 14 1903

APPROVED BY SECRETARY OF INTERIOR.
ENROLLMENT OF NOS. 1 2 3 4 & 5 HEREON APPROVED BY THE SECRETARY OF INTERIOR JAN 13 1905

	NAME OF FATHER	LIVING OR DEAD	NAME OF MOTHER	LIVING OR DEAD	APPLICATION NO.	REMARKS
1	Big John		Sally John		1906	
2	Thompson Kelley	Dead	Fannie Kelley		"	
3	No.1		No.2		"	
4	No.1		No.2		"	
5	No.1		No.2		"	
6						
7						
8						
9						
10						
11						

Nos. 1, 2, 3, 4 & 5: Proof of continuous residence for a period of three years submitted May 16, 1906.

IDENTIFIED MISSISSIPPI CHOCTAWS 1902 - 1909
Volume II

IDENTIFIED MISSISSIPPI CHOCTAWS CARD NO. 413

IDENTIFICATION ADDRESS Tucker, Miss. SETTLEMENT ADDRESS Ardmore, Ind. Ter.
DATE OF IDENTIFICATION Feb. 14, 1903. DATE OF PROOF OF SETTLEMENT July 21, 1903.

APPROVED ROLL No.	DAWES ROLL NO.		NAME	RELATIONSHIP TO PERSON FIRST NAMED	AGE	SEX	BLOOD
		1	Jack, Allen		27	M	Full
		2					
		3					
		4					
		5					
		6					

CITIZENSHIP CERTIFICATE ISSUED FOR NO 1 JUL 22 1903

APPROVED BY SECRETARY OF INTERIOR.
ENROLLMENT OF NOS. 1 HEREON APPROVED BY THE SECRETARY OF INTERIOR JAN 13 1905

	NAME OF FATHER	LIVING OR DEAD	NAME OF MOTHER	LIVING OR DEAD	APPLICATION NO.	REMARKS
1	Billy Jack		Leanna Jack		2070	
2						
3						
4						
5						
6						
7						
8						
9						
10						
11						

No.1 Proof of continuous residence for a period of three years submitted March 31, 1906.

IDENTIFIED MISSISSIPPI CHOCTAWS 1902 - 1909
Volume II

IDENTIFIED MISSISSIPPI CHOCTAWS CARD NO. 414

IDENTIFICATION ADDRESS Hickory, Miss.   SETTLEMENT ADDRESS Ardmore, Ind. Ter.
DATE OF IDENTIFICATION Feb. 14, 1903.   DATE OF PROOF OF SETTLEMENT May 19, 1903.

APPROVED ROLL No.	DAWES ROLL NO.	NAME	RELATIONSHIP TO PERSON FIRST NAMED	AGE	SEX	BLOOD
		1 Simpson, Sookie		30	F	Full
		2				
		3				
		4				
		5				
		6 APPROVED BY SECRETARY OF INTERIOR.				
		7 ENROLLMENT OF NOS. 1 HEREON				
		8 APPROVED BY THE SECRETARY OF INTERIOR JAN 13 1905				
CITIZENSHIP CERTIFICATE ISSUED FOR NO 1 MAY 19 1903		9				
		10				
		11				

	NAME OF FATHER	LIVING OR DEAD	NAME OF MOTHER	LIVING OR DEAD	APPLICATION NO.	REMARKS
1	Simpson	Dead	Eliza Simpson	Dead	1943	
2						
3						
4						
5						
6						
7						
8						
9						
10						
11						

"No.1: Proof of continuous residence for a period of three years submitted August 7-1906."

IDENTIFIED MISSISSIPPI CHOCTAWS 1902 - 1909
Volume II

IDENTIFIED MISSISSIPPI CHOCTAWS CARD NO. 415

IDENTIFICATION ADDRESS Enterprise, Miss.   SETTLEMENT ADDRESS
DATE OF IDENTIFICATION Feb. 14, 1903.   DATE OF PROOF OF SETTLEMENT

APPROVED ROLL No.	DAWES ROLL NO.	NAME	RELATIONSHIP TO PERSON FIRST NAMED	AGE	SEX	BLOOD
		1 Shumake, Charlie		28	M	Full
		2				
		3				
		4				
		5				
		6 APPROVED BY SECRETARY OF INTERIOR.				
		7				
		8				
		9				
		10				
		11				

DID NOT SUBMIT PROOF OF REMOVAL AND BONA-FIDE SETTLEMENT WITHIN ONE YEAR FROM DATE OF IDENTIFICATION.

NAME OF FATHER	LIVING OR DEAD	NAME OF MOTHER	LIVING OR DEAD	APPLICATION NO.	REMARKS
1 Bill Shumake		Liza Shumake		1973	
2					
3					
4					
5					
6					
7					
8					
9					
10					
11					

IDENTIFIED MISSISSIPPI CHOCTAWS 1902 - 1909
Volume II

IDENTIFIED MISSISSIPPI CHOCTAWS   CARD NO. 416

IDENTIFICATION ADDRESS Byram, Miss.   SETTLEMENT ADDRESS Colbert, Indian Territory
DATE OF IDENTIFICATION Feb. 14, 1903.   DATE OF PROOF OF SETTLEMENT June 13-1906.

APPROVED ROLL No.	DAWES ROLL NO.		NAME	RELATIONSHIP TO PERSON FIRST NAMED	AGE	SEX	BLOOD
		1	Johnson, Nochee		21	F	Full
		2					
		3					
		4					
		5					
JUN 13 1906		6	APPROVED BY SECRETARY OF INTERIOR.				
		7	No. 1 DID NOT SUBMIT PROOF OF REMOVAL AND BONA FIDE SETTLEMENT WITHIN ONE YEAR FROM DATE OF IDENTIFICATION				
		8					
		9					
		10	~~1~~				
		11	Feb. 27 07				

	NAME OF FATHER	LIVING OR DEAD	NAME OF MOTHER	LIVING OR DEAD	APPLICATION NO.	REMARKS
1	Taylor Johnson		Jennie Johnson		2689	
2						
3						
4						
5			No.1: Testimony relative to continuous residence			
6			for a period of three years submitted February 19,			
7			1908.			
8						
9						
10						
11						

Proof of removal and settlement within the Choctaw-Chickasaw
country of Nochee Johnson received June 13, 1906, in conformity
with Departmental instructions of November 24, 1905. (I.T.D.-14900-1905).

IDENTIFIED MISSISSIPPI CHOCTAWS 1902 - 1909
Volume II

IDENTIFIED MISSISSIPPI CHOCTAWS CARD NO. 417

IDENTIFICATION ADDRESS Piketon, Miss.   SETTLEMENT ADDRESS
DATE OF IDENTIFICATION Apr 11th, 1903.   DATE OF PROOF OF SETTLEMENT

APPROVED ROLL No.	DAWES ROLL NO.	NAME	RELATIONSHIP TO PERSON FIRST NAMED	AGE	SEX	BLOOD
	1205	1 Gibson, Johnson		30	M	Full
	1206	2 " Emma	Wife	27	F	"
	1207	3 " Robert	Son	9	M	"
		4				
		5				
		6				
		7	DID NOT SUBMIT PROOF OF REMOVAL AND BONA-FIDE SETTLEMENT WITHIN ONE YEAR FROM DATE OF IDENTIFICATION			
		8				
		9				
		10				
		11 APPROVED BY SECRETARY OF INTERIOR.				

NAME OF FATHER	LIVING OR DEAD	NAME OF MOTHER	LIVING OR DEAD	APPLICATION NO.	REMARKS
1 William Gibson	dead	Polly Gibson		4044	
2 Sam Cain (Seahmotubbee)		Susie Cain	dead	4044	
3 No.1		No.2		4044	
4					
5					
6					
7					
8					
9					
10					
11					

JUN 1 1903

IDENTIFIED MISSISSIPPI CHOCTAWS 1902 - 1909
Volume II

IDENTIFIED MISSISSIPPI CHOCTAWS   CARD NO. 418

IDENTIFICATION ADDRESS Trapp, Miss.   SETTLEMENT ADDRESS
DATE OF IDENTIFICATION April 11, 1903.   DATE OF PROOF OF SETTLEMENT

APPROVED ROLL No.	DAWES ROLL NO.	NAME	RELATIONSHIP TO PERSON FIRST NAMED	AGE	SEX	BLOOD
	1208	1 Hinson, Simon		19	M	Full
	1209	2 " Nancy	Wife	23	F	Full

DID NOT SUBMIT PROOF OF REMOVAL AND BONA-FIDE SETTLEMENT WITHIN ONE YEAR FROM DATE OF IDENTIFICATION.

NAME OF FATHER	LIVING OR DEAD	NAME OF MOTHER	LIVING OR DEAD	APPLICATION NO.	REMARKS
1 Hinson	dead	Sophia Willis		4513	
2 Philip [Illegible]	"	don't know	dead	4513	

APPROVED BY SECRETARY OF INTERIOR.   JUN 1 1903

IDENTIFIED MISSISSIPPI CHOCTAWS 1902 - 1909
Volume II

IDENTIFIED MISSISSIPPI CHOCTAWS   CARD NO. 419

IDENTIFICATION ADDRESS Hope, Miss.   SETTLEMENT ADDRESS
DATE OF IDENTIFICATION April 11, 1903.   DATE OF PROOF OF SETTLEMENT

APPROVED ROLL No.	DAWES ROLL NO.	NAME	RELATIONSHIP TO PERSON FIRST NAMED	AGE	SEX	BLOOD
	1210	1 Jimmy, Silas		23	M	Full
	1211	2 " Bicey	Wife	18	F	Full
	1212	3 " Lee	Son	2	M	Full
	1213	4 " Alis	Son	9ms	M	Full
		5				
		6				
		7				
		8 DID NOT SUBMIT PROOF OF				
		9 REMOVAL AND BONA-FIDE SETTLEMENT WITHIN ONE YEAR				
		10 FROM DATE OF IDENTIFICATION.				
		11				

NAME OF FATHER	LIVING OR DEAD	NAME OF MOTHER	LIVING OR DEAD	APPLICATION NO.	REMARKS
1 Tobe Jimmy	dead	Louisa Philip	dead	4502	
2 Isom Comby	dead	Jennie Comby		4502	
3 No.1		No.2		4502	
4 No.1		No.2		4502	
5					
6					
7					
8					
9					
10					
11					

APPROVED BY SECRETARY OF INTERIOR.   JUN 1 1903

IDENTIFIED MISSISSIPPI CHOCTAWS 1902 - 1909
Volume II

IDENTIFIED MISSISSIPPI CHOCTAWS CARD NO. 420
Nos 1-3-4-5 Ardmore I.T.
IDENTIFICATION ADDRESS Pearl River, La.   SETTLEMENT ADDRESS No2 " "
DATE OF IDENTIFICATION April 11, 1903.   DATE OF PROOF OF SETTLEMENT Nos 1-3-4-5 Nov 7/03
No 2 - Nov 28/03

APPROVED ROLL No.	DAWES ROLL NO.	NAME	RELATIONSHIP TO PERSON FIRST NAMED	AGE	SEX	BLOOD
	1214	1 Ok-chi-tubbee, Josephine		40	F	Full
	1215	2 Jim, Filleah	Niece	15	F	Full
	1216	3 " Rosie	Niece	13	F	Full
	1217	4 " Thomas	Neph	10	M	Full
	1218	5 " Salena	Niece	5	F	Full
		6				

CITIZENSHIP CERTIFICATE
ISSUED FOR NO 1
NOV 7 1903

ENROLLMENT
OF NOS. HEREON APPROVED BY THE SECRETARY
OF INTERIOR JAN 13 1905

CITIZENSHIP CERTIFICATE   CITIZENSHIP CERTIFICATE
ISSUED FOR NO 3-4-5   ISSUED FOR NO 2
NOV 21 1903   NOV 30 1903

NAME OF FATHER	LIVING OR DEAD	NAME OF MOTHER	LIVING OR DEAD	APPLICATION NO.	REMARKS
1 Ok-chi-tubbee	dead	Sallie Is-ti-opie	dead	2412	
2 Charley Jim	"	Isabelle Jim	"	2412	
3 " "	"	" " "	"	2412	
4 " "	"	" " "	"	2412	
5 " "	"	" " "	"	2412	
6					
7					
8					
9					
10					
11					

APPROVED BY SECRETARY OF INTERIOR.
JUN 1 1903

Declaration and proof of settlement of Nov. 7/03 apply to Nos 1-3-4-5 only.
Declaration and proof of settlement of Nov. 28/03 apply to No 2 only.
No2: Proof of continuous residence for a period of three years submitted March 11-1907.

IDENTIFIED MISSISSIPPI CHOCTAWS 1902 - 1909
Volume II

IDENTIFIED MISSISSIPPI CHOCTAWS CARD NO. 421

IDENTIFICATION ADDRESS Laurel Hill, Miss.   SETTLEMENT ADDRESS
DATE OF IDENTIFICATION April 11, 1903.   DATE OF PROOF OF SETTLEMENT

APPROVED ROLL No.	DAWES ROLL NO.	NAME	RELATIONSHIP TO PERSON FIRST NAMED	AGE	SEX	BLOOD
	1219	1 Jacoway, Sealy		60	F	Full

DID NOT SUBMIT PROOF OF REMOVAL AND BONAFIDE SETTLEMENT WITHIN ONE YEAR FROM DATE OF IDENTIFICATION.

	NAME OF FATHER	LIVING OR DEAD	NAME OF MOTHER	LIVING OR DEAD	APPLICATION NO.	REMARKS
1	Thompson	dead	Betsey Thompson	dead	4376	

APPROVED BY SECRETARY OF INTERIOR.
JUN 1   1903

IDENTIFIED MISSISSIPPI CHOCTAWS 1902 - 1909
Volume II

IDENTIFIED MISSISSIPPI CHOCTAWS   CARD NO. 422

IDENTIFICATION ADDRESS Philadelphia, Miss.   SETTLEMENT ADDRESS Calloway I.T.
DATE OF IDENTIFICATION April 11, 1903.   DATE OF PROOF OF SETTLEMENT July 23, 1903

APPROVED ROLL No.	DAWES ROLL NO.	NAME	RELATIONSHIP TO PERSON FIRST NAMED	AGE	SEX	BLOOD
	1220	1 Billey, Jim		48	M	Full
	1221	2 " Bud	Son	11	M	Full
		3				
		4				
		5				
		6				

CITIZENSHIP CERTIFICATE
ISSUED FOR NO   1
JUL 23 1903

ENROLLMENT
OF NOS. ___1 & 2___ HEREON
APPROVED BY THE SECRETARY
OF INTERIOR JAN 13 1905.

CITIZENSHIP CERTIFICATE
ISSUED FOR NO   2
AUG 29 1903

NAME OF FATHER	LIVING OR DEAD	NAME OF MOTHER	LIVING OR DEAD	APPLICATION NO.	REMARKS
1 (Oook-a-la-hane-lubbee) Billey	dead	Tim-a-yonah	dead	1998	
2 No.1		Josephine Billey	"	1998	
3					
4					
5					
6					
7					
8					
9					
10					
11					

APPROVED BY SECRETARY OF INTERIOR.
JUN 1 1903

"No.1 and 2: Testimony as to continuous residence for a period of three years submitted July 5, 1906."

IDENTIFIED MISSISSIPPI CHOCTAWS 1902 - 1909
Volume II

IDENTIFIED MISSISSIPPI CHOCTAWS   CARD NO. 423

IDENTIFICATION ADDRESS Walnutgrove, Miss.   SETTLEMENT ADDRESS
DATE OF IDENTIFICATION April 11, 1903.   DATE OF PROOF OF SETTLEMENT

APPROVED ROLL No.	DAWES ROLL NO.		NAME	RELATIONSHIP TO PERSON FIRST NAMED	AGE	SEX	BLOOD
	1222	1	Nelson, Phelia Ann		32	F	Full
	1223	2	" Bessie	Dau	1	F	Full
		3					
		4					
		5	DID NOT SUBMIT PROOF OF				
		6	REMOVAL AND BONA-FIDE SET-				
		7	TLEMENT WITHIN ONE YEAR				
		8	FROM DATE OF IDENTIFICATION.				
		9					
		10					
		11					

	NAME OF FATHER	LIVING OR DEAD	NAME OF MOTHER	LIVING OR DEAD	APPLICATION NO.	REMARKS
1	Peter Ben		Don't know	dead	4240	
2	Harrison Nelson	dead	No.1		4240	
3						
4						
5						
6						
7						
8						
9						
10						
11						

APPROVED BY SECRETARY OF INTERIOR.
JUN 1   1903

IDENTIFIED MISSISSIPPI CHOCTAWS 1902 - 1909
Volume II

IDENTIFIED MISSISSIPPI CHOCTAWS   CARD NO. 424

IDENTIFICATION ADDRESS Hope, Miss.   SETTLEMENT ADDRESS
DATE OF IDENTIFICATION April 11, 1903.   DATE OF PROOF OF SETTLEMENT

APPROVED ROLL No.	DAWES ROLL NO.	NAME	RELATIONSHIP TO PERSON FIRST NAMED	AGE	SEX	BLOOD
	1224	Jim, Adam		31	M	Full
	1225	" Fabie	Wife	21	F	Full

DID NOT SUBMIT PROOF OF REMOVAL AND BONA-FIDE SETTLEMENT WITHIN ONE YEAR FROM DATE OF IDENTIFICATION.

NAME OF FATHER	LIVING OR DEAD	NAME OF MOTHER	LIVING OR DEAD	APPLICATION NO.	REMARKS
Jim Isaac		Mary Isaac		4493	
Tobe Jimmie	dead	Louisa Jimmie		4493	

APPROVED BY SECRETARY OF INTERIOR.

JUN 1 1903

IDENTIFIED MISSISSIPPI CHOCTAWS 1902 - 1909
Volume II

IDENTIFIED MISSISSIPPI CHOCTAWS   CARD NO. 425

IDENTIFICATION ADDRESS
SETTLEMENT ADDRESS Byars, Ind. Ter.
DATE OF IDENTIFICATION April 11, 1903.
DATE OF PROOF OF SETTLEMENT July 11, 1903

APPROVED ROLL No.	DAWES ROLL NO.	NAME	RELATIONSHIP TO PERSON FIRST NAMED	AGE	SEX	BLOOD
	1226	1 Lewis, John Wesley		36	M	Full
	1227	2 " Leanna	Wife	28	F	Full
	1228	3 " William	Son	12	M	Full
	1229	4 " Thomas	Son	10	M	Full
	1230	5 " Nelson	Son	8	M	Full
	1231	6 " Mary	Dau	6	F	Full
	1232	7 " Annie	Dau	4	F	Full
	1233	8 " Easter	Dau	2	F	Full
	1234	9 " Ola	Dau	1mo	F	Full

CITIZENSHIP CERTIFICATE ISSUED FOR NO 2-3-4-5-6-7-8 JUL 13 1903

ENROLLMENT OF NOS. 2 3 4 5 6 7 & 8 HEREON APPROVED BY THE SECRETARY OF INTERIOR JAN. 13. 1905

	NAME OF FATHER	LIVING OR DEAD	NAME OF MOTHER	LIVING OR DEAD	APPLICATION NO.	REMARKS
1	John Lewis	dead	Malissa Lewis	dead	2608	
2	Doctor Dixon			"	2608	
3	No.1		No.2		2608	
4	No.1		No.2		2608	
5	No.1		No.2		2608	
6	No.1		No.2		2608	
7	No.1		No.2		2608	
8	No.1		No.2		2608	
9	No.1		No.2		2608	
10	No.2: Proof of continuous residence from date of					
11	settlement until date of death submitted [Illegible].					

APPROVED BY SECRETARY OF INTERIOR.
JUN 1 1903

No 1&9 DID NOT SUBMIT PROOF OF REMOVAL AND BONA-FIDE SETTLEMENT WITHIN ONE YEAR FROM DATE OF IDENTIFICATION.

No's 3 4 5 6 & 8: Testimony as to continuous residence for a period of 3 years submitted Mch 16, 06.
Declaration and proof of settlement applies to Nos 2 to 8 inclusive only.
No.7 Testimony as to continuous residence of
No.7 for up to time of her death submitted Mch 17, 06.
Proof of continuous residence for a
period of three years submitted Dec. 12-1906.

IDENTIFIED MISSISSIPPI CHOCTAWS 1902 - 1909
Volume II

IDENTIFIED MISSISSIPPI CHOCTAWS CARD NO. 426

IDENTIFICATION ADDRESS North Bend, Miss. SETTLEMENT ADDRESS
DATE OF IDENTIFICATION April 11, 1903. DATE OF PROOF OF SETTLEMENT

APPROVED ROLL No.	DAWES ROLL NO.	NAME	RELATIONSHIP TO PERSON FIRST NAMED	AGE	SEX	BLOOD
	1235	1 Mark, Mingo		54	M	Full
	1236	2 " John	Son	19	M	Full
	1237	3 " Horace	Son	16	M	Full
	1238	4 " Luiza	Dau	14	F	Full
	1239	5 " Solomon	Nephew	20	M	Full
	1240	6 " Lasen	Niece	21	F	Full
	1241	7 " Louisa	Dau	5	F	Full
		8				
		9				
		10				
		11				

NAME OF FATHER	LIVING OR DEAD	NAME OF MOTHER	LIVING OR DEAD	APPLICATION NO.	REMARKS
1 Mark Mingo	dead	Sookey Mark	dead	5106	
2 No.1		Susan Mark	"	5106	
3 No.1		" "	"	5106	
4 No.1		" "	"	5106	
5 Billy Mark	dead	Amy Mark	"	5106	
6 " "		" "	"	5106	
7 No.1		Nancy Mark	dead	5106	
8					
9					
10					
11					

APPROVED BY SECRETARY OF INTERIOR.
JUN 1   1903

IDENTIFIED MISSISSIPPI CHOCTAWS 1902 - 1909
Volume II

IDENTIFIED MISSISSIPPI CHOCTAWS   CARD NO. 427

IDENTIFICATION ADDRESS Rio, Miss.   SETTLEMENT ADDRESS Ft. Towson, I.T.
DATE OF IDENTIFICATION April 11, 1903.   DATE OF PROOF OF SETTLEMENT Oct. 15, 03.

APPROVED ROLL No.	DAWES ROLL NO.		NAME	RELATIONSHIP TO PERSON FIRST NAMED	AGE	SEX	BLOOD
	1242	1	Ha-cubbee, Mollie		60	F	Full
		2					
		3					
		4					
		5					
		6					
		7					
		8					
		9					
		10					
		11					

ZENSHIP ... UED FOR ... CERTIFICATE No 1 OCT 16 1903

ENROLLMENT OF NOS. ~~1~~ HEREON APPROVED BY THE SECRETARY OF INTERIOR JAN 13 1905.

	NAME OF FATHER	LIVING OR DEAD	NAME OF MOTHER	LIVING OR DEAD	APPLICATION NO.	REMARKS
1	Ha-cubbee	dead	Ha-thla-to-nah	Dead	5191	
2						
3						
4						
5						
6						
7						
8			"No.1 died June 14-1904: Proof of continuous			
9			residence up to the time of her death submitted			
10			January 26, 1907."			
11						

APPROVED BY SECRETARY OF INTERIOR.
JUN 1 1903

IDENTIFIED MISSISSIPPI CHOCTAWS 1902 - 1909
Volume II

IDENTIFIED MISSISSIPPI CHOCTAWS CARD NO. 428

IDENTIFICATION ADDRESS Avera, Miss.
DATE OF IDENTIFICATION April 11, 1903.
SETTLEMENT ADDRESS No1 McMillan, I.T. Nos 2-3-5 Shady Point, I.T.
DATE OF PROOF OF SETTLEMENT Nos 2-3-5. Dec. 18-'03
No.1 Sept. 17/03

APPROVED ROLL No.	DAWES ROLL NO.	NAME	RELATIONSHIP TO PERSON FIRST NAMED	AGE	SEX	BLOOD
	1243	1 Thomas, John B.		25	M	Full
	1244	2 " Emma	Wife	35	F	Full
	1245	3 " Ada	Dau	7	F	Full
	1246	4 " Joshua	Son	6	M	Full
	1247	5 " Henry	Son	1	M	Full
		6				
		7 CITIZENSHIP CERTIFICATE ISSUED FOR NO 2-3-5 DEC 18 1903	ENROLLMENT OF NOS. 1 2 3 & 5 HEREON APPROVED BY THE SECRETARY OF INTERIOR JAN 13 1905			

NAME OF FATHER	LIVING OR DEAD	NAME OF MOTHER	LIVING OR DEAD	APPLICATION NO.	REMARKS
1 Elijah Thomas		don't know	dead	1879	
2 Lewis Hawkins	dead	don't know	dead	1879	
3 No.1		No.2		1879	
4 No.1		No.2		1879	
5 No.1		No.2		1879	

APPROVED BY SECRETARY OF INTERIOR.
JUN 1 1903

No.1: Proof of continuous residence for a period of three years submitted June 6, 1906.

Nos 2,3 and 5: Proof of continuous residence for a period of three years submitted March 4-1907.
Declaration and proof of settlement of Sept 17/03 apply to No1 only.
No2 now the wife of Willis Wade No.1 Choc Card 4843 roll #13359 Choc. B.B.
Settlement address of Nos. 2,3&5 Shady point, I.T.
Date of proof of settlement of Nos. 2,3&5 Dec. 18, 1903.
Declaration and proof f settlement of Dec 18/03 apply to Nos 2,3 & 5 only.

IDENTIFIED MISSISSIPPI CHOCTAWS 1902 - 1909
Volume II

IDENTIFIED MISSISSIPPI CHOCTAWS

CARD NO. 429

IDENTIFICATION ADDRESS Conehatta, Miss.　　SETTLEMENT ADDRESS
DATE OF IDENTIFICATION April 11, 1903.　　DATE OF PROOF OF SETTLEMENT

APPROVED ROLL No.	DAWES ROLL NO.	NAME	RELATIONSHIP TO PERSON FIRST NAMED	AGE	SEX	BLOOD
	1248	1 Farmer, Sillman		22	M	Full
		2				
		3				
		4				
		5				
		6				
		7				
		8				
		9				
		10				
		11				

NAME OF FATHER	LIVING OR DEAD	NAME OF MOTHER	LIVING OR DEAD	APPLICATION NO.	REMARKS
1 John Farmer	dead	Polly Farmer		488	
2					
3					
4					
5					
6					
7					
8					
9					
10					
11					

APPROVED BY SECRETARY OF INTERIOR.
JUN 1　1903

IDENTIFIED MISSISSIPPI CHOCTAWS 1902 - 1909
Volume II

IDENTIFIED MISSISSIPPI CHOCTAWS CARD NO. 430

IDENTIFICATION ADDRESS Paulding, Miss. SETTLEMENT ADDRESS Nos 1&3 Kemp, I.T.
DATE OF IDENTIFICATION April 11, 1903. DATE OF PROOF OF SETTLEMENT Nos 1&3 Sept 26/03

APPROVED ROLL No.	DAWES ROLL NO.	NAME	RELATIONSHIP TO PERSON FIRST NAMED	AGE	SEX	BLOOD
	1249	1 John, Jack		22	M	Full
	1250	2 " Sallie	Wife	21	F	Full
	1251	3 " Davis	Son	5	M	Full
4						
5						
6		1 & 3				
7						
8		No2				

CITIZENSHIP CERTIFICATE ISSUED FOR NO 1-3 SEP 26 1903

DID NOT SUBMIT PROOF OF REMOVAL AND BONA FIDE SETTLEMENT WITHIN ONE YEAR FROM DATE OF IDENTIFICATION.

	NAME OF FATHER	LIVING OR DEAD	NAME OF MOTHER	LIVING OR DEAD	APPLICATION NO.	REMARKS
1	Billy John	dead	don't know	dead	2006	
2	Adam Lewis	"	Eliza Lewis		2006	
3	No.1		No.2		2006	
4						
5						
6						
7						
8						
9				Nos. 1 and 3: testimony relative to continuous residence for a period of three years submitted March 12, 1907.		
10						
11						

APPROVED BY SECRETARY OF INTERIOR.
JUN 1 1903

Declaration and proof of settlement apply to Nos. 1 & 3 only.

IDENTIFIED MISSISSIPPI CHOCTAWS 1902 - 1909
Volume II

IDENTIFIED MISSISSIPPI CHOCTAWS   CARD NO. 431

IDENTIFICATION ADDRESS Engine, Miss.   SETTLEMENT ADDRESS Atoka, I.T.
DATE OF IDENTIFICATION April 11, 1903.   DATE OF PROOF OF SETTLEMENT Aug. 18/03

APPROVED ROLL No.	DAWES ROLL NO.	NAME	RELATIONSHIP TO PERSON FIRST NAMED	AGE	SEX	BLOOD
	1252	1 Bob, Mollie		52	F	Full
		2				
		3				
		4				
		5				
		6				
		7	ENROLLMENT			
		8	OF NOS. ~~1~~ HEREON APPROVED BY THE SECRETARY			
CITIZENSHIP CERTIFICATE ISSUED FOR NO 1 AUG 18 1903			OF INTERIOR JAN 13 1905 .			
		11				

NAME OF FATHER	LIVING OR DEAD	NAME OF MOTHER	LIVING OR DEAD	APPLICATION NO.	REMARKS
1 Pis-un-tubbee	dead	Ama	dead	2013	
2					
3					
4					
5					
6					
7					
8	No.1: Testimony as to continuous residence of No.1 up to her death submitted September 21, 1905.				
9		No.1 died 12/22/04			
10					
11					

APPROVED BY SECRETARY OF INTERIOR.
JUN 1 1903

IDENTIFIED MISSISSIPPI CHOCTAWS 1902 - 1909
Volume II

IDENTIFIED MISSISSIPPI CHOCTAWS   CARD NO. 432

IDENTIFICATION ADDRESS Mandeville, La.　　SETTLEMENT ADDRESS Ardmore I.T.
DATE OF IDENTIFICATION April 11, 1903.　　DATE OF PROOF OF SETTLEMENT March 8, 04.

APPROVED ROLL No.	DAWES ROLL NO.	NAME	RELATIONSHIP TO PERSON FIRST NAMED	AGE	SEX	BLOOD
	1253	1 Onah-fal-a-ma-tubbee		52	F	Full
		2				
		3				
		4				
		5				
		6				
		7 1905				
		8				

CITIZENSHIP CERTIFICATE
ISSUED FOR NO --1--
MAR 8 1904

NAME OF FATHER	LIVING OR DEAD	NAME OF MOTHER	LIVING OR DEAD	APPLICATION NO.	REMARKS
1 On-ah-to-bo-ka	dead	Hannah (Ah-be-ho-yo)	dead	2414	
2					
3					
4					
5					
6					
7					
8					
9					
10					
11					

APPROVED BY SECRETARY OF INTERIOR.
JUN 1 1903　　　　"No1. Proof of continuous residence for a period of three years submitted July 17, 1906."

IDENTIFIED MISSISSIPPI CHOCTAWS 1902 - 1909
Volume II

IDENTIFIED MISSISSIPPI CHOCTAWS CARD NO. 433

IDENTIFICATION ADDRESS Cushtusa, Miss. SETTLEMENT ADDRESS Stigler, Ind. Ter.
DATE OF IDENTIFICATION April 11, 1903. DATE OF PROOF OF SETTLEMENT Aug 25, 03

APPROVED ROLL No.	DAWES ROLL NO.	NAME	RELATIONSHIP TO PERSON FIRST NAMED	AGE	SEX	BLOOD
	1254	1 Jacob, Charley		34	M	Full
	1255	2 " Louisa	Wife	31	F	Full
	1256	3 " Ebbie	Dau	4mo	F	Full
		4				
		5				
		6 1 2 & 3				
		7 JAN				
		8				

CITIZENSHIP CERTIFICATE
ISSUED FOR NO 1-2-3
~~DEC 19 1903~~

NAME OF FATHER	LIVING OR DEAD	NAME OF MOTHER	LIVING OR DEAD	APPLICATION NO.	REMARKS
1 Jacob	dead	Betsey Jacob	dead	2649	
2 Thompson	"	Sallie Gibson		2649	
3 No.1		No.2		2649	
4					
5					
6					
7					
8		Testimony Dec 19, 1903 give Ardmore I.T.			
9		as Address taken at Tishomingo			
10		Settlement add. Stigler I.T.			Taken at Atoka Aug 25/03
11		Date proof settlement Aug. 25 03			

APPROVED BY SECRETARY OF INTERIOR
JUN 1 1903

"Nos 1, 2 and 3: Testimony relative to continuous residence for a period of three years submitted September 4, 1906."

IDENTIFIED MISSISSIPPI CHOCTAWS 1902 - 1909
Volume II

IDENTIFIED MISSISSIPPI CHOCTAWS   CARD NO. 434

IDENTIFICATION ADDRESS Carthage, Miss.   SETTLEMENT ADDRESS Calloway, Ind. Ter.
DATE OF IDENTIFICATION April 11, 1903.   DATE OF PROOF OF SETTLEMENT July 6th, 1903

APPROVED ROLL No.	DAWES ROLL NO.	NAME	RELATIONSHIP TO PERSON FIRST NAMED	AGE	SEX	BLOOD
	1257	1 Jim, Simpson		50	M	Full
	1258	2 " Eliza	Wife	45	F	Full
	1259	3 " Robert	Son	15	M	Full
	1260	4 " Egburt	Son	13	M	Full
	1261	5 " Tessie	Dau	10	F	Full
	1262	6 " Clemmon	Son	7	M	Full
	1263	7 " Evan	Son	5	M	Full
		8				
		9				
		10	1 2 3 4 5 6 & 7			
1-3		11				

NAME OF FATHER	LIVING OR DEAD	NAME OF MOTHER	LIVING OR DEAD	APPLICATION NO.	REMARKS
1 Little Jim	dead	Betsey Jim	dead	4368	
2 ~~Solomon York~~ Tuck-a-lam-bee		Martha York	dead	4368	
3 No.1	dead	No.2	"	4368	
4 No.1	"	No.2	"	4368	
5 No.1	"	No.2	"	4368	
6 No.1	"	No.2	"	4368	
7 No.1	"	No.2	"	4368	
8					
9					
10					
11					

CITIZENSHIP CERTIFICATE ISSUED FOR NO 4-5-6-7
JUL 9 1903

APPROVED BY SECRETARY OF INTERIOR.
JUN 1 1903

CITIZENSHIP CERTIFICATE ISSUED FOR NO 2
JUL 21 1903

Nos 1 to 7 - Testimony as to continuous residence of Nos 1 to 7 inclusive, for a period of 3 years submitted February 10, 1906.

IDENTIFIED MISSISSIPPI CHOCTAWS 1902 - 1909
Volume II

IDENTIFIED MISSISSIPPI CHOCTAWS CARD NO. 435

IDENTIFICATION ADDRESS Trapp, Miss. SETTLEMENT ADDRESS Ft. Towson I.T.
DATE OF IDENTIFICATION April 11, 1903. DATE OF PROOF OF SETTLEMENT Oct 15, 03.

APPROVED ROLL No.	DAWES ROLL NO.	NAME	RELATIONSHIP TO PERSON FIRST NAMED	AGE	SEX	BLOOD
	1264	1 Moses, Ike		35	M	Full
	1265	2 " Ann	Wife	27	F	Full
	1266	3 " Nicey	Dau	14	F	Full
	1267	4 " Lottie	Dau	13	F	Full
	1268	5 " Edna	Dau	5	F	Full
	1269	6 " Elsie	Dau	11mo	F	Full
		7				
		8				

CITIZENSHIP CERTIFICATE ISSUED FOR NO 1-2-3-4-5-6 1 2 3 4 5&6
~~OCT 16 1903~~
11

NAME OF FATHER	LIVING OR DEAD	NAME OF MOTHER	LIVING OR DEAD	APPLICATION NO.	REMARKS
1 Tushcanola	dead	Sallie Gamil[sic] (or Moses)		3737	
2 Moses	dead	Bicey Moses	dead	3737	
3 No.1		No.2		3737	
4 No.1		No.2		3737	
5 No.1		No.2		3737	
6 No.1		No.2		3737	
7					
8					
9					
10					
11					

APPROVED BY SECRETARY OF INTERIOR.
JUN 1 1903

"Nos 1 to 6 inclusive; testimony relative to continuous residence for a period of three years submitted December 10, 1906."

IDENTIFIED MISSISSIPPI CHOCTAWS 1902 - 1909
Volume II

IDENTIFIED MISSISSIPPI CHOCTAWS   CARD NO. 436

IDENTIFICATION ADDRESS Coffadeliah, Miss.   SETTLEMENT ADDRESS
DATE OF IDENTIFICATION April 11, 1903.   DATE OF PROOF OF SETTLEMENT

APPROVED ROLL No.	DAWES ROLL NO.	NAME	RELATIONSHIP TO PERSON FIRST NAMED	AGE	SEX	BLOOD
	1270	1 Tubbee, John		22	M	Full
		2 DID NOT SUBMIT PROOF OF				
		3 REMOVAL AND BONA-FIDE SET-				
		4 TLEMENT WITHIN ONE YEAR				
		5 FROM DATE OF IDENTIFICATION				
		6				
		7				
		8				
		9				
		10				
		11				

NAME OF FATHER	LIVING OR DEAD	NAME OF MOTHER	LIVING OR DEAD	APPLICATION NO.	REMARKS
1 Lewis Tubbee		Celia Tubbee	dead	1898	
2					
3					
4					
5					
6					
7					
8					
9					
10					
11					

APPROVED BY SECRETARY OF INTERIOR.
JUN 1 1903

IDENTIFIED MISSISSIPPI CHOCTAWS 1902 - 1909
Volume II

IDENTIFIED MISSISSIPPI CHOCTAWS CARD NO. 437

IDENTIFICATION ADDRESS Ennis, Miss. SETTLEMENT ADDRESS Ardmore I.T.
DATE OF IDENTIFICATION April 11, 1903. DATE OF PROOF OF SETTLEMENT August 21, 1903.

APPROVED ROLL No.	DAWES ROLL NO.	NAME	RELATIONSHIP TO PERSON FIRST NAMED	AGE	SEX	BLOOD
	1271	1 Porter, Jesse		45	M	Full
	1272	2 " Betsey	Wife	40	F	Full
	1273	3 " Jenkins	Son	16	M	Full
	1274	4 " Thornton	Son	9	M	Full

1 2 3&4

CITIZENSHIP CERTIFICATE ISSUED FOR NO 1-2-3-4 AUG 21 1903

NAME OF FATHER	LIVING OR DEAD	NAME OF MOTHER	LIVING OR DEAD	APPLICATION NO.	REMARKS
Ho-yubbee					
1 Jim Porter	dead	Hon-te-mah	Dead	2015	
2 Ah-be-te-tubbee	"	Mary	"	2015	
3 No.1		No.2		2015	
4 No.1		No.2		2015	

"Nos 1,2,3&4: Proof of continuous residence for a period of three years submitted September 4, 1906."

APPROVED BY SECRETARY OF INTERIOR.
JUN 1 1903

IDENTIFIED MISSISSIPPI CHOCTAWS 1902 - 1909
Volume II

IDENTIFIED MISSISSIPPI CHOCTAWS CARD NO. 438

IDENTIFICATION ADDRESS Piketon, Miss.   SETTLEMENT ADDRESS
DATE OF IDENTIFICATION April 11, 1903.   DATE OF PROOF OF SETTLEMENT

APPROVED ROLL No.	DAWES ROLL NO.	NAME	RELATIONSHIP TO PERSON FIRST NAMED	AGE	SEX	BLOOD
	[???]5	1 Williamson, Mack		25	M	Full
	[???]6	2 " Ida	Wife	21	F	Full
	[???]7	3 " Ruby	Dau	1	F	Full
		4				
		5				
		6				
		7				
		8				
		9				
		10				
		11				

DID NOT SUBMIT PROOF OF REMOVAL AND BONA-FIDE SETTLEMENT WITHIN ONE YEAR FROM DATE OF IDENTIFICATION.

NAME OF FATHER	LIVING OR DEAD	NAME OF MOTHER	LIVING OR DEAD	APPLICATION NO.	REMARKS
1 Lewis Williamson	Dead	Becky Williamson	Dead	4013	
2 Sam Cain		Don't know	Dead	4013	
3 No.1		No.2		4013	
4					
5					
6					
7					
8					
9					
10					
11					

APPROVED BY SECRETARY OF INTERIOR.
JUN 1 1903

IDENTIFIED MISSISSIPPI CHOCTAWS 1902 - 1909
Volume II

IDENTIFIED MISSISSIPPI CHOCTAWS   CARD NO. 439

IDENTIFICATION ADDRESS DeKalb, Miss. SETTLEMENT ADDRESS
DATE OF IDENTIFICATION April 11, 1903. DATE OF PROOF OF SETTLEMENT

APPROVED ROLL No.	DAWES ROLL NO.		NAME	RELATIONSHIP TO PERSON FIRST NAMED	AGE	SEX	BLOOD
	[???]8	1	Me-sham-ho-nah		76	F	Full
		2					
		3					
		4					
		5					
		6					
		7					
		8					
		9					
		10					
		11					

DID NOT SUBMIT PROOF OF REMOVAL AND BONA-FIDE SETTLEMENT WITHIN ONE YEAR FROM DATE OF IDENTIFICATION

NAME OF FATHER	LIVING OR DEAD	NAME OF MOTHER	LIVING OR DEAD	APPLICATION NO.	REMARKS
1 Pisahombee	Dead	Mollie-hokee	Dead	2469	
2					
3					
4					
5					
6					
7					
8					
9					
10					
11					

APPROVED BY SECRETARY OF INTERIOR.
JUN 1 1903

IDENTIFIED MISSISSIPPI CHOCTAWS 1902 - 1909
Volume II

IDENTIFIED MISSISSIPPI CHOCTAWS   CARD NO. 440

IDENTIFICATION ADDRESS Cooksey, Miss.   SETTLEMENT ADDRESS #2&4 Atoka I.T.
DATE OF IDENTIFICATION April 11, 1903.   DATE OF PROOF OF SETTLEMENT #2&4 Aug. 18/03.

APPROVED ROLL No.	DAWES ROLL NO.	NAME	RELATIONSHIP TO PERSON FIRST NAMED	AGE	SEX	BLOOD
	1279	1 Lewis, Jim		26	M	Full
	1280	2 " Mollie	Wife	24	F	Full
	1281	3 " Johnnie	Son	6	M	Full
	1282	4 " Martha	Dau	19mo	F	Full
		5				
		6	2 & 4			
		7				
		8				

CITIZENSHIP CERTIFICATE ISSUED FOR NO 2-4 AUG 18 1905

Nos 1&3 DID NOT SUBMIT PROOF OF REMOVAL AND BONA-FIDE SETTLEMENT WITHIN ONE YEAR FROM DATE OF IDENTIFICATION

	NAME OF FATHER	LIVING OR DEAD	NAME OF MOTHER	LIVING OR DEAD	APPLICATION NO.	REMARKS
1	Jim Lewis	Dead	Martha Lewis		2991	
2	Charley Jackson		Frances Jackson		2991	
3	No.1		No.2		2991	
4	No.1		No.2		2991	

Declaration and proof of settlement of Aug 18/03 applies to Nos. 2 & 4 only.

APPROVED BY SECRETARY OF INTERIOR.
JUN 1 1903

"Nos 2 and 4: Testimony as to continuous residence for a period of three years submitted August 22, 1906."

IDENTIFIED MISSISSIPPI CHOCTAWS 1902 - 1909
Volume II

IDENTIFIED MISSISSIPPI CHOCTAWS CARD NO. 441

IDENTIFICATION ADDRESS Conehatta, Miss.   SETTLEMENT ADDRESS
DATE OF IDENTIFICATION April 11, 1903.   DATE OF PROOF OF SETTLEMENT

APPROVED ROLL No.	DAWES ROLL NO.	NAME	RELATIONSHIP TO PERSON FIRST NAMED	AGE	SEX	BLOOD
		1 Farmer, Polly		60	F	Full

NAME OF FATHER	LIVING OR DEAD	NAME OF MOTHER	LIVING OR DEAD	APPLICATION NO.	REMARKS
1 Pi-li-tubbee	dead	Don't know	dead	4059	

APPROVED BY SECRETARY OF INTERIOR.
JUN 1 1903

IDENTIFIED MISSISSIPPI CHOCTAWS 1902 - 1909
Volume II

IDENTIFIED MISSISSIPPI CHOCTAWS CARD NO. 442

IDENTIFICATION ADDRESS Jackson, Miss. SETTLEMENT ADDRESS Ardmore I.T.
DATE OF IDENTIFICATION April 11, 1903. DATE OF PROOF OF SETTLEMENT Nov 16/03.

APPROVED ROLL No.	DAWES ROLL NO.	NAME		RELATIONSHIP TO PERSON FIRST NAMED	AGE	SEX	BLOOD
		1	Robison, Henry		38	M	Full
		2	" Jane	Wife	40	F	Full
		3	" Alice	Dau	7	F	Full
		4	" Eula	Dau	5	F	Full
		5					
		6					
		7	ENROLLMENT				
		8	2 3 & 4				

CITIZENSHIP CERTIFICATE
ISSUED FOR NO 2-3
~~NOV 25 1903~~
JAN 11 04

NAME OF FATHER	LIVING OR DEAD	NAME OF MOTHER	LIVING OR DEAD	APPLICATION NO.	REMARKS
1 Charley Robison	dead	Liza Robison	dead	2684	
2 John Gibson	"	~~~~~~~~~	"	2684	
3 No.1		No.2		2684	
4 No.1		No.2		2684	
5					
6					
7					
8					
9					
10		Nos 2, 3 & 4. Proof of continuous residence for a period of three years submitted June 11, 1906.			
11					

APPROVED BY SECRETARY OF INTERIOR. Declaration and proof of settlement of Nov 16/03 apply to Nos. 2, 3 & 4 only
JUN 1 1903

No.2 is wife of No.1 Miss Choc card No. 555.

IDENTIFIED MISSISSIPPI CHOCTAWS 1902 - 1909
Volume II

IDENTIFIED MISSISSIPPI CHOCTAWS CARD NO. 443

IDENTIFICATION ADDRESS Vernon, Miss.   SETTLEMENT ADDRESS Durwood I.T.
DATE OF IDENTIFICATION April 11, 1903.   DATE OF PROOF OF SETTLEMENT Nov. 24, 03.

APPROVED ROLL No.	DAWES ROLL NO.	NAME	RELATIONSHIP TO PERSON FIRST NAMED	AGE	SEX	BLOOD
		1. Lewis, Caroline		48	F	Full
		2. " Ollie	Dau	10	F	Full
		3. " Martha	Dau	2	F	Full
		4.				
		5.				
		6.				
		7. 2 & 3				
		8.				

CITIZENSHIP CERTIFICATE
ISSUED FOR NO 1-2-3
~~DEC 17 1903~~

	NAME OF FATHER	LIVING OR DEAD	NAME OF MOTHER	LIVING OR DEAD	APPLICATION NO.	REMARKS
1	~~~~~~~~~~		Jennie Lewis		2458	
2	Sancom John		No.1		2458	
3	" "		No.1		2458	
4						
5						
6						
7						
8						
9						
10			"Nos 1, 2 and 3: Proof of continuous residence for a period of three years submitted August 27, 1906."			
11						

APPROVED BY SECRETARY OF INTERIOR.
JUN 1 1903

IDENTIFIED MISSISSIPPI CHOCTAWS 1902 - 1909
Volume II

IDENTIFIED MISSISSIPPI CHOCTAWS

CARD NO. 444

IDENTIFICATION ADDRESS Conehatta, Miss. SETTLEMENT ADDRESS
DATE OF IDENTIFICATION April 11, 1903. DATE OF PROOF OF SETTLEMENT

APPROVED ROLL No.	DAWES ROLL NO.	NAME	RELATIONSHIP TO PERSON FIRST NAMED	AGE	SEX	BLOOD
		1 Farmer, Susan		20	F	Full
		2				
		3				
		4				
		5				
		6				
		7				
		8				
		9				
		10				
		11				

NAME OF FATHER	LIVING OR DEAD	NAME OF MOTHER	LIVING OR DEAD	APPLICATION NO.	REMARKS
1 John Farmer		Jennie Farmer	dead	3956	
2					
3					
4					
5					
6					
7					
8					
9					
10					
11					

APPROVED BY SECRETARY OF INTERIOR.
JUN 1 1903

IDENTIFIED MISSISSIPPI CHOCTAWS 1902 - 1909
Volume II

IDENTIFIED MISSISSIPPI CHOCTAWS

CARD NO. 445

IDENTIFICATION ADDRESS Waldo, Miss.   SETTLEMENT ADDRESS
DATE OF IDENTIFICATION April 11, 1903.   DATE OF PROOF OF SETTLEMENT

APPROVED ROLL No.	DAWES ROLL NO.	NAME	RELATIONSHIP TO PERSON FIRST NAMED	AGE	SEX	BLOOD
		Ock-lo-tubbee				
	1292	1 Steve, Tom		30	M	Full
	1293	2 " Martha	Wife	31	F	Full
	1294	3 " Lucy	Dau	12	F	Full
	1295	4 " Smith	Son	6	M	Full

CITIZENSHIP CERTIFICATE ISSUED FOR NO 1903

NAME OF FATHER	LIVING OR DEAD	NAME OF MOTHER	LIVING OR DEAD	APPLICATION NO.	REMARKS
Con-ne-o tubbee					
1 Steve Tillis		Jane Tillis		4473	
2 Isac[sic] Im-ok-lah	dead	Betsey ~~~~	dead	4473	
3 No.1		No.2		4473	
4 No.1		No.2		4473	

APPROVED BY SECRETARY OF INTERIOR.
JUN 1 1903

IDENTIFIED MISSISSIPPI CHOCTAWS 1902 - 1909
Volume II

IDENTIFIED MISSISSIPPI CHOCTAWS   CARD NO. 446

IDENTIFICATION ADDRESS Newton, Miss.   SETTLEMENT ADDRESS Paucaunla, I.T.
DATE OF IDENTIFICATION April 17, 1903.   DATE OF PROOF OF SETTLEMENT Sept 11/03.

APPROVED ROLL No.	DAWES ROLL NO.	NAME	RELATIONSHIP TO PERSON FIRST NAMED	AGE	SEX	BLOOD
		Kon-ni-ah-tubbee-				
		1 Lewis, Charles		53	M	Full
		2 " Lila	Wife	60	F	Full
		3				
		4				
		5				
		6				
		7				
		8				
CITIZENSHIP CERTIFICATE ISSUED FOR NO 1-2 SEP 11 1903						
		11				

ENROLLMENT OF NOS. 1 & 2 HEREON APPROVED BY THE SECRETARY OF INTERIOR JAN 11 1905

NAME OF FATHER	LIVING OR DEAD	NAME OF MOTHER	LIVING OR DEAD	APPLICATION NO.	REMARKS
1 Old Man Charley	dead	Sallie Charley	dead	3470	
2 Don't know	"	Don't know	"	3470	
3					
4					
5					
6					
7					
8		Nº 2 Testimony relative to continuous residence for a period of three years submitted February 24-1908			
9		"No.1 died February 21, 1904: testimony as to continuous residence up to his death submitted June 21, 1906."			
10					
11					

APPROVED BY SECRETARY OF INTERIOR.
JUN 1 1903

IDENTIFIED MISSISSIPPI CHOCTAWS 1902 - 1909
Volume II

IDENTIFIED MISSISSIPPI CHOCTAWS   CARD NO. 447

IDENTIFICATION ADDRESS Tullis, La.   SETTLEMENT ADDRESS
DATE OF IDENTIFICATION April 17, 1903.   DATE OF PROOF OF SETTLEMENT

APPROVED ROLL No.	DAWES ROLL NO.	NAME	RELATIONSHIP TO PERSON FIRST NAMED	AGE	SEX	BLOOD
		1 Allen, Sally Ann		30	F	Full

NAME OF FATHER	LIVING OR DEAD	NAME OF MOTHER	LIVING OR DEAD	APPLICATION NO.	REMARKS
1 John Allen		Betsey Allen	dead	5951	

APPROVED BY SECRETARY OF INTERIOR.
JUN 1 1903

IDENTIFIED MISSISSIPPI CHOCTAWS 1902 - 1909
Volume II

IDENTIFIED MISSISSIPPI CHOCTAWS   CARD NO. 448

IDENTIFICATION ADDRESS Hays, Miss.   SETTLEMENT ADDRESS
DATE OF IDENTIFICATION April 17, 1903.   DATE OF PROOF OF SETTLEMENT

APPROVED ROLL No.	DAWES ROLL NO.	NAME	RELATIONSHIP TO PERSON FIRST NAMED	AGE	SEX	BLOOD
		1 Isom, Jack		50	M	Full
		2 " Martha	Wife	36	F	Full
		3 " Wes	Son	19	M	Full
		4 " Billie J.	"	11	M	Full
		5 " Bill	"	5	M	Full
		6				
		7				
		8				
		9				
		10				
		11				

NAME OF FATHER	LIVING OR DEAD	NAME OF MOTHER	LIVING OR DEAD	APPLICATION NO.	REMARKS
1 Jacob ~~~	dead	Beckey Jacob		4191	
2 Don't know	dead	Don't know	dead	4191	
3 No.1		No.2		4191	
4 No.1		No.2		4191	
5 No.1		No.2		4191	
6					
7					
8					
9					
10					
11					

APPROVED BY SECRETARY OF INTERIOR.
    JUN 1   1903

IDENTIFIED MISSISSIPPI CHOCTAWS 1902 - 1909
Volume II

IDENTIFIED MISSISSIPPI CHOCTAWS   CARD NO. 449

IDENTIFICATION ADDRESS Saint Anns[sic], Miss.   SETTLEMENT ADDRESS

DATE OF IDENTIFICATION April 17, 1903.   DATE OF PROOF OF SETTLEMENT

APPROVED ROLL No.	DAWES ROLL NO.	NAME	RELATIONSHIP TO PERSON FIRST NAMED	AGE	SEX	BLOOD
		1 Chitto, Pat		24	M	Full
		2 " Laura	Wife	20	F	Full
		3 " Leona	Dau	5	F	Full
		4 " Sissy	Dau	1	F	Full
		5				
		6				
		7				
		8				
		9				
		10				
		11				

NAME OF FATHER	LIVING OR DEAD	NAME OF MOTHER	LIVING OR DEAD	APPLICATION NO.	REMARKS
1 Tom Chitto		Minerva Chitto		2091	
2 Scott York		Sealy York		2091	
3 No.1		Rhoda (Lutie) Chitto		2091	
4 No.1		Laura Chitto		2091	
5					
6					
7					
8					
9					
10					
11					

APPROVED BY SECRETARY OF INTERIOR.
JUN 1 1903

IDENTIFIED MISSISSIPPI CHOCTAWS 1902 - 1909
Volume II

IDENTIFIED MISSISSIPPI CHOCTAWS

CARD NO. 450

IDENTIFICATION ADDRESS Tullis, La.　　SETTLEMENT ADDRESS
DATE OF IDENTIFICATION April 17, 1903.　　DATE OF PROOF OF SETTLEMENT

APPROVED ROLL No.	DAWES ROLL NO.		NAME	RELATIONSHIP TO PERSON FIRST NAMED	AGE	SEX	BLOOD
		1	Allen, Young		Don't Know [32]	M	Full
		2					
		3					
		4					
		5					
		6					
		7					
		8					
		9					
		10					
		11					

DID NOT SUBMIT PROOF OF REMOVAL AND BONA-FIDE SETTLEMENT WITHIN ONE YEAR FROM DATE OF IDENTIFICATION

	NAME OF FATHER	LIVING OR DEAD	NAME OF MOTHER	LIVING OR DEAD	APPLICATION NO.	REMARKS
1	John Allen		Betsey Allen	dead	5952	
2						
3						
4						
5						
6						
7						
8						
9						
10						
11						

APPROVED BY SECRETARY OF INTERIOR.
　　JUN 1　1903

IDENTIFIED MISSISSIPPI CHOCTAWS 1902 - 1909
Volume II

IDENTIFIED MISSISSIPPI CHOCTAWS CARD NO. 451

IDENTIFICATION ADDRESS Cushtusa, Miss.   SETTLEMENT ADDRESS Stigler I.T.
DATE OF IDENTIFICATION April 17, 1903.   DATE OF PROOF OF SETTLEMENT Nov. 25, 03.

APPROVED ROLL No.	DAWES ROLL NO.	NAME	RELATIONSHIP TO PERSON FIRST NAMED	AGE	SEX	BLOOD
		1. Davis, Edna		27	F	Full
		2. " Linnie	Dau	6	F	Full
		3. " Louella	Dau	4	F	Full
		4.				
		5.				
		6.				
		7.				
		8. 1 2 & 3				

CITIZENSHIP CERTIFICATE
ISSUED FOR NO 1-2-3
NOV 25 1903

NAME OF FATHER	LIVING OR DEAD	NAME OF MOTHER	LIVING OR DEAD	APPLICATION NO.	REMARKS
1. Thompson	dead	Sallie Gibson		2053	
2. Ellis Davis	"	No.1		2053	
3. " "	"	No.1		2053	
4.					
5.					
6.		Nos. 1&2 = Testimony relative to continuous residence from date of settlement until date of death submitted September 14, 1908.			
7.					
8.		No.3 = Testimony relative to continuous residence for a period of three years submitted Sept. 14-08.			
9.					
10.					
11.					

APPROVED BY SECRETARY OF INTERIOR.
JUN 1 1903

IDENTIFIED MISSISSIPPI CHOCTAWS 1902 - 1909
Volume II

IDENTIFIED MISSISSIPPI CHOCTAWS   CARD NO. 452

IDENTIFICATION ADDRESS Hope, Miss.   SETTLEMENT ADDRESS
DATE OF IDENTIFICATION April 17, 1903.   DATE OF PROOF OF SETTLEMENT

APPROVED ROLL No.	DAWES ROLL NO.		NAME		RELATIONSHIP TO PERSON FIRST NAMED	AGE	SEX	BLOOD
		1	Ma-hat-sti-ah, Sallie			62	F	Full
		2	" Jefferson		Husb	63	M	Full
		3						
		4						
		5						
		6						
		7						
		8						
		9						
		10						
		11						

NAME OF FATHER		LIVING OR DEAD	NAME OF MOTHER	LIVING OR DEAD	APPLICATION NO.	REMARKS
1 Jim Cun-no-tubbee		dead	Don't know	dead	4492	
2 Ma-hat-sti-ah		dead	Bitsey	dead	4492	
3						
4						
5						
6						
7						
8						
9						
10						
11						

APPROVED BY SECRETARY OF INTERIOR.
JUN 1 1903

IDENTIFIED MISSISSIPPI CHOCTAWS 1902 - 1909
Volume II

IDENTIFIED MISSISSIPPI CHOCTAWS CARD NO. 453

IDENTIFICATION ADDRESS Newton, Miss. SETTLEMENT ADDRESS Paucaunla I.T.
DATE OF IDENTIFICATION April 17, 1903. DATE OF PROOF OF SETTLEMENT Nov 14/03.

APPROVED ROLL No.	DAWES ROLL NO.	NAME	RELATIONSHIP TO PERSON FIRST NAMED	AGE	SEX	BLOOD
		1 Lewis, Sim		20	M	Full
		2 " Minnie	Wife	19	F	Full
		3 " Lonie	Dau	3m	F	Full
		4				
		5				
		6				
		7				
		8	1 2 & 3			
CITIZENSHIP CERTIFICATE ISSUED FOR NO 1-2-3 NOV 13 1903						
		11				

NAME OF FATHER	LIVING OR DEAD	NAME OF MOTHER	LIVING OR DEAD	APPLICATION NO.	REMARKS
1 Charles Lewis		Lila Lewis		3471	
2 John Nickson	dead	Don't know	dead	3471	
3 No.1		No.2		3471	
4					
5					
6					
7					
8					
9		Nº 2 Testimony relative to continuous residence for a period of three years submitted February 19-1908			
10					
11					

APPROVED BY SECRETARY OF INTERIOR.
JUN 1 1903

"Nos. 1 and 3: Testimony as to continuous residence of Nos 1 and 3 up to their death submitted June 21, 1906, and July 24, 1906."

"No1 died February 4, 1904;
No3 died Aug. 5, 1904: evidence received July 24, 1906."

IDENTIFIED MISSISSIPPI CHOCTAWS 1902 - 1909
Volume II

IDENTIFIED MISSISSIPPI CHOCTAWS   CARD NO. 454

IDENTIFICATION ADDRESS Melon, Miss.   SETTLEMENT ADDRESS Kiowa I.T.
DATE OF IDENTIFICATION April 17, 1903.   DATE OF PROOF OF SETTLEMENT Oct 23/03

APPROVED ROLL No.	DAWES ROLL NO.	NAME	RELATIONSHIP TO PERSON FIRST NAMED	AGE	SEX	BLOOD
		1 Lewis, Jesse		23	M	Full
		2				
		3				
		4				
		5				
		6				
		7				
		8				
		9				
		10				
		11				

CITIZENSHIP CERTIFICATE ISSUED FOR NO 1 OCT 23 1903

NAME OF FATHER	LIVING OR DEAD	NAME OF MOTHER	LIVING OR DEAD	APPLICATION NO.	REMARKS
1 John Lewis	dead	Malissa Lewis	dead	2607	
2					
3					
4					
5					
6					
7					
8					
9					
10					
11					

APPROVED BY SECRETARY OF INTERIOR.
JUN 1 1903

"No.1 Testimony as to continuous residence for a period of three years submitted July 21, 1906."

IDENTIFIED MISSISSIPPI CHOCTAWS 1902 - 1909
Volume II

IDENTIFIED MISSISSIPPI CHOCTAWS

CARD NO. 455

IDENTIFICATION ADDRESS Conehatta, Miss.
SETTLEMENT ADDRESS
DATE OF IDENTIFICATION April 17, 1903.
DATE OF PROOF OF SETTLEMENT

APPROVED ROLL No.	DAWES ROLL NO.	NAME	RELATIONSHIP TO PERSON FIRST NAMED	AGE	SEX	BLOOD
		1. Lewis, Lotie		15	F	Full

NAME OF FATHER	LIVING OR DEAD	NAME OF MOTHER	LIVING OR DEAD	APPLICATION NO.	REMARKS
1. Elder Jackson		Sarah Johnson	dead	2992	

APPROVED BY SECRETARY OF INTERIOR.
JUN 1 1903

IDENTIFIED MISSISSIPPI CHOCTAWS 1902 - 1909
Volume II

IDENTIFIED MISSISSIPPI CHOCTAWS CARD NO. 456

IDENTIFICATION ADDRESS Decatur, Miss. SETTLEMENT ADDRESS No.1 Calloway I.T.
DATE OF IDENTIFICATION April 17, 1903. DATE OF PROOF OF SETTLEMENT No.1 Jany 8/04.

APPROVED ROLL No.	DAWES ROLL NO.		NAME	RELATIONSHIP TO PERSON FIRST NAMED	AGE	SEX	BLOOD
		1	Lewis, John		21	M	Full
		2	" Fannie	Wife	17	F	Full
		3					
		4					
		5					
		6					
		7					
		8					

CITIZENSHIP CERTIFICATE
ISSUED FOR NO ~~1~~
JAN 8 1904

	NAME OF FATHER	LIVING OR DEAD	NAME OF MOTHER	LIVING OR DEAD	APPLICATION NO.	REMARKS
1	John Lewis	dead	Malissa Lewis	dead	2826	
2	John William		Jinnie William		2826	
3						
4						
5						
6						
7						
8						
9						
10						
11						

APPROVED BY SECRETARY OF INTERIOR. Declaration and proof of settlement of
JUN 1 1903 Jany 8/04 apply to No1 only.

"No. 1 Testimony relative to continuous residence for a period of three years submitted September 1, 1906."

IDENTIFIED MISSISSIPPI CHOCTAWS 1902 - 1909
Volume II

IDENTIFIED MISSISSIPPI CHOCTAWS   CARD NO. 457

IDENTIFICATION ADDRESS Williston, Miss.   SETTLEMENT ADDRESS
DATE OF IDENTIFICATION April 17, 1903.   DATE OF PROOF OF SETTLEMENT

APPROVED ROLL No.	DAWES ROLL NO.	NAME	RELATIONSHIP TO PERSON FIRST NAMED	AGE	SEX	BLOOD
		1 Johnson, Wesley		52	M	Full
		2 " Nicey	Wife	36	F	Full
		3 " Lula	Dau	18	F	Full
		4 " Henry	Son	14	M	Full
		5 " Martha	Dau	11	F	Full
		6 " Alice	Dau	6	F	Full
		7				
		8				
		9				
		10				
		11				

	NAME OF FATHER	LIVING OR DEAD	NAME OF MOTHER	LIVING OR DEAD	APPLICATION NO.	REMARKS
1	~~Wah-ea-tubbee~~ Johnson	dead	Don't know	dead	4217	
2	Don't know	dead	Don't know	dead	4217	
3	No.1		No.2			
4	No.1		No.2			
5	No.1		No.2			
6	No.1		No.2			
7						
8						
9						
10						
11						

APPROVED BY SECRETARY OF INTERIOR.
JUN 1   1903

IDENTIFIED MISSISSIPPI CHOCTAWS 1902 - 1909
Volume II

IDENTIFIED MISSISSIPPI CHOCTAWS   CARD NO. 458

IDENTIFICATION ADDRESS Gholson, Miss.   SETTLEMENT ADDRESS
DATE OF IDENTIFICATION April 17, 1903.   DATE OF PROOF OF SETTLEMENT

APPROVED ROLL No.	DAWES ROLL NO.	NAME	RELATIONSHIP TO PERSON FIRST NAMED	AGE	SEX	BLOOD
		1 Jones, Henry		20	M	Full
		2				
		3				
		4				
		5				
		6				
		7				
		8				
		9				
		10				
		11				

NAME OF FATHER	LIVING OR DEAD	NAME OF MOTHER	LIVING OR DEAD	APPLICATION NO.	REMARKS
1 Joe Jones		Lucy Jones	dead	3171	
2					
3					
4					
5					
6					
7					
8					
9					
10					
11					

APPROVED BY SECRETARY OF INTERIOR.
JUN 1 1903

IDENTIFIED MISSISSIPPI CHOCTAWS 1902 - 1909
Volume II

IDENTIFIED MISSISSIPPI CHOCTAWS   CARD NO. 459

IDENTIFICATION ADDRESS Lucern, Miss.   SETTLEMENT ADDRESS Byars, Ind. Ter.
DATE OF IDENTIFICATION April 17, 1903.   DATE OF PROOF OF SETTLEMENT July 13, 1903.

APPROVED ROLL No.	DAWES ROLL NO.	NAME	RELATIONSHIP TO PERSON FIRST NAMED	AGE	SEX	BLOOD
		1. Johnson, Cook		23	M	Full
		2. " Eliza	Wife	20	F	Full
		3.				
		4.				
		5.				
		6.				
		7.				
		8.	1&2			
CITIZENSHIP CERTIFICATE ISSUED FOR NO 1-2- JUL 13 1903						
		11.				

NAME OF FATHER	LIVING OR DEAD	NAME OF MOTHER	LIVING OR DEAD	APPLICATION NO.	REMARKS
1. Bob Johnson	dead	Nancy Johnson		3001	
2. John Meely		Leanna Meely		3001	
3.					
4.					
5.					
6.					
7.					
8.					
9.					
10.					
11.					

APPROVED BY SECRETARY OF INTERIOR.
   JUN 1 1903

   Nos. 1&2. Testimony as to continuous residence of Nos 1&2 for a period of three years submitted April 24, 1906.

IDENTIFIED MISSISSIPPI CHOCTAWS 1902 - 1909
Volume II

IDENTIFIED MISSISSIPPI CHOCTAWS CARD NO. 460

IDENTIFICATION ADDRESS Hamlet, Miss. SETTLEMENT ADDRESS
DATE OF IDENTIFICATION April 17, 1903. DATE OF PROOF OF SETTLEMENT

APPROVED ROLL No.	DAWES ROLL NO.	NAME	RELATIONSHIP TO PERSON FIRST NAMED	AGE	SEX	BLOOD
		1 John, Billie		85	M	Full
		2 " Sookey	Wife	80	F	Full
		3				
		4				
		5				
		6				
		7				
		8				
		9				
		10				
		11				

NAME OF FATHER	LIVING OR DEAD	NAME OF MOTHER	LIVING OR DEAD	APPLICATION NO.	REMARKS
1 ~~~~~~	dead	~~~~~~	dead	2994	
2 Tom	dead	~~~~~~	dead	2994	
3					
4					
5					
6					
7					
8					
9					
10					
11					

APPROVED BY SECRETARY OF INTERIOR.
JUN 1 1903

IDENTIFIED MISSISSIPPI CHOCTAWS 1902 - 1909
Volume II

IDENTIFIED MISSISSIPPI CHOCTAWS   CARD NO. 461

IDENTIFICATION ADDRESS Trapp, Miss.   SETTLEMENT ADDRESS
DATE OF IDENTIFICATION April 17, 1903.   DATE OF PROOF OF SETTLEMENT

APPROVED ROLL No.	DAWES ROLL NO.	NAME	RELATIONSHIP TO PERSON FIRST NAMED	AGE	SEX	BLOOD
		1 Jim-Isaac, Wilson		48	M	Full
		2 " " Martha	Wife	36	F	Full
		3 " " Lee	Son	7	M	Full
		4 " " William	Son	6	M	Full
		5 " " Jackson	Son	14mo	M	Full
		6				
		7				
		8				
		9				
		10				
		11				

NAME OF FATHER	LIVING OR DEAD	NAME OF MOTHER	LIVING OR DEAD	APPLICATION NO.	REMARKS
1 Jim Isaac Tin-cha ~~Im-miah-tubbee~~		Mary Isaac He-ka		4501	
2 John Waiter	dead	Emily Waiter	dead	4501	
3 No.1		No.2		4501	
4 No.1		No.2		4501	
5 No.1		No.2		4501	
6					
7					
8					
9					
10					
11					

APPROVED BY SECRETARY OF INTERIOR.
JUN 1 1903

IDENTIFIED MISSISSIPPI CHOCTAWS 1902 - 1909
Volume II

IDENTIFIED MISSISSIPPI CHOCTAWS CARD NO. 462

IDENTIFICATION ADDRESS Conehatta, Miss. SETTLEMENT ADDRESS Byars, Ind. Ter.

DATE OF IDENTIFICATION April 17, 1903. DATE OF PROOF OF SETTLEMENT August 1, 1903.

APPROVED ROLL No.	DAWES ROLL NO.	NAME	RELATIONSHIP TO PERSON FIRST NAMED	AGE	SEX	BLOOD
		1. Meely, Jim		24	M	Full
		2. " Lula	Wife	26	F	Full
		3. " Amos	Son	3	M	Full
		4. " Fannie	Dau	18mo	F	Full
		5.				
		6.				
		7.				
		8. 1 2 3 & 4				

CITIZENSHIP CERTIFICATE ISSUED FOR NO 1-2-3-4 AUG 1 1903

	NAME OF FATHER	LIVING OR DEAD	NAME OF MOTHER	LIVING OR DEAD	APPLICATION NO.	REMARKS
1	John Meely	dead	Leanna Meely		3006	
2	Doctor Dixon		Betsey Dixon	dead	3006	
3	No.1		No.2		3006	
4	No.1		No.2		3006	
5						
6						
7						
8						
9						
10						
11						

APPROVED BY SECRETARY OF INTERIOR.
JUN 1 1903

"Nos 1,2,3 and 4: Proof of continuous residence for a period of three years submitted February 6, 1907."

IDENTIFIED MISSISSIPPI CHOCTAWS 1902 - 1909
Volume II

IDENTIFIED MISSISSIPPI CHOCTAWS CARD NO. 463

IDENTIFICATION ADDRESS Hays, Miss. SETTLEMENT ADDRESS
DATE OF IDENTIFICATION April 17, 1903. DATE OF PROOF OF SETTLEMENT

APPROVED ROLL No.	DAWES ROLL NO.		NAME	RELATIONSHIP TO PERSON FIRST NAMED	AGE	SEX	BLOOD
		1	Martin, Elizabeth		31	F	Full
		2	" Manuel	Son	14	M	Full
		3	" Ona	Dau	12	F	Full
		4					
		5					
		6					
		7					
		8					
		9					
		10					
		11					

	NAME OF FATHER	LIVING OR DEAD	NAME OF MOTHER	LIVING OR DEAD	APPLICATION NO.	REMARKS
1	~John~	dead	Nancy John		4237	
2	Willie Martin	"	No.1		4237	
3	" "	"	No.1		4237	
4						
5						
6						
7						
8						
9						
10						
11						

APPROVED BY SECRETARY OF INTERIOR.
JUN 1 1903

IDENTIFIED MISSISSIPPI CHOCTAWS 1902 - 1909
Volume II

IDENTIFIED MISSISSIPPI CHOCTAWS   CARD NO. 464

IDENTIFICATION ADDRESS Madden, Miss.   SETTLEMENT ADDRESS Roff, I.T.
DATE OF IDENTIFICATION April 17, 1903.   DATE OF PROOF OF SETTLEMENT Sept 28/03.

APPROVED ROLL No.	DAWES ROLL NO.		NAME	RELATIONSHIP TO PERSON FIRST NAMED	AGE	SEX	BLOOD
		1	Martin, Sallie		52	F	Full
		2	" Jacob	Son	19	M	Full
		3					
		4					
		5					
		6					
		7					
		8					
CITIZENSHIP CERTIFICATE ISSUED FOR NO 1-2- SEP 28 1903							
		11					

CITIZENSHIP CERTIFICATE ISSUED FOR NO 1-2- SEP 28 1903

ENROLLMENT 1&2

	NAME OF FATHER	LIVING OR DEAD	NAME OF MOTHER	LIVING OR DEAD	APPLICATION NO.	REMARKS
1	John Billey	dead	Bessie Billey	dead	4487	
2	Martin Weshock	"	No.1		4487	
3						
4						
5						
6						
7						
8						
9						
10						
11						

APPROVED BY SECRETARY OF INTERIOR.
JUN 1   1903

"No.2: Proof of continuous residence for a period of three years submitted December 20, 1906."

"No1: Proof of continuous residence for a period of three years submitted April 24-1907."

IDENTIFIED MISSISSIPPI CHOCTAWS 1902 - 1909
Volume II

IDENTIFIED MISSISSIPPI CHOCTAWS CARD NO. 465

IDENTIFICATION ADDRESS Madden, Miss.   SETTLEMENT ADDRESS
DATE OF IDENTIFICATION April 17, 1903.   DATE OF PROOF OF SETTLEMENT

APPROVED ROLL No.	DAWES ROLL NO.	NAME	RELATIONSHIP TO PERSON FIRST NAMED	AGE	SEX	BLOOD
		1 Martin, Nannie		30	F	Full
		2 Wilson, Neely	Dau	4	F	Full
		3				
		4				
		5				
		6				
		7				
		8				
		9				
		10				
		11				

DID NOT SUBMIT PROOF OF REMOVAL AND BONA FIDE SETTLEMENT WITHIN ONE YEAR FROM DATE OF IDENTIFICATION.

NAME OF FATHER	LIVING OR DEAD	NAME OF MOTHER	LIVING OR DEAD	APPLICATION NO.	REMARKS
1 Wes Amos		Margaret Amos	dead	4488	
2 Grandison Wilson	dead	No.1		4488	
3					
4					
5					
6					
7					
8					
9					
10					
11					

APPROVED BY SECRETARY OF INTERIOR.
JUN 1   1903

IDENTIFIED MISSISSIPPI CHOCTAWS 1902 - 1909
Volume II

IDENTIFIED MISSISSIPPI CHOCTAWS CARD NO. 466

IDENTIFICATION ADDRESS Trapp, Miss. SETTLEMENT ADDRESS
DATE OF IDENTIFICATION April 17, 1903. DATE OF PROOF OF SETTLEMENT

APPROVED ROLL No.	DAWES ROLL NO.	NAME	RELATIONSHIP TO PERSON FIRST NAMED	AGE	SEX	BLOOD
		1 Isaac, Dixon		50	M	Full
		2 " Lucy	Wife	48	F	Full
		3 " Ollie	Dau	18	F	Full
		4 " Rifey	Dau	12	F	Full
		5 " Fannie	Dau	10	F	Full
		6 " Bert	Son	8	M	Full
		7				
		8				
		9				
		10				
		11				

DID NOT SUBMIT PROOF OF REMOVAL AND BONA FIDE SETTLEMENT WITHIN ONE YEAR FROM DATE OF IDENTIFICATION.

NAME OF FATHER	LIVING OR DEAD	NAME OF MOTHER	LIVING OR DEAD	APPLICATION NO.	REMARKS
1 Jim Isaac Tin-cha		Mary Isaac		4856	
2 Billy Ste-ah-tubbee	dead	Mary Ste-ah-tubbee	dead	4856	
3 No.1		No.2		4856	
4 No.1		No.2		4856	
5 No.1		No.2		4856	
6 No.1		No.2		4856	

APPROVED BY SECRETARY OF INTERIOR.
JUN 1 1903

IDENTIFIED MISSISSIPPI CHOCTAWS 1902 - 1909
Volume II

IDENTIFIED MISSISSIPPI CHOCTAWS   CARD NO. 467

IDENTIFICATION ADDRESS Aden, Miss.   SETTLEMENT ADDRESS Ardmore I.T. No.3 Ardmore, I.T.
DATE OF IDENTIFICATION April 17, 1903.   DATE OF PROOF OF SETTLEMENT Aug 27/03

APPROVED ROLL No.	DAWES ROLL NO.	NAME	RELATIONSHIP TO PERSON FIRST NAMED	AGE	SEX	BLOOD
		1 Isaac, King		21	M	Full
		2 " Eliza	Wife	30	F	Full
		3 " Rogers	Bro.	18	M	Full
		4 " Siss	Sister	9	F	Full
		5 Cotton, Willie	Stepson	2	M	Full
		6				

CITIZENSHIP CERTIFICATE ISSUED FOR NO 1-2-4-5 AUG 28 1903

ENROLLMENT 1 2 4 & 5

CITIZEN ──3── 10
Apr 24-07

NAME OF FATHER	LIVING OR DEAD	NAME OF MOTHER	LIVING OR DEAD	APPLICATION NO.	REMARKS
1 Wiley Isaac	dead	Lucy Isaac	dead	5038	
2 Joe Bell	"	Don't know	"	5038	
3 Willy Isaac	"	Lucy Isaac	"	5038	
4 " "	"	" "	"	5038	
5 Charley Cotton	"	Eliza Isaac		5038	
6					
7					
8		"Nos 2 and 5: Proof of continuous residence for a period of three years submitted January 28, 1907."			
9					
10		Declaration and proof of settlement of Aug 27/03 applies to Nos 1-2-4-5 only.			
11					

APPROVED BY SECRETARY OF INTERIOR.
JUN 1 1903

N°3 died January 30-1903 testimony submitted June 30, 1906 as to removal and settlement, considered as proof of continuous residence from date of settlement until date of death.

No3 enrolled under Act of April 26, 1906.

N°4 Proof of continuous residence for a period of three years submitted January 8-1908

No.1 Proof of continuous residence for a period of three years submitted January 28, 1907.

IDENTIFIED MISSISSIPPI CHOCTAWS 1902 - 1909
Volume II

IDENTIFIED MISSISSIPPI CHOCTAWS   CARD NO. 468

IDENTIFICATION ADDRESS Holy Cross, Miss. SETTLEMENT ADDRESS Calloway, Ind. Ter.
DATE OF IDENTIFICATION April 17, 1903.   DATE OF PROOF OF SETTLEMENT July 11, 1903.

APPROVED ROLL No.	DAWES ROLL NO.		NAME	RELATIONSHIP TO PERSON FIRST NAMED	AGE	SEX	BLOOD
		1	Jack, Tom		37	M	Full
		2	" Eliza	Wife	26	F	Full
		3	" Ethel	Dau	8	F	Full
		4	" Silman	Son	7	M	Full
		5	" Evaline	Dau	4	F	Full
		6	" Beaman	Son	3mo	M	Full

CITIZENSHIP CERTIFICATE
ISSUED FOR NO 1-2   1 2 3 4 & 5
JUL 11 1903

CITIZENSHIP CERTIFICATE
ISSUED FOR NO 3-4-5
SEP 9 1903

NAME OF FATHER	LIVING OR DEAD	NAME OF MOTHER	LIVING OR DEAD	APPLICATION NO.	REMARKS
1 Dick Jack	dead	Martha Jack		5176	
2 Jacob	"	Betsey Me-ah-ho-nah	dead	5176	
3 No.1		No.2		5176	
4 No.1		No.2		5176	
5 No.1		No.2		5176	
6 No.1		No.2		5176	
7					
8					
9					
10					
11					

Declaration and proof of settlement applies to Nos. 1,2,3,4 and 5.

APPROVED BY SECRETARY OF INTERIOR.
        JUN 1 1903   "Nos 1,2,3 and 5: Testimony as to continuous residence for
                            a period of three years submitted July 14 and 21, 1906."

                           "No.4 died September 11, 1904: testimony as to
                            continuous residence up to his death submitted July 14 and
                            July 21, 1906."

IDENTIFIED MISSISSIPPI CHOCTAWS 1902 - 1909
Volume II

IDENTIFIED MISSISSIPPI CHOCTAWS   CARD NO. 469

IDENTIFICATION ADDRESS Tullis, Miss.   SETTLEMENT ADDRESS
DATE OF IDENTIFICATION April 17, 1903.   DATE OF PROOF OF SETTLEMENT

APPROVED ROLL No.	DAWES ROLL NO.	NAME	RELATIONSHIP TO PERSON FIRST NAMED	AGE	SEX	BLOOD
		Ah-la-pin-tubbee				
		1 Jackson, Willis		47	M	Full
		2 " Wesley	Son	11	M	Full
		3 " Martha Jane	Dau	10	F	Full
		4 " Chris	Son	8	M	Full
		5				
		6				
		7				
		8				
		9				
		10				
		11				

NAME OF FATHER	LIVING OR DEAD	NAME OF MOTHER	LIVING OR DEAD	APPLICATION NO.	REMARKS
E-la-palo-ubbee					
1 Bill Johnson	dead	Susan	dead	5959	
2 No.1		Roselia Jackson	"	5959	
3 No.1		" "	"	5959	
4 No.1		" "	"	5959	
5					
6					
7					
8					
9					
10					
11					

APPROVED BY SECRETARY OF INTERIOR.
JUN 1 1903

IDENTIFIED MISSISSIPPI CHOCTAWS 1902 - 1909
Volume II

IDENTIFIED MISSISSIPPI CHOCTAWS CARD NO. 470

IDENTIFICATION ADDRESS Tullis, La. SETTLEMENT ADDRESS
DATE OF IDENTIFICATION April 17, 1903. DATE OF PROOF OF SETTLEMENT

APPROVED ROLL No.	DAWES ROLL NO.	NAME	RELATIONSHIP TO PERSON FIRST NAMED	AGE	SEX	BLOOD
		1 Jackson, Willie		21	M	Full
		2 " Mary Ann	Wife	25	F	Full
		3 " Sally	Dau	9mo	F	Full
		4				
		5				
		6				
		7				
		8				
		9				
		10				
		11				

NAME OF FATHER	LIVING OR DEAD	NAME OF MOTHER	LIVING OR DEAD	APPLICATION NO.	REMARKS
1 Willis Jackson		Roselia Jackson	dead	5960	
2 Wilson Williams	dead	Polly	dead	5960	
3 No.1		No.2		5960	
4					
5					
6					
7					
8					
9					
10					
11					

APPROVED BY SECRETARY OF INTERIOR.
JUN 1 1903

IDENTIFIED MISSISSIPPI CHOCTAWS 1902 - 1909
Volume II

IDENTIFIED MISSISSIPPI CHOCTAWS

CARD NO. 471

IDENTIFICATION ADDRESS Freetrade[sic], Miss.　　SETTLEMENT ADDRESS
DATE OF IDENTIFICATION April 17, 1903.　　DATE OF PROOF OF SETTLEMENT

APPROVED ROLL No.	DAWES ROLL NO.	NAME	RELATIONSHIP TO PERSON FIRST NAMED	AGE	SEX	BLOOD
		1 Primus, Nannie		20	F	Full
		2 " Mattie	Dau	2	F	Full
		3				
		4				
		5				
		6				
		7				
		8				
		9				
		10				
		11				

NAME OF FATHER	LIVING OR DEAD	NAME OF MOTHER	LIVING OR DEAD	APPLICATION NO.	REMARKS
		~~Con-che-ho-nah~~			
1 Ellis Sam		Julia Sam		4377	
2 Ben Primus		No.1		4377	
3					
4					
5					
6					
7					
8					
9					
10					
11					

APPROVED BY SECRETARY OF INTERIOR.
JUN 1　1903

IDENTIFIED MISSISSIPPI CHOCTAWS 1902 - 1909
Volume II

IDENTIFIED MISSISSIPPI CHOCTAWS   CARD NO. 472

IDENTIFICATION ADDRESS Hays, Miss.   SETTLEMENT ADDRESS
DATE OF IDENTIFICATION April 17, 1903.   DATE OF PROOF OF SETTLEMENT

APPROVED ROLL No.	DAWES ROLL NO.	NAME	RELATIONSHIP TO PERSON FIRST NAMED	AGE	SEX	BLOOD
	1374	1 Jacoway, Summers		30	M	Full
	1375	2 " Isabell	Wife	26	F	Full
	1376	3 " Mina	Dau	12	F	Full
	1377	4 " Kelley	Son	7	M	Full
	1378	5 " Simmon	Son	6	M	Full
	1379	6 " Cara (Twins)	Dau	3	F	Full
	1380	7 " Cawa	Dau	3	F	Full
	1381	8 " Rufus	Son	1	M	Full
		9				
		10				
		11				

NAME OF FATHER	LIVING OR DEAD	NAME OF MOTHER	LIVING OR DEAD	APPLICATION NO.	REMARKS
1 Charley Jacoway		Malissa Jacoway	dead	4192	
2 Willis	dead	Don't know	dead	4192	
3 No.1		No.2		4192	
4 No.1		No.2		4192	
5 No.1		No.2		4192	
6 No.1		No.2		4192	
7 No.1		No.2		4192	
8 No.1		No.2		4192	
9					
10					
11					

APPROVED BY SECRETARY OF INTERIOR.
     JUN 1 1903

IDENTIFIED MISSISSIPPI CHOCTAWS 1902 - 1909
Volume II

IDENTIFIED MISSISSIPPI CHOCTAWS CARD NO. 473

IDENTIFICATION ADDRESS Hope, Miss. SETTLEMENT ADDRESS
DATE OF IDENTIFICATION April 17, 1903. DATE OF PROOF OF SETTLEMENT

APPROVED ROLL No.	DAWES ROLL NO.	NAME	RELATIONSHIP TO PERSON FIRST NAMED	AGE	SEX	BLOOD
	1382	1 Jacobs, Martha		70	F	Full
		2				
		3				
		4				
		5				
		6				
		7				
		8				
		9				
		10				
		11				

NAME OF FATHER	LIVING OR DEAD	NAME OF MOTHER	LIVING OR DEAD	APPLICATION NO.	REMARKS
1 Don't know	dead	Jennie	dead	4499	
2					
3					
4					
5					
6					
7					
8					
9					
10					
11					

APPROVED BY SECRETARY OF INTERIOR.
JUN 1 1903

IDENTIFIED MISSISSIPPI CHOCTAWS 1902 - 1909
Volume II

IDENTIFIED MISSISSIPPI CHOCTAWS CARD NO. 474

IDENTIFICATION ADDRESS Cushtusa, Miss. SETTLEMENT ADDRESS Nos 1-2-5-6 Stigler I.T.
DATE OF IDENTIFICATION April 17, 1903. DATE OF PROOF OF SETTLEMENT Nos1-2-5-6 Aug 11/03
  No.4 Nov 25/03

APPROVED ROLL No.	DAWES ROLL NO.	NAME	RELATIONSHIP TO PERSON FIRST NAMED	AGE	SEX	BLOOD
	1383	1 Gibson, Ben		47	M	Full
	1384	2 " Sallie	Wife	48	F	Full
	1385	3 " Mullen	Son	19	M	Full
	1386	4 " Lina	Dau	17	F	Full
	1387	5 " Lulu	Dau	14	F	Full
	1388	6 " Sammon	Son	11	M	Full

CITIZENSHIP CERTIFICATE
ISSUED FOR NO 1 2 5&6   1 2 3 4 5&6
AUG 11 1903

CITIZENSHIP CERTIFICATE
ISSUED FOR NO 4
NOV 25 1903

NAME OF FATHER	LIVING OR DEAD	NAME OF MOTHER	LIVING OR DEAD	APPLICATION NO.	REMARKS
1 Gibson (I-ton-i-le-tubbee)	dead	Betsey Gibson	dead	2054	
2 Jim Porter	"	~~~~~~~~~~	"	2054	
3 No.1		No.2		2054	
4 No.1		No.2		2054	
5 No.1		No.2		2054	
6 No.1		No.2		2054	
7					
8					
9					

CITIZENSHIP CERTIFICATE
10 ISSUED FOR NO ~~~3~~~
FEB 9 1904

APPROVED BY SECRETARY OF INTERIOR. Declaration and proof of settlement on Aug 11/03 apply to Nos. 1-2-5&6 only
JUN 1 1903

Nos 1-2-3-4-5&6 = Testimony as to continuous residence for a period of three years submitted September 14, 1908.

Proof settlement No.4 Nov 25/03.

Settlement address No.3. Stigler, I.T.
Date of proof of settlement No3. Feb. 8/04.
Declaration and proof of settlement of Feb 8/04 apply to No3 only.

IDENTIFIED MISSISSIPPI CHOCTAWS 1902 - 1909
Volume II

IDENTIFIED MISSISSIPPI CHOCTAWS

CARD NO. 475

IDENTIFICATION ADDRESS Amite City, La.   SETTLEMENT ADDRESS No1 Atoka I.T. / No.2 Ft. Towson, I.T.
DATE OF IDENTIFICATION April 17, 1903.   DATE OF PROOF OF SETTLEMENT No1 Aug 15/03 No2. Oct 15/03

APPROVED ROLL No.	DAWES ROLL NO.	NAME	RELATIONSHIP TO PERSON FIRST NAMED	AGE	SEX	BLOOD
		1 Isaac, George		53	M	Full
		2 " Mary	Wife	67	F	Full
		3				
		4				
		5				
		6				

CITIZENSHIP CERTIFICATE
ISSUED FOR NO 1   7
AUG 15 1903   1 & 2

CITIZENSHIP CERTIFICATE
ISSUED FOR NO 2
OCT 10 1903
                    11

NAME OF FATHER	LIVING OR DEAD	NAME OF MOTHER	LIVING OR DEAD	APPLICATION NO.	REMARKS
1 William Isaac	dead	Betsie Isaac	dead	2667	
2 Jim Funny	dead	~~~~~~~	"	2667	
3					
4					
5					
6					
7					
8					
9					
10					
11					

APPROVED BY SECRETARY OF INTERIOR.
JUN 1 1903   Declaration and proof of settlement applies to No1 only
Declaration and proof of settlement of Oct 15, 03 apply to No2 only
"No1. Testimony as to continuous residence for a period of three years submitted August 22, 1906."
"No2 Died September 16, 1904: Testimony as to continuous residence up to her death submitted August 22, 1906."

IDENTIFIED MISSISSIPPI CHOCTAWS 1902 - 1909
Volume II

IDENTIFIED MISSISSIPPI CHOCTAWS CARD NO. 476

IDENTIFICATION ADDRESS Madden, Miss.   SETTLEMENT ADDRESS
DATE OF IDENTIFICATION April 17, 1903.   DATE OF PROOF OF SETTLEMENT

APPROVED ROLL No.	DAWES ROLL NO.	NAME	RELATIONSHIP TO PERSON FIRST NAMED	AGE	SEX	BLOOD
		1 Martin, Tom		22	M	Full
		2				
		3				
		4				
		5				
		6				
		7				
		8				
		9				
		10				
		11				

NAME OF FATHER	LIVING OR DEAD	NAME OF MOTHER	LIVING OR DEAD	APPLICATION NO.	REMARKS
1 Martin Weshock	dead	Sallie Martin		3190	
2					
3					
4					
5					
6					
7					
8					
9					
10					
11					

APPROVED BY SECRETARY OF INTERIOR.
JUN 1 1903

IDENTIFIED MISSISSIPPI CHOCTAWS 1902 - 1909
Volume II

IDENTIFIED MISSISSIPPI CHOCTAWS CARD NO. 477

IDENTIFICATION ADDRESS Toles, Miss.　　SETTLEMENT ADDRESS Atoka I.T.
DATE OF IDENTIFICATION April 17, 1903.　　DATE OF PROOF OF SETTLEMENT Aug 17, 03

APPROVED ROLL No.	DAWES ROLL NO.	NAME	RELATIONSHIP TO PERSON FIRST NAMED	AGE	SEX	BLOOD
		1. Martin, Sam B.		29	M	Full
		2. " Winnie	Wife	28	F	Full
		3.				
		4.				
		5.				
		6.				
		7.				
		8.				

CITIZENSHIP CERTIFICATE
ISSUED FOR NO 1-2
AUG 17 1903

NAME OF FATHER	LIVING OR DEAD	NAME OF MOTHER	LIVING OR DEAD	APPLICATION NO.	REMARKS
1. John Martin	dead	Sealy Martin	dead	2050	
2. Sam Phillip	"	Sallie Phillip		2050	
3.					
4.					
5.					
6.					
7.		"Nos 1&2. Testimony relative to continuous residence for a period of three years submitted January 16, 1907."			
8.					
9.					
10.					
11.					

APPROVED BY SECRETARY OF INTERIOR.
　JUN 1 1903

IDENTIFIED MISSISSIPPI CHOCTAWS 1902 - 1909
Volume II

IDENTIFIED MISSISSIPPI CHOCTAWS CARD NO. 478

IDENTIFICATION ADDRESS Conehatta, Miss. SETTLEMENT ADDRESS Byars, Ind. Ter.
DATE OF IDENTIFICATION April 17, 1903. 1/30/03 Prospect, Miss. DATE OF PROOF OF SETTLEMENT August 3, 1903.

APPROVED ROLL No.	DAWES ROLL NO.		NAME	RELATIONSHIP TO PERSON FIRST NAMED	AGE	SEX	BLOOD
		1	Meely, Clark		21	M	Full
		2	" Mary	Wife	20	F	Full
		3					
		4					
		5					
		6					
		7		ENROLLMENT			
		8	1 & 2				
CITIZENSHIP CERTIFICATE ISSUED FOR NO 1-2- AUG 3 1903							
		11					

NAME OF FATHER	LIVING OR DEAD	NAME OF MOTHER	LIVING OR DEAD	APPLICATION NO.	REMARKS
1 John Meely	dead	Leanna Meely		3005	
2 Jimmy John	"	Caroline Ebin		3005	
3					
4					
5					
6					
7					
8					
9					
10					
11		"Nos 1 and 2: Proof of continuous residence for a period of three years submitted February 7-1907."			

APPROVED BY SECRETARY OF INTERIOR.
JUN 1 1903

IDENTIFIED MISSISSIPPI CHOCTAWS 1902 - 1909
Volume II

IDENTIFIED MISSISSIPPI CHOCTAWS CARD NO. 479

IDENTIFICATION ADDRESS Decatur, Miss.   SETTLEMENT ADDRESS
DATE OF IDENTIFICATION April 17, 1903.   DATE OF PROOF OF SETTLEMENT

APPROVED ROLL No.	DAWES ROLL NO.	NAME	RELATIONSHIP TO PERSON FIRST NAMED	AGE	SEX	BLOOD
		1 William, Lewis		23	M	Full
		2				
		3				
		4				
		5				
		6				
		7				
		8				
		9				
		10				
		11				

NAME OF FATHER	LIVING OR DEAD	NAME OF MOTHER	LIVING OR DEAD	APPLICATION NO.	REMARKS
1 John William		Janie William		3019	
2					
3					
4					
5					
6					
7					
8					
9					
10					
11					

APPROVED BY SECRETARY OF INTERIOR.
JUN 1 1903

IDENTIFIED MISSISSIPPI CHOCTAWS 1902 - 1909
Volume II

IDENTIFIED MISSISSIPPI CHOCTAWS   CARD NO. 480

IDENTIFICATION ADDRESS Newton, Miss.   SETTLEMENT ADDRESS
DATE OF IDENTIFICATION April 17, 1903.   DATE OF PROOF OF SETTLEMENT

APPROVED ROLL No.	DAWES ROLL NO.	NAME	RELATIONSHIP TO PERSON FIRST NAMED	AGE	SEX	BLOOD
		1 Harper, John		32	M	Full
		2 " Eunice	Dau	8	F	Full
		3				
		4				
		5				
		6				
		7				
		8				
		9				
		10				
		11				

NAME OF FATHER	LIVING OR DEAD	NAME OF MOTHER	LIVING OR DEAD	APPLICATION NO.	REMARKS
1 John Anderson		Lucy Anderson		3473	
2 No.1		Margaret Harper	dead	3473	
3					
4					
5					
6					
7					
8					
9					
10					
11					

APPROVED BY SECRETARY OF INTERIOR.
JUN 1 1903

IDENTIFIED MISSISSIPPI CHOCTAWS 1902 - 1909
Volume II

IDENTIFIED MISSISSIPPI CHOCTAWS   CARD NO. 481

IDENTIFICATION ADDRESS Hope, Miss.   SETTLEMENT ADDRESS
DATE OF IDENTIFICATION April 17, 1903.   DATE OF PROOF OF SETTLEMENT

APPROVED ROLL No.	DAWES ROLL NO.	NAME	RELATIONSHIP TO PERSON FIRST NAMED	AGE	SEX	BLOOD
		1. Waiter, McNeal		23	M	Full
		2. " Jane Sookey	Wife	18	F	Full
		3.				
		4.				
		5.				
		6.				
		7.				
		8.				
		9.				
		10.				
		11.				

NAME OF FATHER	LIVING OR DEAD	NAME OF MOTHER	LIVING OR DEAD	APPLICATION NO.	REMARKS
1. John Waiter	dead	Emma Waiter	dead	3007	
2. ~~~~~~~~	"	Sookey	"	3007	
3.					
4.					
5.					
6.					
7.					
8.					
9.					
10.					
11.					

APPROVED BY SECRETARY OF INTERIOR.
    JUN 1 1903

IDENTIFIED MISSISSIPPI CHOCTAWS 1902 - 1909
Volume II

IDENTIFIED MISSISSIPPI CHOCTAWS CARD NO. 482

IDENTIFICATION ADDRESS Conehatta, Miss.　　SETTLEMENT ADDRESS Atoka I.T.
DATE OF IDENTIFICATION April 17, 1903.　　DATE OF PROOF OF SETTLEMENT Aug 18/03

APPROVED ROLL No.	DAWES ROLL NO.	NAME	RELATIONSHIP TO PERSON FIRST NAMED	AGE	SEX	BLOOD
		1 Jackson, Annie		19	F	Full
		2				
		3				
		4				
		5				
		6				
		7				
		8				
		9				
		10				
		11				

NAME OF FATHER	LIVING OR DEAD	NAME OF MOTHER	LIVING OR DEAD	APPLICATION NO.	REMARKS
1 Charley Jackson		Frances Jackson		2461	
2					
3					
4					
5					
6					
7					
8					
9					
10					
11			"No1. Testimony as to continuous residence for a period of three years submitted August 22, 1907."		

APPROVED BY SECRETARY OF INTERIOR.
　　JUN 1　1903

IDENTIFIED MISSISSIPPI CHOCTAWS 1902 - 1909
Volume II

IDENTIFIED MISSISSIPPI CHOCTAWS   CARD NO. 483

IDENTIFICATION ADDRESS Williston, Miss.   SETTLEMENT ADDRESS Limestone [Illegible]
DATE OF IDENTIFICATION April 17, 1903.   DATE OF PROOF OF SETTLEMENT Nov 16/03

APPROVED ROLL No.	DAWES ROLL NO.	NAME		RELATIONSHIP TO PERSON FIRST NAMED	AGE	SEX	BLOOD
		1	Isaac, Wilson		34	M	Full
		2	" Siney	Wife	29	F	Full
		3	" Gift	Son	12	M	Full
		4	" Ellen	Dau	7	F	Full
		5	" Jim	Son	5	M	Full
		6	" Lela	Dau	2	F	Full
		7					
		8					
		9					
		10					
		11					

	NAME OF FATHER	LIVING OR DEAD	NAME OF MOTHER	LIVING OR DEAD	APPLICATION NO.	REMARKS
1	Isaac	dead	~~~~~~~~~~	dead	3177	
2	John Mack	"	Nancy Mack		3177	
3	No.1		No.2		3177	
4	No.1		No.2		3177	
5	No.1		No.2		3177	
6	No.1		No.2		3177	
7						
8						
9						
10			Nos 1 to 6 inclusive -- Testimony as to continuous residence of all for a period of 3 years submitted December 2, 1905.			
11						

APPROVED BY SECRETARY OF INTERIOR.
    JUN 1   1903

CITIZENSHIP CERTIFICATE
ISSUED FOR NO 1-2-4-5
    NOV 15 1903

1 2 3 4 5&6

    JAN 13 1905

CITIZENSHIP CERTIFICATE
ISSUED FOR NO 3-6-
    APR 15 1904

IDENTIFIED MISSISSIPPI CHOCTAWS 1902 - 1909
Volume II

IDENTIFIED MISSISSIPPI CHOCTAWS CARD NO. 484

IDENTIFICATION ADDRESS Sebastopol, Miss.   SETTLEMENT ADDRESS
DATE OF IDENTIFICATION April 17, 1903.   DATE OF PROOF OF SETTLEMENT

APPROVED ROLL No.	DAWES ROLL NO.		NAME	RELATIONSHIP TO PERSON FIRST NAMED	AGE	SEX	BLOOD
		1	Isom, Nelson		25	M	Full
		2	" Emma	Wife	20	F	Full
		3	" Mandy	Dau	6	F	Full
		4	" Greer	Son	4	M	Full
		5					
		6					
		7					
		8					
		9					
		10					
		11					

	NAME OF FATHER	LIVING OR DEAD	NAME OF MOTHER	LIVING OR DEAD	APPLICATION NO.	REMARKS
1	Julius Isom		Don't know	dead	4239	
2	Don't know	dead	wife now of Julius Isom Nancy John		4239	
3	No.1		No.2		4239	
4	No.1		No.2		4239	
5						
6						
7						
8						
9						
10						
11						

APPROVED BY SECRETARY OF INTERIOR.
JUN 1 1903

IDENTIFIED MISSISSIPPI CHOCTAWS 1902 - 1909
Volume II

IDENTIFIED MISSISSIPPI CHOCTAWS   CARD NO. 485

IDENTIFICATION ADDRESS Coffadeliah, Miss.   SETTLEMENT ADDRESS
DATE OF IDENTIFICATION April 17, 1903.   DATE OF PROOF OF SETTLEMENT

APPROVED ROLL No.	DAWES ROLL NO.		NAME	RELATIONSHIP TO PERSON FIRST NAMED	AGE	SEX	BLOOD
		1	Hickman, Ellis		35	M	Full
		2	" Susan	Wife	27	F	Full
		3	" Elsie	Dau	6	F	Full
		4	" Ida	Dau	3	F	Full
		5	" Maggie	Dau	1	F	Full
		6	" Johnikin	Stepson	10	M	Full
		7					
		8					
		9					
		10					
		11					

	NAME OF FATHER	LIVING OR DEAD	NAME OF MOTHER	LIVING OR DEAD	APPLICATION NO.	REMARKS
1	Don't know	dead	Mary	dead	5093	
2	Isaac	"	Don't know	"	5093	
3	No.1		No.2		5093	
4	No.1		No.2		5093	
5	No.1		No.2		5093	
6	Jimson Hickman		No.2		5093	
7						
8						
9						
10						
11						

APPROVED BY SECRETARY OF INTERIOR.
     JUN 1   1903

IDENTIFIED MISSISSIPPI CHOCTAWS 1902 - 1909
Volume II

IDENTIFIED MISSISSIPPI CHOCTAWS   CARD NO. 486

IDENTIFICATION ADDRESS Hope, Miss.   SETTLEMENT ADDRESS
DATE OF IDENTIFICATION April 17, 1903.   DATE OF PROOF OF SETTLEMENT

APPROVED ROLL No.	DAWES ROLL NO.	NAME	RELATIONSHIP TO PERSON FIRST NAMED	AGE	SEX	BLOOD
		1 Isaac, Jim (Tincha)		68	M	Full
		2 " Mary (Ho-ki) (Unah-ho-ka)	Wife	75	F	Full
		3				
		4				
		5				
		6				
		7				
		8				
		9				
		10				
		11				

NAME OF FATHER	LIVING OR DEAD	NAME OF MOTHER	LIVING OR DEAD	APPLICATION NO.	REMARKS
1 Nah-kah-ni-o-kah-tubbee Isaac	dead	Ho-ti-nah	dead	4489	
2 We-shock-she-homah	dead	Don't know	dead	4489	
3					
4					
5					
6					
7					
8					
9					
10					
11					

APPROVED BY SECRETARY OF INTERIOR.
JUN 1 1903

IDENTIFIED MISSISSIPPI CHOCTAWS 1902 - 1909
Volume II

IDENTIFIED MISSISSIPPI CHOCTAWS   CARD NO. 487

IDENTIFICATION ADDRESS Coffadeliah, Miss.   SETTLEMENT ADDRESS
DATE OF IDENTIFICATION April 17, 1903.   DATE OF PROOF OF SETTLEMENT

APPROVED ROLL No.	DAWES ROLL NO.	NAME	RELATIONSHIP TO PERSON FIRST NAMED	AGE	SEX	BLOOD
		1 Hickman, Jimpson		45	M	Full
		2				
		3				
		4				
		5				
		6				
		7				
		8				
		9				
		10				
		11				

NAME OF FATHER	LIVING OR DEAD	NAME OF MOTHER	LIVING OR DEAD	APPLICATION NO.	REMARKS
1 John Hickman	dead	Mary Hickman	dead	5092	
2					
3					
4					
5					
6					
7					
8					
9					
10					
11					

APPROVED BY SECRETARY OF INTERIOR.
JUN 1 1903

IDENTIFIED MISSISSIPPI CHOCTAWS 1902 - 1909
Volume II

IDENTIFIED MISSISSIPPI CHOCTAWS CARD NO. 488

IDENTIFICATION ADDRESS Hickory, Miss. Newton Co. SETTLEMENT ADDRESS Ardmore, Ind. Ter.
DATE OF IDENTIFICATION April 22, 1903. DATE OF PROOF OF SETTLEMENT Dec. 23, 1903.

APPROVED ROLL No.	DAWES ROLL NO.	NAME	RELATIONSHIP TO PERSON FIRST NAMED	AGE	SEX	BLOOD
		1 Simpson, Sam		55	M	Full
		2				
		3				
		4				
		5				
		6				
		7				
		8 ~~ 1 ~~				

CITIZENSHIP CERTIFICATE ISSUED FOR NO 1 DEC 23 1903

NAME OF FATHER	LIVING OR DEAD	NAME OF MOTHER	LIVING OR DEAD	APPLICATION NO.	REMARKS
1 Jim Simpson	dead	Liza Simpson		1125	
2					
3					
4					
5					
6					
7					
8					
9					
10					
11					

APPROVED BY SECRETARY OF INTERIOR.
JUN 1 1903

"No.1 Proof of continuous residence for a period of three years submitted June 30, 1906."

IDENTIFIED MISSISSIPPI CHOCTAWS 1902 - 1909
Volume II

IDENTIFIED MISSISSIPPI CHOCTAWS   CARD NO. 489
IDENTIFICATION ADDRESS Freetrade[sic], Miss.   SETTLEMENT ADDRESS Wynnewood, I. T. Atoka, Ind. Ter.
DATE OF IDENTIFICATION April 22, 1903.   DATE OF PROOF OF SETTLEMENT July 11, 1903.

APPROVED ROLL No.	DAWES ROLL NO.		NAME	RELATIONSHIP TO PERSON FIRST NAMED	AGE	SEX	BLOOD
		1	Amos, Wes		62	M	Full
		2	" Lissa	Wife	58	F	Full
		3	" Jasper	Son	20	M	Full
		4	" Dora	Dau	19	F	Full
		5	" Cleveland	Son	17	M	Full
		6	" Bennett	Son	14	M	Full
		7	" Willie	Son	8	M	Full
		8					

No.4 = Testimony relative to continuous residence for a period of three years submitted September 30, 1908.

CITIZENSHIP CERTIFICATE ISSUED FOR NO 1
SEP 17 1903

	NAME OF FATHER	LIVING OR DEAD	NAME OF MOTHER	LIVING OR DEAD	APPLICATION NO.	REMARKS
1	Amos Wah-ko-nah	dead	Becky Ok-in-to-lah	dead	4474	
2	Martin Weshock	dead	Sallie Martin		4474	
3	No.1		No.2		4474	
4	No.1		No.2		4474	
5	No.1		No.2		4474	
6	No.1		No.2		4474	
7	No.1		No.2		4474	
8						

9 Settlement address of #3 Wynnewood I.T. No.2 Testimony as to continuous residence
   Date of Proof of settlement Sept 19, 1903. up to time of her death submitted Mch 17, 06.
10   6&7 Testimony as to continuous residence
                                               for period of 3 years submitted Mch 17, 06.
11 "No1: Proof of continuous residence for a period of three years submitted December 20, 1906."

APPROVED BY SECRETARY OF INTERIOR.

JUN 1 1903
CITIZENSHIP CERTIFICATE
ISSUED FOR NO 3
SEP 19 1903
CITIZENSHIP CERTIFICATE
ISSUED FOR NO 2-4-5-6-7
OCT 13 1903
Testimony relative to
rinuous residence for a
iod of three years
mitted August 31, 1906."

Settlement address No.3 Wynnewood I.T.
Declaration and proof of settlement of Sept 19/03-No3 only.
   Date of proof of settlement No.3 Sept 19/03.

"Additional test. taken at Tish, I.T. 9/16/03 applies to all except No.3."
"Additional test. taken at Tish. I.T. Sept 19/03 applies to No.3 only."
Additional testimony taken January 25, 1909, as to residence of No.3.

IDENTIFIED MISSISSIPPI CHOCTAWS 1902 - 1909
Volume II

IDENTIFIED MISSISSIPPI CHOCTAWS CARD NO. 490

IDENTIFICATION ADDRESS Paulding, Miss. SETTLEMENT ADDRESS No.3 Durwood, I.T.
No.1&2 Ardmore I.T.
DATE OF IDENTIFICATION April 22, 1903. DATE OF PROOF OF SETTLEMENT No.3 Sept 26/03

APPROVED ROLL No.	DAWES ROLL NO.	NAME	RELATIONSHIP TO PERSON FIRST NAMED	AGE	SEX	BLOOD
		1 Washington, Sallie		50	F	Full
		2 Lewis, Mary	Dau	6	F	Full
		3 " Noble	Son	10	M	Full
		4 " Webb	Son	20	M	Full

CITIZENSHIP CERTIFICATE
ISSUED FOR NO 1
JUL 9- 1907

ENROLLMENT OF NOS 1&2 HEREON APPROVED BY THE SECRETARY Mar 2, 1907
4
AUG 7 1903

CITIZENSHIP CERTIFICATE
ISSUED FOR NO 3
SEP 26 1903

NAME OF FATHER	LIVING OR DEAD	NAME OF MOTHER	LIVING OR DEAD	APPLICATION NO.	REMARKS
1 Mose (Lahelah)	dead	Liza	dead	1154	
2 Jim Lewis	"	No.1		1154	
3 " "	"	No.1		1154	
4 " "	"	No.1		1154	
		Nº1 died January 28-1905 testimony submitted			
		June 20-1906, as to removal and settlement			
		considered as proof of continuous residence from			
		date of settlement to date of death.			
		Nº2 died January 28-1903 testimony submitted			
		June 19-1906 as to removal and settlement			
		considered as proof of continuous residence from			
		time of settlement until date of death.			
No.1 enrolled under Act of April 16, 1906.					

APPROVED BY SECRETARY OF INTERIOR.
JUN 1 1903   Settlement address No.4 Kiowa I.T
CITIZENSHIP CERTIFICATE   Date of proof of settlement No4 Aug 7/03.
ISSUED FOR NO ~~2~~   Declaration & proof apply to No.4 only.
MAY 3 1907   Declaration and proof of settlement of Sept 26, 03 apply to No. 3 only.

"No.2 Proof of death filed June 5-1906 No2 enrolled under Act of April 26, 1906.
showing No2 died January 28, 1903."

Nos 3 and 4: Proof of continuous residence for a period of three years submitted January 11-1907.

IDENTIFIED MISSISSIPPI CHOCTAWS 1902 - 1909
Volume II

IDENTIFIED MISSISSIPPI CHOCTAWS CARD NO. 491

IDENTIFICATION ADDRESS Coffadeliah, Miss.   SETTLEMENT ADDRESS
DATE OF IDENTIFICATION April 22, 1903.   DATE OF PROOF OF SETTLEMENT

APPROVED ROLL No.	DAWES ROLL NO.	NAME	RELATIONSHIP TO PERSON FIRST NAMED	AGE	SEX	BLOOD
		1 Wallace, Ikeness		44	M	Full
		2 " Li-cubbee	Son	8	M	Full
		3 " Lah-nubbee	Son	5	M	Full
		4				
		5				
		6				
		7				
		8				
		9				
		10				
		11				

NAME OF FATHER	LIVING OR DEAD	NAME OF MOTHER	LIVING OR DEAD	APPLICATION NO.	REMARKS
1 Tom Wallace	dead	Don't know	dead	5102	
2 No.1		Sis Wallace	"	5102	
3 No.1		" "	"	5102	
4					
5					
6					
7					
8					
9					
10					
11					

APPROVED BY SECRETARY OF INTERIOR.
JUN 1 1903

IDENTIFIED MISSISSIPPI CHOCTAWS 1902 - 1909
Volume II

IDENTIFIED MISSISSIPPI CHOCTAWS CARD NO. 492

IDENTIFICATION ADDRESS Jessie, Miss.　　SETTLEMENT ADDRESS
DATE OF IDENTIFICATION April 27, 1903.　　DATE OF PROOF OF SETTLEMENT

APPROVED ROLL No.	DAWES ROLL NO.	NAME	RELATIONSHIP TO PERSON FIRST NAMED	AGE	SEX	BLOOD
		1 Thompson, Felix		18	M	Full
		2				
		3				
		4				
		5				
		6				
		7				
		8				
		9				
		10				
		11				

NAME OF FATHER	LIVING OR DEAD	NAME OF MOTHER	LIVING OR DEAD	APPLICATION NO.	REMARKS
1 Dennis Thompson	dead	Annie Thompson		2110	
2					
3					
4					
5					
6					
7					
8					
9					
10					
11					

APPROVED BY SECRETARY OF INTERIOR.
　　JUN 1　1903

IDENTIFIED MISSISSIPPI CHOCTAWS 1902 - 1909
Volume II

IDENTIFIED MISSISSIPPI CHOCTAWS   CARD NO. 493

IDENTIFICATION ADDRESS Steele, Miss.   SETTLEMENT ADDRESS 2 to 6 Byars, Ind. Ter
DATE OF IDENTIFICATION April 27, 1903.   DATE OF PROOF OF SETTLEMENT 2 to 6 July 31, 1903

Declaration and proof of settlement applies to Nos 2 to 6 inclus.

APPROVED ROLL No.	DAWES ROLL NO.	NAME Ah-ha-lo-man-tubbee		RELATIONSHIP TO PERSON FIRST NAMED	AGE	SEX	BLOOD
		1	Anderson, John		53	M	Full
		2	" Lucy	Wife	40	F	Full
		3	" Artie	Stepson	9	M	Full
		4	" John Harrison	Son	6	M	Full
794		5	" John Amos	Son	3	M	Full
795		6	" Lola	Dau	8mo	F	Full
		7					
		8					

CITIZENSHIP CERTIFICATE   ENROLLMENT
ISSUED FOR NO 2-3-4-5-6   2-3 4 5 & 6
OCT 13 1903   APPROVED BY THE SECRETARY
                           OF INTERIOR JAN 15, 1907

	NAME OF FATHER Tah-nubbee	LIVING OR DEAD	NAME OF MOTHER	LIVING OR DEAD	APPLICATION NO.	REMARKS
1	John Gibson	dead	Don't know	dead	3996	
2	E-lah-po-nubbee	dead	Don't know	dead	3996	
3	John Hickman		No.2		3996	
4	No.1		No.2		3996	
5	No.1		No.2		3996	
6	No.1		No.2		3996	
7						
8						
9						
10						
11						

APPROVED BY SECRETARY OF INTERIOR.
JUN 1   1903

"No4: Proof of continuous residence for a period of three years submitted December 12, 1906."

"Nos. 2,3,5 and 6: Proof of continuous residence from date of settlement until date of death submitted December 12, 1906."

Nos 3&5 testimony as to continuous residence of Nos. 3&5 up to time of their death submitted Mch 17, 06.

No.4 testimony as to continuous residence for a period of 3 years submitted Mch 17, 06.

IDENTIFIED MISSISSIPPI CHOCTAWS 1902 - 1909
Volume II

IDENTIFIED MISSISSIPPI CHOCTAWS CARD NO. 494

IDENTIFICATION ADDRESS Engine, Miss. SETTLEMENT ADDRESS Atoka I.T. 1&3 No2
DATE OF IDENTIFICATION April 27, 1903. DATE OF PROOF OF SETTLEMENT Aug 17/03

APPROVED ROLL No.	DAWES ROLL NO.	NAME	RELATIONSHIP TO PERSON FIRST NAMED	AGE	SEX	No2 BLOOD
796		1 Toonubbee, Allen		52	M	Full
797		2 " Siss	Dau	16	F	Full
798		3 " Bissie	Dau	5	F	Full
		4				
		5				
		6				
		7				
		8	1 2&3			

CITIZENSHIP CERTIFICATE
ISSUED FOR NO 1-2-3
AUG 17 1903

NAME OF FATHER	LIVING OR DEAD	NAME OF MOTHER	LIVING OR DEAD	APPLICATION NO.	REMARKS
1 Toonubbee	dead	Sti-o-nah	dead	2208	
2 No.1		Lucy Toonubbee	"	2208	
3 No.1		" "	"	2208	
4					
5					
6					
7					
8		Nos 2&3. Testimony as to continuous residence for a period of three years submitted Aug. 5 [illegible]			
9					
10		"No.1 - Testimony as to continuous residence of No1 up to his death			
11		submitted May 24, 1906. No.1 died July 15, 1904."			

APPROVED BY SECRETARY OF INTERIOR.
JUN 1 1903

IDENTIFIED MISSISSIPPI CHOCTAWS 1902 - 1909
Volume II

IDENTIFIED MISSISSIPPI CHOCTAWS CARD NO. 495

IDENTIFICATION ADDRESS St. Anns, Miss.   SETTLEMENT ADDRESS
DATE OF IDENTIFICATION April 27, 1903.   DATE OF PROOF OF SETTLEMENT

APPROVED ROLL No.	DAWES ROLL NO.	NAME	RELATIONSHIP TO PERSON FIRST NAMED	AGE	SEX	BLOOD
		1 Willis, Allen		62	M	Full
		2 " Minerva	Wife	44	F	Full
		3 Chitto, Alma	S.Dau	16	F	Full
		4 " Luella	S.Dau	13	F	Full
		5 " John	S.Son	11	M	Full
		6 " Rufus	S.Son	4	M	Full
		7				
		8				
		9				
		10				
		11				

NAME OF FATHER	LIVING OR DEAD	NAME OF MOTHER	LIVING OR DEAD	APPLICATION NO.	REMARKS
1 Willis	dead	Nancy	dead	2117	
2 Ben	"	Mary	"	2117	
3 Tom Chitto		No.2		2117	
4 " "		No.2		2117	
5 " "		No.2		2117	
6 " "		No.2		2117	
7					
8					
9					
10					
11					

APPROVED BY SECRETARY OF INTERIOR.
JUN 1 1903

IDENTIFIED MISSISSIPPI CHOCTAWS 1902 - 1909
Volume II

IDENTIFIED MISSISSIPPI CHOCTAWS CARD NO. 496

IDENTIFICATION ADDRESS Prospect, Miss.   SETTLEMENT ADDRESS
DATE OF IDENTIFICATION April 27, 1903.   DATE OF PROOF OF SETTLEMENT

APPROVED ROLL No.	DAWES ROLL NO.	NAME	RELATIONSHIP TO PERSON FIRST NAMED	AGE	SEX	BLOOD
		1 Gunsmith, John (Ick-be-tubbee)		70	M	Full
		2 " Eliza (Kah-nah-le-ho-nah)	Wife	68	F	Full
		3				
		4				
		5				
		6				
		7				
		8				
		9				
		10				
		11				

NAME OF FATHER ~~John Davis~~	LIVING OR DEAD	NAME OF MOTHER ~~Ellen Davis~~	LIVING OR DEAD	APPLICATION NO.	REMARKS
1 Ah-cho-nan-tah	dead	Ilah-fi-co-ma-to-mah	dead	4052	
2 Tom Hosh-boh-li	dead	Don't know	dead	4052	
3					
4					
5					
6					
7					
8					
9					
10					
11					

APPROVED BY SECRETARY OF INTERIOR.
JUN 1 1903

IDENTIFIED MISSISSIPPI CHOCTAWS 1902 - 1909
Volume II

IDENTIFIED MISSISSIPPI CHOCTAWS CARD NO. 497

IDENTIFICATION ADDRESS Point, Miss. SETTLEMENT ADDRESS Nos 2-3-4-5 Paucaunla I.T.
DATE OF IDENTIFICATION April 27, 1903. DATE OF PROOF OF SETTLEMENT Nos 2-3-4-5 Nov. 28 03

APPROVED ROLL No.	DAWES ROLL NO.	NAME	RELATIONSHIP TO PERSON FIRST NAMED	AGE	SEX	BLOOD
		1 Gilmore, Henry Jackson		29	M	Full
		2 " Nettie Bessie	Wife	21	F	Full
		3 " Ramond	Son	3½	M	Full
		4 " Emma	Dau	2	F	Full
		5 " Mabell	Dau	1mo	F	Full
		6				
		7				
		8 2 3 4&5				
CITIZENSHIP CERTIFICATE ISSUED FOR NO 2-3-4-5 NOV 28 1903						
		11				

NAME OF FATHER	LIVING OR DEAD	NAME OF MOTHER	LIVING OR DEAD	APPLICATION NO.	REMARKS
1 Squire Gilmore	dead	Winnie Gilmore	dead	3399	
2 Jesse Shoemaker	dead	Becky Shoemaker	dead	3399	
3 No.1		No.2		3399	
4 No.1		No.2		3399	
5 No.1		No.2		3399	
6					
7					
8					
9					
10					
11					

APPROVED BY SECRETARY OF INTERIOR.
JUN 1 1903   Declaration and proof of settlement of Nov. 28/03 apply to Nos. 2-3-4-5 only.
"Nos. 2, 4 and 5: Testimony as to continuous residence for a period of 3 years submitted July 23, 1906."
"No.3 died November 7, 1905: testimony as to continuous residence up to his death submitted July 23, 1906."

IDENTIFIED MISSISSIPPI CHOCTAWS 1902 - 1909
Volume II

IDENTIFIED MISSISSIPPI CHOCTAWS   CARD NO. 498

IDENTIFICATION ADDRESS Hickory, Miss.   SETTLEMENT ADDRESS Paucaunla I.T.
DATE OF IDENTIFICATION April 27, 1903.   DATE OF PROOF OF SETTLEMENT Nov. 28/03

APPROVED ROLL No.	DAWES ROLL NO.	NAME	RELATIONSHIP TO PERSON FIRST NAMED	AGE	SEX	BLOOD
		1 Gibson, Leona		15	F	Full
		2				
		3				
		4				
		5				
		6				
		7				
		8				

CITIZENSHIP CERTIFICATE
ISSUED FOR NO 1
~~NOV 28 1903~~

NAME OF FATHER	LIVING OR DEAD	NAME OF MOTHER	LIVING OR DEAD	APPLICATION NO.	REMARKS
1 William Gibson	dead	Martha Gibson	dead	3491	
2					
3					
4					
5					
6					
7					
8					
9					
10					
11					

APPROVED BY SECRETARY OF INTERIOR.
JUN 1 1903

"No1: Testimony of her husband Sim Wickson, as to continuous residence for a period of three years submitted August 25, 1906."
"Additional testimony November 15, 1906."

IDENTIFIED MISSISSIPPI CHOCTAWS 1902 - 1909
Volume II

IDENTIFIED MISSISSIPPI CHOCTAWS CARD NO. 499

IDENTIFICATION ADDRESS Conehatta, Miss.   SETTLEMENT ADDRESS Ft. Towson I.T.
DATE OF IDENTIFICATION April 27, 1903.   DATE OF PROOF OF SETTLEMENT Oct 15, 03.

APPROVED ROLL No.	DAWES ROLL NO.	NAME	RELATIONSHIP TO PERSON FIRST NAMED	AGE	SEX	BLOOD
		1 Gibson, Billie		35	M	Full
		2 " Christiana	Wife	30	F	Full
		3 " Ethan S.	Son	4	M	Full
		4 " Mattie	Dau	3	F	Full
		5				
		6				
		7				
		8 1 2 3 & 4				

CITIZENSHIP CERTIFICATE
ISSUED FOR NO 12-3-4
~~OCT 16 1903~~

NAME OF FATHER	LIVING OR DEAD	NAME OF MOTHER	LIVING OR DEAD	APPLICATION NO.	REMARKS
1 Jim Gibson	dead	Nancy Gibson (Mishemahtemah)	dead	3967	
2 Don't know	dead	Amy Billey	dead	3967	
3 No.1		No.2		3967	
4 No.1		No.2		3967	
5					
6					
7					
8		"No3 died January 18, 1905 ~~January 23 and 26, 1907.~~"	Proof of continuous residence up to the time of his death submitted		
9		"Nos. 1,2 and 4. Proof of continuous residence for a period of three years submitted January 23 and 26, 1907."			
10					
11					

APPROVED BY SECRETARY OF INTERIOR.
JUN 1 1903

IDENTIFIED MISSISSIPPI CHOCTAWS 1902 - 1909
Volume II

IDENTIFIED MISSISSIPPI CHOCTAWS   CARD NO. 500

IDENTIFICATION ADDRESS Hickory, Miss.   SETTLEMENT ADDRESS Paucaunla I.T.
DATE OF IDENTIFICATION April 27, 1903.   DATE OF PROOF OF SETTLEMENT Oct. 13, 1903

APPROVED ROLL No.	DAWES ROLL NO.		NAME	RELATIONSHIP TO PERSON FIRST NAMED	AGE	SEX	BLOOD
		1	Gibson, Emmie		40	F	Full
		2	" Sallie	Dau	4½	F	Full
		3					
		4					
		5					
		6					
		7					
		8	1&2				
		9					
		10					
		11					

CITIZENSHIP CERTIFICATE ISSUED FOR NO 1&2

NAME OF FATHER	LIVING OR DEAD	NAME OF MOTHER	LIVING OR DEAD	APPLICATION NO.	REMARKS
1 Ben Gibson		Sealy Gibson		3509	
2		No.1			
3					
4					
5					
6					
7					
8					
9					
10					
11		"Nos 1 and 2 Testimony as to continuous residence for a period of three years submitted July 24, 1906."			

APPROVED BY SECRETARY OF INTERIOR.
JUN 1 1903

IDENTIFIED MISSISSIPPI CHOCTAWS 1902 - 1909
Volume II

IDENTIFIED MISSISSIPPI CHOCTAWS   CARD NO. 501

IDENTIFICATION ADDRESS Hickory, Miss.   SETTLEMENT ADDRESS Paucaunla I.T.
DATE OF IDENTIFICATION April 27, 1903.   DATE OF PROOF OF SETTLEMENT Oct. 12, [illegible]

APPROVED ROLL No.	DAWES ROLL NO.	NAME	RELATIONSHIP TO PERSON FIRST NAMED	AGE	SEX	BLOOD
		1 Gibson, Willie		26	M	Full
		2 " Mollie	Wife	24	F	Full
		3 " Mike	Son	2 wks	M	Full
		4				
		5				
		6				
		7				
		8				

CITIZENSHIP CERTIFICATE ISSUED FOR NO 1-2-3

ENROLLMENT OF NOS. 1, 2 & 3 HEREON APPROVED BY THE SECRETARY OF INTERIOR JAN. 11, 1905.

NAME OF FATHER	LIVING OR DEAD	NAME OF MOTHER	LIVING OR DEAD	APPLICATION NO.	REMARKS
1 Ben Gibson		Sealy Gibson		3301	
2 John Allen		Don't know		3301	
3 No.1		No.2		3301	
4					
5					
6					
7					
8					
9					
10					
11			"Nos 1, 2 and 3: Testimony as to continuous residence for a period of three years submitted July 19-1906."		

APPROVED BY SECRETARY OF INTERIOR.
JUN 1 1903

IDENTIFIED MISSISSIPPI CHOCTAWS 1902 - 1909
Volume II

IDENTIFIED MISSISSIPPI CHOCTAWS   CARD NO. 502

IDENTIFICATION ADDRESS Masengale, Miss.   SETTLEMENT ADDRESS
DATE OF IDENTIFICATION April 27, 1903.   DATE OF PROOF OF SETTLEMENT

APPROVED ROLL No.	DAWES ROLL NO.	NAME	RELATIONSHIP TO PERSON FIRST NAMED	AGE	SEX	BLOOD
	[?]469	1 Smith, Willie		22	M	Full
		2				
		3				
		4				
		5				
		6				
		7				
		8				
		9				
		10				
		11				

DID NOT SUBMIT PROOF OF REMOVAL AND BONA-FIDE SETTLEMENT WITHIN ONE YEAR FROM DATE OF IDENTIFICATION.

NAME OF FATHER	LIVING OR DEAD	NAME OF MOTHER	LIVING OR DEAD	APPLICATION NO.	REMARKS
1 Thomas Smith	dead	Annie Smith		1918	
2					
3					
4					
5					
6					
7					
8					
9					
10					
11					

APPROVED BY SECRETARY OF INTERIOR.
JUN 1 1903

IDENTIFIED MISSISSIPPI CHOCTAWS 1902 - 1909
Volume II

IDENTIFIED MISSISSIPPI CHOCTAWS   CARD NO. 503

IDENTIFICATION ADDRESS Freetrade[sic], Miss.   SETTLEMENT ADDRESS
DATE OF IDENTIFICATION April 27, 1903.   DATE OF PROOF OF SETTLEMENT

APPROVED ROLL No.	DAWES ROLL NO.	NAME	RELATIONSHIP TO PERSON FIRST NAMED	AGE	SEX	BLOOD
		1 Sam, Ellis		68	M	Full
		2 " Julia	Wife	45	F	Full
		3 " Fontain	Son	13	M	Full
		4				
		5				
		6				
		7				
		8				
		9				
		10				
		11				

DID NOT SUBMIT PROOF OF REMOVAL AND BONA-FIDE SETTLEMENT WITHIN ONE YEAR FROM DATE OF IDENTIFICATION.

	NAME OF FATHER	LIVING OR DEAD	NAME OF MOTHER	LIVING OR DEAD	APPLICATION NO.	REMARKS
1	Sam	dead	Jennie Sam	dead	4380	
2	Billy Baker	dead	Lucy Baker	dead	4380	
3	No.1		No.2		4380	
4						
5						
6						
7						
8						
9						
10						
11						

APPROVED BY SECRETARY OF INTERIOR.
JUN 1 1903

IDENTIFIED MISSISSIPPI CHOCTAWS 1902 - 1909
Volume II

IDENTIFIED MISSISSIPPI CHOCTAWS   CARD NO. 504
IDENTIFICATION ADDRESS Hero, Miss.   # 1-2-4-5-6-7&8 No.3 Ardmore I.T.
SETTLEMENT ADDRESS Ardmore I.T.
DATE OF IDENTIFICATION April 27, 1903.   DATE OF PROOF OF SETTLEMENT #1-2-4-5-6-7&8 Jany 6/04   No.3 March 25, 04

APPROVED ROLL No.	DAWES ROLL NO.		NAME	RELATIONSHIP TO PERSON FIRST NAMED	AGE	SEX	BLOOD
		1	Shoemaker, Ben		41	M	Full
		2	" Mary (Sti-onah)	Wife	38	F	Full
		3	" Sister	Dau	17	F	Full
		4	" Coleman	Son	14	M	Full
		5	" Henry	Son	10	M	Full
		6	" Selest	Dau	8	F	Full
CITIZENSHIP CERTIFICATE ISSUED FOR NO 8 APR 19 1904		7	" Will	Son	4	M	Full
CITIZENSHIP CERTIFICATE ISSUED FOR NO 1-2-4 JAN 6 1904		8	" Sally	Dau	7mo	F	Full

	NAME OF FATHER	LIVING OR DEAD	NAME OF MOTHER	LIVING OR DEAD	APPLICATION NO.	REMARKS
1	Jim Shoemaker	dead	Sally Shoemaker		1817	
2	Isaac Postoak		Lucy Postoak		1817	
3	No.1		No.2		1817	
4	No.1		No.2		1817	
5	No.1		No.2		1817	
6	No.1		No.2		1817	
7	No.1		No.2		1817	
8	No.1		No.2		1817	

APPROVED BY SECRETARY OF INTERIOR
JUN 1 1903

ENROLLMENT
OF NOS. 1 2 3 4 5 6 7 & 8 HEREON APPROVED BY THE SECRETARY OF INTERIOR. JAN 13 1905.

CITIZENSHIP CERTIFICATE
ISSUED FOR NO   5-6-7
FEB 4 1904
CITIZENSHIP CERTIFICATE
ISSUED FOR NO   3
MAR 25 1904

No.2: Testimony relative to continuous residence for a period of three years submitted September 1, 1906.

Declaration and proof of settlement apply to Nos 1-2-4-5-6-7&8 only.
Declaration and proof of settlement of March 25, 04, apply to No.3 only.
Nos. 1,2,4,5,6,7&8. Proof of continuous residence for a period of three years submitted May 12, 1906.
"No.3. Proof of continuous residence for a period of three years submitted June 2, 1906."

IDENTIFIED MISSISSIPPI CHOCTAWS 1902 - 1909
Volume II

IDENTIFIED MISSISSIPPI CHOCTAWS

CARD NO. 505

IDENTIFICATION ADDRESS Tucker, Miss. SETTLEMENT ADDRESS Atoka, Ind. Ter.
DATE OF IDENTIFICATION April 27, 1903. DATE OF PROOF OF SETTLEMENT Aug 18/03

APPROVED ROLL No.	DAWES ROLL NO.	NAME		RELATIONSHIP TO PERSON FIRST NAMED	AGE	SEX	BLOOD
		1	Phillips, Caroline		36	F	Full
		2	" Lena	Dau	15	F	Full
		3	" Sealia	Dau	12	F	Full
		4	" Germain	Dau	9	F	Full
		5	" Custer	Son	10mo	M	Full
		6					
		7					
		8					

ENROLLMENT
OF NOS. 1 2 3 4 & 5 HEREON
APPROVED BY THE SECRETARY
OF INTERIOR JAN 13 1905

CITIZENSHIP CERTIFICATE ISSUED FOR NO 1-2-3-4-5

	NAME OF FATHER	LIVING OR DEAD	NAME OF MOTHER	LIVING OR DEAD	APPLICATION NO.	REMARKS
1	Joe Jimpson	dead	Don't know	dead	2056	
2	Willie Phillips	dead	No.1		2056	
3	" "	"	No.1		2056	
4	" "	"	No.1		2056	
5	" "	"	No.1		2056	
6						
7						
8						
9			"No.2: Testimony relative to continuous residence for a period of three years submitted September 1, 19[illegible]."			
10			"Nos 1,3,4 and 5: Testimony relative to continuous residence for a period of three years submitted October 10, 1906."			
11						

APPROVED BY SECRETARY OF INTERIOR.
JUN 1 1903

IDENTIFIED MISSISSIPPI CHOCTAWS 1902 - 1909
Volume II

IDENTIFIED MISSISSIPPI CHOCTAWS   CARD NO. 506

IDENTIFICATION ADDRESS Lena, Miss.   SETTLEMENT ADDRESS
DATE OF IDENTIFICATION April 27, 1903.   DATE OF PROOF OF SETTLEMENT

APPROVED ROLL No.	DAWES ROLL NO.	NAME	RELATIONSHIP TO PERSON FIRST NAMED	AGE	SEX	BLOOD
		1 Robison, James		50	M	Full
		2 " Betsy	Wife	35	F	Full
		3 " Fronie	Dau	14	F	Full
		4 " Mattie	Dau	8	F	Full
		5 " Charlie	Son	6mo	M	Full
		6				
		7				
		8				
		9				
		10				
		11				

DID NOT SUBMIT PROOF OF REMOVAL AND BONA FIDE SETTLEMENT WITHIN ONE YEAR FROM DATE OF IDENTIFICATION.

NAME OF FATHER	LIVING OR DEAD	NAME OF MOTHER	LIVING OR DEAD	APPLICATION NO.	REMARKS
1 Charley Robison	dead	Lucy Robison		1599	
2 John Farmer	"	Lucy Farmer	dead	1599	
3 No.1		No.2		1599	
4 No.1		No.2		1599	
5 No.1		No.2		1599	
6					
7					
8					
9					
10					
11					

APPROVED BY SECRETARY OF INTERIOR.
JUN 1 1903

IDENTIFIED MISSISSIPPI CHOCTAWS 1902 - 1909
Volume II

IDENTIFIED MISSISSIPPI CHOCTAWS   CARD NO. 507

IDENTIFICATION ADDRESS Ennis, Miss.   SETTLEMENT ADDRESS Atoka I.T.
DATE OF IDENTIFICATION April 27, 1903.   DATE OF PROOF OF SETTLEMENT Aug 20/03

APPROVED ROLL No.	DAWES ROLL NO.	NAME	RELATIONSHIP TO PERSON FIRST NAMED	AGE	SEX	BLOOD
		1 Philip, Sallie		47	F	Full
		2				
		3				
		4				
		5				
		6				
		7	ENROLLMENT			
		8	~~ 1 ~~			
	1	9	JAN 13 1905			
		10				
		11				

NAME OF FATHER	LIVING OR DEAD	NAME OF MOTHER	LIVING OR DEAD	APPLICATION NO.	REMARKS
1 Jackson	dead	Polly Jackson	dead	2792	
2					
3					
4					
5					
6					
7					
8					
9		"No.1 Testimony relative to continuous residence for a period of three years submitted January 16, 1907."			
10					
11					

APPROVED BY SECRETARY OF INTERIOR.
JUN 1 1903

IDENTIFIED MISSISSIPPI CHOCTAWS 1902 - 1909
Volume II

IDENTIFIED MISSISSIPPI CHOCTAWS   CARD NO. 508

IDENTIFICATION ADDRESS Hickory, Miss.   SETTLEMENT ADDRESS Paucaunla, I.T.
DATE OF IDENTIFICATION April 27, 1903.   DATE OF PROOF OF SETTLEMENT Sept 11/03

APPROVED ROLL No.	DAWES ROLL NO.	NAME	RELATIONSHIP TO PERSON FIRST NAMED	AGE	SEX	BLOOD
		1. Arkansas, Jim		38	M	Full
		2. " Catherine	Wife	27	F	Full
		3. " Marsalina	Dau	8	F	Full
		4. " Fannie	Dau	5	F	Full
		5. " Missie	Dau	3	F	Full
		6. " Linnie	Dau	10mo	F	Full
		7.				
		8.				

CITIZENSHIP CERTIFICATE ISSUED FOR NO 1-2-3-4-5-6 SEP 11 1903

ENROLLMENT OF NOS. 1 2 3 4 5 & 6 HEREON APPROVED BY THE SECRETARY OF INTERIOR JAN 13 1905.

	NAME OF FATHER	LIVING OR DEAD	NAME OF MOTHER	LIVING OR DEAD	APPLICATION NO.	REMARKS
1	John Arkansas	dead	Susie Arkansas		3343	
2	Bob Johnson		Nancy Johnson		3343	
3	No.1		No.2		3343	
4	No.1		No.2		3343	
5	No.1		No.2		3343	
6	No.1		No.2		3343	
7						
8						
9						
10			"Nos 1 to 6 inclusive: Testimony as to continuous residence for a period of three years submitted July 24, 190[?]."			
11						

APPROVED BY SECRETARY OF INTERIOR.
     JUN 1   1903

IDENTIFIED MISSISSIPPI CHOCTAWS 1902 - 1909
Volume II

IDENTIFIED MISSISSIPPI CHOCTAWS CARD NO. 509

IDENTIFICATION ADDRESS Tullis, La. SETTLEMENT ADDRESS
DATE OF IDENTIFICATION April 27, 1903. DATE OF PROOF OF SETTLEMENT

APPROVED ROLL No.	DAWES ROLL NO.	NAME	RELATIONSHIP TO PERSON FIRST NAMED	AGE	SEX	BLOOD
		1 Allen, John (Hatubbee)		80	M	Full
		2				
		3				
		4				
		5				
		6				
		7				
		8				
		9				
		10				
		11				

DID NOT SUBMIT PROOF OF REMOVAL AND BONA-FIDE SETTLEMENT WITHIN ONE YEAR FROM DATE OF IDENTIFICATION.

NAME OF FATHER	LIVING OR DEAD	NAME OF MOTHER	LIVING OR DEAD	APPLICATION NO.	REMARKS
1 John Ah-hoc-la-tubbee	dead	Mollie Satonah	dead	5950	
2					
3					
4					
5					
6					
7					
8					
9					
10					
11					

APPROVED BY SECRETARY OF INTERIOR.
JUN 1 1903

IDENTIFIED MISSISSIPPI CHOCTAWS 1902 - 1909
Volume II

IDENTIFIED MISSISSIPPI CHOCTAWS   CARD NO. 510

IDENTIFICATION ADDRESS Philadelphia, Miss.   SETTLEMENT ADDRESS
DATE OF IDENTIFICATION April 27, 1903.   DATE OF PROOF OF SETTLEMENT

APPROVED ROLL No.	DAWES ROLL NO.	NAME	RELATIONSHIP TO PERSON FIRST NAMED	AGE	SEX	BLOOD
		1 Joe, Langley		50	M	Full
		2 " Emily	Wife	45	F	Full
		3 " Johnnie	Son	15	M	Full
		4 " Edna	Dau	16	F	Full
		5				
		6				
		7				
		8	DID NOT SUBMIT PROOF OF REMOVAL AND BONA FIDE SET-			
		9	TLEMENT WITHIN ONE YEAR			
		10	FROM DATE OF IDENTIFICATION.			
		11				

	NAME OF FATHER	LIVING OR DEAD	NAME OF MOTHER	LIVING OR DEAD	APPLICATION NO.	REMARKS
1	Joe Ah-took-a-lah	dead	Susan Hi-ne-ah	dead	5111	
2	Willis Tah-nah-pah-yah		Don't know	"	5111	
3	No.1		No.2		5111	
4	No.1		No.2		5111	
5						
6						
7						
8						
9						
10						
11						

APPROVED BY SECRETARY OF INTERIOR.
JUN 1 1903

IDENTIFIED MISSISSIPPI CHOCTAWS 1902 - 1909
Volume II

IDENTIFIED MISSISSIPPI CHOCTAWS   CARD NO. 511

IDENTIFICATION ADDRESS Madden, Miss.   SETTLEMENT ADDRESS Roff I.T.
DATE OF IDENTIFICATION April 27, 1903.   DATE OF PROOF OF SETTLEMENT Sept [illegible]

APPROVED ROLL No.	DAWES ROLL NO.		NAME	RELATIONSHIP TO PERSON FIRST NAMED	AGE	SEX	BLOOD
		1	Jacoway, Charlie		52	M	Full
		2	" Mandy	Wife	24	F	Full
		3	" Martin	Son	5	M	Full
		4	" Oma	Dau	4	F	Full
		5	" Elsie	Dau	3	F	Full
		6	" Onus	Son	5mo	M	Full
		7					
		8					
CITI		9	ENROLLMENT OF NOS. 1 2 3 4 5 & 6 HEREON				
ISSU	1-2-3-4-5-6	10	APPROVED BY THE SECRETARY OF INTERIOR JAN. 13, 1905				
		11					

	NAME OF FATHER	LIVING OR DEAD	NAME OF MOTHER	LIVING OR DEAD	APPLICATION NO.	REMARKS
1	Ieneda Jacoway	dead	Sallie Jacoway		3213	
2	Martin Weshock	dead	Sallie Martin		3213	
3	No.1		No.2		3213	
4	No.1		No.2		3213	
5	No.1		No.2		3213	
6	No.1		No.2		3213	
7						
8						
9						
10			"Nos 1,2,3,4,5 and 6: Proof of continuous residence for a period of three years submitted December 20, 1906."			
11						

NAME OF FATHER Chuffatubbee

APPROVED BY SECRETARY OF INTERIOR.
JUN 1 1903

IDENTIFIED MISSISSIPPI CHOCTAWS 1902 - 1909
Volume II

IDENTIFIED MISSISSIPPI CHOCTAWS   CARD NO. 512

IDENTIFICATION ADDRESS Hickory, Miss.   SETTLEMENT ADDRESS Paucaunla I.T.
DATE OF IDENTIFICATION April 27, 1903.   DATE OF PROOF OF SETTLEMENT Oct 30/03

APPROVED ROLL No.	DAWES ROLL NO.	NAME	RELATIONSHIP TO PERSON FIRST NAMED	AGE	SEX	BLOOD
		1 Johnson, Big Wiley		56	M	Full
		2 " Patsie	Wife	42	F	Full
		3 Gilmore, Allen	Nephew	9	M	Full
		4				
		5				
		6				

CITIZENSHIP CERTIFICATE ISSUED FOR NO 1-2- OCT 30 1903

ENROLLMENT OF NOS. 1 2 & 3 HEREON APPROVED BY THE SECRETARY OF INTERIOR JAN 13 1905

CITIZENSHIP CERTIFICATE ISSUED FOR NO 3 MAR 30 1904

NAME OF FATHER	LIVING OR DEAD	NAME OF MOTHER	LIVING OR DEAD	APPLICATION NO.	REMARKS
1 Mon-tah ~~Geo William~~	dead	Che-mah-le	dead	3300	
2 Chuffatubbee	"	Sookey Tah-honah	"	3300	
3 Tom Gilmore	"	Emma Gilmore	"	3300	
4					
5					
6					
7					
8					
9					
10					
11					

APPROVED BY SECRETARY OF INTERIOR.
     JUN 1 1903

"Nos 1 and 3: Testimony as to continuous residence for a period of three years submitted July 23, 1906."

"No2 died February 24, 1904: testimony as to continuous residence up to the time of her death submitted July 23, 1906."

IDENTIFIED MISSISSIPPI CHOCTAWS 1902 - 1909
Volume II

IDENTIFIED MISSISSIPPI CHOCTAWS CARD NO. 513

IDENTIFICATION ADDRESS Conehatta, Miss. SETTLEMENT ADDRESS Atoka I.T.
DATE OF IDENTIFICATION April 27, 1903. DATE OF PROOF OF SETTLEMENT Aug 18/03.

APPROVED ROLL No.	DAWES ROLL NO.	NAME	RELATIONSHIP TO PERSON FIRST NAMED	AGE	SEX	BLOOD
		1. Farmer, Solomon		41	M	Full
		2. " Louisa	Wife	38	F	Full
		3.				
		4.				
		5.				
		6.				
		7.				
		8.				
		9.				
		10.				
		11.				

ENROLLMENT OF NOS. 1&2 HEREON APPROVED BY THE SECRETARY OF INTERIOR JAN. 13, 1905

CITIZENSHIP CERTIFICATE ISSUED FOR NO 1-2 AUG 10 1905

NAME OF FATHER	LIVING OR DEAD	NAME OF MOTHER	LIVING OR DEAD	APPLICATION NO.	REMARKS
1. Yim-mi-ho-nubbee John Farmer	dead	Polly Farmer		4058	
2. ~~~~ Wilson	"	Don't know	dead	4058	
3.					
4.					
5.					
6.					
7.					
8.					
9.					
10.					
11.			Nos 1 and 2: Testimony as to continuous residence for a period of three years submitted August 22, 19[illegible].		

APPROVED BY SECRETARY OF INTERIOR.
1903

IDENTIFIED MISSISSIPPI CHOCTAWS 1902 - 1909
Volume II

IDENTIFIED MISSISSIPPI CHOCTAWS CARD NO. 514

IDENTIFICATION ADDRESS Eady, Miss.   SETTLEMENT ADDRESS Atoka, I.T.
DATE OF IDENTIFICATION April 27, 1903.   DATE OF PROOF OF SETTLEMENT Aug. 19/03.

APPROVED ROLL No.	DAWES ROLL NO.		NAME	RELATIONSHIP TO PERSON FIRST NAMED	AGE	SEX	BLOOD
		1	Fillihemah, Nancy		60	F	Full
		2					
		3					
		4					
		5					
		6					
		7					
	1	8					
		9					
		10					
		11					

ENROLLMENT OF NOS. ~~1~~ HEREON APPROVED BY THE SECRETARY OF INTERIOR JAN 13 1905

	NAME OF FATHER	LIVING OR DEAD	NAME OF MOTHER	LIVING OR DEAD	APPLICATION NO.	REMARKS
1	Sam (Ma-hah-tah-tah)	dead	Sallie (Hi-kah-ti-mah)	dead	4008	
2						
3						
4						
5						
6						
7						
8						
9						
10						
11						

APPROVED BY SECRETARY OF INTERIOR.
JUN 1 1903

"No.1 died Nov. 20, 1904: testimony as to continuous residence up to her death submitted June 15, 1906."
"Additional testimony submitted August 15, 1906."

IDENTIFIED MISSISSIPPI CHOCTAWS 1902 - 1909
Volume II

IDENTIFIED MISSISSIPPI CHOCTAWS   CARD NO. 515

IDENTIFICATION ADDRESS North Bend, Miss.   SETTLEMENT ADDRESS
DATE OF IDENTIFICATION April 27, 1903.   DATE OF PROOF OF SETTLEMENT

APPROVED ROLL No.	DAWES ROLL NO.		NAME Mah-hin-to-nah	RELATIONSHIP TO PERSON FIRST NAMED	AGE	SEX	BLOOD
		1	Frazier, Mary		70	F	Full
		2					
		3					
		4					
		5					
		6					
		7					
		8					
		9					
		10					
		11					

DID NOT SUBMIT PROOF OF REMOVAL AND BONA FIDE SETTLEMENT WITHIN ONE YEAR FROM DATE OF IDENTIFICATION.

	NAME OF FATHER	LIVING OR DEAD	NAME OF MOTHER	LIVING OR DEAD	APPLICATION NO.	REMARKS
1	Joe Ah-took-a-lah	dead	Susan Hi-ne-ah	dead	5110	
2						
3						
4						
5						
6						
7						
8						
9						
10						
11						

APPROVED BY SECRETARY OF INTERIOR.
JUN 1 1903

IDENTIFIED MISSISSIPPI CHOCTAWS 1902 - 1909
Volume II

IDENTIFIED MISSISSIPPI CHOCTAWS   CARD NO. 516

IDENTIFICATION ADDRESS Noxapater, Miss.　　SETTLEMENT ADDRESS
DATE OF IDENTIFICATION April 27, 1903.　　DATE OF PROOF OF SETTLEMENT

APPROVED ROLL No.	DAWES ROLL NO.		NAME	RELATIONSHIP TO PERSON FIRST NAMED	AGE	SEX	BLOOD
		1	Frazier, Henson		21	M	Full
		2					
		3					
		4					
		5					
		6					
		7					
		8					
		9					
		10					
		11					

DID NOT SUBMIT PROOF OF REMOVAL AND BONA-FIDE SETTLEMENT WITHIN ONE YEAR FROM DATE OF IDENTIFICATION

	NAME OF FATHER	LIVING OR DEAD	NAME OF MOTHER	LIVING OR DEAD	APPLICATION NO.	REMARKS
1	Farbis Frazier	dead	Mary Frazier		5036	
2						
3						
4						
5						
6						
7						
8						
9						
10						
11						

APPROVED BY SECRETARY OF INTERIOR.
JUN 1 1903

IDENTIFIED MISSISSIPPI CHOCTAWS 1902 - 1909
Volume II

IDENTIFIED MISSISSIPPI CHOCTAWS CARD NO. 517

IDENTIFICATION ADDRESS Hickory, Miss. SETTLEMENT ADDRESS Kemp, I.T.
DATE OF IDENTIFICATION April 27, 1903. DATE OF PROOF OF SETTLEMENT Oct. 10, 1903.

APPROVED ROLL No.	DAWES ROLL NO.	NAME	RELATIONSHIP TO PERSON FIRST NAMED	AGE	SEX	BLOOD
		1. Gibson, Ben		50	M	Full
		2. " Sealy	Wife	56	F	Full
		3.				
		4.				
		5.				
		6.				
		7.	ENROLLMENT			
		8.	OF NOS. 1&2 HEREON			
CITIZENSHIP CERTIFICATE ISSUED FOR NO 1-2 OCT 10 1903			APPROVED BY THE SECRETARY OF INTERIOR JAN 13 1905.			
		11.				

NAME OF FATHER	LIVING OR DEAD	NAME OF MOTHER	LIVING OR DEAD	APPLICATION NO.	REMARKS
~~Me-ah-she-cubbee~~ 1. John Battiest	dead	Polly Battiest	dead	3298	
2. Mah-yubbee	dead	Ah-tah-le-honah	"	3298	
3.					
4.					
5.					
6.					
7.					
8.					
9.					
10.					
11.		Nos 1 and 2: Testimony as to continuous residence for a period of three years submitted July 24, 1906.			

APPROVED BY SECRETARY OF INTERIOR.
JUN 1 1903

IDENTIFIED MISSISSIPPI CHOCTAWS 1902 - 1909
Volume II

IDENTIFIED MISSISSIPPI CHOCTAWS   CARD NO. 518

IDENTIFICATION ADDRESS Mandeville La.   SETTLEMENT ADDRESS
DATE OF IDENTIFICATION April 27, 1903.   DATE OF PROOF OF SETTLEMENT

APPROVED ROLL No.	DAWES ROLL NO.		NAME	RELATIONSHIP TO PERSON FIRST NAMED	AGE	SEX	BLOOD
	[??]19	1	Jackson, Martha		22	F	Full
	[??]20	2	" Lilly	Dau	7	F	Full
	[??]21	3	" Gibson	Son	1½	M	Full
		4					
		5					
		6	DID NOT SUBMIT PROOF OF				
		7	REMOVAL AND BONA-FIDE SET-				
		8	TLEMENT WITHIN ONE YEAR FROM DATE OF IDENTIFICATION.				
		9					
		10					
		11					

	NAME OF FATHER	LIVING OR DEAD	NAME OF MOTHER	LIVING OR DEAD	APPLICATION NO.	REMARKS
1	~~~~~~~	dead	Con-ne-as	dead	2401	
2	Jackson	"	No.1		2401	
3	"	"	No.1		2401	
4						
5						
6						
7						
8						
9						
10						
11						

APPROVED BY SECRETARY OF INTERIOR.
    JUN 1 1903

IDENTIFIED MISSISSIPPI CHOCTAWS 1902 - 1909
Volume II

IDENTIFIED MISSISSIPPI CHOCTAWS CARD NO. 519

IDENTIFICATION ADDRESS Conehatta, Miss. SETTLEMENT ADDRESS Atoka I.T. #5
DATE OF IDENTIFICATION April 27, 1903. DATE OF PROOF OF SETTLEMENT Aug 19/03 #5

APPROVED ROLL No.	DAWES ROLL NO.	NAME	RELATIONSHIP TO PERSON FIRST NAMED	AGE	SEX	BLOOD
	[??]22	1 Jackson, Billie		35	M	Full
	[??]23	2 " Jennie	Wife	26	F	Full
	[??]24	3 " Leroy	Son	5	M	Full
	[??]25	4 " Mary	Dau	1	F	Full
	[??]26	5 Stoliby, Folsom	Nephew	18	M	Full
		6				
		7	ENROLLMENT OF NOS. 1 2 3 4&5 HEREON			
		8	APPROVED BY THE SECRETARY OF INTERIOR JAN 13 1905.			

CITIZENSHIP CERTIFICATE ISSUED FOR NO 1-2-3-4-5

NAME OF FATHER	LIVING OR DEAD	NAME OF MOTHER	LIVING OR DEAD	APPLICATION NO.	REMARKS
1 Elder Jackson		Betsey Jackson	dead	4086	
2 Don't know	dead	Sarah Jackson	dead	4086	
3 No.1		No.2		4086	
4 No.1		No.2		4086	
5 Hickman Stoliby	dead	Sallie Stoliby	dead	4086	

APPROVED BY SECRETARY OF INTERIOR.
JUN 1 1903

No5 is how husband of No1 on card 38[?]
"No4 died October 24, 1904: testimony as to continuous residence up to her death submitted August 22, 1906."
"Nos 1,2 and 3: Testimony as to continuous residence for a period of three years submitted August 22, 1906."
"No5: Testimony as to continuous residence for a period of three years submitted August 15, 1906."

IDENTIFIED MISSISSIPPI CHOCTAWS 1902 - 1909
Volume II

IDENTIFIED MISSISSIPPI CHOCTAWS

CARD NO. 520

IDENTIFICATION ADDRESS Northbend, Miss. SETTLEMENT ADDRESS #1,2&4 Roff, I.T.
DATE OF IDENTIFICATION April 27, 1903. DATE OF PROOF OF SETTLEMENT Nov. 25/03. #1,2&4

APPROVED ROLL No.	DAWES ROLL NO.	NAME	RELATIONSHIP TO PERSON FIRST NAMED	AGE	SEX	BLOOD
	[??]27	1 Thompson, Allison		40	M	Full
	[??]28	2 " Martha	Wife	55	F	Full
	[??]29	3 Austin[sic], Hortense Thompson	Dau	16	F	Full
	[??]30	4 Thompson, Lena	Dau	14	F	Full
		5				
		6				

CITIZENSHIP CERTIFICATE
ISSUED FOR NO 3
NOV 25 1903

ENROLLMENT
OF NOS. 1 2 3&4 HEREON
APPROVED BY THE SECRETARY
OF INTERIOR JAN 13 1905.

CITIZENSHIP CERTIFICATE
ISSUED FOR NO 1-2-4
NOV 25 1903

NAME OF FATHER	LIVING OR DEAD	NAME OF MOTHER	LIVING OR DEAD	APPLICATION NO.	REMARKS
1 Bill Thompson	dead	Betsey Thompson	dead	1888	
2 Elam Bell	"	Becky Bell	"	1888	
3 No.1		No.2		1888	
4 No.1		No.2		1888	
5					
6					
7					
8					
9					
10					
11		No.3 wife of No1 on card 126			

APPROVED BY SECRETARY OF INTERIOR
JUN 1 1903

"No2. Proof of continuous residence for a period of three years submitted June 14, 1906."
"No4. Proof of continuous residence for a period of three years submitted June 14, 1906."
"No1. Proof of death filed June 14, 1906."
"No1. Proof of continuous residence from date of settlement until date of death submitted June 14, 1906."
"No3. Proof of continuous residence for a period of three years submitted August 20, 1906."

IDENTIFIED MISSISSIPPI CHOCTAWS 1902 - 1909
Volume II

IDENTIFIED MISSISSIPPI CHOCTAWS   CARD NO. 521

IDENTIFICATION ADDRESS Hickory, Miss.   SETTLEMENT ADDRESS Paucaunla, I.T.
DATE OF IDENTIFICATION April 27, 1903.   DATE OF PROOF OF SETTLEMENT Sept 26/03.

APPROVED ROLL No.	DAWES ROLL NO.	NAME	RELATIONSHIP TO PERSON FIRST NAMED	AGE	SEX	BLOOD
	[??]31	1 Gibson, Jeff		28	M	Full
	[??]32	2 " Lucy	Wife	29	F	Full
	[??]33	3 " William	Son	6	M	Full
	[??]34	4 " Ellis	Son	4	M	Full
	[??]35	5 " Snowdon	Son	2	M	Full
	[??]36	6 " Amy	Dau	4mo	F	Full
		7				
		8				

CITIZENSHIP CERTIFICATE
ISSUED FOR NO 1-2-3-4-5-6
SEP 26 1903

ENROLLMENT
OF NOS. 1 2 3 4 5 & 6 HEREON
APPROVED BY THE SECRETARY
OF INTERIOR. JAN. 13. 1905.

	NAME OF FATHER	LIVING OR DEAD	NAME OF MOTHER	LIVING OR DEAD	APPLICATION NO.	REMARKS
1	William Gibson	dead	Becky Gibson	dead	3303	
2	John Lewis	"	Martha Lewis	"	3303	
3	No.1		No.2		3303	
4	No.1		No.2		3303	
5	No.1		No.2		3303	
6	No.1		No.2		3303	
7						
8						
9						
10			"No 2 died April 4, 1904: No 6 died Jan. 15, 1905: testimony as to continuous residence of			
11			Nos 2 and 6 up to their death submitted June 21, 1906."			

APPROVED BY SECRETARY OF INTERIOR.
JUN 1 1903

Nos 1,3,4 and 5: testimony relative to continuous residence for a period of three years submitted November 15, 1906."

IDENTIFIED MISSISSIPPI CHOCTAWS 1902 - 1909
Volume II

IDENTIFIED MISSISSIPPI CHOCTAWS CARD NO. 522

IDENTIFICATION ADDRESS Hero, Miss. SETTLEMENT ADDRESS Ardmore I.T.
DATE OF IDENTIFICATION April 27, 1903. DATE OF PROOF OF SETTLEMENT Nov. 7/03.

APPROVED ROLL No.	DAWES ROLL NO.	NAME	RELATIONSHIP TO PERSON FIRST NAMED	AGE	SEX	BLOOD
	[??]37	1. Davis, Julia		44	F	Full
	[??]38	2. " Mary	Dau	15	F	Full
		3.				
		4.				
		5.				

CITIZENSHIP CERTIFICATE
ISSUED FOR NO 1
NOV 7 1903

ENROLLMENT OF NOS. 1&2 HEREON APPROVED BY THE SECRETARY OF INTERIOR JAN 13 1905.

CITIZENSHIP CERTIFICATE
ISSUED FOR NO 2
MAR 25 1904

NAME OF FATHER	LIVING OR DEAD	NAME OF MOTHER	LIVING OR DEAD	APPLICATION NO.	REMARKS
1. Tom Gibson	dead	Becky Gibson	dead	1932	
2. Jeff Davis	"	No.1		1932	
3.					
4.					
5.					
6.					
7.					
8.					
9.					
10.					
11.					

APPROVED BY SECRETARY OF INTERIOR.
JUN 1 1903

"No1: Proof of continuous residence for a period of three years submitted May 12, 1906."

"No2: Proof of continuous residence for a period of three years submitted May 12, 1906."

IDENTIFIED MISSISSIPPI CHOCTAWS 1902 - 1909
Volume II

IDENTIFIED MISSISSIPPI CHOCTAWS   CARD NO. 523

IDENTIFICATION ADDRESS Red Oak, I.T. (Sugar Loaf Co.)   SETTLEMENT ADDRESS Ardmore, I.T.
DATE OF IDENTIFICATION April 27, 1903.   DATE OF PROOF OF SETTLEMENT Oct. 16/03.

APPROVED ROLL No.	DAWES ROLL NO.		NAME	RELATIONSHIP TO PERSON FIRST NAMED	AGE	SEX	BLOOD
	[??]39	1	Stallaby, Anderson		45	M	Full
		2					
		3					
		4					
		5					
		6					
		7					
		8					

CITIZENSHIP CERTIFICATE ISSUED FOR NO 1
OCT 16 1905

ENROLLMENT
OF NOS. ~~1~~ HEREON
APPROVED BY THE SECRETARY
OF INTERIOR JAN 13 1905.

	NAME OF FATHER	LIVING OR DEAD	NAME OF MOTHER	LIVING OR DEAD	APPLICATION NO.	REMARKS
1	Jno. Stallaby	dead	Mary Stallaby	dead	[?]11	
2						
3						
4						
5						
6						
7			Testimony as to continuous residence for a period of three years submitted December 2, 1908.			
8						
9						
10						
11						

APPROVED BY SECRETARY OF INTERIOR.
JUN 1   1903

IDENTIFIED MISSISSIPPI CHOCTAWS 1902 - 1909
Volume II

IDENTIFIED MISSISSIPPI CHOCTAWS

CARD NO. 524

IDENTIFICATION ADDRESS Tucker, Miss.　　SETTLEMENT ADDRESS Ft. Towson I.T.
DATE OF IDENTIFICATION April 27, 1903.　　DATE OF PROOF OF SETTLEMENT Oct 15/03

APPROVED ROLL No.	DAWES ROLL NO.		NAME	RELATIONSHIP TO PERSON FIRST NAMED	AGE	SEX	BLOOD
	[??]40	1	Scott, Chubby		28	M	Full
		2					
		3					
		4					
		5					
		6					
		7					
		8					

CITIZENSHIP CERTIFICATE ISSUED FOR NO 1
OCT 16 1903

ENROLLMENT
OF NOS. ~~ 1 ~~ HEREON
APPROVED BY THE SECRETARY
OF INTERIOR JAN 13 1905.

	NAME OF FATHER	LIVING OR DEAD	NAME OF MOTHER	LIVING OR DEAD	APPLICATION NO.	REMARKS
1	Scott	dead	Mollie	dead	2331	
2						
3						
4						
5						
6						
7						
8						
9			"No 1. Proof of continuous residence for a period of three years submitted January 26, 1907."			
10						
11						

APPROVED BY SECRETARY OF INTERIOR.
　　JUN 1 1903

IDENTIFIED MISSISSIPPI CHOCTAWS 1902 - 1909
Volume II

IDENTIFIED MISSISSIPPI CHOCTAWS   CARD NO. 525

IDENTIFICATION ADDRESS Hays, Miss.   SETTLEMENT ADDRESS
DATE OF IDENTIFICATION April 27, 1903.   DATE OF PROOF OF SETTLEMENT

APPROVED ROLL No.	DAWES ROLL NO.	NAME	RELATIONSHIP TO PERSON FIRST NAMED	AGE	SEX	BLOOD
	[??]41	1 Isom, Julius		52	M	Full
	[??]42	2 " Nancy	wife	60	F	Full
	[??]43	3 Martin, Lomie	Grand child of No.2	11	M	Full
		4				
		5				
		6				
		7				
		8				
		9				
		10				
		11				

DID NOT SUBMIT PROOF OF REMOVAL AND BONA-FIDE SETTLEMENT WITHIN ONE YEAR FROM DATE OF IDENTIFICATION.

NAME OF FATHER	LIVING OR DEAD	NAME OF MOTHER	LIVING OR DEAD	APPLICATION NO.	REMARKS
1 Isom	dead	Martha Isom		4195	
2 Solomon York		Don't know	dead	"	
3 Willie Martin	dead	Nannie Willis		"	
4					
5					
6					
7					
8					
9					
10					
11					

APPROVED BY SECRETARY OF INTERIOR.
JUN 1 1903

IDENTIFIED MISSISSIPPI CHOCTAWS 1902 - 1909
Volume II

IDENTIFIED MISSISSIPPI CHOCTAWS   CARD NO. 526

IDENTIFICATION ADDRESS Engine, Miss.   SETTLEMENT ADDRESS Atoka I.T.
DATE OF IDENTIFICATION April 27, 1903.   DATE OF PROOF OF SETTLEMENT Aug 17, 03.

APPROVED ROLL No.	DAWES ROLL NO.	NAME	RELATIONSHIP TO PERSON FIRST NAMED	AGE	SEX	BLOOD
		1 Bob, Nancy Jane		42	F	Full
		2 Houston, Willie	Son	20	M	Full
		3 Bob, Herman	Son	9	M	Full
		4 " Woodward	Son	8	M	Full
		5 " Lena	Dau	7	F	Full
		6				
		7 ENROLLMENT OF NOS. 1,2,4&5 HEREON APPROVED BY THE SECRETARY				
		8 OF INTERIOR JAN. 13. 1905.				
CITIZENSHIP CERTIFICATE ISSUED FOR NO 1-2-4-5 AUG 17 1903						

NAME OF FATHER	LIVING OR DEAD	NAME OF MOTHER	LIVING OR DEAD	APPLICATION NO.	REMARKS
1 Wallace Porter	dead	Winnie Solomon		2023	
2 ~~~~~ Houston		No.1		2023	
3 Ianubbee Bob	dead	No.1		2023	
4 " "	"	No.1		2023	
5 " "	"	No.1		2023	
6					
7					
8 No3 DID NOT SUBMIT PROOF OF					
9 REMOVAL AND BONA FIDE SETTLEMENT WITHIN ONE YEAR		"No.1 died June 1, 1905; Testimony as to			
10 FROM DATE OF IDENTIFICATION.		continuous residence up to her death			
11		submitted August 15, 1906."			

APPROVED BY SECRETARY OF INTERIOR.
JUN 1 1903

Declaration and proof of settlement apply to Nos 1-2-4-5.
No3 died in Miss. in Dec. 1902. See test. of No1 taken at Atoka I.T. Aug 17/0[?].
"Nos 2,4 and 5: Testimony as to continuous residence for a period of three years submitted August 15, 1906."

IDENTIFIED MISSISSIPPI CHOCTAWS 1902 - 1909
Volume II

IDENTIFIED MISSISSIPPI CHOCTAWS CARD NO. 527

IDENTIFICATION ADDRESS Brown, Miss. SETTLEMENT ADDRESS Sawyer I.T.
DATE OF IDENTIFICATION April 27, 1903. DATE OF PROOF OF SETTLEMENT Jan'y 20, 1904.

APPROVED ROLL No.	DAWES ROLL NO.		NAME	RELATIONSHIP TO PERSON FIRST NAMED	AGE	SEX	BLOOD
	[??]49	1	Thomas, Charlie		38	M	Full
	[??]50	2	" Mary	Wife	28	F	Full
	[??]51	3	" Peter Foster	Son	14	M	Full
	[??]52	4	" Esau	Son	12	M	Full
	[??]53	5	" Risher	Son	8	M	Full
	[??]54	6	" Enoch	Son	3	M	Full
	[??]55	7	" Nicholas	Son	1	M	Full
		8					
CIT		9	ENROLLMENT OF NOS. 1 2 3 4 5 6 & 7 HEREON APPROVED BY THE SECRETARY OF INTERIOR. JAN. 13 1905.				
ISS	~~1-2-3-4-5-6-7~~	10					
		11					

	NAME OF FATHER	LIVING OR DEAD	NAME OF MOTHER	LIVING OR DEAD	APPLICATION NO.	REMARKS
1	Jake Thomas	dead	Martha Thomas	dead	2010	
2	John Frenchman	"	Polly Frenchman	"	"	
3	No.1		No.2		"	
4	No.1		No.2		"	
5	No.1		No.2		"	
6	No.1		No.2		"	
7	No.1		No.2		"	
8						
9						
10						
11						

APPROVED BY SECRETARY OF INTERIOR.
JUN 1 1903

Nos 1-2-3-4-5&6 = Testimony relative to continuous residence for a period of three years submitted September 21, 1908.
No.7 = Testimony relative to continuous residence from date of settlement until date of death submitted September 21, 1908.

IDENTIFIED MISSISSIPPI CHOCTAWS 1902 - 1909
Volume II

IDENTIFIED MISSISSIPPI CHOCTAWS CARD NO. 528

IDENTIFICATION ADDRESS Rose Hill, Miss. SETTLEMENT ADDRESS Nos 2-3 & 4 Durwood, No1 Ardmore I.T.
DATE OF IDENTIFICATION April 27, 1903. DATE OF PROOF OF SETTLEMENT No1 Sept 3/03 Nos 2-3 & 4 April 19, 04

APPROVED ROLL No.	DAWES ROLL NO.	NAME	RELATIONSHIP TO PERSON FIRST NAMED	AGE	SEX	BLOOD
		1 Ned, Willie		35	M	Full
		2 " Lona	Wife	24	F	Full
		3 " Marvin	Son	9	M	Full
		4 " Russell	Son	2	M	Full
		5				

CITIZENSHIP CERTIFICATE
ISSUED FOR NO 1
SEP 3 1903

ENROLLMENT
OF NOS. 1 2 3 & 4 HEREON
APPROVED BY THE SECRETARY
OF INTERIOR JAN 13 1905.

CITIZENSHIP CERTIFICATE
ISSUED FOR NO 2-3-4
APR 19 1904

	NAME OF FATHER	LIVING OR DEAD	NAME OF MOTHER	LIVING OR DEAD	APPLICATION NO.	REMARKS
1	Ned	dead	Betsy	dead	1144	
2	Jim Lewis		Sallie Lewis		"	
3	No.1		No.2		"	
4	No.1		No.2		"	
5						
6						
7						
8			No.2: Testimony relative to continuous residence from date of settlement until date of death submitted September 24, 1908.			
9			No.1: Testimony as to continuous residence for a period of 3 years submitted 3/29, 06.			
10			Nos. 3 and 4: Testimony relative to continuous residence for a period of three years submitted September 24, 1908.			
11						

APPROVED BY SECRETARY OF INTERIOR.
JUN 1 1903

Declaration and proof of settlement of Sept 3-03 applied to No1 only
Declaration and proof of settlement of April 19/04 apply to Nos 2-3 & 4 only.

IDENTIFIED MISSISSIPPI CHOCTAWS 1902 - 1909
Volume II

IDENTIFIED MISSISSIPPI CHOCTAWS

CARD NO. 529

IDENTIFICATION ADDRESS Decatur, Miss. SETTLEMENT ADDRESS
DATE OF IDENTIFICATION April 27, 1903. DATE OF PROOF OF SETTLEMENT

APPROVED ROLL No.	DAWES ROLL NO.	NAME	RELATIONSHIP TO PERSON FIRST NAMED	AGE	SEX	BLOOD
		1 To-ma-ha-Tubbee, Dave		75	M	Full
		2				
		3				
		4				
		5				
		6				
		7 DID NOT SUBMIT PROOF OF				
		8 REMOVAL AND BONA-FIDE SET-TLEMENT WITHIN ONE YEAR				
		9 FROM DATE OF IDENTIFICATION.				
		10				
		11				

NAME OF FATHER	LIVING OR DEAD	NAME OF MOTHER	LIVING OR DEAD	APPLICATION NO.	REMARKS
1 Cun-ne-tan-Tubbee	dead	Okla-he-ma	dead	3631	
2					
3					
4					
5					
6					
7					
8					
9					
10					
11					

APPROVED BY SECRETARY OF INTERIOR.
JUN 1 1903

IDENTIFIED MISSISSIPPI CHOCTAWS 1902 - 1909
Volume II

IDENTIFIED MISSISSIPPI CHOCTAWS   CARD NO. 530

IDENTIFICATION ADDRESS Ennis, Miss.   SETTLEMENT ADDRESS Atoka I.T.
DATE OF IDENTIFICATION April 27, 1903.   DATE OF PROOF OF SETTLEMENT Aug 17/03

APPROVED ROLL No.	DAWES ROLL NO.	NAME	RELATIONSHIP TO PERSON FIRST NAMED	AGE	SEX	BLOOD
		1. Wilson, Willie		30	M	Full
		2. " Janie	Wife	26	F	Full
		3. " John	Son	2	M	Full
		4. " Donald	Son	3mo	M	Full
		5. Shook, Bettie	Niece	10	F	Full
		6.				
		7.				
CITIZENSHIP CERTIFICATE ISSUED FOR NO 1-2-3-4-5 AUG 17 1903		8.				
		9.				
		10.				
		11.				

ENROLLMENT OF NOS. 1 2 3 4 & 5 HEREON APPROVED BY THE SECRETARY OF INTERIOR JAN 13 1905.

NAME OF FATHER	LIVING OR DEAD	NAME OF MOTHER	LIVING OR DEAD	APPLICATION NO.	REMARKS
1. Willis	dead	Ah-tubbee		2791	
2. John Willis		~~~~~~~~~	dead	"	
3. No.1		No.2		"	
4. No.1		No.2		"	
5. Shook Himmonubbee		Margaret Himmonubbee	dead	"	
6.					
7.					
8.					Nos 1 to 5 inclusive: testimony relative to continuous residence for a period of three years submitted September 4, 1906.
9.					
10.					
11.					

APPROVED BY SECRETARY OF INTERIOR.
JUN 1 1903

IDENTIFIED MISSISSIPPI CHOCTAWS 1902 - 1909
Volume II

IDENTIFIED MISSISSIPPI CHOCTAWS CARD NO. 531

IDENTIFICATION ADDRESS Engine, Miss.   SETTLEMENT ADDRESS
DATE OF IDENTIFICATION April 27, 1903.   DATE OF PROOF OF SETTLEMENT

APPROVED ROLL No.	DAWES ROLL NO.	NAME	RELATIONSHIP TO PERSON FIRST NAMED	AGE	SEX	BLOOD
		1 Bob, Watkin		21	M	Full
		2				
		3				
		4				
		5				
		6 DID NOT SUBMIT PROOF OF				
		7 REMOVAL AND BONA-FIDE SET-				
		8 TLEMENT WITHIN ONE YEAR FROM DATE OF IDENTIFICATION.				
		9				
		10				
		11				

NAME OF FATHER	LIVING OR DEAD	NAME OF MOTHER	LIVING OR DEAD	APPLICATION NO.	REMARKS
1 I-an-ubbee Bob	dead	~~~~~~~~~~	dead	2068	
2					
3					
4					
5					
6					
7					
8					
9					
10					
11					

APPROVED BY SECRETARY OF INTERIOR.
JUN 1 1903

IDENTIFIED MISSISSIPPI CHOCTAWS 1902 - 1909
Volume II

IDENTIFIED MISSISSIPPI CHOCTAWS

CARD NO. 532

IDENTIFICATION ADDRESS Dossville, Miss. SETTLEMENT ADDRESS
DATE OF IDENTIFICATION April 27, 1903. DATE OF PROOF OF SETTLEMENT

APPROVED ROLL No.	DAWES ROLL NO.		NAME	RELATIONSHIP TO PERSON FIRST NAMED	AGE	SEX	BLOOD
		1	Bob, Charlie		85	M	Full
		2					
		3					
		4					
		5					
		6					
		7					
		8					
		9					
		10					
		11					

DID NOT SUBMIT PROOF OF REMOVAL AND BONA-FIDE SETTLEMENT WITHIN ONE YEAR FROM DATE OF IDENTIFICATION.

	NAME OF FATHER	LIVING OR DEAD	NAME OF MOTHER	LIVING OR DEAD	APPLICATION NO.	REMARKS
1	Bob Onubbee	dead	Betsey Onubbee	dead	2111	
2						
3						
4						
5						
6						
7						
8						
9						
10						
11						

APPROVED BY SECRETARY OF INTERIOR.
JUN 1 1903

IDENTIFIED MISSISSIPPI CHOCTAWS 1902 - 1909
Volume II

IDENTIFIED MISSISSIPPI CHOCTAWS   CARD NO. 533

IDENTIFICATION ADDRESS Tucker, Miss.   SETTLEMENT ADDRESS Atoka I.T.
DATE OF IDENTIFICATION April 27, 1903.   DATE OF PROOF OF SETTLEMENT Aug 17, 03

APPROVED ROLL No.	DAWES ROLL NO.	NAME	RELATIONSHIP TO PERSON FIRST NAMED	AGE	SEX	BLOOD
		1. Bob, Boyd		44	M	Full
		2. " Lisby	Wife	38	F	Full
		3. " Preston	Son	13	M	Full
		4. " Rainey	Dau	8	F	Full
		5. " Lexis	Son	18mo	M	Full
		6.				
		7. ENROLLMENT				
		8. 1 2 3 4 & 5				

CITIZENSHIP CERTIFICATE ISSUED FOR NO 1-2-3-4-5
AUG 17 1903

	NAME OF FATHER	LIVING OR DEAD	NAME OF MOTHER	LIVING OR DEAD	APPLICATION NO.	REMARKS
1	Bob	dead	(Pis-un-tubbee) Sookie Bob	dead	2000	
2	Jimson Porter		~~~~~~~~~~	"	"	
3	No.1		No.2	"		
4	No.1		No.2	"		
5	No.1		No.2	"		
6						
7						
8						
9						
10					"Nos 1 to 5 inclusive. Testimony relative to continuous residence for a period of three years submitted October 11, 1906."
11						

APPROVED BY SECRETARY OF INTERIOR.
JUN 1 1903

IDENTIFIED MISSISSIPPI CHOCTAWS 1902 - 1909
Volume II

IDENTIFIED MISSISSIPPI CHOCTAWS CARD NO. 534

IDENTIFICATION ADDRESS Tucker, Miss.   SETTLEMENT ADDRESS Nos 1&3 Atoka I.T.
                                                            No. 2 Atoka I.T.
DATE OF IDENTIFICATION April 27, 1903.   DATE OF PROOF OF SETTLEMENT Nos 1&3 Aug 17/03
                                                                     No. 2 Sept 4/03

APPROVED ROLL No.	DAWES ROLL NO.		NAME	RELATIONSHIP TO PERSON FIRST NAMED	AGE	SEX	BLOOD
		1	Billey, Nolie		50	F	Full
		2 "	Charley Columbus	Son	16	M	Full
		3 "	Paulina	Dau	4	F	Full
		4					
		5					
		6					

CITIZENSHIP CERTIFICATE
ISSUED FOR NO 1-3
        AUG 17 1903

ENROLLMENT OF NOS 1, 2 & 3 HEREON APPROVED BY THE SECRETARY OF INTERIOR JAN 13 1905.

CITIZENSHIP CERTIFICATE
ISSUED FOR NO 2
        SEP 4 1903

NAME OF FATHER (Ah-no-sa-cubbee)	LIVING OR DEAD	NAME OF MOTHER	LIVING OR DEAD	APPLICATION NO.	REMARKS
1 John Smith		Mollie Smith	dead	2039	
2 Tom Billey	dead	No.1		"	
3 " "	"	No.1		"	
4					
5		No.2: Testimony of one witness relative to continuous			
6		residence from date of settlement until date of death submitted September 18, 1908.			
7		No.2: Additional testimony relative to continuous			
8		residence from date of settlement until date of death submitted December 7, 1908.			
9					
10					
11					

APPROVED BY SECRETARY OF INTERIOR.
    JUN 1   1903

Declaration and proof of settlement of Aug 17, 03 apply to Nos 1 & 3 only.
"Nos 1 and 3: testimony relative to continuous residence for a period of three years submitted September 21, 1906."

IDENTIFIED MISSISSIPPI CHOCTAWS 1902 - 1909
Volume II

IDENTIFIED MISSISSIPPI CHOCTAWS   CARD NO. 535

IDENTIFICATION ADDRESS Tucker, Miss.   SETTLEMENT ADDRESS No2. Atoka I.T.
DATE OF IDENTIFICATION April 27, 1903.   DATE OF PROOF OF SETTLEMENT No2. Aug 15/03

APPROVED ROLL No.	DAWES ROLL NO.		NAME	RELATIONSHIP TO PERSON FIRST NAMED	AGE	SEX	BLOOD
		1	Billey, Summers		19	M	Full
		2	" Frank Bishop	Bro.	18	M	Full
		3					
		4					
		5	ENROLLMENT No. DID NOT SUBMIT PROOF OF				
		6	OF NOS. 2 HEREON REMOVAL AND BONA-FIDE SET-				
		7	OF INTERIOR JAN. 13, 1905. FROM DATE OF IDENTIFICATION				
		8					
CITIZENSHIP CERTIFICATE ISSUED FOR NO 2 AUG 15 1903		9 10 11					

NAME OF FATHER	LIVING OR DEAD	NAME OF MOTHER	LIVING OR DEAD	APPLICATION NO.	REMARKS
1 Jim Billey	dead	Susie Billey	dead	2063	
2 " "	"	" "	"	"	
3					
4					
5					
6					
7					
8					
9					
10					
11					

APPROVED BY SECRETARY OF INTERIOR.
JUN 1   1903

No.1 is dead. See test. taken Aug 15/093.
Also letter of Comms. dated 9/4/03 enclosing letter 8/24/03.
"No2 Testimony relative to continuous residence for a period of three years submitted September 10, 1906."

IDENTIFIED MISSISSIPPI CHOCTAWS 1902 - 1909
Volume II

IDENTIFIED MISSISSIPPI CHOCTAWS

CARD NO. 536

IDENTIFICATION ADDRESS Carthage, Miss.
SETTLEMENT ADDRESS
DATE OF IDENTIFICATION April 27, 1903.
DATE OF PROOF OF SETTLEMENT

APPROVED ROLL No.	DAWES ROLL NO.	NAME	RELATIONSHIP TO PERSON FIRST NAMED	AGE	SEX	BLOOD
		1 Dixon, Philip		25	M	Full
		2 " Annie	Wife	19	F	Full
		3				
		4				
		5				
		6				
		7				
		8				
		9				
		10				
		11				

DID NOT SUBMIT PROOF OF REMOVAL AND BONA-FIDE SETTLEMENT WITHIN ONE YEAR FROM DATE OF IDENTIFICATION.

NAME OF FATHER	LIVING OR DEAD	NAME OF MOTHER	LIVING OR DEAD	APPLICATION NO.	REMARKS
1 Dixon	dead	Ho-pah-ki / Annie Dixon	dead	4406	
2 Simpson Jim		Eliza Jim		"	
3					
4					
5					
6					
7					
8					
9					
10					
11					

APPROVED BY SECRETARY OF INTERIOR.
JUN 1 1903

IDENTIFIED MISSISSIPPI CHOCTAWS 1902 - 1909
Volume II

IDENTIFIED MISSISSIPPI CHOCTAWS   CARD NO. 537

IDENTIFICATION ADDRESS Cushtusa, Miss.   SETTLEMENT ADDRESS Atoka I.T.
DATE OF IDENTIFICATION April 27, 1903.   DATE OF PROOF OF SETTLEMENT Aug. 15/03.

APPROVED ROLL No.	DAWES ROLL NO.		NAME		RELATIONSHIP TO PERSON FIRST NAMED	AGE	SEX	BLOOD
		1	Billy, Putwood			23	M	Full
		2	" Fannie		Wife	21	F	Full
		3	" John		Son	1mo	M	Full
		4						
		5						
		6						
		7		ENROLLMENT				
		8		1 2 & 3				
CITIZENSHIP CERTIFICATE ISSUED FOR NO 1-2-3 AUG 15 1903								
		11						

	NAME OF FATHER	LIVING OR DEAD	NAME OF MOTHER	LIVING OR DEAD	APPLICATION NO.	REMARKS
1	John Billy		Elizabeth Billy	dead	2043	
2	Buckhorn Phillip	dead	Lucy Phillip		"	
3	No.1		No.2		"	
4						
5						
6						
7						
8						
9			"Nos 1,2 and 3: Testimony relative to continuous residence for a period of three years submitted October 6, 1906."			
10						
11						

APPROVED BY SECRETARY OF INTERIOR.
JUN 1 1903

IDENTIFIED MISSISSIPPI CHOCTAWS 1902 - 1909
Volume II

IDENTIFIED MISSISSIPPI CHOCTAWS   CARD NO. 538

IDENTIFICATION ADDRESS Conehatta, Miss.   SETTLEMENT ADDRESS
DATE OF IDENTIFICATION April 27, 1903.   DATE OF PROOF OF SETTLEMENT

APPROVED ROLL No.	DAWES ROLL NO.		NAME	RELATIONSHIP TO PERSON FIRST NAMED	AGE	SEX	BLOOD
		1	Cooper, Jennie (Imathlehonah)		50	F	Full
		2	" Gaston	Son	13	M	Full
		3					
		4					
		5					
		6	DID NOT SUBMIT PROOF OF				
		7	REMOVAL AND BONA-FIDE SET-				
		8	TLEMENT WITHIN ONE YEAR				
		9	FROM DATE OF IDENTIFICATION.				
		10					
		11					

NAME OF FATHER	LIVING OR DEAD	NAME OF MOTHER	LIVING OR DEAD	APPLICATION NO.	REMARKS
1 Ah-ho-na-ubbee	dead	Nancy (Ok-a-in-chuk-a-ma)	dead	3987	
2 George Cooper		No.1		"	
3					
4					
5					
6					
7					
8					
9					
10					
11					

APPROVED BY SECRETARY OF INTERIOR.
    JUN 1 1903

IDENTIFIED MISSISSIPPI CHOCTAWS 1902 - 1909
Volume II

IDENTIFIED MISSISSIPPI CHOCTAWS CARD NO. 539

IDENTIFICATION ADDRESS Hosey, Miss.
SETTLEMENT ADDRESS No2 Durwood Ind Ter
Nos 4&5: Tishomingo, Ind. Territory
DATE OF IDENTIFICATION April 27, 1903.
DATE OF PROOF OF SETTLEMENT Nos 2 & 5: January 12-1907

APPROVED ROLL No.	DAWES ROLL NO.	NAME	RELATIONSHIP TO PERSON FIRST NAMED	AGE	SEX	BLOOD
		1 Amos, Josephine		30	F	Full
		2 " Jeff	Son	14	M	Full
		3 " Becky	Dau	10	F	Full
		4 " Lucinda	Dau	2	F	Full
		5 " Roselle	Dau	1	F	Full
		6				
		7				
		8				
		9				
		10				
		11				

DID NOT SUBMIT PROOF OF REMOVAL AND BONA-FIDE SETTLEMENT WITHIN ONE YEAR FROM DATE OF IDENTIFICATION.

	NAME OF FATHER	LIVING OR DEAD	NAME OF MOTHER	LIVING OR DEAD	APPLICATION NO.	REMARKS
1	Sam	dead	Nancy (Emithla)	dead	1947	
2	Amos	"	No.1	"		
3	"	"	No.1	"		
4	"	"	No.1	"		
5	"	"	No.1	"		
6						
7			Declaration and proof of settlement January 12-1907 applies to			
8			Nos 2, 4 & 5.			
9			"No.2 Proof of continuous residence for a period of three years submitted January 26, 1907"			
10			Nos 4 and 5: Proof of continuous residence for a period of three			
11			years submitted January 26, 1907.			

APPROVED BY SECRETARY OF INTERIOR.
JUN 1 1903

CITIZENSHIP CERTIFICATE
ISSUED FOR NO 4
JUL 9 1907

CITIZENSHIP CERTIFICATE
ISSUED FOR NO 5
JUL 19 1907

ENROLLMENT
OF NOS. 2-4 & 5 HEREON
APPROVED BY THE SECRETARY
OF INTERIOR Feb. 16, 1907.

IDENTIFIED MISSISSIPPI CHOCTAWS 1902 - 1909
Volume II

IDENTIFIED MISSISSIPPI CHOCTAWS CARD NO. 540

IDENTIFICATION ADDRESS Engine, Miss. SETTLEMENT ADDRESS No1 Atoka, I.T.
DATE OF IDENTIFICATION April 27, 1903. DATE OF PROOF OF SETTLEMENT No1 Aug 18/03

APPROVED ROLL No.	DAWES ROLL NO.	NAME	RELATIONSHIP TO PERSON FIRST NAMED	AGE	SEX	BLOOD
		1. Wilkinson, Harrison		77	M	Full
		2. " Sallie	Wife	52	F	Full
		3.				
		4.				
		5.				
		6.				
		7.				
		8.				

ENROLLMENT OF NOS. 1 HEREON APPROVED BY THE SECRETARY OF INTERIOR JAN. 13. 1905.

CITIZENSHIP CERTIFICATE ISSUED FOR NO 1
AUG 18 1903

NAME OF FATHER	LIVING OR DEAD	NAME OF MOTHER	LIVING OR DEAD	APPLICATION NO.	REMARKS
1. Ahconeubbee	dead	Okishmulle	dead	2041	
2. John Billy	"	Martha Billy	"	"	
3.					
4.					
5.					
6.					
7.					Declaration & proof of settlement applies to No.1 only.
8.					
9.					
10.					No.2 is dead. See test. taken Aug 18/03 in MCI jacket 1590. Also letter of Com. dated
11.					

APPROVED BY SECRETARY OF INTERIOR. 9/4/03 enclosing copy of letter of [illegible]
JUN 1 1903

"No.1 died August 20, 1904: Testimony relative to continuous residence up to his death submitted September 10, 1906."

IDENTIFIED MISSISSIPPI CHOCTAWS 1902 - 1909
Volume II

IDENTIFIED MISSISSIPPI CHOCTAWS CARD NO. 541

IDENTIFICATION ADDRESS Conehatta, Miss.   SETTLEMENT ADDRESS
DATE OF IDENTIFICATION April 27, 1903.   DATE OF PROOF OF SETTLEMENT

APPROVED ROLL No.	DAWES ROLL NO.		NAME	RELATIONSHIP TO PERSON FIRST NAMED	AGE	SEX	BLOOD
		1	Gibson, Bard		25	M	Full
		2	" Susanna	Wife	17	F	Full
		3	" Lela	Dau	2	F	Full
		4	" Kima	Dau	1mo	F	Full
		5					
		6					
		7					
		8	DID NOT SUBMIT PROOF OF REMOVAL AND BONA-FIDE SETTLEMENT WITHIN ONE YEAR FROM DATE OF IDENTIFICATION.				
		9					
		10					
		11					

	NAME OF FATHER	LIVING OR DEAD	NAME OF MOTHER	LIVING OR DEAD	APPLICATION NO.	REMARKS
1	William Gibson	dead	Martha Gibson	dead	4043	
2	Henry Johnson		Sealy Johnson		"	
3	No.1		No.2		"	
4	No.1		No.2		"	
5						
6						
7						
8						
9						
10						
11						

APPROVED BY SECRETARY OF INTERIOR.
JUN 1 1903

IDENTIFIED MISSISSIPPI CHOCTAWS 1902 - 1909
Volume II

IDENTIFIED MISSISSIPPI CHOCTAWS   CARD NO. 542

IDENTIFICATION ADDRESS Hickory, Miss.   SETTLEMENT ADDRESS Kemp I.T.
DATE OF IDENTIFICATION April 27, 1903.   DATE OF PROOF OF SETTLEMENT Sept 25/03.

APPROVED ROLL No.	DAWES ROLL NO.		NAME	RELATIONSHIP TO PERSON FIRST NAMED	AGE	SEX	BLOOD
		1	Gilmore, Tom		33	M	Full
		2	" Martha	Wife	25	F	Full
		3	" Johnnie	Son	2	M	Full
		4	" Mamie	Dau	1	F	Full
		5	" Ludie	Dau	1mo	F	Full
		6					
		7					
		8	ENROLLMENT				
		9	OF NOS. 1,2,3,4 & 5 HEREON APPROVED BY THE SECRETARY				
1-2-3-4-5		10	OF INTERIOR JAN. 13, 1905.				
		11					

	NAME OF FATHER	LIVING OR DEAD	NAME OF MOTHER	LIVING OR DEAD	APPLICATION NO.	REMARKS
1	William	Dead	Sookey	dead	3096	
2	Tom		Don't know	dead	"	
3	No.1		No.2		"	
4	No.1		No.2		"	
5	No.1		No.2		"	
6						
7						
8						
9			Nos 1 to 5 inclusive: testimony relative to continuous residence for a period of three years submitted February 18, 1907.			
10						
11						

APPROVED BY SECRETARY OF INTERIOR.
JUN 1 1903

IDENTIFIED MISSISSIPPI CHOCTAWS 1902 - 1909
Volume II

IDENTIFIED MISSISSIPPI CHOCTAWS

CARD NO. 543

IDENTIFICATION ADDRESS Hickory, Miss.
SETTLEMENT ADDRESS No.1 Colbert, I.T. / No.2 Ardmore, Ind. Ter.
DATE OF IDENTIFICATION April 27, 1903.
DATE OF PROOF OF SETTLEMENT No.1 Aug. 29/03 / No.2 July 30, 1903

APPROVED ROLL No.	DAWES ROLL NO.	NAME	RELATIONSHIP TO PERSON FIRST NAMED	AGE	SEX	BLOOD
		1 Gilmore, Benjamin		37	M	Full
		2 " Jane	Wife	24	F	Full
		3				
		4				
		5				
		6				

CITIZENSHIP CERTIFICATE
ISSUED FOR NO 2 — JUL 30 1903

CITIZENSHIP CERTIFICATE
ISSUED FOR NO 1 — AUG 29 1903

ENROLLMENT OF NOS. 1 & 2 HEREON APPROVED BY THE SECRETARY OF INTERIOR JAN 11, 1905

10 Declaration and proof of settlement of Jul 30/03 applies to No2 only

11   7/30/03

NAME OF FATHER	LIVING OR DEAD	NAME OF MOTHER	LIVING OR DEAD	APPLICATION NO.	REMARKS
1 William George Gilmore	dead	Sookey Gilmore Mak-ta-ho-nah	dead	3392	
2 John Willis Chuff-e-tubbee	dead	Julia Willis		"	
3					
4					
5					
6		No 1 died January 16, 1904. Testimony relative to continuous residence from date of settlement until date of death submitted July 19, 1904.			
7					
8					
9		"No.2 Proof of continuous residence for a period of three years submitted July 5, 1907."			
10					
11		Declaration and proof of settlement applies to No1 only - 8/29/03.			

APPROVED BY SECRETARY OF INTERIOR.
JUN 1 1903

IDENTIFIED MISSISSIPPI CHOCTAWS 1902 - 1909
Volume II

IDENTIFIED MISSISSIPPI CHOCTAWS CARD NO. 544

IDENTIFICATION ADDRESS Toles, Miss. SETTLEMENT ADDRESS Atoka I.T.
DATE OF IDENTIFICATION April 27, 1903. DATE OF PROOF OF SETTLEMENT Aug 17, 03.

APPROVED ROLL No.	DAWES ROLL NO.	NAME	RELATIONSHIP TO PERSON FIRST NAMED	AGE	SEX	BLOOD
		Il-le-mah-ho-ki				
		1 Ha-cubbee, Amie		75	F	Full
		2 Pistubbee, Tinsley	Grandson	15	M	Full
		3 " Archie	"	17	M	Full
		4				
		5				
		6				
		7				
		8				
CITIZENSHIP CERTIFICATE ISSUED FOR NO 1-2-3 AUG 17 1903						
		11				

ENROLLMENT
OF NOS. 1, 2 & 3 HEREON
APPROVED BY THE SECRETARY
OF INTERIOR JAN 13 1905.

NAME OF FATHER	LIVING OR DEAD	NAME OF MOTHER	LIVING OR DEAD	APPLICATION NO.	REMARKS
1 Ha-cubbee	dead	Ha-thla-cha-mah	dead	5197	
2 Elan Pistubbee	"	Martha Pistubbee	"	"	
3 " "	"	" "	"	"	
4					
5					
6					
7					
8					
9		"Nos 1,2 and 3, testimony relative to continuous residence for a period of three years submitted November 30, 1906."			
10		"Additional testimony submitted December 7, 1906."			
11					

APPROVED BY SECRETARY OF INTERIOR.
JUN 1 1903

IDENTIFIED MISSISSIPPI CHOCTAWS 1902 - 1909
Volume II

IDENTIFIED MISSISSIPPI CHOCTAWS CARD NO. 545

IDENTIFICATION ADDRESS Wickware, Miss. SETTLEMENT ADDRESS Nos 1-2-3 Durwood I.T. Nos 5&6
DATE OF IDENTIFICATION April 27, 1903. DATE OF PROOF OF SETTLEMENT Sept 12/03 Nos 1-2-3 Sept 17/03

APPROVED ROLL No.	DAWES ROLL NO.	NAME	RELATIONSHIP TO PERSON FIRST NAMED	AGE	SEX	BLOOD
		1 Henry, John		35	M	Full
		2 " Sarah	Dau	8	F	Full
		3 " Dennis	Son	7	M	Full
		4 Lewis, Mary	S.Dau	15	F	Full
		5 " Jim	S.Son	10	M	Full
		6 " Jeffie	S.Son	9	M	Full
		7				
		8				

CITIZENSHIP CERTIFICATE ISSUED FOR NO 1-2-3 SEP 12 1903

ENROLLMENT OF NOS. 1,2,3,4,5&6 HEREON APPROVED BY THE SECRETARY OF INTERIOR JAN 13 1905.

NAME OF FATHER	LIVING OR DEAD	NAME OF MOTHER	LIVING OR DEAD	APPLICATION NO.	REMARKS
1 Doctor John	dead	Sookey John		3214	
2 No.1		Martha Henry		"	
3 No.1		"		"	
4 Jim Lewis		"		"	
5 "		"		"	
6 "		"		"	

7 No.4: Proof of continuous residence for a period of three years submitted January 14-1907
8
9 Nos 5&6: Testimony relative to continuous
residence for a period of three years submitted
10 September 18, 1908 and September 24, 1908.
11

APPROVED BY SECRETARY OF INTERIOR.
JUN 1 1903

CITIZENSHIP CERTIFICATE
ISSUED FOR NO 5-6
SEP 17 1903

CITIZENSHIP CERTIFICATE
ISSUED FOR NO 4
SEP 13 1904

Settlement address No4 Kiowa, I.T.
Date of proof of settlement No4, Aug 7/03.
Declaration and proof of settlement on Aug 7/03 applies to No4 only.

Declaration and proof of settlement of Sept 17/03 apply to Nos 5 & 6 only.

Declaration and proof of settlement of Sept 12,03 apply to Nos 1-2 & 3 only.

"Nos 1,2 and 3: Proof of continuous residence for a period of three years submitted a November 30, 1906."

IDENTIFIED MISSISSIPPI CHOCTAWS 1902 - 1909
Volume II

IDENTIFIED MISSISSIPPI CHOCTAWS CARD NO. 546

IDENTIFICATION ADDRESS Battlefield Miss. SETTLEMENT ADDRESS Ft. Towson I.T.
DATE OF IDENTIFICATION April 27, 1903. DATE OF PROOF OF SETTLEMENT Oct 15, 03.

APPROVED ROLL No.	DAWES ROLL NO.	NAME		RELATIONSHIP TO PERSON FIRST NAMED	AGE	SEX	BLOOD
		1	Himonubbe, Shook		50	M	Full
		2	" Bobbie	Dau	19	F	Full
		3	" Laben	Son	12	M	Full
		4					
		5					
		6					
		7					
		8					
CITIZENSHIP CERTIFICATE ISSUED FOR NO 1-2-3 OCT 16 1903		9					
		10					
		11					

ENROLLMENT OF NOS. 1 2 & 3 HEREON APPROVED BY THE SECRETARY OF INTERIOR JAN 13 1905

NAME OF FATHER	LIVING OR DEAD	NAME OF MOTHER	LIVING OR DEAD	APPLICATION NO.	REMARKS
1 Him-o-nubbe	dead	Hochemah		2912	
2 No.1		Maggie Jane Himonubbe	dead	"	
3 No.1		" " "	"	"	
4					
5					
6					
7					
8		"No 2 died October 16, 1904; testimony relative to continuous residence up to her death submitted August 30, 1906."			
9		"Nos 1 and 3: testimony relative to continuous residence for a period of three years submitted November 17, 1906."			
10					
11					

APPROVED BY SECRETARY OF INTERIOR.
JUN 1 1903

IDENTIFIED MISSISSIPPI CHOCTAWS 1902 - 1909
Volume II

IDENTIFIED MISSISSIPPI CHOCTAWS CARD NO. 547

IDENTIFICATION ADDRESS Stamper, Miss.   SETTLEMENT ADDRESS
DATE OF IDENTIFICATION April 27, 1903.   DATE OF PROOF OF SETTLEMENT

APPROVED ROLL No.	DAWES ROLL NO.	NAME	RELATIONSHIP TO PERSON FIRST NAMED	AGE	SEX	BLOOD
		1 Tookolo, George		35	M	Full
		2 " Emaline	Wife	28	F	Full

DID NOT SUBMIT PROOF OF REMOVAL AND BONA-FIDE SETTLEMENT WITHIN ONE YEAR FROM DATE OF IDENTIFICATION

NAME OF FATHER	LIVING OR DEAD	NAME OF MOTHER	LIVING OR DEAD	APPLICATION NO.	REMARKS
1 Olis Tookolo	dead	Mary Tookolo		3004	
2 John Lewis	"		dead	"	

APPROVED BY SECRETARY OF INTERIOR.
JUN 1 1903

IDENTIFIED MISSISSIPPI CHOCTAWS 1902 - 1909
Volume II

IDENTIFIED MISSISSIPPI CHOCTAWS CARD NO. 548

IDENTIFICATION ADDRESS Hays, Miss. SETTLEMENT ADDRESS
DATE OF IDENTIFICATION April 27, 1903. DATE OF PROOF OF SETTLEMENT

APPROVED ROLL No.	DAWES ROLL NO.	NAME	RELATIONSHIP TO PERSON FIRST NAMED	AGE	SEX	BLOOD
		1 Wesley, John		70	M	Full
		2 " Louisa	Wife	59	F	Full
		3 Davis, Alice	G.Dau	18	F	Full
		4 " Sulena	"	16	F	Full
		5 " Jamison	G.Son	12	M	Full
		6				
		7				
		8				
		9				
		10				
		11				

DID NOT SUBMIT PROOF OF REMOVAL AND BONA-FIDE SETTLEMENT WITHIN ONE YEAR FROM DATE OF IDENTIFICATION.

NAME OF FATHER	LIVING OR DEAD	NAME OF MOTHER	LIVING OR DEAD	APPLICATION NO.	REMARKS
1 Don't know	dead	Jennie	dead	4187	
2 Don't know	"	Don't know	"	"	
3 Jeff Davis	"	Maria Davis	"	"	
4 " "	"	" "	"	"	
5 " "	"	" "	"	"	
6					
7					
8					
9					
10					
11					

APPROVED BY SECRETARY OF INTERIOR.
JUN 1 1903

IDENTIFIED MISSISSIPPI CHOCTAWS 1902 - 1909
Volume II

IDENTIFIED MISSISSIPPI CHOCTAWS   CARD NO. 549

IDENTIFICATION ADDRESS Thomastown, Miss.   SETTLEMENT ADDRESS
DATE OF IDENTIFICATION April 27, 1903.   DATE OF PROOF OF SETTLEMENT

APPROVED ROLL No.	DAWES ROLL NO.	NAME		RELATIONSHIP TO PERSON FIRST NAMED	AGE	SEX	BLOOD
		1	Lewis, Moses		55	M	Full
		2	Isaac, Polly (E-la-ho-te-mah)	Mother	92	F	Full
		3	Lewis, Susan	Wife	48	F	Full
		4	" Calvin	Son	12	M	Full
		5	" Marshall	Son	15	M	Full
		6	" Lissa	Dau	10	F	Full
		7					
		8	DID NOT SUBMIT PROOF OF				
		9	REMOVAL AND BONA-FIDE SET-				
		10	TLEMENT WITHIN ONE YEAR				
		11	FROM DATE OF IDENTIFICATION.				

	NAME OF FATHER	LIVING OR DEAD	NAME OF MOTHER	LIVING OR DEAD	APPLICATION NO.	REMARKS
	Apesamby		Elahotemah			
1	Moses Lewis	dead	Polly Isaac		3397	
2	Don't know	dead	Sallie	dead	"	
3	Wallace Sockey	dead	Liza Sockey	dead	"	
4	No.1		No.3		"	
5	No.1		No.3		"	
6	No.1		No.3		"	
7						
8						
9						
10						
11						

APPROVED BY SECRETARY OF INTERIOR.
JUN 1 1903

IDENTIFIED MISSISSIPPI CHOCTAWS 1902 - 1909
Volume II

IDENTIFIED MISSISSIPPI CHOCTAWS CARD NO. 550

IDENTIFICATION ADDRESS Steel, Miss. SETTLEMENT ADDRESS
DATE OF IDENTIFICATION April 27, 1903. DATE OF PROOF OF SETTLEMENT

APPROVED ROLL No.	DAWES ROLL NO.	NAME	RELATIONSHIP TO PERSON FIRST NAMED	AGE	SEX	BLOOD
		1 John, Alex		57	M	Full
		2 " Sarah	Wife	48	F	Full
		3 " Rhoda	Dau	20	F	Full
		4 " Grundy	Son	17	M	Full
		5 " Lee	Son	16	M	Full
		6				
		7				
		8 *DID NOT SUBMIT PROOF OF*				
		9 *REMOVAL AND BONA-FIDE SET-*				
		10 *TLEMENT WITHIN ONE YEAR*				
		11 *FROM DATE OF IDENTIFICATION.*				

NAME OF FATHER	LIVING OR DEAD	NAME OF MOTHER	LIVING OR DEAD	APPLICATION NO.	REMARKS
1 Don't know	dead	Don't know	dead	4218	
2 Don't know	dead	Don't know	dead	"	
3 No.1		No.2		"	
4 No.1		No.2		"	
5 No.1		No.2		"	
6					
7					
8					
9					
10					
11					

APPROVED BY SECRETARY OF INTERIOR.
JUN 1 1903

IDENTIFIED MISSISSIPPI CHOCTAWS 1902 - 1909
Volume II

IDENTIFIED MISSISSIPPI CHOCTAWS   CARD NO. 551

IDENTIFICATION ADDRESS Cooksey, Miss.   SETTLEMENT ADDRESS
DATE OF IDENTIFICATION April 27, 1903.   DATE OF PROOF OF SETTLEMENT

APPROVED ROLL No.	DAWES ROLL NO.	NAME	RELATIONSHIP TO PERSON FIRST NAMED	AGE	SEX	BLOOD
		1 Lewis, Little		78	M	Full
		2 " Liney	Wife	66	F	Full
		3 " Mary	Dau	20	F	Full
		4				
		5				
		6				
		7				
		8				
		9				
		10				
		11				

DID NOT SUBMIT PROOF OF REMOVAL AND BONA-FIDE SETTLEMENT WITHIN ONE YEAR FROM DATE OF IDENTIFICATION.

NAME OF FATHER	LIVING OR DEAD	NAME OF MOTHER	LIVING OR DEAD	APPLICATION NO.	REMARKS
1 ~~~~~~~~	dead	~~~~~~~~	dead	2990	
2 Big Lewis	"	Patsey Lewis	"	"	
3 No.1		No.2		"	
4					
5					
6					
7					
8					
9					
10					
11					

APPROVED BY SECRETARY OF INTERIOR.
JUN 1 1903

IDENTIFIED MISSISSIPPI CHOCTAWS 1902 - 1909
Volume II

IDENTIFIED MISSISSIPPI CHOCTAWS   CARD NO. 552

IDENTIFICATION ADDRESS Sebastopol, Miss.   SETTLEMENT ADDRESS
DATE OF IDENTIFICATION April 27, 1903.   DATE OF PROOF OF SETTLEMENT

APPROVED ROLL No.	DAWES ROLL NO.	NAME		RELATIONSHIP TO PERSON FIRST NAMED	AGE	SEX	BLOOD
		1	Tom, William		26	M	Full
		2	" Sarah	Wife	22	F	Full
		3	" Mollie	Dau	5	F	Full
		4	" Elan	Son	1	M	Full
		5					
		6					
		7	DID NOT SUBMIT PROOF OF REMOVAL AND BONA-FIDE SETTLEMENT WITHIN ONE YEAR FROM DATE OF IDENTIFICATION.				
		8					
		9					
		10					
		11					

NAME OF FATHER	LIVING OR DEAD	NAME OF MOTHER	LIVING OR DEAD	APPLICATION NO.	REMARKS
1 Don't know	~~	Martha Tom		4267	
2 Don't know	dead	Don't know	dead	"	
3 No.1		No.2		"	
4 No.1		No.2		"	
5					
6					
7					
8					
9					
10					
11					

APPROVED BY SECRETARY OF INTERIOR.
JUN 1 1903

IDENTIFIED MISSISSIPPI CHOCTAWS 1902 - 1909
Volume II

IDENTIFIED MISSISSIPPI CHOCTAWS   CARD NO. 553

IDENTIFICATION ADDRESS Engine, Miss.   SETTLEMENT ADDRESS Atoka I.T.
DATE OF IDENTIFICATION April 27, 1903.   DATE OF PROOF OF SETTLEMENT Aug 18/03

APPROVED ROLL No.	DAWES ROLL NO.	NAME	RELATIONSHIP TO PERSON FIRST NAMED	AGE	SEX	BLOOD
		1 Tom, Nicholas		38	M	Full
		2 " Watson	Son	15	M	Full
		3 " Moses	Son	13	M	Full
		4 " Sicily	Dau	5	F	Full
		5				
		6				
		7				
		8				
CITIZENSHIP CERTIFICATE ISSUED FOR NO 1-2-3-4 AUG 18 1903						
		11				

ENROLLMENT OF NOS. 1 2 3 & 4 HEREON APPROVED BY THE SECRETARY OF INTERIOR JAN 13 1905

	NAME OF FATHER	LIVING OR DEAD	NAME OF MOTHER	LIVING OR DEAD	APPLICATION NO.	REMARKS
1	Tom	dead	Betsie Tom	dead	2207	
2	No. 1		Susan Tom	"	"	
3	No. 1		" "	"	"	
4	No. 1		" "	"	"	
5						
6						
7						
8					"Nos 1,2,3 and 4: Testimony relative to continuous residence for a period of three years submitted September 10, 1906."
9						
10						No1 is husband of No.4 on card 193.
11						

APPROVED BY SECRETARY OF INTERIOR.
JUN 1 1903

IDENTIFIED MISSISSIPPI CHOCTAWS 1902 - 1909
Volume II

IDENTIFIED MISSISSIPPI CHOCTAWS CARD NO. 554

IDENTIFICATION ADDRESS Bay Spring, Miss. SETTLEMENT ADDRESS
DATE OF IDENTIFICATION April 27, 1903. DATE OF PROOF OF SETTLEMENT

APPROVED ROLL No.	DAWES ROLL NO.	NAME	RELATIONSHIP TO PERSON FIRST NAMED	AGE	SEX	BLOOD
		Con-che-ha-tubbee				
		1 Tom, William		68	M	Full
		2				
		3				
		4				
		5				
		6				
		7				
		8 DID NOT SUBMIT PROOF OF				
		9 REMOVAL AND BONA-FIDE SET-				
		10 TLEMENT WITHIN ONE YEAR				
		11 FROM DATE OF IDENTIFICATION.				

NAME OF FATHER	LIVING OR DEAD	NAME OF MOTHER	LIVING OR DEAD	APPLICATION NO.	REMARKS
1 Tubbish Tom	dead	Sallie Tom	dead	3798	
2					
3					
4					
5					
6					
7					
8					
9					
10					
11					

APPROVED BY SECRETARY OF INTERIOR.
JUN 1 1903

IDENTIFIED MISSISSIPPI CHOCTAWS 1902 - 1909
Volume II

IDENTIFIED MISSISSIPPI CHOCTAWS CARD NO. 555

IDENTIFICATION ADDRESS Hickory, Miss. SETTLEMENT ADDRESS Ardmore, I.T.
DATE OF IDENTIFICATION April 27, 1903. DATE OF PROOF OF SETTLEMENT Nov 16/03

APPROVED ROLL No.	DAWES ROLL NO.	NAME	RELATIONSHIP TO PERSON FIRST NAMED	AGE	SEX	BLOOD
		1 Johnston, Isham		43	M	Full
		2 " Lemma	Dau	11	F	Full
		3				
		4				
		5				
		6				
		7				
		8				
CITIZENSHIP CERTIFICATE ISSUED FOR NO 1-2 NOV 25 1903						
		11				

ENROLLMENT OF NOS. 1 & 2 HEREON APPROVED BY THE SECRETARY OF INTERIOR JAN 13 1905.

NAME OF FATHER	LIVING OR DEAD	NAME OF MOTHER	LIVING OR DEAD	APPLICATION NO.	REMARKS
1 Isaac Billy		Nancy Billy	dead	1103	
2 No.1		Emma Johnston	"	"	
3					
4					
5					
6					
7					
8					
9					
10					
11			"No1 Proof of continuous residence for a period of three years submitted May 26, 1906."		

APPROVED BY SECRETARY OF INTERIOR.
JUN 1 1903

No.1 is husband of No2 on Miss Choc. card 442.

"No2: Proof of continuous residence for a period of three years submitted February 6, 1907."

IDENTIFIED MISSISSIPPI CHOCTAWS 1902 - 1909
Volume II

IDENTIFIED MISSISSIPPI CHOCTAWS   CARD NO. 556

IDENTIFICATION ADDRESS Hickory, Miss.   SETTLEMENT ADDRESS Ardmore I.T.
DATE OF IDENTIFICATION April 27, 1903.   DATE OF PROOF OF SETTLEMENT Nov. 16/03.

APPROVED ROLL No.	DAWES ROLL NO.	NAME	RELATIONSHIP TO PERSON FIRST NAMED	AGE	SEX	BLOOD
		1 Johnston, Jesse		18	M	Full
		2 " Lena	Wife	20	F	Full
		3 " Malissie	Dau	2mo	F	Full
		4				
		5				
		6				
		7				
		8	ENROLLMENT OF NOS. 1, 2 & 3 HEREON APPROVED BY THE SECRETARY OF INTERIOR JAN 13 1905			
CITIZENSHIP CERTIFICATE ISSUED FOR NO 1-2-3 DEC 1 1903		9				
		10				
		11				

NAME OF FATHER	LIVING OR DEAD	NAME OF MOTHER	LIVING OR DEAD	APPLICATION NO.	REMARKS
1 Isham Johnston		Emily Johnston	dead	2188	
2 Jim Thomas		Melissa Thomas	"	"	
3 No.1		No.2		"	
4					
5					
6					
7					
8					
9					
10					"Nos 1, 2 & 3: Proof of continuous residence for a period of three years submitted May 26, 1906."
11					

APPROVED BY SECRETARY OF INTERIOR.
    JUN 1 1903

IDENTIFIED MISSISSIPPI CHOCTAWS 1902 - 1909
Volume II

IDENTIFIED MISSISSIPPI CHOCTAWS CARD NO. 557

IDENTIFICATION ADDRESS Avera, Miss.   SETTLEMENT ADDRESS Durwood I.T.
DATE OF IDENTIFICATION April 27, 1903.   DATE OF PROOF OF SETTLEMENT Sept 16/03

APPROVED ROLL No.	DAWES ROLL NO.	NAME	RELATIONSHIP TO PERSON FIRST NAMED	AGE	SEX	BLOOD
		1 Tom, Willie		35	M	Full
		2				
		3				
		4				
		5				
		6				
		7				
		8				

CITIZENSHIP CERTIFICATE ISSUED FOR NO 1
SEP 16 1903

ENROLLMENT OF NO ~~~ 1 ~~~

NAME OF FATHER	LIVING OR DEAD	NAME OF MOTHER	LIVING OR DEAD	APPLICATION NO.	REMARKS
1 Wm Tom	dead	~~~~~~	dead	1953	
2					
3					
4					
5					
6					
7					
8					
9					
10					
11		"No1: Proof of continuous residence for a period of three years submitted December 22, 1906."			

APPROVED BY SECRETARY OF INTERIOR.
JUN 1 1903

IDENTIFIED MISSISSIPPI CHOCTAWS 1902 - 1909
Volume II

IDENTIFIED MISSISSIPPI CHOCTAWS CARD NO. 558

IDENTIFICATION ADDRESS Brown, Miss. SETTLEMENT ADDRESS Nos 1-2-3-4-6 Kiowa I.T.
DATE OF IDENTIFICATION April 27, 1903. DATE OF PROOF OF SETTLEMENT Nos 1-2-3-4-6 Aug 7/03

APPROVED ROLL No.	DAWES ROLL NO.	NAME	RELATIONSHIP TO PERSON FIRST NAMED	AGE	SEX	BLOOD
		1 Taylor, Willie		26	M	Full
		2 " Jennie	Wife	38	F	Full
		3 " Elizabeth	Dau	3	F	Full
		4 " Johnson	Son	2	M	Full
		5 Jeff, Ludie	S.Dau	14	F	Full
		6 " Alice	S.Dau	11	F	Full

ISSUED FOR NO 1-2-3-4
AUG 7 1903

CITIZE
ISSUED 6
AUG 7 1903

ENROLLMENT
OF NOS. 1 2 3 4 & 6 HEREON
APPROVED BY THE SECRETARY
OF INTERIOR JAN. 13. 1905.

NAME OF FATHER	LIVING OR DEAD	NAME OF MOTHER	LIVING OR DEAD	APPLICATION NO.	REMARKS
1 Billbo Taylor	dead	Merceline Taylor	dead	2005	
2 Jake Thomas	"	~~~~~ Thomas	"	"	
3 No.1		No.2		"	
4 No.1		No.2		"	
5 John Jeff	dead	No.2		"	
6 " "	"	No.2		"	

No 5 DID NOT SUBMIT PROOF OF REMOVAL AND BONA FIDE SETTLEMENT WITHIN ONE YEAR FROM DATE OF IDENTIFICATION.

Nos 1-2-3-4-6 = Testimony of one witness relative to continuous residence for a period of three years submitted a September 16-1908.

APPROVED BY SECRETARY OF INTERIOR.
JUN 1 1903

Nos. 1-2-3-4-6: Additional testimony relative to continuous residence for a period of three years submitted Dec. 4, 1908.

Declaration and proof of settlement applies to Nos. 1-2-3-4-6 only.

IDENTIFIED MISSISSIPPI CHOCTAWS 1902 - 1909
Volume II

IDENTIFIED MISSISSIPPI CHOCTAWS CARD NO. 559

IDENTIFICATION ADDRESS Toles, Miss.   SETTLEMENT ADDRESS Atoka I.T.
DATE OF IDENTIFICATION April 27, 1903.   DATE OF PROOF OF SETTLEMENT Aug 17/03

APPROVED ROLL No.	DAWES ROLL NO.	NAME	RELATIONSHIP TO PERSON FIRST NAMED	AGE	SEX	BLOOD
		Ok-lah-nah-nubbee				
		1 Brokeshoulder, Adam		70	M	Full
		2				
		3				
		4				
		5				
		6				
		7				
		8				
CITIZENSHIP CERTIFICATE ISSUED FOR NO 1 AUG 17 1903		9				
		10				
		11				

ENROLLMENT OF NOS. ~~1~~ HEREON APPROVED BY SECRETARY OF INTERIOR JAN. 13, 1905.

NAME OF FATHER	LIVING OR DEAD	NAME OF MOTHER	LIVING OR DEAD	APPLICATION NO.	REMARKS
Alomatubbee					
1 Brokeshoulder	dead	~~~~~~	dead	2049	
2					
3					
4					
5					
6					
7					
8					
9					
10				"No1: testimony relative to continuous residence for a period of three years submitted December 7, 1906."	
11					

APPROVED BY SECRETARY OF INTERIOR.
JUN 1 1903

IDENTIFIED MISSISSIPPI CHOCTAWS 1902 - 1909
Volume II

IDENTIFIED MISSISSIPPI CHOCTAWS CARD NO. 560

IDENTIFICATION ADDRESS Conehatta, Miss. SETTLEMENT ADDRESS Atoka, I.T.
DATE OF IDENTIFICATION April 27, 1903. DATE OF PROOF OF SETTLEMENT Aug 19/03

APPROVED ROLL No.	DAWES ROLL NO.		NAME	RELATIONSHIP TO PERSON FIRST NAMED	AGE	SEX	BLOOD
		1	Jackson, Charlie		49	M	Full
		2	" Frances	Wife	48	F	Full
		3	" Ben	Son	9	M	Full
		4	" Stephen	Son	6	M	Full
		5					
		6					
		7					
		8					

ENROLLMENT OF NOS. 1 2 3 & 4 HEREON APPROVED BY THE SECRETARY OF INTERIOR JAN 13 1905.

CITIZENSHIP CERTIFICATE ISSUED FOR NO 1-2-3-4 AUG 10 1905

	NAME OF FATHER	LIVING OR DEAD	NAME OF MOTHER	LIVING OR DEAD	APPLICATION NO.	REMARKS
1	(Kah-no-nubbee) Johnson Charlie	dead	(Me-hah-te-mah) Sophia Charlie	dead	3959	
2	(Toh-ha-le-chubbee) Sam Wilson	dead	(Pis-ah-to-she-mah) Eliza Wilson	"	"	
3	No.1		No.2		"	
4	No.1		No.2		"	

APPROVED BY SECRETARY OF INTERIOR.
JUN 1 1903

"Nos 1, 2, 3 and 4: Testimony as to continuous residence for a period of three years submitted August 2, 1906."

IDENTIFIED MISSISSIPPI CHOCTAWS 1902 - 1909
Volume II

IDENTIFIED MISSISSIPPI CHOCTAWS   CARD NO. 561

IDENTIFICATION ADDRESS Madden, Miss.   SETTLEMENT ADDRESS Roff Ind. Ter.
DATE OF IDENTIFICATION April 27, 1903.   DATE OF PROOF OF SETTLEMENT Sept 25, 1903

APPROVED ROLL No.	DAWES ROLL NO.	NAME	RELATIONSHIP TO PERSON FIRST NAMED	AGE	SEX	BLOOD
		1 Jacoway, Davis		50	M	Full
		2 " Sealy	Wife	38	F	Full
		3 " Rose	Dau	7mo	F	Full
		4 Jamus, Lulu	S.Dau	12	F	Full
		5				
		6				
		7				
	1-2-3	8 1 2 3 & 4				
CIT ISS		9				
		10				
		11				

NAME OF FATHER	LIVING OR DEAD	NAME OF MOTHER	LIVING OR DEAD	APPLICATION NO.	REMARKS
~~Chuffatubbee~~ 1 Jacoway	dead	Sallie Jacoway	dead	3012	
2 ~~~~~~	"	~~~~~~	"	"	
3 No.1		No.2		"	
4 Jamus	dead	No.2		"	
5					
6					
7					
8					
9					
10 CITIZENSHIP CERTIFICATE ISSUED FOR NO. 4					
11 OCT 17 1903					

APPROVED BY SECRETARY OF INTERIOR.
JUN 1 1903

"Nos 1, 2 and 3: Proof of continuous residence for a period of three years submitted December 20, 1906."
"No4: Proof of continuous residence for a period of three years submitted April 24-1907."

IDENTIFIED MISSISSIPPI CHOCTAWS 1902 - 1909
Volume II

IDENTIFIED MISSISSIPPI CHOCTAWS   CARD NO. 562

IDENTIFICATION ADDRESS Ennis, Miss.   SETTLEMENT ADDRESS
DATE OF IDENTIFICATION April 27, 1903.   DATE OF PROOF OF SETTLEMENT

APPROVED ROLL No.	DAWES ROLL NO.	NAME	RELATIONSHIP TO PERSON FIRST NAMED	AGE	SEX	BLOOD
		1 Philip, Simon		26	M	Full
		2				
		3				
		4				
		5				
		6				
		7				
		8				
		9				
		10				
		11				

DID NOT SUBMIT PROOF OF REMOVAL AND BONA-FIDE SETTLEMENT WITHIN ONE YEAR FROM DATE OF IDENTIFICATION.

NAME OF FATHER	LIVING OR DEAD	NAME OF MOTHER	LIVING OR DEAD	APPLICATION NO.	REMARKS
1 Sam Philip	dead	Sallie Philip		2650	
2					
3					
4					
5					
6					
7					
8					
9					
10					
11					

APPROVED BY SECRETARY OF INTERIOR.
JUN 1 1903

IDENTIFIED MISSISSIPPI CHOCTAWS 1902 - 1909
Volume II

IDENTIFIED MISSISSIPPI CHOCTAWS   CARD NO. 563

IDENTIFICATION ADDRESS Tucker, Miss.   SETTLEMENT ADDRESS Colbert, I.T.
DATE OF IDENTIFICATION April 27, 1903.   DATE OF PROOF OF SETTLEMENT Nov. 27/03

APPROVED ROLL No.	DAWES ROLL NO.	NAME	RELATIONSHIP TO PERSON FIRST NAMED	AGE	SEX	BLOOD
		1. Lick, John (Hintubbee)		72	M	Full
		2.				
		3.				
		4.				
		5.				
		6.				
		7.				
		8.				
CITIZENSHIP CERTIFICATE ISSUED FOR NO 1 NOV 27 1905		9.				
		10.				
		11.				

ENROLLMENT OF NOS ~~~1~~~ HEREON APPROVED BY THE SECRETARY OF INTERIOR JAN 13, 1905

NAME OF FATHER	LIVING OR DEAD	NAME OF MOTHER	LIVING OR DEAD	APPLICATION NO.	REMARKS
1. Con-cha-tubbee	dead	Betsey	dead	1857	
2.					
3.					
4.					
5.					No.1: Proof of continuous residence from date of settlement until date of death submitted November 17, 1905.
6.					
7.					
8.					
9.					
10.					
11.					

APPROVED BY SECRETARY OF INTERIOR.
JUN 1 1903

IDENTIFIED MISSISSIPPI CHOCTAWS 1902 - 1909
Volume II

IDENTIFIED MISSISSIPPI CHOCTAWS CARD NO. 564

IDENTIFICATION ADDRESS Newton, Miss.   SETTLEMENT ADDRESS
DATE OF IDENTIFICATION April 27, 1903.   DATE OF PROOF OF SETTLEMENT

APPROVED ROLL No.	DAWES ROLL NO.	NAME	RELATIONSHIP TO PERSON FIRST NAMED	AGE	SEX	BLOOD
		1. Lish, John		28	M	Full
		2. " Mattie	Wife	23	F	Full
		3. " John Roy	Son	3	M	Full
		4. " Annie	Dau	1	F	Full
		5.				
		6.				
		7.				
		8.				
		9.				
		10.				
		11.				

DID NOT SUBMIT PROOF OF REMOVAL AND BONA FIDE SETTLEMENT WITHIN ONE YEAR FROM DATE OF IDENTIFICATION.

NAME OF FATHER	LIVING OR DEAD	NAME OF MOTHER	LIVING OR DEAD	APPLICATION NO.	REMARKS
1. John Anderson		Lucy Anderson		3472	
2. Doctor Lewis	Dead	Mary Lewis	dead	"	
3. No.1		No.2		"	
4. No.1		No.2		"	
5.					
6.					
7.					
8.					
9.					
10.					
11.					

APPROVED BY SECRETARY OF INTERIOR.
JUN 1 1903

IDENTIFIED MISSISSIPPI CHOCTAWS 1902 - 1909
Volume II

IDENTIFIED MISSISSIPPI CHOCTAWS   CARD NO. 565

IDENTIFICATION ADDRESS Philadelphia, Miss.   SETTLEMENT ADDRESS Stigler, I.T.
DATE OF IDENTIFICATION April 27, 1903.   DATE OF PROOF OF SETTLEMENT Nov. 25, 03

APPROVED ROLL No.	DAWES ROLL NO.		NAME	RELATIONSHIP TO PERSON FIRST NAMED	AGE	SEX	BLOOD
		1	Marris, Elizabeth		36	F	Full
		2					
		3					
		4					
		5					
		6					
		7					
		8					
CITIZENSHIP CERTIFICATE ISSUED FOR NO 1 NOV 25 1903		9					
		10					
		11					

	NAME OF FATHER	LIVING OR DEAD	NAME OF MOTHER	LIVING OR DEAD	APPLICATION NO.	REMARKS
1	Dickson	dead	Nancy Jackson		1993	
2						
3						
4						
5						
6			Testimony relative to continuous residence for a period of three years submitted September 14, 1903.			
7						
8						
9						
10						
11						

APPROVED BY SECRETARY OF INTERIOR.
JUN 1 1903

IDENTIFIED MISSISSIPPI CHOCTAWS 1902 - 1909
Volume II

IDENTIFIED MISSISSIPPI CHOCTAWS CARD NO. 566

IDENTIFICATION ADDRESS Ennis, Miss. SETTLEMENT ADDRESS Ardmore, I.T.
DATE OF IDENTIFICATION April 27, 1903. DATE OF PROOF OF SETTLEMENT August 24th 1903.

APPROVED ROLL No.	DAWES ROLL NO.	NAME	RELATIONSHIP TO PERSON FIRST NAMED	AGE	SEX	BLOOD
		1 Philip, George		23	M	Full
		2 " Bettie	Wife	18	F	Full
		3 " Sissy	Dau	2mo	F	Full

ENROLLMENT OF NOS. 1 2 & 3 HEREON APPROVED BY THE SECRETARY OF INTERIOR JAN 13 1905

CITIZENSHIP CERTIFICATE ISSUED FOR NO 1-2-3 AUG 24 1905

NAME OF FATHER	LIVING OR DEAD	NAME OF MOTHER	LIVING OR DEAD	APPLICATION NO.	REMARKS
1 Williamson Philip		Jinnie Philip		2016	
2 Jesse Porter		Betsey Porter		"	
3 No.1		No.2		"	

APPROVED BY SECRETARY OF INTERIOR.
JUN 1 1903

"Nos 2 and three: Proof of continuous residence for a period of three years submitted December 18, 1906."
"No.1: Proof of death filed showing No1 died January 4, 1906."
"No1: Proof of continuous residence from date of settlement until date of death submitted December 18, 1906."

IDENTIFIED MISSISSIPPI CHOCTAWS 1902 - 1909
Volume II

IDENTIFIED MISSISSIPPI CHOCTAWS   CARD NO. 567

IDENTIFICATION ADDRESS Gip[sic], Miss.   SETTLEMENT ADDRESS
DATE OF IDENTIFICATION April 27, 1903.   DATE OF PROOF OF SETTLEMENT

APPROVED ROLL No.	DAWES ROLL NO.		NAME	RELATIONSHIP TO PERSON FIRST NAMED	AGE	SEX	BLOOD
		1	Stoliby, Solomon		31	M	Full
		2	" Missouri	Wife	40	F	Full
		3	Allen, Bob	S.Son	17	M	Full
		4	" Allie	S.Son	15	M	Full
		5	" Joe	S.Son	13	M	Full
		6	" Lacy	S.Son	10½	M	Full
		7	" Willis	S.Son	5	M	Full
		8					
		9	DID NOT SUBMIT PROOF OF				
		10	REMOVAL AND BONA-FIDE SET-				
		11	TLEMENT WITHIN ONE YEAR FROM DATE OF IDENTIFICATION				

NAME OF FATHER	LIVING OR DEAD	NAME OF MOTHER	LIVING OR DEAD	APPLICATION NO.	REMARKS
1 Bill Stoliby	dead	Lucy Stoliby		3304	
2 Don't know	"	Don't know	dead	"	
3 Kit Allen	"	No.2		"	
4 " "	"	No.2		"	
5 " "	"	No.2		"	
6 " "	"	No.2		"	
7 " "	"	No.2		"	
8					
9					
10					
11					

APPROVED BY SECRETARY OF INTERIOR.
JUN 1 1903

IDENTIFIED MISSISSIPPI CHOCTAWS 1902 - 1909
Volume II

IDENTIFIED MISSISSIPPI CHOCTAWS

CARD NO. 568

IDENTIFICATION ADDRESS Toles, Miss.
SETTLEMENT ADDRESS
DATE OF IDENTIFICATION April 27, 1903.
DATE OF PROOF OF SETTLEMENT

APPROVED ROLL No.	DAWES ROLL NO.		NAME	RELATIONSHIP TO PERSON FIRST NAMED	AGE	SEX	BLOOD
		1	Vaughn, John		26	M	Full
		2					
		3					
		4					
		5					
		6					
		7					
		8					
		9					
		10					
		11					

DID NOT SUBMIT PROOF OF REMOVAL AND BONA-FIDE SETTLEMENT WITHIN ONE YEAR FROM DATE OF IDENTIFICATION.

NAME OF FATHER	LIVING OR DEAD	NAME OF MOTHER	LIVING OR DEAD	APPLICATION NO.	REMARKS
(Lin-tubbee)					
1 Jim Vaughn	dead	Sookey Vaughn	dead	1861	
2					
3					
4					
5					
6					
7					
8					
9					
10					
11					

APPROVED BY SECRETARY OF INTERIOR.
JUN 1 1903

IDENTIFIED MISSISSIPPI CHOCTAWS 1902 - 1909
Volume II

IDENTIFIED MISSISSIPPI CHOCTAWS CARD NO. 569

IDENTIFICATION ADDRESS Rose Hill, Miss. SETTLEMENT ADDRESS
DATE OF IDENTIFICATION April 27, 1903. DATE OF PROOF OF SETTLEMENT

APPROVED ROLL No.	DAWES ROLL NO.	NAME	RELATIONSHIP TO PERSON FIRST NAMED	AGE	SEX	BLOOD
		1 Jim, Ben		17	M	Full
		2				
		3				
		4				
		5				
		6				
		7				
		8				
		9				
		10				
		11				

DID NOT SUBMIT PROOF OF REMOVAL AND BONA-FIDE SETTLEMENT WITHIN ONE YEAR FROM DATE OF IDENTIFICATION.

NAME OF FATHER	LIVING OR DEAD	NAME OF MOTHER	LIVING OR DEAD	APPLICATION NO.	REMARKS
1 Billy Jim		Sookie Jim		2504	
2					
3					
4					
5					
6					
7					
8					
9					
10					
11					

APPROVED BY SECRETARY OF INTERIOR.
JUN 1 1903

IDENTIFIED MISSISSIPPI CHOCTAWS 1902 - 1909
Volume II

IDENTIFIED MISSISSIPPI CHOCTAWS

CARD NO. 570

IDENTIFICATION ADDRESS Conehatta, Miss.   SETTLEMENT ADDRESS
DATE OF IDENTIFICATION April 27, 1903.   DATE OF PROOF OF SETTLEMENT

APPROVED ROLL No.	DAWES ROLL NO.	NAME	RELATIONSHIP TO PERSON FIRST NAMED	AGE	SEX	BLOOD
		1. Williamson, Will		30	M	Full
		2. " Mollie	Wife	30	F	Full
		3. " Nancy	Dau	11	F	Full
		4. " Lingum	Son	9	M	Full
		5. " Adeline	Dau	6	F	Full
		6. " Sistine	Dau	3	F	Full
		7. " Eliza	Dau	2mo	F	Full
		8.				
		9. DID NOT SUBMIT PROOF OF REMOVAL AND BONA-FIDE SETTLEMENT WITHIN ONE YEAR FROM DATE OF IDENTIFICATION.				
		10.				
		11.				

	NAME OF FATHER	LIVING OR DEAD	NAME OF MOTHER	LIVING OR DEAD	APPLICATION NO.	REMARKS
1	John Williamson	dead	Lucy Williamson		1614	
2	Lewis Williamson	"	Becky Williamson	dead	"	
3	No.1		No.2		"	
4	No.1		No.2		"	
5	No.1		No.2		"	
6	No.1		No.2		"	
7	No.1		No.2		"	
8						
9						
10						
11						

APPROVED BY SECRETARY OF INTERIOR.
JUN 1 1903

IDENTIFIED MISSISSIPPI CHOCTAWS 1902 - 1909
Volume II

IDENTIFIED MISSISSIPPI CHOCTAWS   CARD NO. 571

IDENTIFICATION ADDRESS Battlefield, Miss.   SETTLEMENT ADDRESS Ft. Towson I.T.
DATE OF IDENTIFICATION April 27, 1903.   DATE OF PROOF OF SETTLEMENT Oct 15/03

APPROVED ROLL No.	DAWES ROLL NO.	NAME	RELATIONSHIP TO PERSON FIRST NAMED	AGE	SEX	BLOOD
		1 Hochemah, Mary		57	F	Full
		2				
		3				
		4				
		5				
		6				
		7				
		8				

CITIZENSHIP CERTIFICATE ISSUED FOR NO 1 OCT 16 1905

ENROLLMENT OF NOS. 1 HEREON
APPROVED BY THE SECRETARY OF INTERIOR JAN 13 1905.

NAME OF FATHER	LIVING OR DEAD	NAME OF MOTHER	LIVING OR DEAD	APPLICATION NO.	REMARKS
1 Him-o-nubbe	dead	Ho-che-mah	dead	2910	
2					
3					
4					
5					
6					
7					
8					
9					
10					No.1 testimony relative to continuous residence for a period of three years submitted November 17, 1906.
11					

APPROVED BY SECRETARY OF INTERIOR.
JUN 1 1903

IDENTIFIED MISSISSIPPI CHOCTAWS 1902 - 1909
Volume II

IDENTIFIED MISSISSIPPI CHOCTAWS

CARD NO. 572

IDENTIFICATION ADDRESS Holy Cross, Miss. SETTLEMENT ADDRESS Calloway, Ind. Ter.
DATE OF IDENTIFICATION April 27, 1903. DATE OF PROOF OF SETTLEMENT July 22, 1903.

APPROVED ROLL No.	DAWES ROLL NO.		NAME	RELATIONSHIP TO PERSON FIRST NAMED	AGE	SEX	BLOOD
		1	Jack, Martha		75	F	Full
		2					
		3					
		4					
		5					
		6					
		7					
		8					
CITIZENSHIP CERTIFICATE ISSUED FOR NO 1 JUL 22 1903		9					
		10					
		11					

ENROLLMENT
OF NOS. 1 HEREON
APPROVED BY THE SECRETARY
OF INTERIOR JAN 13 1905.

	NAME OF FATHER	LIVING OR DEAD	NAME OF MOTHER	LIVING OR DEAD	APPLICATION NO.	REMARKS
1	Don't know	dead	Don't know	dead	5177	
2						
3						
4						
5						
6						
7						
8						
9						
10						
11						

"No1 died December 14, 1904; testimony as to continuous residence up to her death submitted July 14 and July 21, 1906."

APPROVED BY SECRETARY OF INTERIOR.
JUN 1 1903

IDENTIFIED MISSISSIPPI CHOCTAWS 1902 - 1909
Volume II

IDENTIFIED MISSISSIPPI CHOCTAWS   CARD NO. 573

IDENTIFICATION ADDRESS Franks, Miss.　　SETTLEMENT ADDRESS
DATE OF IDENTIFICATION April 27, 1903.　　DATE OF PROOF OF SETTLEMENT

APPROVED ROLL No.	DAWES ROLL NO.		NAME	RELATIONSHIP TO PERSON FIRST NAMED	AGE	SEX	BLOOD
		1	Hickman, Davis		47	M	Full
		2					
		3					
		4					
		5					
		6					
		7					
		8					
		9					
		10					
		11					

DID NOT SUBMIT PROOF OF REMOVAL AND BONA-FIDE SETTLEMENT WITHIN ONE YEAR FROM DATE OF IDENTIFICATION

	NAME OF FATHER	LIVING OR DEAD	NAME OF MOTHER	LIVING OR DEAD	APPLICATION NO.	REMARKS
1	~~~~ Hickman	dead	Don't know	dead	4853	
2						
3						
4						
5						
6						
7						
8						
9						
10						
11						

APPROVED BY SECRETARY OF INTERIOR.
JUN 1 1903

IDENTIFIED MISSISSIPPI CHOCTAWS 1902 - 1909
Volume II

IDENTIFIED MISSISSIPPI CHOCTAWS   CARD NO. 574

IDENTIFICATION ADDRESS Battlefield, Miss.   SETTLEMENT ADDRESS Ft. Towson I.T.
DATE OF IDENTIFICATION April 27, 1903.   DATE OF PROOF OF SETTLEMENT Oct 15, 03.

APPROVED ROLL No.	DAWES ROLL NO.	NAME	RELATIONSHIP TO PERSON FIRST NAMED	AGE	SEX	BLOOD
		1 Him-o-nubbe, Davis		52	M	Full
		2 " Emmon	Son	20	M	Full
		3 " Ella	Dau	19	F	Full
		4 " Carson	Dau	18	F	Full
		5 " Larbin	Son	14	M	Full
		6				
		7				
		8				

CITIZENSHIP CERTIFICATE ISSUED FOR NO 1-2-3-4-5 OCT 16 1903

ENROLLMENT OF NOS. 1 2 3 4 & 5 HEREON APPROVED BY THE SECRETARY OF INTERIOR JAN 13 1905.

	NAME OF FATHER	LIVING OR DEAD	NAME OF MOTHER	LIVING OR DEAD	APPLICATION NO.	REMARKS
1	Him-mo-nubbe[sic]	dead	Hochemah	dead	2911	
2	No.1		Mattie Him-mo-nubb[sic]	Dead	"	
3	No.1		" "	"	"	
4	No.1		" "	"	"	
5	No.1		" "	"	"	

APPROVED BY SECRETARY OF INTERIOR.
JUN 1 1903

"Nos 1, 3, 4 and 5: testimony relative to continuous residence for a period of three years submitted November 9, 1906."

No2. died September 15, 1906: testimony relative to continuous residence up to his death submitted November 9, 1906.

IDENTIFIED MISSISSIPPI CHOCTAWS 1902 - 1909
Volume II

IDENTIFIED MISSISSIPPI CHOCTAWS   CARD NO. 575

IDENTIFICATION ADDRESS Boyce, La.   SETTLEMENT ADDRESS

DATE OF IDENTIFICATION April 27, 1903.   DATE OF PROOF OF SETTLEMENT

APPROVED ROLL No.	DAWES ROLL NO.	NAME	RELATIONSHIP TO PERSON FIRST NAMED	AGE	SEX	BLOOD
		1 Jack, John		45	M	Full
		2 " Isaac	Son	10	M	Full
		3				
		4				
		5				
		6				
		7				
		8				
		9				
		10				
		11				

DID NOT SUBMIT PROOF OF REMOVAL AND BONA-FIDE SETTLEMENT WITHIN ONE YEAR FROM DATE OF IDENTIFICATION

NAME OF FATHER	LIVING OR DEAD	NAME OF MOTHER	LIVING OR DEAD	APPLICATION NO.	REMARKS
1 Jack	dead	Eliza	dead	5126	
2 No.1		Celeste	"	"	
3					
4					
5					
6					
7					
8					
9					
10					
11					

APPROVED BY SECRETARY OF INTERIOR.
JUN 1 1903

IDENTIFIED MISSISSIPPI CHOCTAWS 1902 - 1909
Volume II

IDENTIFIED MISSISSIPPI CHOCTAWS

CARD NO. 576

IDENTIFICATION ADDRESS Conehatta, Miss. SETTLEMENT ADDRESS Atoka I.T.
DATE OF IDENTIFICATION April 27, 1903. DATE OF PROOF OF SETTLEMENT Aug. 18/03

APPROVED ROLL No.	DAWES ROLL NO.	NAME	RELATIONSHIP TO PERSON FIRST NAMED	AGE	SEX	BLOOD
		1 Jack, Lena		16	F	Full
		2 " Sara Jane	Dau	8mo	F	Full
		3				
		4				
		5				
		6				
		7	ENROLLMENT			
		8	OF NOS. 1 & 2 HEREON			
CITIZENSHIP CERTIFICATE			APPROVED BY THE SECRETARY OF INTERIOR JAN 13 1905.			
ISSUED FOR NO 1-2						
AUG 18 1903		10				
		11				

NAME OF FATHER	LIVING OR DEAD	NAME OF MOTHER	LIVING OR DEAD	APPLICATION NO.	REMARKS
1 Tecumseh Jackson		Don't know	dead	3920	
2 Tom Jack		No.1		"	
3					
4					
5					
6					
7					
8					
9					"Nos 1 and 2: Testimony relative to continuous residence for a period of three years submitted August 31, 1906."
10					
11					

APPROVED BY SECRETARY OF INTERIOR.
JUN 1 1903

IDENTIFIED MISSISSIPPI CHOCTAWS 1902 - 1909
Volume II

IDENTIFIED MISSISSIPPI CHOCTAWS   CARD NO. 577

IDENTIFICATION ADDRESS Standing Pine, Miss.   SETTLEMENT ADDRESS Lime Stone Gap I.T.
DATE OF IDENTIFICATION April 27, 1903.   DATE OF PROOF OF SETTLEMENT Nov 16/03

APPROVED ROLL No.	DAWES ROLL NO.	NAME	RELATIONSHIP TO PERSON FIRST NAMED	AGE	SEX	BLOOD
		1 Jack, Willie		32	M	Full
		2 " Nancy	Wife	31	F	Full
		3 " Ellen	Dau	12	F	Full
		4 " Lillie	Dau	2½	F	Full
		5 " Robert	Son	2mo	M	Full
		6				

CITIZENSHIP CERTIFICATE ISSUED FOR NO 1-2-3 NOV 16 1903
CITIZENSHIP CERTIFICATE ISSUED FOR NO 4-5 MAR 9 1904

ENROLLMENT OF NOS. 1 2 3 4 & 5 HEREON APPROVED BY THE SECRETARY OF INTERIOR JAN 13 1905.

	NAME OF FATHER	LIVING OR DEAD	NAME OF MOTHER	LIVING OR DEAD	APPLICATION NO.	REMARKS
1	Columbus Jack	dead	Winnie Jack		2155	
2	Josie	"	~~~~~~~~~	dead	"	
3	No.1		No.2		"	
4	No.1		No.2		"	
5	No.1		No.2		"	
6						
7	Nos 1 to 5 inclusive. Testimony as to continuous residence of all					
8	for a period of 3 years submitted December 2, 1905.					

APPROVED BY SECRETARY OF INTERIOR.
JUN 1 1903

IDENTIFIED MISSISSIPPI CHOCTAWS 1902 - 1909
Volume II

IDENTIFIED MISSISSIPPI CHOCTAWS CARD NO. 578

IDENTIFICATION ADDRESS Conehatta, Miss. SETTLEMENT ADDRESS Atoka I.T.
DATE OF IDENTIFICATION April 27, 1903. DATE OF PROOF OF SETTLEMENT Aug. 19/03

APPROVED ROLL No.	DAWES ROLL NO.	NAME	RELATIONSHIP TO PERSON FIRST NAMED	AGE	SEX	BLOOD
		1 Jackson, Tecumseh		37	M	Full
		2 " Sophia	Wife	24	F	Full
		3 " Walter	Son	11	M	Full
		4 " McElroy	Son	5	M	Full
		5 " Salina	Dau	4	F	Full
		6 " Winnie	Dau	2	F	Full
		7				
		8				

CITIZENSHIP CERTIFICATE ISSUED FOR NO 1-2-3-4-5-6 AUG 19 1903

ENROLLMENT OF NOS. 1 2 3 4 5 & 6 HEREON APPROVED BY THE SECRETARY OF INTERIOR. JAN. 13. 1905.

	NAME OF FATHER	LIVING OR DEAD	NAME OF MOTHER	LIVING OR DEAD	APPLICATION NO.	REMARKS
1	Sam Jackson	dead	Becky Jackson		3968	
2	Don't know		Amy Billey	dead	"	
3	No.1		Nancy Jackson	dead	"	
4	No.1		No.2		"	
5	No.1		No.2		"	
6	No.1		No.2		"	
7						
8			"Nos 1 to 6 inclusive: Testimony relative to continuous residence for a period of three years submitted August 31, 1906."			
9						
10						
11			"No3 died August 26, 1906."			

APPROVED BY SECRETARY OF INTERIOR.
JUN 1 1903

IDENTIFIED MISSISSIPPI CHOCTAWS 1902 - 1909
Volume II

IDENTIFIED MISSISSIPPI CHOCTAWS   CARD NO. 579

IDENTIFICATION ADDRESS Melon, Miss.   SETTLEMENT ADDRESS Kiowa I.T.
DATE OF IDENTIFICATION April 27, 1903.   DATE OF PROOF OF SETTLEMENT Feby 3, 1904.

APPROVED ROLL No.	DAWES ROLL NO.	NAME		RELATIONSHIP TO PERSON FIRST NAMED	AGE	SEX	BLOOD
		1	Lewis, Sam		30	M	Full
		2	" Pollie	Wife	27	F	Full
		3	" Jim	Son	11	M	Full
		4	" Dorano	Son	7	M	Full
		5	" Ump	Son	5	M	Full
		6	" Claire	Dau	1mo	F	Full

CITIZENSHIP CERTIFICATE
ISSUED FOR NO 1-3-4-5-6
FEB 3 1904

ENROLLMENT
OF NOS. 1,2,3,4,5&6 HEREON
APPROVED BY THE SECRETARY
OF INTERIOR JAN. 13. 1905.

CITIZENSHIP CERTIFICATE
ISSUED FOR NO 2
MAY 9 1904

	NAME OF FATHER	LIVING OR DEAD	NAME OF MOTHER	LIVING OR DEAD	APPLICATION NO.	REMARKS
1	John Lewis	dead	Melissa Lewis	dead	2584	
2	Isaac Johnson	"	~~~~~	"	"	
3	No.1		No.2	"	"	
4	No.1		No.2	"	"	
5	No.1		No.2	"	"	
6	No.1		No.2	"	"	
7						
8						
9						
10						
11						

APPROVED BY SECRETARY OF INTERIOR.
JUN 1 1903

"Nos 1, 3, 4 and 6: testimony relative to continuous residence
for a period of three years submitted October 13, 1906."
{ No2 died March 27, 1906: testimony relative to
No5 died May 12, 1906: continuous residence up to
their death submitted October 13, 1906."

IDENTIFIED MISSISSIPPI CHOCTAWS 1902 - 1909
Volume II

IDENTIFIED MISSISSIPPI CHOCTAWS CARD NO. 580

IDENTIFICATION ADDRESS Ofahoma, Miss.   SETTLEMENT ADDRESS
DATE OF IDENTIFICATION April 27, 1903.   DATE OF PROOF OF SETTLEMENT

APPROVED ROLL No.	DAWES ROLL NO.	NAME	RELATIONSHIP TO PERSON FIRST NAMED	AGE	SEX	BLOOD
		1. Joshua, Sam		49	M	Full
		2. " Jane	Wife	39	F	Full
		3. " Sillian	Dau	19	F	Full
		4. " Mollie	Dau	4	F	Full
		5. " Eva	Dau	2	F	Full
		6. Anderson, Ollie	S.Son	16	M	Full
		7.				
		8. ~~DID NOT SUBMIT PROOF OF~~				
		9. ~~REMOVAL AND BONA-FIDE SET-~~				
		10. ~~TLEMENT WITHIN ONE YEAR~~				
		11. ~~FROM DATE OF IDENTIFICATION~~				

	NAME OF FATHER	LIVING OR DEAD	NAME OF MOTHER	LIVING OR DEAD	APPLICATION NO.	REMARKS
1	Joshua	dead	Liza	dead	3305	
2	John Wilson	"	Martha Wilson		"	
3	No.1		Hoka Joshua	dead	"	
4	No.1		Jane Joshua		"	
5	No.1		" "		"	
6	Bob Anderson		" "		"	
7						
8						
9						
10						
11						

APPROVED BY SECRETARY OF INTERIOR.
JUN 1 1903

IDENTIFIED MISSISSIPPI CHOCTAWS 1902 - 1909
Volume II

IDENTIFIED MISSISSIPPI CHOCTAWS   CARD NO. 581

IDENTIFICATION ADDRESS Stringer, Miss.   SETTLEMENT ADDRESS McMillan I.T.
DATE OF IDENTIFICATION May 5, 1903.   DATE OF PROOF OF SETTLEMENT March 1, 04.

APPROVED ROLL No.	DAWES ROLL NO.	NAME	RELATIONSHIP TO PERSON FIRST NAMED	AGE	SEX	BLOOD
		1 Lewis, Charlie		45	M	Full
		2 " Sallie	Wife	35	F	Full
		3 " Larnie	Son	10	M	Full
		4 " Minnie	Dau	8	F	Full
		5 " Bud	Son	6	M	Full
		6 " Rody	Dau	[?]	F	Full
		7				
		8				

CITIZENSHIP CERTIFICATE ISSUED FOR NO 3-4-5 MAR 1 1904

ENROLLMENT OF NOS. 1,2,3,4,5&6 HEREON APPROVED BY THE SECRETARY OF INTERIOR JAN. 13. 1905.

	NAME OF FATHER	LIVING OR DEAD	NAME OF MOTHER	LIVING OR DEAD	APPLICATION NO.	REMARKS
1	Big John		Jennie John		1965	
2	Jim Lewis	dead	~~~~~~	dead	"	
3	No.1		No.2		"	
4	No.1		No.2		"	
5	No.1		No.2		"	
6	No.1		No.2		"	
7						
8						
9						
10						
11						

CITIZENSHIP CERTIFICATE ISSUED FOR NO ~1-2-6~ APR 27 1904

APPROVED BY SECRETARY OF INTERIOR.
JUN 1   1903

"Nos 1 to 6 inclusive: Proof of continuous residence for a period of three years submitted July 8-1907."

IDENTIFIED MISSISSIPPI CHOCTAWS 1902 - 1909
Volume II

IDENTIFIED MISSISSIPPI CHOCTAWS   CARD NO. 582

IDENTIFICATION ADDRESS Hero, Miss.   SETTLEMENT ADDRESS Marsden I.T.
DATE OF IDENTIFICATION May 5, 1903.   DATE OF PROOF OF SETTLEMENT Jan'y 6, 04

APPROVED ROLL No.	DAWES ROLL NO.	NAME	RELATIONSHIP TO PERSON FIRST NAMED	AGE	SEX	BLOOD
		1 Shoemaker, Wiggin		30	M	Full
		2 " Margaret (Ish-te-mah)	Wife	30	F	Full
		3 " Emerson	Son	1	M	Full
		4				
		5				
		6				
		7				
		8				

CITIZENSHIP CERTIFICATE ISSUED FOR NO 1-2-3 JAN 6 1904

ENROLLMENT OF NOS. 1, 2 & 3 HEREON APPROVED BY THE SECRETARY OF INTERIOR JAN 13 1905.

NAME OF FATHER	LIVING OR DEAD	NAME OF MOTHER	LIVING OR DEAD	APPLICATION NO.	REMARKS
1 Jim Shoemaker	dead	Sallie Shoemaker	dead	1839	
2 Simpson	"	Eliza Simpson	"	"	
3 No.1		No.2		"	
4					
5					
6					
7					
8					
9					
10					
11					

APPROVED BY SECRETARY OF INTERIOR.
JUN 1 1903

"Nos 1&2: Proof of continuous residence for a period of three years submitted May 16, 1906."
"No3: Proof of death filed showing No3 died May 14, 1904."
"No3: Proof of continuous residence from date of settlement until date of death submitted June 2, 1906."

IDENTIFIED MISSISSIPPI CHOCTAWS 1902 - 1909
Volume II

IDENTIFIED MISSISSIPPI CHOCTAWS CARD NO. 583

IDENTIFICATION ADDRESS Ardmore, Ind. Ter.   SETTLEMENT ADDRESS
DATE OF IDENTIFICATION May 28th, 1903.   DATE OF PROOF OF SETTLEMENT

APPROVED ROLL No.	DAWES ROLL NO.	NAME	RELATIONSHIP TO PERSON FIRST NAMED	AGE	SEX	BLOOD
	1736	1 Mose, Laura		2	F	Full
		2				
		3				
		4				
		5 See identified Mississippi Choctaw Card #367.				
		6				
		7 APPROVED BY SECRETARY OF INTERIOR. SEP 14 1903				
		8				
		9 ENROLLMENT OF NOS. 1 HEREON APPROVED BY THE SECRETARY OF INTERIOR Sept 4/05	DID NOT SUBMIT PROOF OF REMOVAL AND BONA-FIDE SETTLEMENT WITHIN ONE YEAR FROM DATE OF IDENTIFICATION.			
		11				

	NAME OF FATHER	LIVING OR DEAD	NAME OF MOTHER	LIVING OR DEAD	APPLICATION NO.	REMARKS
1	John Mose		Lula Mose		1145	No 1 is the daughter of Nos 1068 and 1069 on approved schedule of identified Mississippi Choctaws
2						
3						
4						
5						
6						
7						
8						
9						
10						
11						

IDENTIFIED MISSISSIPPI CHOCTAWS 1902 - 1909
Volume II

IDENTIFIED MISSISSIPPI CHOCTAWS CARD NO. 584

IDENTIFICATION ADDRESS Kiowa Ind Ter   SETTLEMENT ADDRESS Kiowa, I.T.
DATE OF IDENTIFICATION May 28th 1903.   DATE OF PROOF OF SETTLEMENT May 22, 1906

APPROVED ROLL No.	DAWES ROLL NO.		NAME	RELATIONSHIP TO PERSON FIRST NAMED	AGE	SEX	BLOOD
1364	1737	1	Golden, Margaret Ann		1	F	Full
		2					
		3					
		4					
		5	See identified Mississippi Choctaw Card #46.				
		6	~~1~~				
		7	Sept 18, 06				
~~1~~		8	APPROVED BY SECRETARY				
10-23-1906		9					
		10					
		11					

	NAME OF FATHER	LIVING OR DEAD	NAME OF MOTHER	LIVING OR DEAD	APPLICATION NO.	REMARKS
1	Abe Golden		Louisa Golden		1639	No1 is the daughter of ~~Nos 131 and 132 on approved schedule of identified Mississippi Choctaws~~
2						
3						
4						
5						
6						
7						
8	~~DID NOT SUBMIT PROOF OF REMOVAL AND BONA-FIDE SETTLEMENT WITHIN ONE YEAR FROM DATE OF IDENTIFICATION.~~		No1 died Sept 14, 03			
9						
10						
11						

Nº1 - Proof of settlement taken May 22, 1906 under authority Act of Congress Approved April 26, 1906.

No1. Margaret Ann Golden enrolled as a Mississippi Choctaw by Commissioner under Act of Congress of Apr 26, 03.

Dead Oct 1903. See test. Abe Golden MCI 46 taken Nov 2, 03.

Testimony as to removal and settlement taken May 22, 1906, considered as proof of continuous residence from date of settlement until date of death.

Additional testimony as to continuous residence from date of settlement until date of death submitted September 16, 1908.

IDENTIFIED MISSISSIPPI CHOCTAWS 1902 - 1909
Volume II

IDENTIFIED MISSISSIPPI CHOCTAWS

CARD NO. 585

IDENTIFICATION ADDRESS Ravia, Ind. Ter. SETTLEMENT ADDRESS Ravia, I.T.
DATE OF IDENTIFICATION May 28th, 1903. DATE OF PROOF OF SETTLEMENT Nov. 7/03

APPROVED ROLL No.	DAWES ROLL NO.	NAME	RELATIONSHIP TO PERSON FIRST NAMED	AGE	SEX	BLOOD
	1738	1 James, Ore		6mo	F	Full
		2				
		3				
		4				
		5 See identified Mississippi Choctaw Card #397.				
		6				
		7				

APPROVED BY SECRETARY OF INTERIOR.

CITIZENSHIP CERTIFICATE
ISSUED FOR NO 1
NOV - 7 1905

ENROLLMENT
OF NOS. ~~1~~ HEREON
APPROVED BY THE SECRETARY
OF INTERIOR JAN. 13. 1905.

NAME OF FATHER	LIVING OR DEAD	NAME OF MOTHER	LIVING OR DEAD	APPLICATION NO.	REMARKS
1 Wash James		Easter James		1645	No1 is the
2					daughter of
3					Nos 1155
4					and 1156 on
5					approved
6					schedule of
7					identified
8					Mississippi
9					Choctaws.
10					
11					

"No1" Proof of continuous [sic] for a period of three years submitted June 19, 1906."

IDENTIFIED MISSISSIPPI CHOCTAWS 1902 - 1909
Volume II

IDENTIFIED MISSISSIPPI CHOCTAWS   CARD NO. 586

IDENTIFICATION ADDRESS Ravia, Ind. Ter.   SETTLEMENT ADDRESS Madill, Ind. Ter.
DATE OF IDENTIFICATION May 28th, 1903.   DATE OF PROOF OF SETTLEMENT Dec. 14, 1903.

APPROVED ROLL No.	DAWES ROLL NO.	NAME	RELATIONSHIP TO PERSON FIRST NAMED	AGE	SEX	BLOOD
	1739	1 Lewis, Betty		6ms	F	Full
		2				
		3				
		4				
		5 See identified Mississippi Choctaw Card #98				
		6				
		7				
		8				

CITIZENSHIP CERTIFICATE ISSUED FOR NO 1 DEC 14 1903

ENROLLMENT OF NOS. ~~ 1 ~~ HEREON APPROVED BY THE SECRETARY OF INTERIOR JAN 13 1905.

NAME OF FATHER	LIVING OR DEAD	NAME OF MOTHER	LIVING OR DEAD	APPLICATION NO.	REMARKS
1 Smith Lewis		Chuly Lewis		2306	No 1 is the daughter of Nos 314 and 315 approved schedule of identified Mississippi Choctaws.

APPROVED BY SECRETARY OF INTERIOR. SEP 14 1903

No1 Proof of continuous residence for a period of three years submitted February 4, 1907.

IDENTIFIED MISSISSIPPI CHOCTAWS 1902 - 1909
Volume II

IDENTIFIED MISSISSIPPI CHOCTAWS   CARD NO. 587

IDENTIFICATION ADDRESS Ravia, Ind. Ter.   SETTLEMENT ADDRESS Teller, Ind. Ter.
DATE OF IDENTIFICATION May 28th, 1903.   DATE OF PROOF OF SETTLEMENT July 11, 1903

APPROVED ROLL No.	DAWES ROLL NO.	NAME	RELATIONSHIP TO PERSON FIRST NAMED	AGE	SEX	BLOOD
1740	1	Shoemaker, Susie		1	F	Full
	2					
	3					
	4	ENROLLMENT				
	5	OF NOS. ~~~ 1 ~~~ HEREON APPROVED BY THE SECRETARY				
	6	OF INTERIOR June 19-1906				
	7	See identified Mississippi Choctaw Card #283				
	8					

CITIZENSHIP CERTIFICATE
ISSUED FOR NO ~~~ 1 ~~~
MAY 29 1906

	NAME OF FATHER	LIVING OR DEAD	NAME OF MOTHER	LIVING OR DEAD	APPLICATION NO.	REMARKS
1	Willie Shoemaker		Lucy Shoemaker		2462	No1 is the daughter of Nos 841 and 842 approved schedule of identified Mississippi Choctaws.
2						
3						
4						
5						
6						
7						
8						
9					Testimony relative to continuous residence from date of settlement until date of death submitted September 24, 1908.	
10						
11						

IDENTIFIED MISSISSIPPI CHOCTAWS 1902 - 1909
Volume II

IDENTIFIED MISSISSIPPI CHOCTAWS CARD NO. 588

IDENTIFICATION ADDRESS Kiowa, Ind. Ter. SETTLEMENT ADDRESS Kiowa, I.T.
DATE OF IDENTIFICATION May 28th, 1903. DATE OF PROOF OF SETTLEMENT June 4, 1906.

APPROVED ROLL No.	DAWES ROLL NO.		NAME	RELATIONSHIP TO PERSON FIRST NAMED	AGE	SEX	BLOOD
1365	1741	1	Tookolo, John Henry		1	M	Full
		2					
		3					
		4	DID NOT SUBMIT PROOF OF				
		5	REMOVAL AND BONA-FIDE SET-TLEMENT WITHIN ONE YEAR				
		6	FROM DATE OF IDENTIFICATION.				
		7					
		8	See identified Mississippi Choctaw Card #316				
		9	~~~1~~~				
		10	Sept 18				
		11					

ISSUED 10-18-06

	NAME OF FATHER	LIVING OR DEAD	NAME OF MOTHER	LIVING OR DEAD	APPLICATION NO.	REMARKS
1	William O. Tookolo		Lillie Tookolo		2668	No1 is the
2						son of Nos
3						921 and 922
4						approved
5						~~schedule of~~
6						identified
7						Mississippi
8						Choctaws.

9 "No1. Proof of death showing No1 died October 20, 1903, submitted June 4, 1906."
10 "No1. Proof of settlement taken June 4, 1906, under authority of Act of Congress approved April 26, 1906."
11 ~~Testimony taken June 4, 1906, to be considered as proof of continuous residence from~~ date of settlement until date of death.

No1. died Oct 20, 1903
No1. John Henry Tookolo enrolled as a
Mississippi Choctaw by the Commissioner
under Act of Congress of Apr 26, 1906.

IDENTIFIED MISSISSIPPI CHOCTAWS 1902 - 1909
Volume II

IDENTIFIED MISSISSIPPI CHOCTAWS   CARD NO. 589

IDENTIFICATION ADDRESS Stringer, Miss.   SETTLEMENT ADDRESS Durwood, I.T.
DATE OF IDENTIFICATION May 28th, 1903.   DATE OF PROOF OF SETTLEMENT Dec. 22, 1903.

APPROVED ROLL No.	DAWES ROLL NO.		NAME	RELATIONSHIP TO PERSON FIRST NAMED	AGE	SEX	BLOOD
	1742	1	Johnson, Jesse Porter		8ms	M	Full
		2					
		3	ENROLLMENT				
		4	OF NOS. ~~1~~ HEREON				
		5	APPROVED BY THE SECRETARY OF INTERIOR				
		6					
		7					
		8	See identified Mississippi Choctaw Card #92				
CITIZENSHIP CERTIFICATE ISSUED FOR NO 1 DEC 22 1903							
		11					

NAME OF FATHER	LIVING OR DEAD	NAME OF MOTHER	LIVING OR DEAD	APPLICATION NO.	REMARKS
1 Louis Johnson		Nettie Johnson		2229	No1 is the son of Nos 297 and 298 approved schedule of identified Mississippi Choctaws.
2					
3					
4					
5					
6					
7					
8					
9					
10 APPROVED BY SECRETARY OF INTERIOR.					
11					

No1. Proof of continuous residence for a period of three years submitted June 20-1906.

IDENTIFIED MISSISSIPPI CHOCTAWS 1902 - 1909
Volume II

IDENTIFIED MISSISSIPPI CHOCTAWS   CARD NO. 590

IDENTIFICATION ADDRESS Ardmore, Ind. Ter. SETTLEMENT ADDRESS Ardmore I.T.
DATE OF IDENTIFICATION May 28th, 1903. DATE OF PROOF OF SETTLEMENT Feby 2-04.

APPROVED ROLL No.	DAWES ROLL NO.	NAME	RELATIONSHIP TO PERSON FIRST NAMED	AGE	SEX	BLOOD
	1743	1 Reese, Lelia		8ms	F	Full
		2				
		3				
		4				
		5				
		6 See identified Mississippi Choctaw Card #208				
		7				
		8				

CITIZENSHIP CERTIFICATE ISSUED FOR NO ~~1~~ FEB 2 1904

ENROLLMENT OF NOS. ~~1~~ HEREON APPROVED BY THE SECRETARY OF INTERIOR JAN 13 1905.

NAME OF FATHER	LIVING OR DEAD	NAME OF MOTHER	LIVING OR DEAD	APPLICATION NO.	REMARKS
1 John Reese		Fannie Reese		5195	No1 is the daughter of 615 and 616 ~~approved schedule of~~ identified Mississippi Choctaws.

APPROVED BY SECRETARY OF INTERIOR.

"No1: Proof of continuous residence for a period of three years submitted August 20-1907."

IDENTIFIED MISSISSIPPI CHOCTAWS 1902 - 1909
Volume II

IDENTIFIED MISSISSIPPI CHOCTAWS CARD NO. 591

IDENTIFICATION ADDRESS Ardmore, Ind. Ter.   SETTLEMENT ADDRESS Ardmore I.T.
DATE OF IDENTIFICATION May 28th, 1903.   DATE OF PROOF OF SETTLEMENT March 15-04.

APPROVED ROLL No.	DAWES ROLL NO.	NAME	RELATIONSHIP TO PERSON FIRST NAMED	AGE	SEX	BLOOD
	1744	1 Williams, Telan		1	F	Full
		2				
		3				
		4				
		5 See identified Mississippi Choctaw Card #247				
		6				
		7				

CITIZENSHIP CERTIFICATE ISSUED FOR NO ─── 8
MAR 15 1904 9
MAR 15 1904 10
ISSUED FOR NO
CITIZENSHIP CERTIFICATE

ENROLLMENT
OF NOS. ~~~1~~~ HEREON
APPROVED BY THE SECRETARY
OF INTERIOR JAN 13 1905.

	NAME OF FATHER	LIVING OR DEAD	NAME OF MOTHER	LIVING OR DEAD	APPLICATION NO.	REMARKS
1	Jack Williams		Emaline Williams		1964	No1 is the
2						daughter of
3						Nos 734 and
4						735 approved
5						schedule of
6						identified
7						Mississippi
8						Choctaws.
9						
10						
11	APPROVED BY SECRETARY OF INTERIOR.					

"No1. Proof of continuous residence for a period of three years submitted August 27, 1906."

IDENTIFIED MISSISSIPPI CHOCTAWS 1902 - 1909
Volume II

IDENTIFIED MISSISSIPPI CHOCTAWS   CARD NO. 592

IDENTIFICATION ADDRESS Dossville, Miss.   SETTLEMENT ADDRESS Nos 1-3-5 Ardmore I.T. Nos 2-4-6 Durwood I.T.
DATE OF IDENTIFICATION July 8th, 1903.   DATE OF PROOF OF SETTLEMENT Nos 1-3-5 Oct 29/03 Nos 2-4-6 Jany 7/04

APPROVED ROLL No.	DAWES ROLL NO.		NAME	RELATIONSHIP TO PERSON FIRST NAMED	AGE	SEX	BLOOD
	1745	1	Simpson, William		33	M	Full
	1746	2	" Caroline	Wife	26	F	Full
	1747	3	" Ben	Son	7	M	Full
	1748	4	" Fannie	Dau	5	F	Full
	1749	5	" Ira	Son	3	M	Full
	1750	6	" Mabel	Dau	5mo	F	Full

CITIZENSHIP CERTIFICATE ISSUED FOR NO 1-3-5 OCT 29 1903

ENROLLMENT OF NOS. 1 2 3 4 5 & 6 HEREON APPROVED BY THE SECRETARY OF INTERIOR JAN 13 1905.

CITIZENSHIP CERTIFICATE ISSUED FOR NO 2-4-6 JAN 7 1904

APPROVED BY SECRETARY OF INTERIOR. SEP 14 1903

	NAME OF FATHER	LIVING OR DEAD	NAME OF MOTHER	LIVING OR DEAD	APPLICATION NO.	REMARKS
1	Sam Simpson		Mary Simpson		1572	
2	John Hall		Melissa Hall		"	
3	No.1		No.2		"	
4	No.1		No.2		"	
5	No.1		No.2		"	
6	No.1		No.2		"	
7						
8						
9			N°5 proof of continuous residence from the time settlement until date of death filed February 15-08			
10						
11						

"No1: Proof of continuous residence from date of settlement until date of death submitted September 25, 1906."
"No1: Proof of death filed filed[sic] showing No1 died January 17, 1906."

Declaration and proof of settlement of Oct 29, 03 apply to Nos 1-3 & 5 only.
Declaration and proof of settlement of Jany 7/04 apply to Nos 2-4 & 6 only.
"Nos 2, 3, 4 and 6: Proof of continuous residence for a period of three years submitted August 4, 1906."
No2 is now wife of No.1 on card 34.

IDENTIFIED MISSISSIPPI CHOCTAWS 1902 - 1909
Volume II

IDENTIFIED MISSISSIPPI CHOCTAWS CARD NO. 593

IDENTIFICATION ADDRESS Masengale, Miss. { SETTLEMENT ADDRESS Roff, Ind. Ter.
DATE OF IDENTIFICATION July 8th, 1903. DATE OF PROOF OF SETTLEMENT Dec. 10, 1903.

APPROVED ROLL No.	DAWES ROLL NO.	NAME (This applies to No.2, only.)	RELATIONSHIP TO PERSON FIRST NAMED	AGE	SEX	BLOOD
	1751	1 Smith, Amie (A-ha-ka-te-ma)		40	F	Full
	1752	2 " Mack	Son	10	M	"
		3				
		4				
		5				

6 ENROLLMENT
OF NOS. ~~2~~ HEREON
APPROVED BY THE SECRETARY
OF INTERIOR JAN. 13. 1905.

No1 DID NOT SUBMIT PROOF OF REMOVAL AND BONA-FIDE SETTLEMENT WITHIN ONE YEAR FROM DATE OF IDENTIFICATION.

CITIZENSHIP CERTIFICATE ISSUED FOR NO 2
DEC 10 1908

10 APPROVED BY SECRETARY OF INTERIOR SEP 14 1903
11

NAME OF FATHER	LIVING OR DEAD	NAME OF MOTHER	LIVING OR DEAD	APPLICATION NO.	REMARKS
1 Willis (No-ubbee)	Dead	Eliza (Ha-ka-ya-to-ma)	Dead	1934	
2 Thomas Smith	"	No.1	Dead	"	
3					
4					
5					
6					
7					
8					
9					
10					
11					

See test. taken [remainder illegible]

No.2: Proof of continuous residence for a period of three years submitted February 27-1907.

IDENTIFIED MISSISSIPPI CHOCTAWS 1902 - 1909
Volume II

IDENTIFIED MISSISSIPPI CHOCTAWS CARD NO. 594

IDENTIFICATION ADDRESS Thomastown, Miss. SETTLEMENT ADDRESS Marlow I.T.
DATE OF IDENTIFICATION July 8th, 1903. DATE OF PROOF OF SETTLEMENT Oct. 23/03.

APPROVED ROLL No.	DAWES ROLL NO.	NAME	RELATIONSHIP TO PERSON FIRST NAMED	AGE	SEX	BLOOD
	1753	1 York, Amos		22	M	Full
	1754	2 " Lettie Lee	Dau	2	F	Full
		3				
		4				
		5 APPROVED BY SEC	SEP	14	1903	
		6				
		7				
		8				

CITIZENSHIP CERTIFICATE ISSUED FOR NO 1-2 OCT 23 1903

ENROLLMENT OF NOS. 1 & 2 HEREON APPROVED BY THE SECRETARY OF INTERIOR JAN. 13 1905.

NAME OF FATHER	LIVING OR DEAD	NAME OF MOTHER	LIVING OR DEAD	APPLICATION NO.	REMARKS
1 Rufus York		Malissa York		4421	
2 No.1		Sealy York	Dead	"	
3					
4					
5					
6					
7					
8					
9					
10					
11					

"Nos 1 and 2: Proof of continuous residence for a period of three years submitted August 1-1907."

IDENTIFIED MISSISSIPPI CHOCTAWS 1902 - 1909
Volume II

IDENTIFIED MISSISSIPPI CHOCTAWS CARD NO. 595

IDENTIFICATION ADDRESS Engine, Miss.   SETTLEMENT ADDRESS Nos 2&3 Ft Towson I.T.
DATE OF IDENTIFICATION July 8th, 1903. DATE OF PROOF OF SETTLEMENT Nos 2&3 Oct 15/03

APPROVED ROLL No.	DAWES ROLL NO.	NAME	RELATIONSHIP TO PERSON FIRST NAMED	AGE	SEX	BLOOD
	1755	1 Bob, Henry		44	M	Full
	1756	2 " Sallie	Wife	32	F	Full
	1757	3 " Emma	Dau	5	F	Full
		4				
		5		SEP 14 1903		
		6				

ENROLLMENT No 1 DID NOT SUBMIT PROOF
7 OF NOS. 2 & 3 HEREON OF REMOVAL AND BONA-FIDE
APPROVED BY THE SECRETARY SET-TLEMENT WITHIN ONE YEAR
8 OF INTERIOR JAN. 13, 1905. FROM DATE OF IDENTIFICATION.

CITIZENSHIP CERTIFICATE
ISSUED FOR NO 2-3
OCT 16 1905

	NAME OF FATHER	LIVING OR DEAD	NAME OF MOTHER	LIVING OR DEAD	APPLICATION NO.	REMARKS
1	Bob (Pis-un-tubbee)	Dead	Amy Bob	Dead	1987	
2	(Kah-tubbee) William Thompson	"	Sockia	"	"	
3	No.1		No.2		"	
4						
5						
6						
7						
8						
9						
10						
11						

Declaration and proof of settlement apply to Nos 2 & 3 only.
No1 died in Miss. See test of No2 taken at Ft. Towson Oct 15/03.
"Nos 2 and 3. testimony relative to continuous residence for a period of three years submitted Dec. 14, 1906."

IDENTIFIED MISSISSIPPI CHOCTAWS 1902 - 1909
Volume II

IDENTIFIED MISSISSIPPI CHOCTAWS   CARD NO. 596

IDENTIFICATION ADDRESS Sterrett, Ind. Ter.   SETTLEMENT ADDRESS Durwood I.T.
DATE OF IDENTIFICATION July 8th, 1903.   DATE OF PROOF OF SETTLEMENT Oct 7/03.

APPROVED ROLL No.	DAWES ROLL NO.		NAME	RELATIONSHIP TO PERSON FIRST NAMED	AGE	SEX	BLOOD
	1758	1	Johnson, Wiley		21	M	Full
	1759	2	" Stella	Wife	16	F	Full
		3					
		4					
		5					
		6					
		7					
		8					
		9					
		10					
		11					

CITIZENSHIP CERTIFICATE ISSUED FOR NO 1-2 OCT 5 1905

ENROLLMENT OF NOS. 1 & 2 HEREON APPROVED BY THE SECRETARY OF INTERIOR JAN. 13, 1905.

APPROVED BY SECRETARY OF INTERIOR SEP 14 1903

	NAME OF FATHER	LIVING OR DEAD	NAME OF MOTHER	LIVING OR DEAD	APPLICATION NO.	REMARKS
1	Isaac Johnson		Susie Johnson		1960	
2	Henry Larndeen		Sookey Peters		"	
3						
4						
5						
6						
7						
8						
9			"Nos 1 and 2: Proof of continuous residence for a period			
10			of three years submitted January 14, 1907."			
11						

IDENTIFIED MISSISSIPPI CHOCTAWS 1902 - 1909
Volume II

IDENTIFIED MISSISSIPPI CHOCTAWS   CARD NO. 597

IDENTIFICATION ADDRESS Adamsville, Miss.   SETTLEMENT ADDRESS McMillan, I.T.
DATE OF IDENTIFICATION July 8th, 1903.   DATE OF PROOF OF SETTLEMENT Oct. 7, 03

APPROVED ROLL No.	DAWES ROLL NO.	NAME		RELATIONSHIP TO PERSON FIRST NAMED	AGE	SEX	BLOOD
	1760	1	Jackson, Willis		50	M	Full
	1761	2	" Eliza	Wife	30	F	Full
	1762	3	" Jameson	Son	15	M	Full
	1763	4	" Ida	Dau	13	F	Full
	1764	5	" Alice	Dau	9	F	Full
	1765	6	" Albert	Son	7	M	Full
	1766	7	" Nixie	Dau	4	F	Full
		8	APPROVED BY SECRETARY OF INTERIOR. SEP 14 1903				

CITIZENSHIP CERTIFICATE ISSUED FOR NO 1-3-4-6-7 OCT 7 1905

ENROLLMENT OF NOS. 1 3 4 6 & 7 HEREON APPROVED BY THE SECRETARY OF INTERIOR JAN 13 1905.

	NAME OF FATHER	LIVING OR DEAD	NAME OF MOTHER	LIVING OR DEAD	APPLICATION NO.	REMARKS
1	Jackson	Dead	~~~~~	Dead	1961	No1
2	George Gibson	"	~~~~~	Dead	"	
3	No.1		No.2		"	
4	No.1		No.2		"	
5	No.1		No.2		"	
6	No.1		No.2		"	
7	No.1		No.2		"	

No2&5 DID NOT SUBMIT PROOF OF REMOVAL AND BONA-FIDE SETTLEMENT WITHIN ONE YEAR FROM DATE OF IDENTIFICATION.

Declaration and proof of settlement apply to Nos 1-3-4-6-7 only - Oct 7, 03
"Nos 1,3,4,6 and 7: Proof of continuous residence for a period of three years submitted November 23-1906."

IDENTIFIED MISSISSIPPI CHOCTAWS 1902 - 1909
Volume II

IDENTIFIED MISSISSIPPI CHOCTAWS CARD NO. 598

IDENTIFICATION ADDRESS Hays, Mississippi SETTLEMENT ADDRESS
DATE OF IDENTIFICATION July 8th, 1903. DATE OF PROOF OF SETTLEMENT

APPROVED ROLL No.	DAWES ROLL NO.	NAME	RELATIONSHIP TO PERSON FIRST NAMED	AGE	SEX	BLOOD
	1767	Williamson, Malissa		35	F	Full
	1768	" Bike	Son	11	M	"
		APPROVED BY SECRETARY OF INTERIOR.			1903	
		DID NOT SUBMIT PROOF OF REMOVAL AND BONA-FIDE SETTLEMENT WITHIN ONE YEAR FROM DATE OF IDENTIFICATION				

NAME OF FATHER	LIVING OR DEAD	NAME OF MOTHER	LIVING OR DEAD	APPLICATION NO.	REMARKS
Don't know	Dead	Mary	Dead	4190	
Mike Williamson	Separated from No.1	No.1		"	

IDENTIFIED MISSISSIPPI CHOCTAWS 1902 - 1909
Volume II

IDENTIFIED MISSISSIPPI CHOCTAWS CARD NO. 599

IDENTIFICATION ADDRESS Saint Anns[sic], Miss.   SETTLEMENT ADDRESS

DATE OF IDENTIFICATION July 8th, 1903.   DATE OF PROOF OF SETTLEMENT

APPROVED ROLL No.	DAWES ROLL NO.	NAME	RELATIONSHIP TO PERSON FIRST NAMED	AGE	SEX	BLOOD
	1769	1 Billey, Sampson		36	M	Full
	1770	2 " Nicey	Wife	29	F	Full
	1771	3 " Basie	Son	13	M	Full
	1772	4 " Williston	Son	7	M	Full
	1773	5 " Davis	Son	4	M	Full
		6				
		7				
		8 APPROVED BY SECRETARY OF INTERIOR.		4	1903	
		9 DID NOT SUBMIT PROOF OF				
		10 REMOVAL AND BONA-FIDE SET- TLEMENT WITHIN ONE YEAR				
		11 FROM DATE OF IDENTIFICATION.				

NAME OF FATHER	LIVING OR DEAD	NAME OF MOTHER	LIVING OR DEAD	APPLICATION NO.	REMARKS
1 Billey Willis	Dead	Lucy Joshua		2106	
2 Amos	"	Eliza	Dead	"	
3 No.1		No.2		"	
4 No.1		No.2		"	
5 No.1		No.2		"	
6					
7					
8					
9					
10					
11					

IDENTIFIED MISSISSIPPI CHOCTAWS 1902 - 1909
Volume II

IDENTIFIED MISSISSIPPI CHOCTAWS   CARD NO. 600

IDENTIFICATION ADDRESS Cushtusa, Miss. SETTLEMENT ADDRESS Atoka I.T.
DATE OF IDENTIFICATION July 8th, 1903. DATE OF PROOF OF SETTLEMENT Aug 15/03.

APPROVED ROLL No.	DAWES ROLL NO.		NAME	RELATIONSHIP TO PERSON FIRST NAMED	AGE	SEX	BLOOD
	1774	1	Phillip, Williamson		55	M	Full
	1775	2	" Jinnie	Wife	55	F	Full
	1776	3	" Leanna	Dau	20	F	Full
	1777	4	" Sina	Dau	14	F	Full
	1778	5	" Albert	Son	16	M	Full
	1779	6	" Dibin	Son	8	M	Full
	1780	7	" Bob	Son	5	M	Full
		8	APPROVED BY SECRETARY OF INTERIOR.		14	1903	

CITIZENSHIP CERTIFICATE ISSUED FOR NO 1-2-3-4-5-6-7 OCT 22 1903

ENROLLMENT OF NOS. 1 2 3 4 5 6 & 7 HEREON APPROVED BY THE SECRETARY OF INTERIOR JAN. 13. 1905.

	NAME OF FATHER	LIVING OR DEAD	NAME OF MOTHER	LIVING OR DEAD	APPLICATION NO.	REMARKS
1	Simon Phillip	Dead	Nancy Phillip	Dead	2044	
2	John Ah-to-blechy	Dead	~~~~~~~~~~	Dead	"	
3	No.1		No.2		"	
4	No.1		No.2		"	
5	No.1		No.2		"	
6	No.1		No.2		"	
7	No.1		No.2		"	
8						
9						
10						
11						

Nos 1,2,4,6 and 7: Testimony relative to continuous residence for a period of three years submitted October 11, 1906.

No.3 died June 30, 1906:   { Testimony relative to continuous
No.5 died June 4, 1904:   { residence up to the time of their death
                           { submitted October 11, 1906.

IDENTIFIED MISSISSIPPI CHOCTAWS 1902 - 1909
Volume II

IDENTIFIED MISSISSIPPI CHOCTAWS CARD NO. 601

IDENTIFICATION ADDRESS Sterrett, Ind. Ter. SETTLEMENT ADDRESS Kemp, I.T.
DATE OF IDENTIFICATION July 8th, 1903. DATE OF PROOF OF SETTLEMENT March 12-1904

APPROVED ROLL No.	DAWES ROLL NO.		NAME	RELATIONSHIP TO PERSON FIRST NAMED	AGE	SEX	BLOOD
	1781	1	Williamson, Tom		18	M	Full
	1782	2	" Mary	Wife	19	F	Full
	1783	3	" Davie	Son	1mo	M	Full
		4					
		5					
		6					
		7		4 1903			
		8	APPROVED BY SEC RETARY OF INTERIOR				

CITIZENSHIP CERTIFICATE ISSUED FOR NO 1-2-3- MAR 12 1904

ENROLLMENT OF NOS. 1, 2 & 3 HEREON APPROVED BY THE SECRETARY OF INTERIOR JAN. 13. 1905.

	NAME OF FATHER	LIVING OR DEAD	NAME OF MOTHER	LIVING OR DEAD	APPLICATION NO.	REMARKS
1	Little Charley	Dead	Amie Williamson		2454	
2	John Cooks	Dead	Sophie Frenchman		"	
3	No.1		No.2		"	
4						
5						
6						
7						
8						
9			"No.2 died March 27, 1904: testimony as to continuous residence up to her death submitted June 21, 1906."			
10			Nos 1 and 3. Testimony as to continuous residence for a period of three years submitted July 24, 1906			
11						

IDENTIFIED MISSISSIPPI CHOCTAWS 1902 - 1909
Volume II

IDENTIFIED MISSISSIPPI CHOCTAWS   CARD NO. 602

IDENTIFICATION ADDRESS Rose Hill, Miss.   SETTLEMENT ADDRESS No.8 Ardmore, I.T.
DATE OF IDENTIFICATION July 8th, 1903.   DATE OF PROOF OF SETTLEMENT No.8 Feb. 23-04

APPROVED ROLL No.	DAWES ROLL NO.	NAME	RELATIONSHIP TO PERSON FIRST NAMED	AGE	SEX	BLOOD
	1784	1 Jim, Billy		50	M	Full
	1785	2 " Sookie	Wife	40	F	Full
	1786	3 " Logan	Son	18	M	Full
	1787	4 " Tom George	Son	15	M	Full
	1788	5 " Henry	Son	12	M	Full
	1789	6 " Tycoolie	Son	10	M	Full
	1790	7 " Lissie	Dau	8	F	Full
	1791	8 Tom, Willie	Neph	18	M	Full

CITIZENSHIP CERTIFICATE ISSUED FOR NO ~~8~~   ENROLLMENT OF NOS. 8 HEREON APPROVED BY THE SECRETARY OF INTERIOR.
APR 26 1904

No.8 - Died November 21st 1906.

NAME OF FATHER	LIVING OR DEAD	NAME OF MOTHER	LIVING OR DEAD	APPLICATION NO.	REMARKS
1 Jim On-tubbee	Dead	Jennie Jim	Dead	2505	No1
2 ~~~~~~~~	"	Eliza		"	
3 No.1		No.2		"	
4 No.1		No.2		"	
5 No.1		No.2		"	
6 No.1		No.2		"	
7 No.1		No.2		"	
8 Little Tom		Julia Tom	Dead	"	

APPROVED BY SECRETARY OF INTERIOR.   SEP 4 1903

No1 to 7 DID NOT SUBMIT PROOF OF REMOVAL AND BONA-FIDE SETTLEMENT WITHIN ONE YEAR FROM DATE OF IDENTIFICATION.

Declaration and proof of settlement Feb. 23-04 apply to No8 only.

No.8. Proof of continuous residence from date of settlement to date of death submitted Sept. 27th 1907.
" " Died on 21st day of Nov 1906 proof filed 27 day of Sept-1907

IDENTIFIED MISSISSIPPI CHOCTAWS 1902 - 1909
Volume II

IDENTIFIED MISSISSIPPI CHOCTAWS   CARD NO. 603

IDENTIFICATION ADDRESS Ardmore, Ind. Ter.   SETTLEMENT ADDRESS Nos 1-2-5-6 M°Millan I.T. Nos. 3&4 M°Millan I.T.
DATE OF IDENTIFICATION July 8th, 1903.   DATE OF PROOF OF SETTLEMENT Nos 1-2-5-6 March 23-04 Nos. 3&4 May 4, 04

APPROVED ROLL No.	DAWES ROLL NO.		NAME	RELATIONSHIP TO PERSON FIRST NAMED	AGE	SEX	BLOOD
	1792	1	Emi-yah-tubbe, Wallace		55	M	Full
	1793	2	" Nancy	Wife	54	F	Full
	1794	3	" Martha	Dau	18	F	Full
	1795	4	" Minnie	Dau	16	F	Full
	1796	5	" Flemmon	Son	14	M	Full
	1797	6	" Johnnie	Son	11	M	Full
		7					

CITIZENSHIP CERTIFICATE ISSUED FOR NO 1-2-5-6 MAR 22 1904
CITIZENSHIP CERTIFICATE ISSUED FOR NO ~~3-4~~ MAY 4 1904

ENROLLMENT OF NOS. 1 2 3 4 5&6 HEREON APPROVED BY THE SECRETARY OF INTERIOR JAN 13 1905.

APPROVED BY SECRETARY OF INTERIOR.   4 1903

	NAME OF FATHER	LIVING OR DEAD	NAME OF MOTHER	LIVING OR DEAD	APPLICATION NO.	REMARKS
1	Emi-yah-tubbe	Dead	~~~~~~~	Dead	2066	
2	~~~~~~~	"	~~~~~~~	"	"	
3	No.1		No.2		"	
4	No.1		No.2		"	
5	No.1		No.2		"	
6	No.1		No.2		"	
7						
8						
9						
10						
11			"No4: Proof of continuous residence for a period of three years submitted December 17-1906."			

"Nos 1,2,5&6: Proof of continuous residence for a period of three years submitted August 15, 1906."

Declaration and proof of settlement of Mar 22,04 apply to Nos 1-2-5&6 only.
Settlement address Nos 3&4 M°Millan, I.T.
Date of proof of settlement Nos 3&4 May 4/04.
Declaration and proof of settlement of May 4/04 apply to Nos 3&4 only.
No3: Proof of continuous residence for a period of three years submitted August 15, 1906.

IDENTIFIED MISSISSIPPI CHOCTAWS 1902 - 1909
Volume II

IDENTIFIED MISSISSIPPI CHOCTAWS

CARD NO. 604

IDENTIFICATION ADDRESS Tucker, Miss.   SETTLEMENT ADDRESS Atoka I.T.
DATE OF IDENTIFICATION July 8th, 1903.   DATE OF PROOF OF SETTLEMENT Aug 17, 03.

APPROVED ROLL No.	DAWES ROLL NO.	NAME	RELATIONSHIP TO PERSON FIRST NAMED	AGE	SEX	BLOOD
	1798	1 Billey, Lem		21	M	Full
		2				
		3				
		4				
		5				
		6 APPROVED BY SECRETARY OF INTERIOR. 1903				
		7 ENROLLMENT				
		8 OF NOS. ~1~ HEREON APPROVED BY THE SECRETARY				
CITIZENSHIP CERTIFICATE		OF INTERIOR JAN 13 1905.				
ISSUED FOR NO 1 SEP 24 190	10					
		11				

NAME OF FATHER	LIVING OR DEAD	NAME OF MOTHER	LIVING OR DEAD	APPLICATION NO.	REMARKS
		Te-chubbee			
1 Billey	dead	Kissie Billey	Dead	2048	
2					
3					
4					
5					
6					
7					
8					Testimony as to residence taken Dec. 7, 1908 and
9					January 20 and 23, 1909. Question as to whether
10					he forfeited his rights by returning to Mississippi.
11					

IDENTIFIED MISSISSIPPI CHOCTAWS 1902 - 1909
Volume II

IDENTIFIED MISSISSIPPI CHOCTAWS   CARD NO. 605

IDENTIFICATION ADDRESS Hickory, Miss.   SETTLEMENT ADDRESS Ardmore, I.T.
DATE OF IDENTIFICATION July 8th, 1903.   DATE OF PROOF OF SETTLEMENT Feb. 25-04

APPROVED ROLL No.	DAWES ROLL NO.	NAME	RELATIONSHIP TO PERSON FIRST NAMED	AGE	SEX	BLOOD
	1799	1 Sam, Wallace		21	M	Full
		2				
		3				
		4				
		5				
		6				
		APPROVED BY SECRETARY OF INTERIOR 1903				
		8				

CITIZENSHIP CERTIFICATE ISSUED FOR NO 1 FEB 25 1904

ENROLLMENT OF NOS. 1 HEREON APPROVED BY THE SECRETARY OF INTERIOR JAN. 13. 1905.

NAME OF FATHER	LIVING OR DEAD	NAME OF MOTHER	LIVING OR DEAD	APPLICATION NO.	REMARKS
1 Little Sam	Dead	Martha Sam	Dead	2120	
2					
3					
4					
5					
6					
7					
8					
9			No1 Proof of continuous residence for a period of three		
10			years submitted February 20, 1907.		
11					

IDENTIFIED MISSISSIPPI CHOCTAWS 1902 - 1909
Volume II

IDENTIFIED MISSISSIPPI CHOCTAWS   CARD NO. 606

IDENTIFICATION ADDRESS McGlothin, La.   SETTLEMENT ADDRESS Mill Creek I.T.
DATE OF IDENTIFICATION July 8th, 1903.   DATE OF PROOF OF SETTLEMENT Jan'y 19-04.

APPROVED ROLL No.	DAWES ROLL NO.		NAME	RELATIONSHIP TO PERSON FIRST NAMED	AGE	SEX	BLOOD
	1800	1	Scott, Liza		21	F	Full
	1801	2	" Aline	Dau	6	F	Full
		3					
		4					
		5					
		6					
		7	APPROVED BY SECRETARY OF INTERIOR. SEP 14 1903				
		8					
		9	ENROLLMENT OF NOS. 1 & 2 HEREON APPROVED BY THE SECRETARY OF INTERIOR June 19-1906.				
		10					
		11					

	NAME OF FATHER	LIVING OR DEAD	NAME OF MOTHER	LIVING OR DEAD	APPLICATION NO.	REMARKS
1	John Scott		Celeste	Dead	5127	
2	Scott	Dead	No.1		"	
3						
4						
5						
6			Nos. 1 & 2 returned to Louisiana before selecting allotments.			
7			Did they abandon their residence and forfeit their rights?			
8						
9						
10						
11						

IDENTIFIED MISSISSIPPI CHOCTAWS 1902 - 1909
Volume II

IDENTIFIED MISSISSIPPI CHOCTAWS   CARD NO. 607

IDENTIFICATION ADDRESS Sterrett, Ind. Ter. SETTLEMENT ADDRESS Nos.1,3,4,5&6 Kemp, I.T.
                                                                No2 Paucaunla, I.T.
DATE OF IDENTIFICATION July 8th, 1903. DATE OF PROOF OF SETTLEMENT Nos.1,3,4,5&6 Dec 18,1903

APPROVED ROLL No.	DAWES ROLL NO.	NAME	RELATIONSHIP TO PERSON FIRST NAMED	AGE	SEX	BLOOD
	1802	1 Thompson, Lem		21	M	Full
	1803	2 " Suala	Sis	18	F	Full
	1804	3 " Lonie	Sis	16	F	Full
	1805	4 " Sydney	Bro	17	M	Full
	1806	5 " Leona	Sis	12	F	Full
	1807	6 " Marsaline	Sis	10	F	Full
		7				

No2 Nov. 13/03

CITIZENSHIP CERTIFICATE
ISSUED FOR NO 1,3,4,5&6   APPROVED BY SECRETARY OF INTERIOR. SEP 14 1903
DEC 18 1903 9
CITIZENSHIP CERTIFICATE
ISSUED FOR NO ~~2~~   11

NAME OF FATHER FEB 19 1904	LIVING OR DEAD	NAME OF MOTHER	LIVING OR DEAD	APPLICATION NO.	REMARKS
1 Alex Thompson	Dead	Jane Thompson	Dead	2119	
2 "	"	"	"	"	
3 "	"	"	"	"	
4 "	"	"	"	"	
5 "	"	"	"	"	
6 "	"	"	"	"	
7		Nos 1,2,3,4,5 and 6: additional testimony relative			
8		to continuous residence submitted January 29-1908			

ENROLLMENT
OF NOS. 1 2 3 4 5&6 HEREON   No2 wife of No1 Identified 26
APPROVED BY THE SECRETARY
OF INTERIOR JAN 13 1905

Declaration and proof of settlement of Nov 13/03
apply to No2 only
Declaration and proof of settlement of Dec 18/03
apply to Nos 1-3-4-5&6 only.

"Nos 2,4,5 and 6: testimony relative to continuous residence for a period
of three years submitted February 18, 1907."
No1 died about May 26-1904. No3 died about March 28, 1904:
testimony relative to continuous residence up to the time of their deaths
submitted February 18, 1907.

IDENTIFIED MISSISSIPPI CHOCTAWS 1902 - 1909
Volume II

IDENTIFIED MISSISSIPPI CHOCTAWS CARD NO. 608
IDENTIFICATION ADDRESS Decatur, Miss.   SETTLEMENT ADDRESS Ardmore I.T.
DATE OF IDENTIFICATION July 8th, 1903.   DATE OF PROOF OF SETTLEMENT March 16, 04.

APPROVED ROLL No.	DAWES ROLL NO.		NAME	RELATIONSHIP TO PERSON FIRST NAMED	AGE	SEX	BLOOD
	1808	1	Wallace, Wesley		27	M	Full
	1809	2	" Letitia	Wife	32	F	Full
	1810	3	Jackson, Tom	StepSon	13	M	Full
	1811	4	Wallace, Lemmie	Dau	3	F	Full
	1812	5	" Earley	Son	1	M	Full
		6					
		7					
		8	APPROVED BY SECRETARY OF INTERIOR. SEP 4 1903				

CITIZENSHIP CERTIFICATE ISSUED FOR NO 1-2-3-4-5 MAR 16 1904

ENROLLMENT OF NOS. 1 2 3 4 & 5 HEREON APPROVED BY THE SECRETARY OF INTERIOR JAN 13 1905.

	NAME OF FATHER	LIVING OR DEAD	NAME OF MOTHER	LIVING OR DEAD	APPLICATION NO.	REMARKS
1	John Wallace		Sarah Wallace	Dead	3921	No 1
2	Ah-no-sa-chubbee		Don't know	Dead	"	
3	Jim Jackson	Dead	No.2		"	
4	No.1		No.2		"	
5	No.1		No.2		"	
6			Nos 1 and 2 = Testimony relative to continuous residence from date of settlement until date of death submitted September 25, 1908.			
7						
8						
9			Nos. 3,4 and 5 = Testimony relative to continuous residence for a period of three years submitted September 25, 1908.			
10						
11						

IDENTIFIED MISSISSIPPI CHOCTAWS 1902 - 1909
Volume II

IDENTIFIED MISSISSIPPI CHOCTAWS CARD NO. 609

IDENTIFICATION ADDRESS Philadelphia, Miss.   SETTLEMENT ADDRESS Kiowa I.T.
DATE OF IDENTIFICATION July 8th, 1903.   DATE OF PROOF OF SETTLEMENT Oct 9/03.

APPROVED ROLL No.	DAWES ROLL NO.		NAME	RELATIONSHIP TO PERSON FIRST NAMED	AGE	SEX	BLOOD
	1813	1	Jackson, Nancy		65	F	Full
	1814	2	" Bessie	Dau	6	F	Full
	1815	3	" Patsey	Dau	9	F	Full
		4					
		5					
		6					
		7					
		8					
CITIZENSHIP CERTIFICATE ISSUED FOR NO 1-2-3 OCT 9 1903		10					
		11	APPROVED BY SECRETARY OF INTERIOR. 1903				

ENROLLMENT OF NOS. 1 2 & 3 HEREON APPROVED BY THE SECRETARY OF INTERIOR JAN 13 1905.

	NAME OF FATHER	LIVING OR DEAD	NAME OF MOTHER	LIVING OR DEAD	APPLICATION NO.	REMARKS
1	Big Jack	Dead	Martha Big Jack	Dead	1991	
2	Jackson	"	No.1	"		
3	"	"	No.1	"		
4						
5						
6						
7						
8						
9						
10						
11						

"Nos 1,2 and 3: Testimony relative to continuous residence for a period of three years submitted September 10, 1906."

IDENTIFIED MISSISSIPPI CHOCTAWS 1902 - 1909
Volume II

IDENTIFIED MISSISSIPPI CHOCTAWS   CARD NO. 610

IDENTIFICATION ADDRESS Brown, Mississippi   SETTLEMENT ADDRESS Nos 1,2&4 Mannsville, I.T.
   No.3 Durwood, I.T.
DATE OF IDENTIFICATION July 8th, 1903.   DATE OF PROOF OF SETTLEMENT Nos 1,2&4 Dec. 23, 1903
   No.3 May 18 and 25, 1906

APPROVED ROLL No.	DAWES ROLL NO.		NAME			RELATIONSHIP TO PERSON FIRST NAMED	AGE	SEX	BLOOD
	1816	1	Reed, Kit				27	M	Full
	1817	2	" Victoria			Wife	26	F	Full
1366	1818	3	" Linnie			Dau	1	F	Full
	1819	4	Hawkins, Sillie			S. Dau	4	F	Full

	5	ENROLLMENT				
	6	OF NOS. ~~3~~ HEREON APPROVED BY THE SECRETARY				
CITIZENSHIP CERTIFICATE ISSUED FOR NO 1-2-4 DEC 23 1903		OF INTERIOR Sept 18-06				
CITIZENSHIP CERTIFICATE ISSUED FOR NO ~~3~~ Sept 20-06	10	ENROLLMENT OF NOS. 1, 2 & 4 HEREON APPROVED BY THE SECRETARY OF INTERIOR JAN 13, 1905.				1903
	11	APPROVED BY SECRETARY OF INTERIOR				

	NAME OF FATHER	LIVING OR DEAD	NAME OF MOTHER	LIVING OR DEAD	APPLICATION NO.	REMARKS
1	Willis Chubby	Dead	Betsy Chubby	Dead	2087	
2	Jule Favre		~~~~ Favre	"	"	
3	No.1		No.2		"	
4	Henry Hawkins	Dead	No.2		"	
5			No3 died Aug 8, 03.			
6			No3 Linnie Reed enrolled as a Mississippi			
7			Choctaw by Commissioner under Act of Congress of Apr 26, 1906			
8			No.3 DID NOT SUBMIT PROOF OF			
9			REMOVAL AND BONA-FIDE SET-			
10			TLEMENT WITHIN ONE YEAR			
11			FROM DATE OF IDENTIFICATION.			

No.3. Proof of death filed showing No2 died August 8th 1903.
No.3. Prof of settlement taken May 18 and 25, 1906 under authority Act of Congress Approved April 26, 1906.
"Nos 2 and 4. Proof of continuous residence for a period of three years submitted July 25, 1906."
No.1. Testimony as to continuous residence from date of settlement until date of death submitted October 28, 1905 and November 9, 1905.

IDENTIFIED MISSISSIPPI CHOCTAWS 1902 - 1909
Volume II

IDENTIFIED MISSISSIPPI CHOCTAWS CARD NO. 611

IDENTIFICATION ADDRESS Hays, Mississippi SETTLEMENT ADDRESS
DATE OF IDENTIFICATION July 8th, 1903. DATE OF PROOF OF SETTLEMENT

APPROVED ROLL No.	DAWES ROLL NO.	NAME	RELATIONSHIP TO PERSON FIRST NAMED	AGE	SEX	BLOOD
		(O-ti-hi-mah)				
	1820	1 Farmer, Mary		45	F	Full
	1821	2 Billy, Jim	Son	18	M	Full
	1822	3 Farmer, Miley	Son	5	M	Full
		4				
		5				
		6 APPROVED BY INTERIOR.		1903		
		7				
		8				
		9 DID NOT SUBMIT PROOF OF				
		10 REMOVAL AND BONA-FIDE SET- TLEMENT WITHIN ONE YEAR				
		11 FROM DATE OF IDENTIFICATION.				

	NAME OF FATHER	LIVING OR DEAD	NAME OF MOTHER	LIVING OR DEAD	APPLICATION NO.	REMARKS
1	Jacob	Dead	Don't know		4269	
2	Jim Billy	Dead	No.1		"	
3	Wilson Farmer		No.1		"	
4						
5						
6						
7						
8						
9						
10						
11						

IDENTIFIED MISSISSIPPI CHOCTAWS 1902 - 1909
Volume II

IDENTIFIED MISSISSIPPI CHOCTAWS CARD NO. 612

IDENTIFICATION ADDRESS Avera, Mississippi   SETTLEMENT ADDRESS Durwood, Ind. Ter.
DATE OF IDENTIFICATION July 8th, 1903.   DATE OF PROOF OF SETTLEMENT Dec. 16, 1903

APPROVED ROLL No.	DAWES ROLL NO.	NAME	RELATIONSHIP TO PERSON FIRST NAMED	AGE	SEX	BLOOD
	1823	1 Tom, Sealy Ann		18	F	Full
		2				
		3				
		4				
		5				
		6				
		7				
		8				

CITIZENSHIP CERTIFICATE ISSUED FOR NO 1 DEC 16 1903

ENROLLMENT OF NOS. ~~1~~ HEREON APPROVED BY THE SECRETARY OF INTERIOR JAN 13 1905.

NAME OF FATHER	LIVING OR DEAD	NAME OF MOTHER	LIVING OR DEAD	APPLICATION NO.	REMARKS
Pis-a-ha-tubbee		A-cha-fa			
1 Tom Billy	Dead	Polly Billy		1956	
2					
3					
4					
5					
6					
7					
8					
9					
10		"No1: Proof of continuous residence for a period of three years submitted December 22, 1906."			
11					

IDENTIFIED MISSISSIPPI CHOCTAWS 1902 - 1909
Volume II

IDENTIFIED MISSISSIPPI CHOCTAWS CARD NO. 613

IDENTIFICATION ADDRESS Engine, Mississippi SETTLEMENT ADDRESS Ft. Towson I.T.
DATE OF IDENTIFICATION July 8th, 1903. DATE OF PROOF OF SETTLEMENT Oct 15,03

APPROVED ROLL No.	DAWES ROLL NO.	NAME	RELATIONSHIP TO PERSON FIRST NAMED	AGE	SEX	BLOOD
	1824	1 Solomon, Fannie		10	F	Full
	1825	2 Dixey, Jim	H. Bro	7	M	Full
		3				
		4				
		5				
		6				
		7	APPROVED BY SECRETARY OF INTERIOR. SEP 14 1903			
		8				

CITIZENSHIP CERTIFICATE ISSUED FOR NO 1-2 OCT 16 1903

ENROLLMENT OF NOS. 1 & 2 HEREON APPROVED BY THE SECRETARY OF INTERIOR JAN. 13. 1905.

NAME OF FATHER	LIVING OR DEAD	NAME OF MOTHER	LIVING OR DEAD	APPLICATION NO.	REMARKS
1 Charley Bob		Sallie Bob		2012	
2 John Dixey		" "		"	
3					
4					
5					
6					
7					
8					
9					
10		"Nos 1 and 2: testimony relative to continuous			
11		residence for a period of three years submitted Dec. 14, 1906."			

IDENTIFIED MISSISSIPPI CHOCTAWS 1902 - 1909
Volume II

IDENTIFIED MISSISSIPPI CHOCTAWS CARD NO. 614

IDENTIFICATION ADDRESS Conehatta, Miss.   SETTLEMENT ADDRESS Atoka I.T.
DATE OF IDENTIFICATION July 8th, 1903.   DATE OF PROOF OF SETTLEMENT Aug. 19/03.

APPROVED ROLL No.	DAWES ROLL NO.		NAME	RELATIONSHIP TO PERSON FIRST NAMED	AGE	SEX	BLOOD
	1826	1	Wallace, John B.		32	M	Full
	1827	2	" Lillie	Wife	26	F	Full
	1828	3	" Arna	Dau	3	F	Full
	1829	4	" Ora	Dau	1	F	Full
		5					
		6					
		7	APPROVED BY SECRETARY OF INTERIOR. SEP 14 1903				
		8					

CITIZENSHIP CERTIFICATE ISSUED FOR NO 1-2-3-4 SEP 24 1903

ENROLLMENT OF NOS. 1 2 3&4 HEREON APPROVED BY THE SECRETARY OF INTERIOR JAN. 13 1905.

	NAME OF FATHER	LIVING OR DEAD	NAME OF MOTHER	LIVING OR DEAD	APPLICATION NO.	REMARKS
1	Billy John		Betsey John	Dead	4045	
2	John Nickson		Don't know	Dead	"	
3	No.1		No.2		"	
4	No.1		No.2		"	
5						
6						
7						
8						
9						
10			"Nos 1, 3 and 4: Testimony as to continuous residence for a period of three years submitted August 22, 1906."			
11						

No2 died February 21, 1905: Testimony as to continuous residence up to her death submitted August 22, 1906.

Research Books

Campbell, Will D., Marietta, Georgia, 1992, *Providence*, Longstreet Press, Inc.

Carson, James Taylor, Lincoln and London, 2003, *Searching For The Bright Path The Mississippi Choctaws From Prehistory To Removal*, University of Nebraska Press, published by author 1999.

Carter, Kent, Orem, Utah, 1999, *The Dawes Commission And The Allotment Of The Five Civilized Tribes, 1893-1914*, Ancestry.com.

Cohen, Felix S., Charlottesville, Virginia, 1982, *Felix S. Cohen's Handbook Of Federal Indian Law 1982 Edition*, The Michie Company.

Debo, Angie, Norman, 1975, *The Rise and Fall of the Choctaw Republic*, University of Oklahoma Press, published by author 1934.

Foreman, Grant, Norman, 1989, *Indian Removal*, University of Oklahoma Press, published by author 1932.

Kidwell, Clara Sue, Norman, 1995, *Choctaws and Missionaries in Mississippi, 1818-1918*, University of Oklahoma Press.

Reeves, Carolyn Keller, Jackson, 1985, *The Choctaw Before Removal*, University Press of Mississippi and Choctaw Heritage Press.

Wells, Samuel J. and Tubby, Roseanna, Jackson and London, 1986, *After Removal, The Choctaw in Mississippi*, University Press of Mississippi and Choctaw Heritage Press.

Index

~~~, Betsey 139
A-CHA-FA 306
ACHE-HO-NAH 10
ADAM 98
   Toney 98
A-HA-KA-TE-MA 287
AHBEHOKE 46
AH-BE-HO-YO 126
AH-BE-TE-TUBBEE 131
AH-BE-TU-TAH 53
AH-BIN-AH-TUBBEE, Alex 35
AH-CHE-BAH 30,86
AH-CHO-NAN-TAH 190
AHCONEUBBEE 234
AH-HA-LO-MAN-TUBBEE 187
AH-HOC-LA-TUBBEE, John 203
AH-HO-NA-UBBEE 232
AH-LA-PIN-TUBBEE 163
AH-LE-MO-TUBBEE 71
AH-NO-SA-CHUBBEE 11,302
AH-NO-SA-CUBBEE 228
AH-TAH-LE-HONAH 211
AH-TO-BLECHY, John 294
AH-TOOK-A-LAH, Joe 204,209
AH-TUBBEE 224
ALDERMAN
   Christian 57
   John 57
   Sealy 57
ALLEN 101
   Allie 261
   Betsey 141,144
   Bob 261
   Joe 261
   John 141,144,195,203
   Kit 47,261
   Lacy 261
   Martha 47
   Newton 47
   Rosie 47
   Sally Ann 141
   Willis 261
   Young 144
ALMAN, John 96
ALOMATUBBEE 253
AMA 125
AMELIA 63
AMOS 233,293
   Becky 233
   Bennett 183
   Cleveland 183
   Dora 183
   Giffin 54
   Jasper 183
   Jeff 233
   Josephine 233
   Lissa 183
   Lucinda 233
   Margaret 159
   Roselle 233
   Stemala 19
   Wes 19,159,183
   Willie 183
ANCHAUNUBBEE 63
ANDERSON
   Artie 187
   Bob 274
   John 174,187,258
   John Amos 187
   John Harrison 187
   Lola 187
   Lucy 174,187,258
   Ollie 274
ANN 89
APESAMBY 243
ARKANSAS
   Catherine 202
   Fannie 202
   Jim 202
   John 202
   Linnie 202
   Marsalina 202
   Missie 202
   Susie 202
AUSTIN, Hortense Thompson 214
BAKER
   Billy 197
   Lucy 197
BARNEY
   Alex 19
   Eve 19
   George 19
   Jinnie 19
   Martha 19
   Willis 40
BATTIEST

Index

John 211
Polly 211
BELL
   Becky 214
   Bud 87
   Elam 214
   Joe 161
   Kelly 87
   Sally 87
BEN 189
   Eliza 2
   Madison 2
   Peter 117
BETSEY 44,86,257
BETSIE 98
BETSY 222
BIG JACK 303
   Martha 303
BIG JOHN 106,275
BILLEY 116,298
   Alam 46
   Amy 6,193,272
   Basie 293
   Bessie 158
   Betty 46
   Bud 116
   Captain 31,85
   Charley 46
   Charley Columbus 228
   Davis 293
   Esther 85
   Fabie 46
   Frank Bishop 229
   Harrison 85
   Ina 46
   Jesse 6
   Jim 17,116,229
   John 158
   Josephine 116
   Kissie 298
   Lem 298
   Lilie 56
   Lizzie 85
   Mack 91
   Martha 85
   Mary 17
   Nicey 293
   Nolie 228

Paulina 228
Richmond 85
Sallie 31,46,85,86
Sam 56
Sampson 293
Summers 229
Susie 229
Thompson 56
Tom 228
Welsh 6
Williston 293
Yahfin 46
Young 46
BILLY
   Ada 96
   Elizabeth 231
   Fannie 231
   Hullison 96
   Isaac 249
   Isbey 96
   Jim 305
   John 231,234
   Martha 234
   Moss 96
   Nancy 249
   Polly 306
   Putwood 231
   Tom 306
   Young 96
BITSEY 146
BOB 227,289
   Ama 10
   Amy 10,97,289
   Betsie 10
   Boyd 227
   Charles 37
   Charley 307
   Charlie 226
   Emma 289
   Henry 289
   Herman 220
   I-an-ubbee 225
   Ianubbee 220
   John 10
   Johnnie 97
   Johnnis 10
   Lena 220
   Lexis 227

Index

Lisby 227
Martha 97
Mollie 96,125
Nancy Jane 220
Preston 227
Rainey 227
Sallie 289,307
Sookie 227
Sophie 37
Watkin 225
William 97
Willis 10
Woodward 220
BOLEY, Eliza 19
BROKESHOULDER 253
   Adam 253
BULL
   Emma 54
   Houston 88
   John 5,42,54,88
   Leah 42
   Pink 54
   Robert E 5
   Susan 88
CAIN
   Sam 111,132
   Susie 111
CARTER
   Jubal Braxton 41
   Nettie Frances 41
CASEY 49
CELESTE 269,300
CHARLEY
   Little 295
   Sallie 140
   Simon 60
CHARLIE
   Dave 73
   Donie 73
   Fannie 84
   Herman E 75
   Jane 75
   John H 84
   Johnson 75,254
   Leona 75
   Lillie 73
   Lula 84
   Nettie 73

   Salena 84
   Seaborn 84
   Sophia 254
   William 84
CHATHAM
   Eliza 104
   Lewis 104
CHE-FA-NO-AH 24
CHE-MAH-LE 206
CHITTO
   Alma 189
   John 189
   Laura 143
   Leona 143
   Luella 189
   Minerva 143
   Pat 143
   Rhoda 143
   Rufus 189
   Sissy 143
   Tom 143,189
CHUBBEE
   Agnes 25
   Anna 25
   Janie 25
   John 25,93
   Julia 25
   Lucy 25
   Pink 25
   Rosanna 25
   Sallie 25
   Sam 25
   Susan 93
   Susie 25
   Willie 25
CHUBBY
   Betsy 304
   Willis 304
CHUFFATUBBEE 205,206,255
CHUFF-E-TUBBEE 237
COMBY
   Isom 113
   Jennie 113
CON-CHA-TUBBEE 257
CON-CHE-HA-TUBBEE 248
CON-CHE-HO-NAH 165
CON-NE-AS 212
CONNE-MA-HONAH 53

Index

CON-NE-MA-TUBBEE 53
CON-NE-O-TUBBEE 139
COOKS, John 295
COOPER
    Annie 59
    Betsey 59
    Billy 72
    Gaston 232
    George 72,232
    James 59
    Jennie 72,232
    Lonnie 59
    Mary 59
    Nancy 59
    Peter 59
COTTON
    Charley 161
    Willie 161
CUN-NE-O-TE-MAH 50
CUN-NE-TAN-TUBBEE 223
CUN-NO-TUBBEE, Jim 146
DANSBY
    Betsie 65
    Isom 65,82
    Lewis 65
DAVID 91
DAVIS
    Alice 242
    Anna 71
    Beny 71
    Culberson 71
    Edna 145
    Ellen 190
    Ellis 145
    Jamison 242
    Jeff 216,242
    John 53,71,190
    Julia 216
    Leanna 71
    Linnie 145
    Louella 145
    Maria 242
    Mary 216
    Nancy 71
    Sulena 242
    Thomas 71
DICKSON 259
DIXEY

    Jim 307
    John 307
DIXON 76,230
    Annie 230
    Beauty 83
    Benjamin 74
    Betsey 156
    Columbus 76
    Doctor 83,95,119,156
    John 83
    Julia 74
    Leanna 83
    Lena 83
    Mary 83
    Nancy 95
    Philip 230
    Sallie 76
    Sarah Jane 83
    Sealy 76
    Simpson 74
EBIN, Caroline 172
E-LA-HO-TE-MAH 243
ELAHOTEMAH 243
ELAH-PE-AH 99
E-LAH-PO-NUBBEE 187
E-LA-PALO-UBBEE 163
ELIZA 269,287,293,296
ELLIS 85
    Jim 93
    Leroy 93
    Mary 93
    Nancy 93
EMITHLA 233
EMI-YAH-TUBBE 297
    Flemmon 297
    Johnnie 297
    Martha 297
    Minnie 297
    Nancy 297
    Wallace 297
FARMER
    Jennie 138
    John 83,123,138,200,207
    Louisa 207
    Lucy 200
    Mary 305
    Miley 305
    Polly 83,123,135,207

Index

Sillman 123
Solomon 207
Susan 138
Wilson 305

FAVRE

~~~~ 304
Jule 304

FILLIHEMAH, Nancy 208

FOLEY

Betsie 24
John 24
Oscar 24
Stella 24

FORBES 92
Alice 92
Josephine 92
Lala 92
Mary 92
William 92

FRAZER 21
Echols 20
Forbes 20
John 21
Mary 20
Mollie 20
Will Marshall 20
Winston 20

FRAZIER

Farbis 210
Henson 210
Mary 209,210

FRENCHMAN

John 221
Polly 221
Sophie 295

FUNNY, Jim 169

GAMIL, Sallie 129

GIBSON 168
Amy 215
Bard 235
Becky 215,216
Ben 168,194,195,211
Betsey 168
Billie 193
Christiana 193
Ellis 215
Emma 111
Emmie 194
Ethan S 193
George 291
Jeff 215
Jim 193
John 136,187
Johnson 111
Kima 235
Lela 235
Leona 192
Lina 168
Lucy 215
Lulu 168
Martha 192,235
Mattie 193
Mike 195
Mollie 195
Mullen 168
Nancy 193
Polly 111
Robert 111
Sallie 127,145,168,194
Sammon 168
Sealy 194,195,211
Snowdon 215
Susanna 235
Tom 216
William 111,192,215,235
Willie 195

GILMORE

Allen 206
Benjamin 237
Emma 191,206
Henry Jackson 191
Jane 237
Johnnie 236
Ludie 236
Mabell 191
Mamie 236
Martha 236
Nettie Bessie 191
Ramond 191
Sookey 237
Squire 191
Tom 206,236
William George 237
Winnie 191

GOLDEN

Abe 278

Index

Louisa 278
Margaret Ann 278
GOLDTHORPE, Laura Belle 41
GUNSMITH
   Eliza 190
   John 190
HA-CUBBEE 121,238
   Amie 238
   Mollie 121
HA-KA-YA-TO-MA 287
HALL
   John 286
   Melissa 286
HA-NA-KA-UBBEE 99
HANNAH 126
HARPER
   Eunice 174
   John 174
   Margaret 174
HA-THLA-CHA-MAH 238
HA-THLA-TO-NAH 121
HATUBBEE 203
HAWKINS
   Henry 304
   Lewis 59,122
   Nancy 59
   Sillie 304
HE-KA 155
HE-LE-HO-NAH 99
HENRY
   Dennis 239
   John 239
   Martha 239
   Sarah 239
HICKMAN
   ~~~ 267
   Davis 267
   Ellis 179
   Elsie 179
   Ida 179
   Jimpson 181
   Jimson 179
   John 181,187
   Johnikin 179
   Maggie 179
   Mary 181
   Susan 179
HI-KAH-TI-MAH 208

HIM-MO-NUBB, Mattie 268
HIM-MO-NUBBE 268
HIMMONUBBEE
   Margaret 224
   Shook 224
HIM-O-NUBBE 240,265
   Carson 268
   Davis 268
   Ella 268
   Emmon 268
   Larbin 268
HIMONUBBE
   Bobbie 240
   Laben 240
   Maggie Jane 240
   Shook 240
HI-NE-AH, Susan 204,209
HINSON 112
   Nancy 112
   Simon 112
HINTUBBEE 257
HO-CHE-MAH 265
HOCHEMAH 240,268
   Mary 265
HO-KI 180
HON-TE-MAH 131
HO-PAH-KI 230
HO-PH-KA 76
HOSH-BOH-LI, Tom 190
HO-TI-NAH 180
HOTINLUBBEE 95
HOUSTON
   ~~~ 220
   Willie 220
HUFF
   Phyllis 69
   Zeno 69
ICK-BE-TUBBEE 190
ILAH-FI-CO-MA-TO-MAH 190
ILLAHOTIMAH 103
ILLAYOCUBBEE 74
IL-LE-AH-TUBBEE 50
IL-LE-MAH-HO-KI 238
ILLE-NOWAH 38
IMA-CAH-TUBBEE 10
IMATHLEHONAH 72,232
IM-MIAH-TUBBEE 155
IM-OK-LAH, Isac 139

Index

ISAAC 177,179,180
   Bert 160
   Betsie 169
   Dixon 34,36,160
   Eliza 161
   Ellen 177
   Fannie 160
   George 169
   Gift 177
   Jim 23,118,155,160,177,180
   King 161
   Lela 177
   Lucy 160,161
   Maggie 36
   Malissa 36
   Margaret 34
   Mary 23,118,155,160,169,180
   Ollie 160
   Polly 103,243
   Rifey 160
   Rogers 161
   Siney 177
   Siss 161
   Wiley 161
   William 169
   Willy 161
   Wilson 177
ISH-MA-TE-MAH 71
ISH-TE-MAH 276
ISOM 219
   Bill 142
   Billie J 142
   Emma 178
   Greer 178
   Jack 142
   Julius 178,219
   Mandy 178
   Martha 142,219
   Nancy 219
   Nelson 178
   Wes 142
IS-TI-OPIE, Sallie 114
ISTUBBEE 28
ITHLAHOKE 95
I-TON-I-LE-TUBBEE 168
JACK 269
   Allen 107
   Beaman 162
   Big 67
   Billy 64,67,107
   Camille 67
   Columbus 271
   Dick 162
   Eliza 162
   Ellen 271
   Ethel 162
   Evaline 162
   Isaac 269
   Jim 64
   John 269
   Leanna 64,67,107
   Lena 270
   Lillie 271
   Liza 64
   Martha 162,266
   Minnie 67
   Nancy 271
   Nettie 67
   Robert 271
   Sara Jane 270
   Silman 162
   Tom 162,270
   Willie 271
   Winnie 271
JACKSON 61,201,212,291,303
   Albert 291
   Alex 3
   Alice 291
   Annie 176
   Becky 272
   Ben 254
   Bessie 303
   Betsey 213
   Billey 91
   Billie 213
   Callie 3
   Caway 3
   Charley 134,176
   Charlie 254
   Chris 163
   Cornelia 95
   Elder 149,213
   Eliza 74,291
   Fannie 3
   Frances 134,176,254
   Franklin 3

Index

Gibson 212
Henry 95
Ida 291
Jameson 291
Jeff 74,99
Jennie 213
Jim 4,302
Leroy 213
Lilly 212
Lottie 99
Lulie 95
Martha 99,212
Martha Jane 163
Mary 3,213
Mary Ann 164
McElroy 272
Nancy 259,272,303
Nixie 291
Patsey 303
Polly 201
Roselia 163,164
Salina 272
Sally 164
Sam 99,272
Sarah 149,213
Solomon 3
Sonie 3
Sophia 272
Stephem 254
Tecumseh 270,272
Tom 99,302
Walter 272
Wesley 163
Willie 164
Willis 163,164,291
Winnie 272
JACOB 44,127,142,162,305
   Beckey 142
   Betsey 127
   Charley 127
   Ebbie 127
   Louisa 127
JACOBS, Martha 167
JACOWAY 255
   Cara 166
   Cawa 166
   Charley 166
   Charlie 205

Davis 255
Elsie 205
Ieneda 205
Isabell 166
Kelley 166
Malissa 166
Mandy 205
Martin 205
Mina 166
Oma 205
Onus 205
Rose 255
Rufus 166
Sallie 205,255
Sampson 78
Sealy 115,255
Simmon 166
Summers 166
JAMES
   Doctor 91
   Easter 91,279
   Harbar 91
   Ore 279
   Sophie 91
   Wash 91,279
JAMUS 255
   Lulu 255
JANIE 28
JEFF
   Alice 252
   John 252
   Ludie 252
JENNIE 167,242
JIM 43,58
   Adam 118
   Ben 263
   Betsey 128
   Billy 263,296
   Charley 114
   Clemmon 128
   Dr. 25
   Egburt 128
   Eliza 128,230
   Evan 128
   Fabie 118
   Filleah 114
   Goodman 77
   Henry 296

Index

Isabelle 114
Lillie 77
Lissie 296
Logan 296
Mary 77
Robert 128
Rosie 114
Salena 114
Sallie 77
Simpson 128,230
Sookie 263,296
Sophie 25
Steve 77
Tessie 128
Thomas 114
Tom George 296
Tycoolie 296
Wash 32
JIM-ISAAC
   Jackson 155
   Lee 155
   Martha 155
   William 155
   Wilson 155
JIMMIE
   Louisa 118
   Tobe 118
JIMMY
   Alis 113
   Bicey 113
   Ike 66
   Lee 113
   Mabel 2
   Silas 113
   Tobe 2,66,113
   Viola 2
   Will 2
JIMPSON, Joe 199
JOE
   Edna 204
   Emily 204
   Johnnie 204
   Langley 204
JOHN 38,49,157
   Alex 106,244
   Betsey 308
   Big 63
   Billie 154
   Billy 124,308
   Charley 63
   Davis 124
   Doctor 239
   Georgia 106
   Grundy 244
   Jack 124
   Jennie 275
   Jimmy 172
   Johnnie 106
   Julia 63
   Lee 244
   Lena 63
   Lucy 63
   Minnie 106
   Nancy 38,157,178
   Polly 38
   Rhoda 244
   Sallie 124
   Sally 63,106
   San 38
   Sancom 137
   Sarah 244
   Simon 106
   Sookey 154,239
   Sukey 91
JOHNSON 151
   Alice 151
   Big Wiley 206
   Bill 163
   Bob 153,202
   Charley 73,84
   Charlie 75
   Cook 153
   Eliza 73,75,84,153
   Frank 70,105
   Freeman 58
   Henry 151,235
   Isaac 273,290
   Jennie 58,110
   Jesse Porter 283
   John P 70
   Josephine 105
   Louis 283
   Lula 151
   Mamie 105
   Martha 151
   Nancy 153,202

Index

Nettie 283
Nicey 151
Nochee 110
Patsie 206
Sealy 235
Stella 290
Susie 290
Taylor 58,110
Wesley 151
Wiley 290
JOHNSTON
   Emily 250
   Emma 249
   Isham 249,250
   Jesse 250
   Lemma 249
   Lena 250
   Malissie 250
JONES
   Henry 152
   Joe 94,152
   Lucy 152
JOSHUA 274
   Eva 274
   Hoka 274
   Jane 274
   Lucy 47,293
   Mollie 274
   Sam 274
   Sillian 274
   Simon 47
JOSIE 271
KAH-NAH-LE-HO-NAH 190
KAH-NO-NUBBEE 254
KAH-TUBBEE 289
KANIATUBBEE 63
KELLEY
   Fannie 106
   Thompson 106
KON-NI-AH-TUBBEE 140
LAHBIN 52
   Ben 52
   Elizabeth 52
LAHELAH 184
LARNDEEN, Henry 290
LEWIS 13
   Adam 124
   Alice 13
Annie 119
Becky 36
Betsy 13
Betty 280
Big 245
Bud 275
Calvin 243
Caroline 137
Charles 140,147
Charlie 275
Chuly 280
Claire 273
Doctor 258
Dorano 273
Easter 119
Ed 36
Eliza 124
Emma 36
Fannie 150
Isaac 36
Jeffie 239
Jennie 13,137
Jesse 148
Jim 43,134,184,222,239,273,275
John 13,119,148,150,215,241,273
John Wesley 119
Johnnie 134
Larnie 275
Leanna 119
Lila 140,147
Liney 245
Lissa 243
Little 245
Lonie 147
Lotie 149
Malissa 119,148,150
Mamie 13
Marshall 243
Martha 39,134,137,215
Mary 119,184,239,245,258
Melissa 273
Minnie 147,275
Mollie 134
Moses 243
Nelson 119
Noble 184
Ola 119
Ollie 137

Index

Patsey 245
Pollie 273
Rody 275
Sallie 222,275
Sam 36,39,273
Sim 147
Smith 280
Susan 243
Thomas 119
Ump 273
Webb 184
William 119
LICK, John 257
LIN-TUBBEE 262
LISE
   John 95
   Lissie 95
   Mary J 95
LISH
   Annie 258
   John 258
   John Roy 258
   Mattie 258
LITTLE JIM 128
LITTLE SAM 299
LITTLE TOM 296
LIZA 89,184,274
LONDINE
   James 12
   Julie 12
LOW-AH-HOKA 82
LUCY 1,63,101
LUTIE, Rhoda 143
MACK
   John 177
   Nancy 177
MA-HAH-TAH-TAH 208
MA-HAT-STI-AH 146
   Jefferson 146
   Sallie 146
MAH-HIN-TO-NAH 209
MAH-YUBBEE 211
MAK-TA-HO-NAH 237
MALEY
   John 97
   Noley 97
MARK
   Amy 120

Billy 120
Horace 120
John 120
Lasen 120
Louisa 120
Luiza 120
Mingo 120
Nancy 120
Solomon 120
Sookey 120
Susan 120
MARRIS, Elizabeth 259
MARTHA 20
MARTIN
   Bettie 76
   Ed 76
   Elizabeth 157
   Jacob 158
   John 171
   Lomie 219
   Louisa 76
   Manuel 157
   Nannie 159
   Ona 157
   Sallie 158,170,183,205
   Sam B 171
   Sealy 171
   Tom 170
   Willie 157,219
   Winnie 171
MARY 131,179,189
MA-SHONE-TAH-TUBBEE 50
MA-TE-HO-NAH 71
ME-AH-HO-NAH, Betsey 162
MEALY 67
MEELY
   Amos 156
   Clark 172
   Fannie 156
   Jim 156
   John 71,153,156,172
   Leanna 153,156,172
   Lula 156
   Mary 172
ME-HAH-TE-MAH 254
MEHAN
   Sally 16
   Tom 16

Index

ME-SHAM-HO-NAH 133
MINGO, Gibson 15
MISHEMAHTEMAH 193
MOLLIE 218
MOLLIE-HOKEE 133
MOMINTUBBEE 16
MONK
    Mingo 15
    Susie 15
MON-TAH 206
MORRIS 45
    Bessie 45
    J P 45
MOSE 61,184
    Frank 61
    John 61,277
    Lark 61
    Laura 277
    Lula 61,277
    Steen 61
    William Davis 61
MOSES 129
    Ann 129
    Bicey 129
    Edna 129
    Elsie 129
    Ike 129
    Lottie 129
    Nicey 129
    Sallie 129
NAH-KAH-NI-O-KAH-TUBBEE 180
NANCY 49,189,232,233
NED 222
    Lona 222
    Marvin 222
    Russell 222
    Willie 222
NELSON
    Bessie 117
    Harrison 117
    Phelia Ann 117
NICKSON, John 147,308
NO-UBBEE 287
NUBBEE
    Billy 8
    Jennie 8
NUN-TA-O-TUBBEE 94

OCK-LO-TUBBEE 139
OK-A-IN-CHUK-A-MA 232
OK-CHI-TUBBEE 114
    Josephine 114
OK-IN-TO-LAH, Becky 183
OKISHMULLE 234
OKLA-HE-MA 223
OK-LAH-NAH-NUBBEE 253
OLD MAN CHARLEY 140
O-MOLLIE-HOKE 94
ONAH-FAL-A-MA-TUBBEE 126
ON-AH-TO-BO-KA 126
ON-CHA-LEY 11
ONDOCHATUBBEE 63
ON-TA-MAH-CHUBBEE 49
ON-TUBBEE
    Jennie 296
    Jim 296
ONUBBEE
    Betsey 226
    Bob 226
OON-TE-AH-TUBBE 94
OOOK-A-LA-HANE-LUBBEE 116
OSCAR, Billy 33
O-TI-HI-MAH 305
PARKER
    Jim 90
    John 90
    Lizzie 90
    Logan 90
    Sally 24
    Sidney 90
    Susan 90
    Tom 24
PELIONAH 63
PETERS, Sookey 290
PHILIP 112
    Bettie 260
    George 260
    Jinnie 260
    Louisa 2,66,113
    Sallie 9,80,81,201,256
    Sam 9,80,81,256
    Simon 256
    Sissy 260
    Tom 81
    Williamson 260
    Winston 80

Index

PHILLIP
- Albert 294
- Arlena 79
- Bob 294
- Buckhorn 231
- Dibin 294
- Jinnie 79,294
- Leanna 294
- Lucy 231
- Mack 79
- Mary 79
- Nancy 294
- Sallie 79,171
- Sam 171
- Simon 294
- Sina 294
- Williamson 79,294

PHILLIPS
- Caroline 199
- Custer 199
- Germain 199
- Lena 199
- Sealia 199
- Willie 199

PHYLLIS 38
PI-LI-TUBBEE 135
PIS-A-HA-TUBBEE 306
PISAHOMBEE 133
PIS-AH-TO-SHE-MAH 254
PISAMBY, Lewis 103
PIS-AN-TUBBEE 10
PISTUBBEE 64
- Amy 64
- Archie 238
- Elan 238
- Martha 238
- Tinsley 238

PIS-UN-TUBBEE 125,227,289
PO-KI 49
POLK
- Jim 22
- Mary 22
- Winston 22

POLLY 12,164
PORTER
- Betsey 131,260
- Betsie 79
- Jenkins 131
- Jesse 79,131,260
- Jim 131,168
- Jimson 227
- Thornton 131
- Wallace 220

POST-OAK, Malissa 16
POSTOAK
- Isaac 198
- Lucy 198

PRIMUS
- Ben 165
- Mattie 165
- Nannie 165

REED
- Kit 304
- Linnie 304
- Victoria 304

REESE
- Fannie 284
- John 284
- Lelia 284

RICHARD 102
ROBISON
- Alice 136
- Betsy 200
- Charley 136,200
- Charlie 200
- Eula 136
- Fronie 200
- Henry 136
- James 200
- Jane 136
- Liza 136
- Lucy 200
- Mattie 200

RUSH, Eliza 36
SALLIE 12,95,208,243
SAM 10,48,49,89,197,208,233
- Acy 86
- Amos 89
- Delia 89
- Dennis 86
- Eliza 48
- Ellis 165,197
- Fontain 197
- George 89
- Houston 48
- Jennie 197

Jimsie 48
Joe 89
Julia 165,197
Martha 299
Mattie 48
Minnie 89
Nancy 89,93
Oscar 48
Porter 93
Raymond 48
Rena 86
Sis 89
Sophie 48
Thomas 89
Tilwa 10
Wallace 299
Wash 86

SAMPSON
   Johnson 32
   Lillie 32
   Sallie 32
   Salonie 32

SATONAH, Mollie 203
SCOTT 218,300
   Aline 300
   Chubby 218
   John 300
   Liza 300

SEAHMOTUBBEE 111
SHOEMAKER
   Becky 191
   Ben 198
   Coleman 198
   Emerson 276
   Henry 198
   Jesse 191
   Jim 198,276
   Lucy 281
   Margaret 276
   Mary 198
   Sallie 276
   Sally 198
   Selest 198
   Sister 198
   Sti-onah 198
   Susie 281
   Wiggin 276
   Will 198

Willie 281
SHOOK, Bettie 224
SHUMAKE
   Bill 109
   Charlie 109
   Liza 109
SHUN-I-O-TUBBEE 66
SIEL-LA-HONAH 16
SIMON
   Albert 60
   Amos 60
   Charley 60
   Fannie 60
   Jane 60
   Mary Jane 60
SIMPSON 108,276
   Adaline 1
   Ben 286
   Caroline 286
   Celia 1
   Cinda 1
   Eliza 108,276
   Fannie 286
   George 1
   Gill 33
   Ira 286
   Jim 182
   John 1,33
   Johnnie 1
   Leanna 33
   Leta 1
   Lewis 1
   Liza 182
   Mabel 286
   Mary 286
   Meely 1
   Mertine 33
   Minnie 33
   Mollie 1
   Rosie 33
   Sam 182,286
   Simms 1
   Sissie 33
   Sookie 108
   William 286
SISMAN, Milljean 33
SMITH
   Amie 287

Index

Annie..................................196
John....................................228
Mack..................................287
Mollie................................228
Thomas......................196,287
Willie................................196
SOCKEY
   Elsie................................. 29
   Ethel................................ 29
   John................................. 29
   Liza...........................103,243
   Louis................................ 29
   Martha............................. 29
   Mary................................103
   Phoebe............................103
   Riley................................. 29
   Sally................................. 29
   Sarah................................ 29
   Solomon..........................103
   Wallace......................103,243
SOCKIA...............................289
SOLOMON
   Fannie..............................307
   Sallie................................ 82
   Squire............................... 82
   Winnie.............................220
SOOKEY......................175,236
STALLABY
   Anderson.........................217
   Jno....................................217
   Mary.................................217
STE-AH-TUBBEE
   Billy.................................160
   Mary.................................160
STEMONA
   Eliza................................. 18
   Jim................................... 18
   Sallie................................ 18
STEPHEN
   Allie.................................101
   Betsie...............................101
   Eliza.................................101
   Frank................................101
   Jim...................................101
   Lissie................................101
STEVE
   Lucy.................................139
   Martha..............................139
   Smith................................139
   Tom..................................139
STI-O-NAH..........................188
STOLIBY
   Bill....................................261
   Folsom........................74,213
   Hickman..........................213
   Lucy.................................261
   Missouri......................47,261
   Sallie................................213
   Solomon..........................261
STURDEVANT, Charley............. 68
SUKEY................................. 68
SUSAN................................163
TAH-HONAH, Sookey..............206
TAH-NAH-PAH-YAH.................204
TAH-NUBBEE.......................187
TAYLOR
   Billbo...............................252
   Elizabeth.........................252
   Jennie..............................252
   Johnson............................252
   Lawrence.......................... 14
   Madeline.......................... 14
   Merceline........................252
   Sam.................................. 14
   Willie...............................252
TE-CHUBBEE.......................298
TEH-E-CUBBEE..................... 82
THOMAS............................... 28
~~~~......................................252
   Ada..................................122
   Charlie.............................221
   Elijah........................100,122
   Emma..............................122
   Enoch..............................221
   Esau.................................221
   George.............................. 28
   Henry...............................122
   Jake......................100,221,252
   Jim...................................250
   John B..............................122
   Joshua..............................122
   Lewis................................ 28
   Martha.......................100,221
   Mary.................................221
   Melissa.............................250
   Nicholas...........................221

Index

Peter Foster 221
Risher 221
Sally 28
Susie 28
THOMPSON 51,115,127,145
   Alex 301
   Allison 214
   Annie 186
   Ben 44
   Betsey 115,214
   Bill 44,214
   Dennis 186
   Felix 186
   Jane 301
   Lem 301
   Lena 214
   Leona 44,301
   Lonie 301
   Maggie 44
   Marsaline 301
   Martha 44,214
   Sookie 44
   Suala 301
   Sydney 301
   Thomas 44
   William 289
TICK-A-BAH-TI-MAH 207
TILLIS
   Jane 139
   Steve 139
TIM-A-YONAH 116
TIN-CHA 23,155
TINCHA 180
TISH-O-CUBBEE 49
TOH-HA-LE-CHUBBEE 254
TOM 46,154,236,247
   Betsie 247
   Elan 246
   Julia 296
   Martha 8,246
   Mollie 246
   Moses 247
   Nicholas 247
   Sallie 248
   Sarah 246
   Sealy Ann 306
   Sicily 247
   Susan 247
   Tubbish 248
   Watson 247
   William 246,248
   Willie 251
   Wm 251
TO-MA-HA-TUBBEE, Dave 223
TOOKOLO
   Elan 9
   Emaline 241
   George 241
   John Henry 282
   Lillie 9,282
   Lissie 9
   Mary 241
   Olis 241
   William O 9,282
TOONUBBEE 188
   Allen 188
   Bissie 188
   Lucy 188
   Siss 188
TUBBEE
   Caroline 48
   Celia 130
   John 130
   Lewis 130
   Sampson 48
   Willis 102
TUCK-A-LAM-BEE 128
TUCK-A-LUM-BEE 30
TUF-FA-MAH
   Amos 49
   Exa 49
   Lucy 49
   Willis 49
TUSHCANOLA 129
UNAH-HO-KA 180
UN-TEH-YAH-BEE 99
VAUGHN
   Jim 262
   John 262
   Sookey 262
WADE, Willis 122
WAH-CA-TUBBEE 151
WAH-KO-NAH, Amos 183
WAIT 23
   Liza 23
   Nancy 23

Index

Sawil 23
WAITER
   Caleb 31
   Emily 155
   Emma 175
   Jane 35
   Jane Sookey 175
   John 35,155,175
   Martha 31
   McNeal 175
   Minnie 35
   Robert 31
   Tom 35
WALLACE
   Aben 4
   Arna 308
   Earley 302
   Ikeness 185
   John 4,45,302
   John B 308
   Lah-nubbee 185
   Latisha 4
   Lemmie 302
   Letitia 302
   Li-cubbee 185
   Lillie 308
   Ora 308
   Sarah 4,45,302
   Sis 185
   Sota 4
   Tom 185
   Wesley 302
WASHINGTON
   Billy 27
   George 27
   Hannah 27
   Liza 27
   Lucy 27
   Martha 27
   Sallie 184
   Susan 27
WEEKS
   John 104
   Masleke 104
WESHOCK
   Jane 40
   John 40
   Martin 158,170,183,205

Massy 40
Nona 40
Sallie 40
Sampson 40
WE-SHOCK-SHE-HOMAH 180
WESLEY
   John 73,75,84,242
   Louisa 73,75,84,242
WEST 39
   John 39
   Ollie 39
WICKSON
   Amie 17
   Cleo 17
   Holiston 17
   John 17,53
   Leotie 17
   Malinda 17
   Mike 17
   Nancy 17
   Sim 192
WILKINSON
   Harrison 234
   Sallie 234
WILLIAM 1,204,236
   Geo 206
   Janie 173
   Jinnie 150
   John 150,173
   Lewis 173
WILLIAMS 51
   Chlorie 51
   Emaline 285
   Harvey 51
   Jack 285
   Mary 51
   Sam 51
   Susan 51
   Telan 285
   Tom 51
   Wilson 164
WILLIAMSON
   Adeline 264
   Amie 295
   Becky 132,264
   Bike 292
   Davie 295
   Eliza 264

Index

Ida 132
John 264
Lewis 132,264
Lingum 264
Lucy 99,264
Mack 132
Malissa 292
Mary 295
Mike 292
Mollie 264
Nancy 264
Ruby 132
Sistine 264
Tom 295
Will 264
WILLIS 58,166,189,204,224,287
   Allen 189
   Almond 102
   Billey 293
   Camblin 34
   Charley 55
   Ely 34
   Gus 34
   John 50,55,224,237
   Julia 237
   Katie 78
   Louisa 34
   Mahala 78
   Minerva 189
   Mose W 102
   Nannie 219
   Rachael 102
   Sookey 55
   Sophia 112
WILSON
   ~~~~ 207
   Donald 224
   Eliza 254
   Grandison 159
   Janie 224
   John 224,274
   Martha 274
   Neely 159
   Sam 254
   Willie 224
YEARBY
   Ellis 62
   Jesse 62

Margaret 62
YIM-MI-HO-NUBBEE 207
YORK
   Amos 288
   Annie 7,37
   Charley 7
   Ida 37
   Jamison 37
   Jesse 37
   Lettie Lee 288
   Malissa 37,288
   Martha 76,128
   Mimie 37
   Nannie 7
   Nicey 7
   Pickens 7
   Rufus 37,288
   Scott 143
   Sealy 143,288
   Solomon 30,76,128,219
   Tom 37
   Ya-con-ya 30

www.ingramcontent.com/pod-product-compliance
Lightning Source LLC
Chambersburg PA
CBHW020238030426
42336CB00010B/528